D1523648

Mission in the Spirit

Towards a Pentecostal/Charismatic Missiology

Series Preface

Regnum Studies in Mission are born from the lived experience of Christians and Christian communities in mission, especially but not solely in the fast growing churches among the poor of the world. These churches have more to tell than stories of growth. They are making significant impacts on their cultures in the cause of Christ. They are producing 'cultural products' which express the reality of Christian faith, hope and love in their societies.

Regnum Studies in Mission are the fruit often of rigorous research to the highest international standards and always of authentic Christian engagement in the transformation of people and societies. And these are for the world. The formation of Christian theology, missiology and practice in the twenty-first century will depend to a great extent on the active participation of growing churches contributing biblical and culturally appropriate expressions of Christian practice to inform World Christianity.

Series Editors

Julie C. Ma	Oxford Centre for Mission Studies, Oxford, UK
Wonsuk Ma	Oxford Centre for Mission Studies, Oxford, UK
Doug Petersen	Vanguard University, Costa Mesa, CA, USA
Terence Ranger	University of Oxford, Oxford, UK
C.B. Samuel	Emmanuel Hospital Association, Delhi, India
Chris Sugden	Anglican Mainstream, Oxford, UK

A full listing of titles in this series
appears at the end of this book

REGNUM STUDIES IN MISSION

Mission in the Spirit

Towards a Pentecostal/Charismatic Missiology

Julie C. Ma and Wonsuk Ma

Foreword by Andrew F. Walls

First published 2010 by Regnum Books International

Regnum is an imprint of the Oxford Centre for Mission Studies
St. Philip & St. James Church
Woodstock Road, Oxford, OX2 6HR, UK

16 15 14 13 12 11 10 8 7 6 5 4 3 2 1

British Library Cataloguing in Publication Data
A catalogue record for this book is available from the British Library

ISBN 978-1-506477-72-5

Typeset by RBI

The publication of this title is made possible through the generous
financial assistance of The Commission on Theological Education of
Evangelisches Missionswerk in Deutschland (EMW, Dr. Verena
Grüter), Hamburg, Germany

Distributed by 1517 Media in the US and Canada

In honour and memory of our mothers
who believed not only in God but also in His plan for their children

Contents

Part II On the Frontline

Foreword

During the twentieth century, Christianity underwent several transformations. One change was demographic; at the century's beginning, as for several centuries before it, the Christian centre lay in Europe and North America, whereas by the century's end the majority of professing Christians belonged to Africa, Asia and Latin America. Further, the centuries of Western pre-eminence meant that the models used for understanding movements in Christianity, and the terminology and classifications used to describe and assess them, arose from Western, and especially from European history. Developments in the twentieth century began to show the limitations of these typologies as African and Asian and Latin American Christianity came into their own. In the early years of the century a movement arose in the Western United States that brought together features, such as prophecy, tongues and healing, that had appeared from time to time in earlier Christian history, with a coherent theology which gave special prominence to the Holy Spirit and a dynamic and distinctive expression of worship and spirituality. The spread of this movement in the old Western Christendom was modest, if sometimes dramatic; but in various parts of Asia, Latin America and Africa, then thought of in the West as mission fields, its leading features intersected with similar features already native to Christian groups there. In the course of the twentieth century this process has flourished among the burgeoning Christian communities of Africa, Asia and Latin America. In much of the world it is now the most visible face of Christianity,

The name early given to the movement was Pentecostal, since its various manifestations share a profound consciousness of the Holy Spirit as the mainspring of Christian life; but in much of the world, it can no longer be described or assessed in denominational terms. It has become one of the major traditions of Christianity, deeply affecting parts of the Roman Catholic Church and in some countries transforming the life of the historic Protestant denominations; another sign that the old Europe-based ways of classifying Christian communities are no longer adequate.

For anyone who wishes to understand this transforming current within contemporary Christianity, the present work will prove invaluable. The authors, Asian Christians and international citizens with years of cross-cultural experience, speak from within this crucially important manifestation of contemporary Christianity, sharing its characteristic consciousness of the Holy Spirit as the interpreter of Christ in the world, while remaining alert and sensitive to the whole Christian *oikumene*. They engage the reader in biblical exploration, in doctrinal reflection, in striking accounts of the modes of Christian life and witness in various Asian contexts. They address topics not always associated with Pentecostal Christianity – social justice, care of creation, the ancient religious traditions and worldviews of Asia, the goal of Christian unity. They reveal the situations where conventional Western theology is disabled, because the West has bracketed out of its world view spiritual entities with which people in much of the world wrestle daily. The theology here represented takes the principalities and powers seriously, as it confronts us arrestingly with the theme of Mission in the Spirit. Here is a valuable contribution to modern missiology, for which those who belong to the Pentecostal or Charismatic tradition and those who do not should equally be grateful.

Andrew F Walls
Honorary Professor, University of Edinburgh
Professor of the History of Mission, Liverpool Hope University
Professor in the Akrofi-Christaller Institute, Ghana

Preface

The book is the first work that we, as a couple, have undertaken as a joint project, although we have previously published an edited monograph. We are looking back over thirty years of our missionary engagement, research and teaching, and the book is a culmination of our missionary life so far. It is also fitting that, while the global mission community celebrates the centenary of the Edinburgh Missionary Conference in 2010, the unique contribution that Pentecostals have made to mission for the last hundred years is widely recognized. And this book is an expression of this awareness. Indeed, both of us are deeply involved in the Edinburgh 2010 process: Julie as a general council member, and Wonsuk as the leader of three study groups. Furthermore, Regnum, the imprint of the Oxford Centre for Mission Studies where both of us are teaching, is publishing all the Edinburgh 2010 titles.

We were part of the early missionary movement of Korea. We began our missionary service in the Philippines in the late 1970s, even before our church, the Korean Assemblies of God, organized its missions department. In many ways, we began mission without knowing what that was. We had to learn almost everything, including English, to launch our missionary work. Our post-graduate studies were an after-thought: intercultural studies for Julie and Old Testament studies for Wonsuk. As Pentecostals, our perspectives have been consistently Pentecostal, regardless of our academic disciplines. Of course, our 'newness' to rapidly changing mission realities is evident within the pages of this book.

Most of the chapters were originally published in different places as stand-alone pieces, as the acknowledgement page shows. This brought several practical challenges: firstly, some of the information was rather dated; and secondly, some of the chapters contained repetition. Putting the different articles into a book, therefore, has been a great challenge. In spite of our earnest efforts to correct this situation, it is inevitable that some of the repetition remains. Along with this problem, a larger question remains: Is it really necessary to add this less-than-perfect book to the already crowded world of mission publications? The Introduction chapter briefly mentions several important contributions on Pentecostal mission. An informed scan, however, quickly reveals that the majority of them are written from western perspectives. This raises the question of whether having a Korean or Asian perspective on this topic makes any significant difference. We believe it does. A perspective from a missionary-receiving end is valuable for practical reasons, as we quickly learned through our own missionary work. My (Wonsuk's) Old Testament perspective can also shed important light on foundations for mission.

The book is divided into two large sections: foundational (or theological/theoretical) and praxis level. However, the division is not as clear as the Table of Contents would suggest. Even the theoretical discussion is quickly joined and enriched by the 'ground-level' experiences, and the same can be said for the praxis discussion which is often 'invaded' by theological reflection. Nonetheless, we felt this division to be useful. In spite of the sometimes random nature of each original chapter, we have carefully brought them together to form a larger unit in the form of this book. How successful we have been in this difficult process should be judged by the readers. However, we are aware that gaps remain. For example, we wish we could have included separate chapters on Social Engagement and the Creation/Environmental aspect of Pentecostal mission. We hope that in future years there will be an opportunity to return to this topic and expand on the ideas and material which have been gathered together in this book.

Some words on the title of the book: we struggled a great deal to reach the present title, *Mission in the Spirit.* At first, we thought of 'empowerment' as the main theme of the title. However, two considerations quickly led us to decide against this concept. Firstly, the idea of 'power' for mission, regardless of its context, has been seriously questioned in recent mission discussions. For example, in the Edinburgh 2010 circle, the reflection on the western missionary paradigm of power led to stress mission 'with humility'. Although the Pentecostal argument of mission with power has its justification, the relationship between (em)power(ment) and triumphalism requires a serious rethink. Secondly, as the 'Charismatic Spirit' chapter demonstrates, the most mature form of empowerment is found not in the demonstration and wielding of (whatever) power, but in the sustaining power of the Spirit in the faithful obedience of a person to the calling of the Lord. It is only then that the combination of 'mission' and 'the Spirit' becomes a viable option. However, the question of how to link the two themes remained a serious question: 'mission with the Spirit' fails to recognize the truth of *missio Dei,* mission that is God's. We eventually concluded that mission *in the Spirit* recognises not only his lordship and resourcing in mission, but also human partnership in this mysterious plan of God.

The authors are extremely grateful to many who patiently walk with us in our missionary journey. These precious partners, mostly from the Philippines, will remain unnamed. Judy Gilliland has been gladly helping us to improve our manuscript, as learning a language remains a life-long process. We want to thank her for this service, and also for her friendship which spans more than a decade. Kaye Cole, our colleague in the Philippines, went through the entire manuscript to make the scattered pieces into a coherent whole. This process involved a myriad of tasks and required an extremely attentive and discerning eye. We are grateful for her help. Kate Harris, my (Wonsuk's) executive officer at Oxford Centre for Mission Studies read most of the manuscript and ran the publication project as Managing Editor of Regnum. We want to thank the editors of the Regnum Studies in Mission series for including this study in its prestigious series. The Regnum editorial team should also be thanked for their efficient handling of the project, in particular Tony Gray of Bound Biographies. Whilst we acknowledge these valuable contributions, the final responsibility, of course, rests on us as the authors.

Our good friends provided very generous comments in the form of a Foreword, and commendations. We want to thank them for their time in reading the manuscript and thoughtfulness in providing valuable comments.

The publication of the book was made possible through the kind financial assistance of Evangelisches Missionswerk in Deutschland (EMW) of Germany. We want to record our appreciation to EMW director, Dr Verena Gruter.

We want to thank the Lord for taking us along a path through which He has taught us His own deep commitment in bringing his creation back to Him, while his people, created in His image, have been graciously invited to be partners of His plan for restoration.

Julie & Wonsuk Ma
Oxford
Easter, 2010

Acknowledgements

The authors acknowledge the kind permissions various publishers for the use of our studies previously published in their publications. A varying degree of editorial work has been applied to them for the including in this book.

APTS Press, the publisher of *Reflections on Developing Asian Pentecostal Leaders* (2004) for 'Church Planting'

Asia Graduate School of Theology-Philippines, the publisher of *Journal of Asian Mission* for: 'Growing Churches in Manila' (1997); 'Asian Religious Worldviews' (2005)

Faculty of Asia Pacific Theological Seminary for the following studies originally published in *Asian Journal of Pentecostal Studies*: 'Santuala' (1999); 'Korean Pentecostal Spirituality' (2002); 'Full Circle Mission' (2005); 'Pentecostal Worship in Asia' (2007)

Lausanne World Pulse for 'Two Ripples of Pentecostal Mission' and 'Third Ripple of Pentecostal Mission' (2008)

OMF Lit. (Manila) for 'Proclamation and Manifestation' in *Asian Church and God's Mission: Studies Presented at the International Symposium on Asian Mission, Manila, January 2002* (2003); '"In Jesus' Name...": Power Encounter from an Asian Pentecostal Perspective', appeared in *Principalities and Powers: Biblical Reflections in the Asian Context* (2007)

Oxford Centre for Mission Studies, the publisher of *Transformation* for: 'The Spirit of God in Creation: Lessons for Christian Mission' (2007); 'Discerning What God Is Doing among His People Today' (2010)

Pentecostal-Charismatic Theological Inquiry International, the publisher of *Cyberjournal for Pentecostal-Charismatic Research* for 'Mission with Power' (1998)

Regnum Books International for 'Social Context of Pentecostal Mission' in *The Globalization of Pentecostalism* (1999); 'Asian Women in Ministry' in *Asian and Pentecostal* (2005)

Abbreviations

ADB	Asian Development Bank, Manila, Philippines
AG	Assemblies of God
AJPS	*Asian Journal of Pentecostal Studies*
CWME	Commission on World Mission and Evangelism, World Council of Churches
DPCM	*Dictionary of Pentecostal and Charismatic Movements*
EMSS	Evangelical Missiological Society Series
IBMR	*International Bulletin of Missionary Research*
IRM	*International Review of Mission*
JAM	*Journal of Asian Mission*
JPT	*Journal of Pentecostal Theology*
JPTSS	Journal of Pentecostal Theological Supplement Series
NIDPCM	*New International Dictionary of Pentecostal and Charismatic Movements*
NT	New Testament
OT	Old Testament
WCC	World Council of Churches

Chapter 1

Introduction

The Pentecostal movement was born at the turn of the twentieth century. In that same decade, a historic global mission gathering took place, which is known as the Edinburgh Missionary Conference (EMC) of 1910. The former has grown into a massive and often almost chaotic global Christian movement, while the latter gave birth to the modern ecumenical movement, thus, evolving into an ecumenical mission movement. Both are hailed as the two major Spirit movements in the twentieth century, but whether everyone would agree with that opinion is a matter of debate. For the century, in addition to the two Christian 'mega-movements', it would be well not to forget that the Catholic Church, the largest of the global Christian family, came through a revolutionary reform called the Vatican II, and this can equally be hailed as an epochal work of the Spirit.

Global Christianity

It will also be useful to quickly survey the movements of global Christianity in the last 100 years since the EMC made a firm commitment to complete the 'evangelisation of the world in this [their] generation'.[1] However, the generation after the conference was overshadowed by horrible destruction through two world wars and their aftermath.

The post-war era saw the birth of many nations out of the colonial period. The colonial political grip did not help the missionary aspirations of the western churches at all, and independence and nation-building brooded nationalism, often making the missionary climate more hostile than conducive. The political polarization of the world caused every nation to pick a superpower to align with, and this was how most of the so-called 'developing nations' survived in the cruel climate of the cold war era. At the same time, a group of 'developing' nations, dissatisfied with the dominant world order, formed a third group of nations of non-alliance. The gospel and modernization, the seemingly winning formula for mission, in general, failed to deliver what the EMC hoped for. Then came the

---

[1] Even before this was taken up by the conference, John R. Mott published a book under the same title, *The Evangelisation of the World in This Generation* (London: Student Volunteer Missionary Union, 1910). For a useful reflection, see, for example, David A. Kerr and Kenneth R. Ross, 'Introduction', in David A. Kerr and Kenneth R. Ross (eds.), *Edinburgh 2010: Mission Then and Now* (Oxford: Regnum Books, 2009), 3-20.

collapse of Communism and the end of the cold war era. The world, then, was no longer the same.

The rise of churches in the Global South[2] (or 'Southern Church' in shorthand) has been prophetically declared by Andrew Walls.[3] Recently Todd Johnson convincingly argues that Christianity oscillated in every millennium between South and North. In the first millennium, it was a religion of the south of Israel, the birth place of Christianity. Then it made a west and northward move in the second millennium, making it a 'western' religion. According to him, from the 1970s, global Christianity again made a southward as well as an eastward, turn making it a 'southern' religion again.[4] Thus, in our own lifetime, the centre of global Christian gravity has moved to the south. An average world Christian is an African female youth, as now almost 7 out of every 10 world Christians are found in the Global South.

It is not only the numerical redistribution of world Christians, but more importantly a reshaping of the very nature of 'being Christian'. As Philip Jenkins presented and convincingly argues, Southern Christianity in general, and those initiated by nationals in particular, exhibit radically different religious orientations. Evidently informed by a rich religious environment, Christianity is no longer a set of rational arguments, but something that is taken as a 'given' with full awareness of the active spiritual world intimately interfacing with the visible world. As a result, the Bible is read to believe it and to expect to experience the same healings and miracles, and God is expected to 'speak' to his people through visions, dreams, voices and the like.[5] The net result is that Christianity becomes a live and dynamic experience. This ethos makes a good proportion of Southern Christianity 'Pentecostal' although the term is never used in many church groups. The evangelistic and missionary zeal of these emerging churches is but a natural consequence of this type of Christianity, often coupled with voluntary and involuntary displacement of massive numbers of people,

---

[2] This is a problematic term, as the 'emerging churches' are also found in the north of the equator, including Eastern Europe, newly independent former Soviet states, and equally critical, the increasing number of 'Southerners' now living in the North. 'Southern Christianity' as a designation for the emerging Christianity outside the western world was used, for example, by Philip Jenkins, 'Next Christianity', *The Atlantic Monthly*, Oct 2002 (http://www.theatlantic.com/past/docs/issues/ 2002/10/jenkins.htm). Other terms, such as the 'Two-Thirds World', and the 'Majority World', have also been used to refer to the same reality.
[3] Andrew F. Walls, *The Missionary Movement in Christian History: Studies in the Transmission of Faith* (Maryknoll, NY: Orbis, 1996).
[4] Todd M. Johnson and Sun Young Chung, 'Christianity's Centre of Gravity, AD 33-2100', in Todd M. Johnson and Kenneth R. Ross (eds.), *Atlas of Global Christianity* (Edinburgh: Edinburgh University Press, 2009), 50-53.
[5] Philip Jenkins, *The New Faces of Christianity: Believing the Bible in the Global South* (Oxford: Oxford University Press, 2006).

including Christians. This has already changed the landscape of global Christianity and mission.

This also comes with several formidable challenges, and only a few will be outlined here, particularly relevant to Pentecostalism and Pentecostal mission. The first is the 'religiously fundamental' orientation, which has also fuelled the exponential growth. With its extremely conservative theology, it replicates a sort of 'imperialistic' type of mission engagement, which is all too familiar from the western missionary enterprise. Living mostly in religiously pluralistic environments, where sometimes Christianity is a tiny minority, suspicion and persecution from neighbours leads to a challenging Christian life, as the most number of churches burned by Muslim mobs in Indonesia were Pentecostal. In spite of the validity of martyrdom spirituality, Christians and a local congregation are called on to promote a peaceful community life. This extreme evangelism outlook continues its campaign for the other world, while ignoring the church's missionary call to 'this life' matters.

Equally alarming is a strong leaning towards theology of (this worldly) blessing. Although perfectly understandable considering the immediate felt needs of daily struggles, such a message often is indistinguishable from the western-born, self-centred prosperity gospel and can turn Christianity into another self-serving religion, as many indigenous ones have been. Pentecostal-type Christianity can also create popular religious heroes for their charisma of healings and miracles. By commanding a large group of followers, some leaders' celebrity lifestyles, in commensurate to the social context of the majority of believers, can further reinforce the consumerist 'commoditization' of Christian religion.

The bottom line of these challenges is theological construction. Criticisms like [theologically] 'mile wide but inch deep' indicates the need for a serious theological formation, faithful to the scripture and relevant to the context. The regurgitation of western theologians will not serve the Southern church; neither will a theological process to describe or to 'decently' present a super-leader's thoughts point to the future direction of Southern Christianity. It will take a fresh way to read the Bible in its original and our contemporary contexts, and to communicate the message in a way understood and appreciated by the growing churches in the Global South. This will obviously require serious investment in raising up a small number of good theologians. With the increasing awareness of such a need among western church leaders, opportunities are present both in the south and the north. For example, for decades John Stott's Langham Partnership has been instrumental in encouraging the global church to make this serious investment. Langham scholars are now leading theologians in the south, and their contribution is making impact beyond the southern hemisphere. With growing Christianity and also the economy, resources do not have to come only from the west. Emerging churches are also beginning to pay attention to this critical investment for the future.

Pentecostalism

During the one-hundred years of the modern Pentecostal-charismatic movement, it has made many impacts on Christianity in general, but its role in mission is extremely significant. The explosive growth of churches, particularly in the non-western continents, is but one example. Various topics on Pentecostalism such as its origin, theological distinctive, various groupings of Pentecostal/charismatic Christianity, and its inherent missionary values and orientation have been studied by theologians as well as social scientists. Also regional studies are increasing, particularly on North America, Europe, Africa and Latin America, but in a lesser degree on Asia and Eastern Europe. The following discussion is not meant to be comprehensive, but to briefly highlight only those that are relevant to Pentecostal mission.

Then who are Pentecostals today? Already the incredible diversity of Pentecostalism is further complicated by the 'discovery' of new indigenous groups, as well as the constant 'evolution' of the movement. Its neat and clean theological definition was possible only in the first half of the twentieth century, before the advent of the Charismatic movement and the 'discovery' of indigenous Pentecostal-like groups, completely unconnected to the North American roots of Pentecostalism. Although the term is often narrowly used to refer to the denominational or 'classical' Pentecostal groups, its generic use is increasingly adopted to be interchangeably used with 'charismatic Christianity'. This then refers to a wide range of Christians who are open to, believe in, and expect the work—particularly a supernatural kind—of the Holy Spirit, often characterized by an emphasis on experiential and emotive dimension of religious life. The outward expression of such a value includes vibrant and participatory worship, commitment to prayer for God's direct intervention to human needs, zealousness for evangelism, and the like. This form of Christianity tends to attract the marginalized and the poor in society. As the religion *of* the poor, Pentecostalism has brought an empowering effect to masses who are socially and even eccelestically marginalized.

The profile of an average global Pentecostal or charismatic believer is perhaps a female African youth. This fastest-growing segment of global Christianity is extremely difficult to broadly classify. Until now, three divisions have been commonly used: classical (or denominational) Pentecostals, Charismatic (or Neo-) Pentecostals, and indigenous (or Neo-Charismatic) Pentecostals. Although the first category remains relatively unchanged, the second group has been significantly altered by the addition of independent congregations who do not identify themselves with classical Pentecostals, to the traditional Pentecostal Christians found within established churches. With the increase of evangelically oriented congregations and their networks, the landscape of this group is changing and will continue to change. The last category has been particularly problematic, because of its fluidity and diversity, the 'discovery' of new groups, and also because of some groups that appear to be 'more Pentecostal but less

Christian'. The 'new discovery' includes the majority of the African Initiated churches and Chinese house church networks. What is agreed by many are: 1) The character of global Pentecostal Christianity will be increasingly less western, but more Asian, African and Latin American; and 2) The growth of Pentecostal Christianity is, therefore, 'messy' and yet dynamic, and this chaotic situation is expected to continue in the coming generations.

Mission

Equally impossible in this limited space is a discussion on mission and its contemporary issues. A short discussion then is only in the area concerning Pentecostal mission.

What is mission? This is the subject of detailed discussion by important mission scholars today.[6] For Pentecostals how mission is understood is better seen in their mission practices. Mission is predominantly perceived as 'soul winning'. Two major influences have shaped this. The first is the general evangelical perception of mission such as the North American Holiness movement. The second is eschatological urgency, which was closely linked with the evangelization of the whole world (Matt. 24:14). All other activities such as Bible school ministry, caring for children or relief work (which is sometimes called 'mercy ministry') are to contribute to evangelism and church planting.

This narrowly focused notion of mission is well in line with the general evangelical understanding and practice of mission. One can say that the strong impetus for this understanding is rooted in what is called the Great Commission:

> Therefore go and make disciples of all nations, baptizing them in the name of the Father and of the Son and of the Holy Spirit, and teaching them to obey everything I have commanded you. And surely I am with you always, to the very end of the age (Matt. 28:19-20).[7]

However, there has been growing signs of a broader and more holistic understanding of mission. Again, this has to do, in part, with the development of evangelical mission, particularly from the creation of the Lausanne movement from 1974. The Lausanne Covenant broke a theological ground making social service one of the two 'pillars of mission', along with traditional evangelism. Some Pentecostal churches, called 'progressive Pentecostals' are more intentional in making social service a serious part of their mission work. In addition to the shift in evangelical mission scope, the rise of new mission players from the Global South has also played an important role. The social context of the 'developing' societies requires Christians to take social issues into their

---

[6] For example, Andrew J. Kirk, *What Is Mission?: Theological Explorations* (Minneapolis, MN: Fortress, 2000).

[7] Scripture quotations are taken from the New International Version (NIV) unless indicated otherwise.

mission thinking, such as poverty, health issues (HIV/AIDS, etc), women and children, education, etc.

The biblical base for this broader understanding may be found in John 17:18: 'As you sent me into the world, I have sent them into the world'. According to this model of mission, the move from God's kingdom (or church) toward the world itself is an act of mission. In spite of a danger of making 'everything mission, thus, nothing mission' according to some critics,[8] this model provides an important ground for a broader understanding of mission. According to this model, every issue that society wrestles with is a mission agenda, be it corruption, poverty, or racial conflict. This argument also makes the proposition that the very existence of a church is important in society, even if Christianity is only a tiny minority. This public role of the gospel is an integral part of Christian mission. The vision of Pentecostal mission, however, must go beyond caring for the needy and poor, and this will be further elaborated below.

Towards Pentecostal Missiology

The book intends to present reflections both from biblical/theological and contextual fronts, with the hope to contribute towards the making of a Pentecostal missiology. Here Pentecostalism is taken more generically, or as an umbrella word for the wide range of worldwide charismatic Christianity. As discussed above, mission is also taken beyond evangelism. The chapter on mission and creation theology will attempt to explore the concept of God's plan for restoration and his invitation to human agents in this divine plan. Therefore, mission belongs to God, thus, *missio dei*. Discussions often include practical dimensions of mission engagement, and they come primarily from Asia where the authors' orientation and experience are grounded. The book is an attempt to articulate theological orientation and motivation of certain unique Pentecostal mission practices. Therefore, the approach is a descriptive analysis. Based on the reading of the scripture, the book is also intended to point to a direction, if Pentecostal mission is to be faithful to its theological roots.

Of course, this is not the first attempt for Pentecostal missiology. As a powerful missionary movement, various reflections on the role of the Holy Spirit in mission abound. However, the first systematic presentation of unique Pentecostal mission assumptions and practices is by Melvin Hodges, an American missionary to Latin America. His 'indigenous church' principle proposes a radical strategy to empower national workers as early as possible.[9] Then an extremely useful collection of Pentecostal mission-thinking was

---

[8] Stephen Neill, *Creative Tension* (London: Edinburgh House, 1959), 81 introduced the famous quote, 'If everything is mission, then nothing is mission'.
[9] Melvin L. Hodges, *The Indigenous Church: A Complete Handbook on How to Grow Young Churches* (Springfield, MO: Gospel Publishing House, 1976).

produced by three Pentecostal mission theologian practitioners.[10] In this valuable work, various authors presented biblical and theological basis of Pentecostal mission thinking and approaches. This book has remained as an important resource for Pentecostal mission. Pomerville produced a useful book arguing that Pentecostalism is the third Christian force in mission. This historical and theological study places Pentecostal mission within the large historical and theological context of Christian mission. Gary McGee, in addition to his prolific contributions, produced a historical work of the US Assemblies of God mission.[11] In this two volume work, he incorporated theological motivations. Douglas Petersen published a valuable contribution on Pentecostal social work based on his mission engagement in Latin America. Andrew Lord, an Anglican Charismatic, made an important contribution on Charismatic missiology, which in fact serves as a challenge to typical Pentecostal mission.[12] Allan Anderson researched several cases of Pentecostal mission from early days and forcefully argues that Pentecostalism from the beginning has been a missionary movement.[13] It is clear that there are other important works that deserve more close attention, but this brief survey is to introduce some representative studies on the subject.

Three Ripples of Pentecostal Mission

In its short history of slightly more than one hundred years, Pentecostal/ Charismatic Christianity has not only grown, but has also made a significant contribution to Christian mission. At the time of the 1910 Edinburgh Missionary Conference, which presented a master roadmap to world evangelization 'in our [their] generation', the movement was only four years old (if we count from the 1906 Azusa Street Mission in Los Angeles, California, USA).

It is not surprising that no mention was made in Edinburgh of this deeply controversial group; nor is it surprising that there was no delegate at the conference to represent this new form of Christianity. However, a century later Pentecostal/Charismatic Christianity claims about half a billion adherents worldwide. And it does not show any signs of slowing. The movement is here to stay—or more accurately, 'to travel'— for quite some time.

---

[10] Murray W. Dempster, Byron D. Klaus, and Douglas Petersen (eds.), *Called and Empowered: Global Mission in Pentecostal Perspective* (Peabody, MA: Hendrickson, 1991).
[11] Gary B. McGee, *This Gospel Shall Be Preached: A History and Theology of Assemblies of God Foreign Missions*, 2 vols. (Springfield, MO: Gospel Publishing House, 1986-1989).
[12] Andrew Lord, *Spirit-Shaped Mission: A Holistic Charismatic Missiology* (Bletchley: Paternoster, 2005).
[13] Allan Anderson, *Spreading Fires: The Missionary Nature of Early Pentecostalism* (Maryknoll, NY: Orbis, 2007).

Spheres of Pentecostal mission are divided into three sections: This first is proclamation with the establishment of local congregations as a goal; the second is care for the needy; and the third deeper and wider mission engagement. As each is related to the other, an analogy of three ripples, or three concentric circles, is used.

Pentecostal mission has demonstrated its genius in two specific areas of mission engagement and they roughly correspond with the development of the Pentecostal movement itself.

The First Ripple: The Other Side of Heaven

The first stage of the Pentecostal movement is found in its global expansion, especially in the first half of the twentieth century. Armed with and compelled by eschatological urgency, and a Spirit-filled sense of missionary calling, the expansion of Pentecostal Christianity through missionary activities is unprecedented.

Several Pentecostal mission scholars have provided useful characterizations of their mission force. Allan Anderson, for example, lists six characteristics:

1) Pneumatocentric mission, highlighting the role of the Holy Spirit in mission;
2) Dynamic mission praxis with zeal and commitment;
3) Evangelism as the central mission thrust;
4) Contextualization of leadership or development of local leadership as early as possible;
5) Mobilization in mission where everyone is called and empowered for witness;
6) Contextual missiology with creativity in packaging the gospel to be relevant to the local cultural and social setting.[14]

In a 2007 article, I portrayed the Pentecostal mission forces as 'the poor now fired up'.[15] Their marginality in various settings has made them fittingly 'poor' in every sense. They are even marginalized by other churches. The mission forces are characterized by:

1) Their deep zeal and commitment (exemplified by 'one-way ticket missionaries' of the early days of the movement);
2) Everyone's involvement in mission by its democratized theology of mission and ministry (or their belief in the 'prophet hood of all believers');

---

[14] Allan Anderson, 'Towards a Pentecostal Missiology for the Majority World', *AJPS* 8:1 (2005), 28-47.

[15] Wonsuk Ma, '"When the Poor Are Fired Up": The Role of Pneumatology in Pentecostal-Charismatic Mission', *Transformation* 24:1 (2007), 28-34.

3) Mission with healing and miracles;
4) A priority of inner change and evangelism with other ministries such as 'care', ultimately contributing to evangelism;
5) Empowerment missiology with implications not only for the church, missionaries, but also for the new recipient lands;
6) Their unique ecumenical potential as demonstrated in the Azusa Street Mission with its ecumenical and interracial congregation and leadership.

Pentecostals have been more engaged in practitioner work rather than reflection; thus, there is far more 'fruit' of their mission engagement than there is literature about their missionary work. Many reports have exclaimed the exponential growth of this movement. Equally impressive is the movement's unusual ability to engage with the context (social and cultural) to create forms of Christianity that are dynamic and engaging. The sheer size and dynamism of the movement has turned its churches, particularly those in the Global South, into a powerful mission force 'from South to South' as well as 'reverse mission to the West'.

Theologically, classical Pentecostals provided leadership and a theological basis for this mission thrust. Highly motivated by the unique empowerment theology for witness—and further fuelled by the eschatological urgency of the return of the Lord—evangelism was the most logical consequence. The continuing mission energy and commitment in spite of the unfulfilled eschatological 'prophecies' proves that the main motivation for Pentecostal mission lies in its unique pneumatological missiology rather than the eschatological drive.

The Second Ripple: This Side of Heaven
From the 1960s, the movement expanded its influence and experienced a significant transformation in its mission engagement. The rise of the Charismatic or Neo-Pentecostal movement brought Pentecostalism to the Christian mainstream as the spiritual dynamic spread throughout the established denominations, including the Roman Catholic Church. It also spread among the social mainstream as the middle classes embraced the 'religion of the poor'.

This period also witnessed the quick disappearance of eschatological expectations among Pentecostal minds and pulpits. At the same time, Pentecostalism began to grow in significance in Latin America, Asia, and Africa. The spread of the controversial 'prosperity gospel' also contributed to the development of the 'Southern' Pentecostalism. That is when some social scientists began to notice Pentecostal's unique contribution to the social and economic upward mobility of its members. This interest has been increasing and the recent publication of Donald Miller and Tetsunao Yamamori's four-year research project is a good example of this.[16]

In mission settings, care for those in need is a strong part of Pentecostal mission practice. Specific approaches include orphanages, feeding programs, vocational schools, medical clinics, and educational programs. Even social contexts hostile towards open evangelism have led Pentecostals in some countries to develop drug rehabilitation centres, children's homes, and elderly homes.

Recently, a new breed of Pentecostal churches, particularly in the Global South, has taken social service seriously. Miller and Yamamori call them 'progressive Pentecostals'. It is worth noting that such churches are increasing in the southern continents as their social contexts demand that churches provide a more proactive response to social issues. The uniqueness of the 'progressive Pentecostals' is characterized by a 'bottom up' and a 'one-person-at-a-time' approach.

This second stage of Pentecostal mission has resulted in social and economic upward mobility. Many studies have focused on the correlation between one's spiritual experience and behavioural changes, which inevitably creates a ripple effect from personal life to family and community life. Although there is a risk of privatization of the religious experience and a self-centred or materialistic-centred 'prosperity gospel', studies have proven the critical role of having an inner or spiritual change in one's social life and economic activities.

Pentecostals, including 'progressives', are expected to continue to push their mission envelope to include social issues in the life 'this side of heaven', or 'life before death'. Pentecostal scholars have a daunting task to provide a solid theology that is distinctly Pentecostal in various social contexts around the world.

The Third Ripple: Deeper and Wider Mission Engagement

The final section of the chapter will deal with a third area of Pentecostal mission, a deeper and more strategic level of social engagement and beyond. This level of mission engagement often aims at 'justice' in social, economic, political, racial and environmental areas. 'Reconciliation' is another term used for this sphere of mission engagement, which includes ecumenism, peace initiatives, and environmental stewardship. Although the third level takes place on the same social level as the 'care' and 'service' of the second level, this will require a quantum leap in Pentecostal mission thinking and practice.

This section presents a concrete setting as a launching point and poses challenging questions for Pentecostal mission engagement. This issue deserves deep reflection by both insiders (Pentecostals) and outsiders (friends of Pentecostals).

---

[16] Donald E. Miller and Yamamori Tetsunao, *Global Pentecostalism: The New Face of Christian Social Engagement* (Berkeley, CA: University of California Press, 2007).

My first visit to Nairobi exposed me to three types of Pentecostal congregations. The first congregation was on the outskirts of Nairobi. It was full of the urban poor and rural immigrants. Its construction-in-progress sanctuary seemed to suggest its growth, spontaneity and creative responses to emerging circumstances, as seen in the creative, impromptu moves of their dynamic worship. The primary interest of the worshippers seemed to be focused on daily survival and God's help in enabling them to live today and tomorrow. My admonition in mission did not excite them very much.

The second congregation was in the heart of the city. It was full of young adults who appeared to be mostly professionals. This energetic congregation was in stark contrast to the first one I had ministered to just an hour earlier. Undoubtedly organized by the middle classes, the worship was presented professionally (evidently coming from first-class musicians, singers, and dancers and the first-class audio and lighting facilities). My unplanned message was on the Azusa Street story and its missionary call. The pastor's humble request for me to pray that his church would obey the great missionary calling, in turn, humbled me. My friends and I apologetically excused ourselves as a samba dance presentation brought the whole congregation into another height of excitement in worship.

The third congregation was a more 'settled' Pentecostal church in an exclusive, middle-class, residential area known for its active mission engagements, including gospel outreach work and social service. I did not participate in their worship, as by the time we passed by the area, people had begun to jam the parking lot and nearby streets. A casual look at its demography showed a contrast between this church and the highly-charged youth congregation on the other side of the city. The presence of many children suggested a wider age distribution. Also, the presence of vehicles in the overflowing parking lot and the nearby streets, and the way people dressed revealed that the congregation had a relatively higher social and economic level. This church also had the best building among the three.

Although the churches may be different, and the people may worship in different ways, there is no question that Kenya has experienced a surge of Charismatic Christianity, both in urban and rural communities. This is not limited to just Pentecostal denominations, African initiated churches, and independent Charismatic groups. New expressions of spirituality and worship (which some argue is rooted in African religiosity) are increasingly found in the historic churches as well. Pentecostal Christianity has been shifting African religious demography. I returned home genuinely impressed.

An entirely different scene was presented less than a month later in the aftermath of the December, 2007 Kenyan general election. I do not need to go into the painful details of the political, social, and now racial, conflict. The situation can be analyzed in many ways, but it also poses some challenging questions to Christians.

First, how could this robust economy and peaceful society be shattered overnight by a political tilt? If the majority of Kenyans are Christians—and a good number of them evangelical and Spirit-filled—then one cannot deny that church-goers must have participated in the destruction of their neighbours' lives, including those of fellow Christians. Secondly, if this is the case, then how do one's social values quickly override his or her spiritual commitment? My own focus has been on how the growing 'spiritual capital' of the country has played so small a role in the face of this social unrest. I am not trying to suggest that growing Christianity was expected to prevent such social conflict, as the social dynamic is extremely complex. However, it is natural to expect that the growing spiritual 'capital' should have promoted more Kingdom signs in the society.

TOWARDS ENGAGEMENT WITH SOCIAL ISSUES

This section will introduce some guiding thoughts to encourage already 'progressive' Pentecostals to engage more deeply and broadly with social issues and beyond:

1) The success and sustenance of much of the micro-mission engagement (or the second ripple) depends on the stability of the macro-level structure, although the spiritual dimension (evangelized souls) may continue to remain unchanged. For example, many cases of social and economic upward mobility are extremely vulnerable to social stability. Here lies the essential nature of this level of mission engagement, and Pentecostals have to move beyond the first two levels of mission activities.

2) The unique 'Pentecostal' approach to this mission engagement begins with the assessment of Pentecostal mission resources. Several studies, as briefly mentioned above, inform us of Pentecostalism's unique resources. However, two stand out: a) the dynamism coming from the unique Pentecostal spirituality and experience with the 'divine', and b) its sheer number of adherents, which can easily turn into a political resource. The empowerment missiology of Pentecostalism also has an extraordinary potential to mobilize massive numbers of front-line mission practitioners among its laity.

3) Equally important is the 'bottom up' or 'from individual to community' movement. This 'people's movement' comes with strong motivation and relevance; it includes a real-life setting in their mission engagement. Related is the 'from inside out' movement: the inner or spiritual change becomes the fundamental basis of changes in the physical, the behavioural, the family, and the community.

In fact, the Pentecostal approach towards deeper mission engagement should employ these unique Pentecostal mission resources. This will make its mission contribution distinctly Pentecostal.

STRUGGLE WITH DEEPER ISSUES

So how can Pentecostals continue to strengthen the dynamic growth in church, mission, and influence, while renewing this powerful movement with the more intentional goal of mission? How can the powerful mission force, which has prepared people for heaven so well, be made equally powerful in empowering people for this world as well? Or to put the question differently, why are Pentecostals so miserably ill-prepared for life this side of heaven, especially in the face of macro-scale challenges (be it social unrest, ethnic conflicts, corruption, oppressive political systems, economic injustice, church divisions, or environmental degradation)? Why is the characteristic dynamism of Pentecostals confined or trapped in the spiritual sphere? Three points to bring Pentecostal mission forward:

First, Pentecostals, like their evangelical cousins, need to seriously revisit their understanding of mission. Pentecostals never lack in missionary activities. In fact, they are 'sold out to mission' as their exponential growth attests. Since this is true, the disconnection may be blamed on the kind of theological orientation of mission that prevails among the believers as well as the leadership. A narrowly-defined concept of mission is now hurting the overgrown church. The 'rescue boat' mode of mission is not going to serve the highly complex lifestyles of today. Mission engagement now stretches from soul-saving to earth-saving for the next generation.

Secondly, Pentecostal missiology is characterized by its emphasis on 'power' or 'empowerment'. There have been two issues related to power. The first is the early Pentecostals' narrow understanding of power. Based on Acts 1:8, the 'power' was generally understood as a spiritual one (i.e., power to overcome evil, heal, or prophecy). This narrow view has been gradually corrected and expanded, not through an intentional theological revision, but more intuitively and circumstantially, to include non-spiritual components such as economic advancement. An example of this is found where some Pentecostals begin to turn the swelling size of their Pentecostal constituencies into political capital. Some leaders now run for public offices. If sound theological guidance is not provided, this will follow the path of the prosperity gospel. The second issue is the weakest part of power: corruptibility. As the old saying goes, 'power tends to corrupt'. Unfortunately, Pentecostals do not lack examples to prove this, as we have seen enough charismatic 'stars' fall. Thus, every power requires serious regulation and guidance. This is why the Pentecostal theological task is more pressing than other less power-oriented groups. The seduction of power is so great that Pentecostals must develop an equally rigorous theology of power, so that power will be wielded for God's mission, and not for an individual's ambitions.

Thirdly, a change in outlook concerning leadership is needed. The height of wonderful charismatic leadership also comes with a long shadow. Often organisational power is in the hands of the leader of a congregation. Therefore, leadership plays a decisive role not only in causing good growth and mission expansion, but also in threatening its very existence, not to mention its mission.

One large African indigenous church has been going through a leadership crisis, and its vibrant church life and mission has been critically affected by this. Leadership is a complex phenomenon and a good theological treaty will not be sufficient to resolve the issue. Culture, social dynamism, and changes in social life are to be studied carefully as well.

Summary

This reflection has only touched the surface of many urgent and important issues. I invite Pentecostal mission thinkers and practitioners from every part of the globe to join in this important discussion. In speaking about the ripples, it is important to further explore the idea that the ripple is not the result of a single stone dropping into a lake. Rather, the ripples are created by an underwater spring which constantly provides energy to create the ripples. This analogy teaches two important lessons:

First, the unique Pentecostal spirituality is the springhead of the mission dynamism and ethos. Pentecostals need to acquire an historical and ecumenical sense that its theological and spiritual tradition is a unique gift from God to the global church and to the world.

Secondly, Pentecostals should be careful not to 'graduate' from their 'primal' form of spirituality as they begin to attain social and ecclesial respectability. We have some painful historical lessons from spiritual renewal movements which later turned into sophisticated ecclesial forms by acquiring all the academic and social amenities. They lost what once made them unique and powerful.

Further, the ripple analogy suggests the interrelatedness of the ripples. One ripple (e.g., the evangelism thrust with spiritual fervour) resources the next one (individual behaviours and values and family life), while the latter informs the former by providing resources for theological reflection and revision. With the rise of the Southern Pentecostal communions, the creativity of Pentecostal mission will expand, while equally formidable challenges are discovered. After all, the journey of Pentecostal mission is not much different from what its evangelical cousins are struggling with in mission engagement. This makes mission a kingdom business.

PART ONE

Reflections

Chapter 2

Spirit, Creation Theology, and Mission

Introduction

Pentecostals rightly consider Acts 2 as the birth of the church through the outpouring of the Holy Spirit upon Christ's disciples. Therefore, the involvement of the Spirit is essential in the life of the church, as well as in its mission to the world. From the beginning of the Pentecostal movement, Acts 1:8 has been the bedrock of its *raison d'etre*: 'But you will receive power when the Holy Spirit comes on you; and you will be my witnesses in Jerusalem, and in all Judea and Samaria, and to the ends of the earth'. Naturally, Pentecostal pneumatology is focused on the empowerment work of the Holy Spirit, and its pneumatology has a strong missiological motif.[1] This may explain at least in part the explosive growth of the global Pentecostal-charismatic churches in the last hundred years.

Just as a sharply focused energy can become extremely powerful, so has this power-oriented, or charismatic, Pentecostal missiology, drawn from Lukan pneumatology. However, from a historical observation, it has also become evident that this intensely focused mission movement has created several serious blind spots. Some of the ignored areas of mission are ecumenism, social justice, poverty, environmental concerns, and others. In other words, Pentecostal mission has not been holistic in its thinking and practice; but rather, evangelism and church planning has been the primary focus and the full extent of Pentecostal mission until recently.[2] This narrow focus was increased by eschatological urgency as people understood that the modern outpouring of the Spirit signified the last hour of human history.[3] Naturally, that increased the extent of the blind

---

[1] For the empowerment motif of Pentecostal missiology, see W. Ma, '"When the Poor Are Fired Up"', 28-34.

[2] In 2003, US Assemblies of God World Mission added 'Touching' as a new 'pillar' to their mission practice to the existing three: 'reaching' (that is, evangelism), 'planting' (churches) and 'training' (local workers and leaders). See Assemblies of God World Mission, 'Our Mission' (http://worldmissions.ag.org/about/about_mission.cfm, 2005), accessed: April 4, 2008. It is 'touching poor and suffering people with the compassion of Jesus Christ and inviting them to become His followers'.

[3] For the role of eschatology in Pentecostal life, see Wonsuk Ma, 'Pentecostal Eschatology: What Happened When the Wave Hit the West of the Ocean', in Harold D.

spots within Pentecostal mission thinking and practices. This raises the question of how we maintain the unique dynamism in mission whilst minimizing its blind spots?

One way to resolve this dilemma is to trace God's mission and the work of the Spirit much further back than in the book of Acts. In fact, I am suggesting that we go all the way back to the theology of creation in the Old Testament, particularly from the book of Genesis.

In this study, we will pursue three major aspects of creation theology through studying selected passages which refer to the role of God's Spirit.[4] The passages also include those with reference to God's restoration. After studying the passages, we will consider the implications for Pentecostal mission thinking and practice, with the hope that broadening mission scope and deepening mission roots will provide a much wider foundation. This in turn, we pray, will strengthen Pentecostal mission without diminishing its uniquely focused dynamism.

Pneumatology of God's Creation

For each heading, there will be two groups of passages: for the creation in the beginning and for the restoration of God's people at the end of the age. It is possible that a short discussion will link between the two.

The Spirit as Creator

IN CREATION

In Genesis 1:2, God's Spirit is above the water which is part of the chaotic disorder. The undisclosed role of God's Spirit is explored in various passages throughout the Old Testament.

In Job 26, we hear Job's response to a charge lodged by two of his friends based on God's power and splendour in creation. Job counter-argues using the same creation motif: 'By his power he churned up the sea; by his wisdom he cut Rahab to pieces; by his breath ('Spirit') the skies became fair; his hand pierced the gliding serpent' (Job 26:12, 13). Here God's Spirit is responsible for making the skies fair: the Spirit is the creator.

Similarly, Isaiah 40 records God's challenge to the idols of nations to match God's power. In fact, God provokes the idols to present any counter-evidence to prove that he is not the unchallenged supreme God. The main point is clearly

---

Hunter and Cecil M. Robeck, Jr. eds., *The Azusa Street Revival and Its Legacy* (Cleveland, TN: Pathway, 2006), 227-42.

[4] For the OT references to God's spirit, the lower case 's' is the accurate usage, as the spirit was not yet understood by ancient Israelites as a person of the Godhead. However, as this study extends beyond the OT, often referring to the Holy Spirit, the capital 'S' is consistently adopted.

God's supremacy as displayed in his creative acts: 'Who has understood the
mind (or 'Spirit') of the Lord, or instructed him as his counsellor?' (Isa. 40:13).
Yahweh's supreme wisdom required no counsel from any deity. In fact, there is
no god who could fathom God's mind.

Isaiah 32:15-18 may serve as the best example:

> ...till the Spirit is poured upon us from on high,
> and the desert becomes a fertile field,
> and the fertile field seems like a forest.
> Justice will dwell in the desert
> and righteousness live in the fertile field.
> The fruit of righteousness will be peace;
> the effect of righteousness will be quietness and confidence forever.
> My people will live in peaceful dwelling places,
> in secure homes, in undisturbed places of rest.

After an oscillation between restoration and judgment in 32:1-14, v. 15
introduces a radically new era. And this new day is ushered in through the
outpouring of the Spirit from on high. The language is unmistakable in its
abundance. Also noted is its 'democratic' scope: God's Spirit is going to be
present among his people, unlike the limited presence among selected leaders in
the past. The first change that occurs is the transformation of the land. The desert
or parched land will become a fertile field, now arable for abundant farming, and
the fertile field will be like a forest. The coming of the Spirit actually brings
fertility to the land (e.g., Isa. 44:3). Then v. 16 moves to the ethical dimension of
the society: the presence of justice and righteousness will flourish. It is important
to note that Israel was judged due to the lack of justice in the society, and the
idolatry. The link between the presence of social justice and the Spirit of God has
been established in Isaiah 11. The immediate effect of justice and righteousness
is a society that is peace itself. Peacefulness is confidence in one another, in God
and his presence, and in the future ('forever') of the community of faith.

The Spirit as the Giver and Sustainer of Life

This is a most common role for God's Spirit, as we will see in Genesis 2. God is
viewed specifically as the giver of life and his Spirit is frequently associated with
'breath'.

Job 33:4 is a clear expression of this belief: 'The Spirit of God has made me;
the breath of the Almighty gives me life'. Here the Spirit of God is responsible
for creating humans, and this act is specifically identified as the giving of breath.
In the same way, sustenance of human life is linked to the continual presence of
such Spirit/breath. Job 34:14-15 tells, 'If he should take back his Spirit to

himself, and gather to himself his breath, all flesh would perish together and all mortals return to dust' (NRSV). The passage emphasises that the breath in humans is indeed God's Spirit and he has the prerogative to keep it in, or withdraw it from, humans. This makes humans extremely vulnerable and human existence is completely dependent upon God's continual creative care. Sustenance of human life, or in this case, the maintenance of God's Spirit in humans, is part of God's creative activity.

A similar expression is found in Psalm 104:29 which reads: 'When you hide your face, they [creation] are terrified; when you take away their breath, they die and return to the dust'. In this passage, the concept of sustenance is extended to all creation, while God's provision goes beyond mere existence: the creation is 'satisfied with good things'. However, when he hides his face and takes away breath, the creation is terrified and eventually perishes. Verse 30 reverses this gloomy fate: 'When you send your Spirit, they are created, and you renew the face of the earth'. God is the giver of life through his Spirit, hence, in complete control over his creation. He can also renew his creation through the same Spirit. This opens a surprising possibility that when Israel went through the exilic experience they were terrified, 'died and returned to the dust'. The God of creation is also the God of re-creation.

A series of passages in the book of Ezekiel seem to allude to the role of the Spirit in giving strength to humans. In the prophet's first visionary experience (Ezek. 1:28), he fell face down (1:28), presumably describing a state, '…when I lost physical and mental strength'. Then the Spirit of God 'came into him and raised' the prophet to his feet (2:2). Similarly, in 3:23, he faced the glory of Yahweh, and as a result, he 'fell face down'. In this case too, the Spirit came into the prophet and 'raised' him. It is plausible then to think that the Spirit strengthened and energized the prophet, and this is in line with the life-giving and life-sustaining work of God's Spirit.

IN RE-CREATION

In Ezekiel 37, the prophet was brought to the valley of vast dry bones by the Spirit of God. The complete hopelessness of the 'whole house of Israel' (v. 12) is a stark reality, and there is no possibility of restoration in a normal process (v. 3). It takes God's re-creation. The resurrection of the dry bones takes two stages: the restoration of the body and the entering of 'breath' (or 'Spirit'), just as in the original creation in Genesis 2.

The 'spirit' or 'breath' is described as coming from 'four winds' or 'four corners' of the world (cf. Gen. 1:2). This distinct life-giving work of the Spirit is identical to the original creation, but this time, it is only applied to the nation as a whole. The exile is the grave of the nationhood and also of the covenant relationship. The return to the promised land will be another exodus, but this time a greater miracle of redemption, not from slavery but from death (v. 12). His Spirit will bring this dead nation into life. 'These bones' (e.g., v. 4) will become 'my people' (v. 12), a tender covenant designation for Israel. They also are to become a 'vast army' (v. 10).

Allen observes rightly that in this passage, the agency of the prophet is a unique feature.[5] The prophet's command has brought about the process of bodily 'assembly' and another command caused the coming of the Spirit into the lifeless bodies.

The Spirit as Divine in Human

This idea has been suggested by scholars when the two creation reports in Genesis 1 and 2 are discussed. It has to do with the uniqueness of human creation. However, its relationship with the Spirit of God has not been explored. There are three passages to discuss, but only one of them has a direct reference to God's Spirit.

IN CREATION

'Image' (Gen. 1:26-28)
Humans were made according to God's 'image' (1:27), but the exact meaning is not known. But this makes humans distinct from, and superior to, other creations, especially animals. What is commonly agreed upon among scholars is that the 'image' represents a reality, in this case the reality of the creator. Throughout Ancient Near East and the Old Testament, the term often refers to religious images. The wooden or metal image of a deity, once consecrated to a sanctuary, is believed to contain some aspects of the deity's presence. Then the image is believed to be a receptacle of the extended presence of the deity or figure it represents.

This provides a reasonable basis for us to conclude that humans were made in God's 'image', first of all, to have a certain, although unknown, aspect(s) of God's being, and secondly, through that imparted element, humans represent God, the creator, in his creation. One can then reasonably conclude that the 'image' represents 'divine (aspects) in humans'. This also provides a basis for the human's authority to rule over God's creation as his regent, a kingly role.

'Breath of Life'
In this microscopic presentation of creation in Genesis 2, it is now God's breath of life that makes the first man different from the animals. As a result he became 'a living being'. The Hebrew word here is not 'Spirit', but we have already observed a close parallelism between these two words in several passages. Again, this is something of the divine granted to the human, as Gunkel suggests. Therefore, it is suspected that the 'breath' which Adam received from God is more than just a life-giving and sustaining force, commonly noted as the

---

[5] Leslie C. Allen, *Ezekiel 20-48*, Word Biblical Commentary 29 (Dallas: Word, 1990), 185.

movement of air through the nostrils. For Adam, it was 'God's breath' making him a 'living being', different from the animals: thus, it is 'breath plus'. The 'plus' is an element of God that was graciously granted to humans. In this way, humans are sharers of an unspecified character and nature of God in a limited degree, along with authority and responsibility.

This 'plus' notion is further confirmed in the report of the human fall. Death as predicted by God was more than a physical death, which did not occur immediately, but severance from God the creator and the alienated relationship with the rest of creation took place immediately. This loss signifies that what is lost is this 'plus' factor, that is, 'divine (aspects) in human'. Thus, humans were created in God's image, and 'powered' by his breath-Spirit to fulfil God's creation purpose!

'Sons of God(s)' (Gen. 6)

Genesis 6:1-3 includes an ancient myth, which was later appropriated by the Genesis author:

> When men began to increase in number on the earth and daughters were born to them, the sons of God saw that the daughters of men were beautiful, and they married any of them they chose. Then the LORD said, 'My Spirit will not abide in man forever, for he is mortal; his days will be a hundred and twenty years'.

Although ambiguity looms especially over the identity of the 'sons' and the 'daughters', it is evident that the 'sons' are meant to be 'a class that is utterly superior'.[6] Also obvious is the fact that the union between the 'sons of God/gods' and the 'daughters of human' is seen in a negative way, being a serious offence to God's creation order. As a result, 'My [God's] Spirit shall not abide in mortals forever, for they are flesh...' (v. 3).[7] Through this verdict, we learn that the immortality of the 'sons of God/gods' is attributed to the presence of God's Spirit, as the mortals will not have the same Spirit indefinitely. This state is called 'flesh' and this is quite different from 'the living being' in our previous discussion. Thus, the presence of God's Spirit distinguished them from the humans as well as their daughters. The Spirit, then, is something of God that had been graciously granted to the 'sons of God/gods', thus giving them a special status in contrast to other creations including 'mortals'. Even though the limitation of the life span suggests 'breath' as the primary meaning of the Hebrew word used here (which is normally translated as 'Spirit'), the Spirit also made them the 'sons of God/gods'.

---

[6] Claus Westermann, *Genesis 1-11: A Commentary*, trans. John J. Scullion (Minneapolis: Augsburg, 1984), 367.

[7] E.A. Speiser, *Genesis* (Garden City, NY: Doubleday, 1964), 44, translates רוח as 'shield' thus providing protection. That the Spirit of God protects humans is not a known usage in the Old Testament. Others translate this as 'contends' (e.g., NIV).

IN RE-CREATION (EZEK. 36:24-28)

The passage to bring God's restoration of this 'divine in human' comes from Ezekiel 36. Before we look at the passage in detail, it is important to form a link between God's creation and Israel. The election of Israel follows closely the creation of humans. The creation of humans with 'divine in them' is much like the creation of the nation Israel with its divine covenant relationship. As the humans are to represent their creator among creation, so Israel is to represent God among the nations. As humans lost by sin their special status with privilege and responsibility, Israel lost its God-given special status with privilege and calling. Therefore, the restoration of Israel in its land with a renewed covenant is analogous to the restoration of humans with the 'divine' in them. Here is the promise of God to Israel:

> For I will take you out of the nations; I will gather you from all the countries and bring you back into your own land. I will sprinkle clean water on you, and you will be clean; I will cleanse you from all your impurities and from all your idols. I will give you a new heart and put a new spirit in you; I will remove from you your heart of stone and give you a heart of flesh. And I will put my Spirit in you and move you to follow my decrees and be careful to keep my laws. You will live in the land I gave your forefathers; you will be my people, and I will be your God.

In this plan of restoration, God will recover his people (v. 24). This 'return' is entirely God's initiative, as it was his name that had been profaned among the nations (Ezek. 36:20-22). The restoration of the people, however, cannot be completed unless there is an inner change; only then will the land be truly restored.

Verses 25-27 are our main focus: the Spirit of God and the inner restoration of God's people. God brings inner transformation by removing impurities and idolatry. Therefore, the foundational issue is the 'heart' problem. God is going to remove their stony hearts, and give them a new heart of flesh, warm and responding toward God's gracious covenantal relationship with them. This spiritual and national 'heart transplant' is completed by putting a new spirit in them. This spirit is identified as God's own Spirit in v. 27, and the result is the reversal of the old 'stone' age: God's empowerment ('move') to become a faithful people of the covenant relationship by following God's decrees and observing his laws. Here God, by putting in his own Spirit, is restoring Israel's special status among the nations. Once this heart problem is resolved through the coming of God's Spirit, the people of God are restored.

Now, How about Mission in the Spirit?

The brief study of the Spirit's role in the process of God's creation and re-creation points us to several key issues of Christian mission, or more specifically of Pentecostal mission.

Mission as the Centre of God's Activity in History

If creation is the beginning of God's engagement with creation and humans in history, the ultimate goal of God's activity in history is the restoration of his creation. History, then, is the platform where he unfolds and executes his mission plans. Therefore, the mission is the centre of God's revelation and historical engagements with the world and humans. From hindsight, it is tempting to say that the 'word' and the 'Spirit' were with God as the creator, the Trinity. The re-creation also involves God's plan for restoration, the 'word' initiating the process (as in the dry bone experience in Ezek. 37), and the 'Spirit' giving life to the whole army, again the Trinity.

What can be argued is that the revelation and history cannot be interpreted without God's clear plan for the mission. This foundational understanding provides guidance to any theological study: if the mission is missing as the motivation and goal of God's activity in human history, the study is not complete. This also makes the mission the ultimate purpose of the calling of God's people, be it Israel or the church, or individually or collectively, and the very reason for their existence.

Mission as the Restoration of God's Creation

'What is mission' has become a bewildering question among Christians. However, our study makes it clear that mission begins with God's commitment to restore his creation. For this reason, the church's mission is indeed participation in God's mission of restoration. In a number of ways, Pentecostals have taken this element seriously. First of all, the movement itself is a restorationist one: restoring the dynamics of the early church, for example. Secondly, the charismatic evolution in the 1960s demonstrated its 'renewal' potential to many historic churches through the presence and work of the Holy Spirit. Ultimately, such a reform or renewal results in the renewing of the missionary commitment of the church.

Several concepts are related to this idea of restoration. Particularly significant to Pentecostal thinking is healing. With its long-standing tradition of divine healing, mission as God's restoration of individual and communal life is at the heart of Pentecostal mission. However, the ministry and idea of healing has been confined to physical and, at most, mental and emotional spheres of individual lives. Popular Pentecostal-charismatic healing evangelists such as Oral Roberts and ordinary pastors with regular healing ministry exemplify this emphasis. However, the scripture, particularly the Old Testament, uses the term 'to heal' in a much broader way, surely including physical healing. One common example is Isaiah 53. In this Servant Song, the vicarious suffering Servant is portrayed. His affliction is, first of all, for 'our infirmities', 'our transgressions', and 'for our iniquities' (v. 5). Immediately, the restoration of a community of faith is the object of restoration, which includes, no doubt, physical healing (as the same verse is often quoted by Pentecostals to claim healing). However, physical healing is part of the much broader restoration of the community. In the same vein, Jeremiah declared God's promise: 'I will bring health and healing to it [the city, that is, Jerusalem]; I will heal my people and will let them enjoy abundant peace and security...' (Jer. 33:6). This clearly shows that the biblical concept of healing is much broader and comprehensive, from physical to emotional, social, communal and national. If Pentecostals develop the theological capability to apply their prized heritage of healing to the broken families, relationships, divided churches and societies, racial conflicts and moral decay, the impact of Pentecostal mission will be unimaginable.

The broad scope of God's mission found in the theology of creation, however, immediately challenges Pentecostal mission, which has narrowly focused its efforts on evangelism and church planting. The Isaiah 32 passage is especially informative, as the Spirit not only ushers in the long-awaited new era, but the re-creative power of the Spirit brings about fertility and prosperity, physical wholeness (which Pentecostals have well augmented), and also moral transformation in the society. The restoration of social justice, therefore, is definitely part of God's mission agenda. The 'peace', which seems to be the final goal of God's restoration, compels God's people to be more involved in various socio-political issues. In fact, almost every social agenda, or struggle of the people, should be a Christian agenda, thus, mission agenda. Mission engagement, however, is to be focused on its final goal: restoration of God's creation to the state of 'goodness' (e.g., Gen. 1:4) through the creative power of the Spirit.

Another important issue is that God's entire creation is the target of the church's missionary calling. This makes environmental stewardship an important mission agenda. It is understandable that Pentecostal ideology was shared not only by its pneumatic experience but also by the urgency of the Lord's return as informed by pre-millennial eschatology. Equally inadequate is the extremely spiritualized New Testament pneumatology in dealing with any physical and material aspect of God's restoration. The only exception is physical healing (and the lately popularized 'theology of blessing'). The theological polarization between liberals and conservatives does not help, as social and environmental concerns have become a hallmark of 'liberal' theology. However, the modern environmental disasters, especially in the Southern regions, have challenged evangelical and Pentecostal Christians to be more serious about environmental stewardship. This necessitates the revisitation of creation theology. Pentecostals as 'people of the Spirit' need to develop a heightened awareness of, and take responsible action towards, God's creation. The whole earth is God's creation and humans have a special responsibility to care for it.

Centrality of Humans in God's Mission

In the creation theology, God intentionally set humans apart from the rest of creation by placing something 'divine' in humans. This also afforded humans a unique role to play in God's creation and in the process of re-creation. It was humans who defiled God's image by sin, and, as a consequence, the whole creation suffered. As God saves Israel because his name has been defiled among the nations (Ezek. 36:22), he is committed to redeeming humans as the bearer of his image.

Humans also become God's agency of restoration. The election of Israel was part of God's plan, and so was the coming of Christ as man. Therefore, the outpouring of the Spirit upon humans (or God's people) triggers a chain of restorational actions in various aspects of human society (as in Isa. 32). In Isaiah 11:6-9, this effect is further expanded to the entire creation. The righteous rule of the eschatological king through the empowerment of the Spirit results in a perfect harmony in God's created world.

For this reason, the Pentecostals' traditional emphasis on 'saving [human] souls' is the right focus. In fact, its empowerment theology has prepared the 'saved souls' to be empowered witnesses to the ends of the earth (Acts 1:8). The instrumentality of human agents is further brought forward by the critical role of the prophet in restoring the dry bones (Ezek. 37). This also challenges Pentecostals to view the entirety of human life as a 'mission field'. Especially important is human suffering as a critical mission agenda. Suffering is the sign of anti-creation, and God's people are called not only to care for those who suffer, but also to fight the roots of human suffering. This includes poverty, corruption, materialism, human trafficking, child labour, HIV-AIDS, women's issues, and other issues. Pentecostals are called to develop their missiology so that God's mission will truly empower those who suffer.

The Spirit's Work in Community Context

It is very interesting to note that all the passages we have discussed for God's re-creation have a community setting as their context. Equally significant is the Spirit's presence within the community of people of God so that they will experience the restoration of the covenant relationship (Ezek. 36). The S/spirit of God draws his people into the company of a worshiping and serving community (e.g., 1 Sam. 10:5-6). The community-forming power of the Spirit is well attested historically and it challenges mission in the Spirit to act consciously in a community context. This parameter is particularly challenging to Pentecostals, as the modern renewal movement has tended to accentuate the individualized form of Christianity. As part of the large modern evangelicalism, salvation, suffering, blessing, healing, baptism in the Spirit, spiritual gifts and miracles are theologically perceived as a personal matter. Granted that individualistic western culture has become part of Pentecostal spirituality (as it was made in the U.S.A.), it is important that a concerted effort is made, especially by the churches in the Global South, that the authentic form of Pentecostal theology and spirituality is recovered in its worship, church life and mission practices.

In the modern missionary context, highly individualistic Pentecostal behaviour works against the path of the Spirit. Although a spiritual renewal may cause some fall outs, the presence of the Spirit should also bring divided churches and communities together. In the 1960s and 70s the way in which various traditional churches celebrated common faith and the working of the

Spirit together, is a powerful demonstration of the Spirit's potential for bringing people together. As the ecumenical movement has strongly argued, the presence of a divided church in a non-Christian society is against the mission of God. From the work of the Spirit uniting his people together, God's people can, in turn, bring the power of the Spirit to divided nations, people, groups and conflicts. Therefore, mission in the Spirit has a broader mandate.

Last Words

Having stated this broad spectrum of God's mission agenda, there are several important points of caution.

The first is a disclaimer: the theology of creation is only one of several bases that motivate Christian mission. For Pentecostal missiology, the most influential theological ground is its theology of empowerment, often anchored on the unique experience called baptism in the Holy Spirit. What is discussed here is something which Pentecostal mission has failed to pay serious attention to. Therefore, in order to have a full perspective on mission in the Spirit, it will be important to consider other theological contributions to the shaping of their mission thinking and practice. A healthy dose of eschatology, which was characteristic of early Pentecostalism, should guide Christian mission so that the ultimate restoration is an eschatological reality, and Christian mission is an attempt to bring a 'foretaste' of kingdom life through proclamation, serving, and miracles, but also with humble surrender to the Almighty's sovereignty.

The second, continuing the first point, is the eschatological reality of the full consummation. All good attempts to alleviate poverty through social development and care, ministry of healing, either through prayer or medical service, transformation of society with justice and righteousness, the restoration of human dignity, environmental justice, and many others, are pressing mission agenda. As mission is fulfilled at the appearance of the Lord, so are the various mission agendas. The motivation for mission engagement does not come with the expectation that the full restoration is viable in this world, but with the commitment that God's church is a visible sign of God's reign and hope, thus, God's people are called to live out its mission mandate. Pentecostals have an understanding that the advent of the Spirit in the modern times is the sign of the beginning of the end of the end time, *vis-à-vis* the first outpouring of the Spirit being the beginning of the end. Consequently their mission engagement should be the expression of their eschatological conviction.

The third is an appeal to the uniqueness of the Pentecostal contribution to Christian mission. The past hundred years of growth and expansion in various forms has demonstrated that this family of Christianity, like any other community throughout church history, is a unique gift from the Lord to the wider church, often as a response to a specific social, historical and spiritual context in society. If we follow the body analogy of Paul (1 Cor. 11), Pentecostals, like others, have a unique gift to edify the body of Christ and make a contribution to its mission. The call for Pentecostals is *not* to spread themselves too thin in an attempt to fulfil every mission mandate; but, on the contrary, Pentecostalism should remain as a powerful spiritual movement, perhaps continuing its trademark church planting and church growth, while bringing renewal to other churches.

The last is the possible danger of mission triumphalism among Pentecostals, or even arrogance in their attitude toward other missionary approaches and other churches, especially those that are dwindling in their membership and strength. To counter this very human tendency, it is important for Pentecostals to fully acknowledge that the same Holy Spirit uses different Christian communities in different ways, to fulfil the same call for restoration. Broad Christian fellowship and partnership will help, along with a diligent study of church history and other churches. A humble learning spirit will, in fact, bring a maximum contribution to Christian mission.

Chapter 3

The Charismatic Spirit of God

In the Old Testament, there are several traditions of the Spirit of God. They can be divided into two broader categories based on its role and function: charismatic and non-charismatic Spirit. The Spirit in the context of creation and wisdom fall in the latter, while the Spirit tradition upon selected leaders and prophets belongs to the charismatic tradition. In the charismatic Spirit tradition, God's Spirit is given to call, equip, enable or empower one to perform a divinely commissioned task.

The leadership Spirit tradition is well represented among several judges and the first two kings of the united Israelite kingdom. The prophetic Spirit tradition is found in early narratives such as the Balaam episodes (Num. 24) and several prophets (prominently in Ezekiel). In both traditions, the Spirit enables ordinary people to perform with extraordinary ability: often military tasks for the leaders and prophetic inspiration and utterance for the prophets. In both categories, the Spirit's coming initiates God's specific call upon individuals and empowerment for the given task. There are several passages where both Spirit traditions are coming together, and for this discussion two will be examined to trace the roots of Pentecostal mission theology and practice.

Passages

The Spirit upon the Seventy Elders (Num. 19)

This whole episode is set in the context of Israel's wilderness journey, particularly in one of their complaints about food. God's anger against Israel's complaint over the lack of food in turn became Moses' undeserved burden to bear. God's response was the provision of junior leaders who would assist him.

> The Lord said to Moses: 'Bring me seventy of Israel's elders who are known to you as leaders and officials among the people. Have them come to the Tent of Meeting, that they may stand there with you. I will come down and speak with you there, and I will take of the Spirit that is on you and put the Spirit on them. They will help you carry the burden of the people so that you will not have to carry it alone (Num. 11:16-17).

The details of God's actions are interesting: God is going to withdraw 'some of the Spirit' which has been upon Moses. Similarly, God commands him to 'bestow some of your [his] ray upon him [Joshua]' (Num. 27:20). A certain portion of something ('Spirit' or 'ray'), which is upon Moses is going to be shared with someone else. And it is something of God, presumably bestowed previously on Moses. This 'sharing', however, does not diminish the presence of the Spirit (or the 'ray') on Moses.

The narrative reports the bestowal of the Spirit upon the seventy elders as God promised to Moses: 'Then the LORD came down in the cloud and spoke with him, and he took of the Spirit that was on him and put the Spirit on the seventy elders. When the Spirit rested on them, they prophesied, but they did not do so again' (v. 25). The immediate effect of the Spirit's presence is prophesying. The hithpael form of the verb 'to prophesy' is often viewed as a reference to an ecstatic behaviour (for example, 1 Sam. 10:5 and following).[1] The absence of any oracular activity supports this notion.

However, they are not to serve as prophets. Prophesying here functions as the sign of the Spirit's coming upon the seventy, which in turn authenticates and legitimizes the election of the seventy elders. The prophetic phenomenon is perceived by the Israelites as the cultural and religious symbol of the presence of the spirit of Yahweh. In full view of the entire Israelites, their ecstatic behaviour caused by the coming of God's Spirit must have convinced them that their election for leadership was fully authenticated. The temporary nature of their prophesying further supports this. Therefore, reading the passage as 'a divine empowerment giving all necessary resources for the leadership of God's people'[2] is beyond evidence.

The connection between the Spirit's presence and prophesying does not end here. Two leaders, Eldad and Medad, failed to appear in the Tent of Meeting and to join the seventy in their experience with the Spirit. Yet they prophesied in their own camps and this raises a strong objection in the mind of Joshua, Moses' faithful aide. The issue was the legitimacy and authenticity of their experience, as they do this outside of the appointed location (and perhaps outside of the appointed time, as well). This further questions the source of the Spirit, as others received the portion of the Spirit which was upon Moses. Since these two do not 'share' the spirit of Moses, the source of the Spirit is questioned. On one hand, it can be from an unknown illegitimate source, thus, not God's Spirit; but on the other hand, it may have come from God himself without Moses' mediation. Moses' response supports the latter, as Joshua appears to be concerned about Moses' authority. At the urge of Joshua to stop them from prophesying, Moses makes a profound statement: 'Are you jealous for my sake? I wish that all the Lord's people were prophets and that the Lord would put his Spirit on them!' (Num. 11:29).

---

[1] For example, Baruch Levine, *Numbers 1-20* (New York: Doubleday, 1993), 324.

[2] Philip Budd, *Numbers* (Waco, TX: Word, 1984), 128.

Moses' statement expresses his desire and perhaps eschatological expectation that every one of God's people would be 'prophets' as God puts his Spirit upon the entire nation. Many consider that Joel's description of the coming age in 2:28-29 is the fulfilment of this expectation: 'And afterward, I will pour out my Spirit on all people. Your sons and daughters will prophesy, your old men will dream dreams, your young men will see visions. Even on my servants, both men and women, I will pour out my Spirit in those days'. This passage also attests that prophesying is the primary and external sign of the Spirit's presence, and 'prophesying' is elaborated in various modes: dreams and visions. Nonetheless, the literary context of Numbers 11 puts Moses' wish not to make every Israelite a prophet, but to have the presence of the Spirit which is authenticated by prophetic experience.

What began as God's response to the complaints of the Israelites and Moses ends not only with the practical provision of a group of leaders to assist Moses, but also with a spectacular revelation of the leader's vision for the nation (and God's plan for the future).

The Spirit upon the Messianic Prophet (Isa. 61)

The book of Isaiah contains several important passages providing valuable windows to the age of restoration, or simply the Old Testament understanding of the end time. This is the age of restoration, not only of the nation of Israel but also the entire creation under God's rule. The previous chapter discussed the renewed creation, community and ethical life. At the centre of this eschatological vision, however, is the ideal ruler, presented in various figures such as the Servant of Yahweh (e.g., Isa. 42:1-4).

> The Spirit of the Sovereign Lord is on me, because the Lord has anointed me to preach good news to the poor. He has sent me to bind up the broken-hearted, to proclaim freedom for the captives and release from darkness for the prisoners, to proclaim the year of the Lord's favour and the day of vengeance of our God, to comfort all who mourn, and provide for those who grieve in Zion-- to bestow on them a crown of beauty instead of ashes, the oil of gladness instead of mourning, and a garment of praise instead of a spirit of despair (Isa. 61:1-3a).

In this Servant song-like, self-claim of the future leader, the leader reveals his understanding of God-given call. In the long-standing call tradition both for leaders and prophets, several elements are evident.[3]

The first is 'anointing'. Generally found among kings and priests, the anointing is linked with the endowment of the Spirit. And two ancient traditions are immediately thought of: the anointing of Saul (1 Sam. 10:1-13) and David (1 Sam. 16:13). Through the anointing by the hand of Samuel, both became kings of Israel, and in both cases they were endowed with the Spirit. As the rite of

---

[3] Mic. 3:8 is often pointed out as a parallel in the prophetic call tradition, e.g., George T. Montague, *The Holy Spirit: Growth of a Biblical Tradition* (New York: Paulist, 1976), 53.

anointing heralds public introduction of the kings, although still in concealed ways, the presence of the Spirit served to authenticate God's election of them. For this reason, the prophesying of Saul reinforced this 'sign' function of the Spirit's coming. However, in David's case, the lack of anything displayable resulting from the Spirit's coming, it may be reasonable to assume that the Spirit's presence had an empowering role. However, it is premature to conclude, based on this observation, that the figure has more of a royal role than prophetic. The anointing here can be interpreted as a metaphorical use, as it is not with oil but with the Spirit.[4]

The second is the clear sense of tasks for which he is called and anointed. One is immediately reminded of the introduction of the ideal king in Isaiah 11. He is endowed with the Spirit, which brings royal virtues such as wisdom, understanding, counsel, power, knowledge, the fear of the Lord (11:2), righteousness, and faithfulness (11:4-5). As a result, he will have proper discernment to judge the wicked, to uphold the righteous, and to protect the powerless. Under his rule, individuals, society and the whole creation will enjoy peace and harmony (11:5-9). Similarly, the Servant of God in the first Servant Song (Isa. 42:1-4) makes a clear link between the coming of the Spirit and his task to bring justice and Torah to the nations and coastlands. In both cases, the coming of the Spirit is directly tied to the task. In a similar way, this prophet-like individual is anointed to minister to the deprived and suffering. They are the poor, the broken-hearted, the captives, prisoners, and those who mourn and grieve. Unlike the Servant in Isaiah 42 whose call has an international nature, this individual's call is to his own community, particularly to those who are neglected and marginalized.

The third is the realization of God's rule as an ultimate goal. The ideal king's rule in Isaiah 11 brings a paradise-like restoration to individual, societal and natural life. The Servant in Isaiah 42 brings God's justice and law to many nations. Through the caring ministry through the anointed in the present passage, the physical restoration of Zion will be accomplished (61:4). Only after that will God's people be served by foreigners and strangers (v. 5) as the nations offer homage to Zion (v. 10). Israel is now fully restored to be 'priests of Yahweh' and 'ministers of God' (v. 6).

As the identity of the 'I' is not known, the exact nature of his task is not known from one tradition. As discussed, anointing is practiced for a king, but seldom for a prophet, and this may lead to his royal nature. Also some of the tasks would require royal authority, for example, in the release of the captives.[5] However, the metaphorical use of the anointing and more importantly most of

---

[4] Norman H. Snaith, 'Isaiah 40-66: A Study of the Teaching of the Second Isaiah and Its Consequences', in *Studies on the Second Part of the Book of Isaiah* (Leiden: Brill, 1967), 199; R.N. Whybray, *Isaiah 40-66* (London: Marshall, Morgan & Scott, 1975), 241.

[5] Particularly Helmer Ringgren, *The Messiah in the Old Testament*, trans. David E. Green (Philadelphia: Fortress, 1966), 33.

his work done through 'proclamation' brings the prophetic character forward.[6] The solution may be found in the hybridizing tendency of the future leader encompassing both the leadership and prophetic characters. The Servant Song (Isa. 42) is a good example of both traditions coming together.

The presence of the Spirit here is to equip the individual for the task, although the self-claim of the Spirit anointing may also serve to prove God's election to an unknown audience. Similarly, the Servant, although introduced by God, has the Spirit of God primarily to equip him for the task, but secondarily to authenticate God's call to the unknown audience.

Acts 1:8

Luke's understanding of the Holy Spirit has been an important source for Pentecostal missiology. Throughout Luke and Acts, references to the Holy Spirit are found and many of them used Old Testament passages or expressions. It is the charismatic Spirit tradition which Luke used most.[7] Above all, however, Acts 1:8 has been the most popularly recited passage by Pentecostals: 'But you will receive power when the Holy Spirit comes on you; and you will be my witnesses in Jerusalem, and in all Judea and Samaria, and to the ends of the earth'. This passage should be read along with two other pre-ascension sayings of Jesus: Luke 24:49 and Acts 1:4-5.

Luke 24:49 contains the command of the Lord between his resurrection and ascension: 'I am going to send you what my Father has promised; but stay in the city until you have been clothed with power from on high'. His promise of the Holy Spirit is for the empowerment of the disciples for the specific task of witnessing: '...and repentance and forgiveness of sins will be preached in his name to all nations, beginning at Jerusalem. You are witnesses of these things'. (24:47-48) A link between Luke 24:49 and several Isaiah passages, namely 8:9; 48:20; 49:6; 62:11 is argued by a Pentecostal scholar.[8]

Acts 1:4-5, a repetition of Luke 24:49, forms part of the transitional link between the Gospel of Luke and the book of Acts, while it provides the literary context for Acts 1:8: 'On one occasion, while he was eating with them, he gave them this command: 'Do not leave Jerusalem, but wait for the gift my Father promised, which you have heard me speak about. For John baptized with water, but in a few days you will be baptized with the Holy Spirit'. However, the

---

[6] For example, A. Joseph Everson, 'Isaiah 61:1-6 (To Give Them a Garland Instead of Ashes)', *Interpretation* 32 (1978), p. 70; J. McKenzie, *Second Isaiah* (Garden City, NY: Doubleday, 1968), 181; S. Mowinckel, 'The 'Spirit' and the 'Word' in the Pre-Exilic Reforming Prophets', *Journal of Biblical Literature* 53 (1934), 203.

[7] Wonsuk Ma X, 'The Empowerment of the Spirit of God in Luke-Acts: An Old Testament Perspective', in Wonsuk ma and Robert P. Menzies, eds., *The Spirit and Spirituality: Essays in Honor of Russell P. Spittler* (London: T. & T. Clark, 2004), 28-40.

[8] Robert P. Menzies, *Empowered for Witness: The Spirit in Luke-Acts*, JPTSS 6 (Sheffield: Sheffield Academic Press, 1994), 169 n. 3.

comparison to John's baptism exhibits a unique Lukan interpretation of the Holy Spirit. All the Synoptic Gospels, including Luke himself, quote John the Baptist's testimony of Christ who would baptize in the Holy Spirit (Mark 1:8) and fire (Matt. 3:11; Luke 3:16), instead of water. In all of these cases, the baptism in the Holy Spirit is presented in the context of the baptism for repentance. However, in Acts 1:5, the baptism in the Holy Spirit is specifically for the empowerment of the disciples for witnessing.

Acts 1:8 climaxes the Lord's commission for witnessing and promise of the Holy Spirit's empowerment. Menzies detects a link between Acts 1:8 and Isaiah 49:6.[9] The geographical progression and expansion reminds of the Servant's mission to the nations and coastlands in Isaiah 42:1-4, rather than the Zion-orientated Isaiah 61 passage.

Between the leadership and prophetic Spirit traditions consistent with increasing overlap, in this passage, the prophetic nature is predominant, as being 'witnesses' in this context does not involve any political or military elements either in its process or its result. The following accounts of the book of Acts inform that it is either through direct verbal proclamation or living out a life as followers of Christ.

On the other hand, the coming of the Holy Spirit is to empower or to equip the disciples of Jesus to be effective witnesses, following the traditional function of the Spirit's presence upon the leaders. But there is no reference to authentication, or the Spirit's presence to serve as a sign of something. In Acts 2, the Holy Spirit functions both for authentication with a visible sign of tongues of fire, an audible sign of speaking in tongues, and now this empowerment function assumes two actions before and after the presence of the Holy Spirit: calling and commissioning. However, whether these implied actions can be considered as parts of the same process of the Holy Spirit remains another matter. Also assumed is the democratized development of the Spirit, as Peter's interpretation of the Day of Pentecost proves (Acts 2:16-21).

Implications

Having studied selected passages on the charismatic Spirit of God, what features of modern Pentecostal mission trace its influence to this Spirit tradition? This tradition proves to be the most important resources for Pentecostal mission thinking and practice.

Calling

In the Old Testament, a divine call is an important experience. In older Israelite history, many call records involve God's direct election (or 'handpick') of leaders. This may be attributed to the lack of established social systems for leadership emergence. For example, the two kings of Israel, like the judges

---

[9] D.P. Seccombe, 'Luke and Isaiah', *New Testament Studies* 27 (1981), 258-59.

before them, are elected by God himself, while subsequent kings followed more or less an established succession system, especially for the southern kingdom of Judah. For the northern kingdom of Israel, the social system is less stable and sometimes volatile, as royal successions are often bloody. Sklba argues that such an unstable social context promotes the rise of charismatic leaders, be they prophets or kings.[10]

Such a direct call of God is limited to political leaders and prophets, but not to priests and scribes. That is, this 'charismatic' call is limited to the categories which are to represent God to his people and beyond. Yahweh is the real king of Israel, and a human king is to faithfully administer God's kingship on his behalf. Prophets in a similar way are to bring God's message to his people, reminding them of God's demand for faithfulness to God and to fellow citizens in justice and righteousness.

For the prophetic tradition, an institutionalized system exists. The expression 'sons of the prophet' (or 'the company of the prophets' in NIV) reveals that a prominent prophetic figure attracts a group of followers for a prophetic training process (e.g., Elisha's case in 2 Kings 6:1). Also references to royal prophets suggest that a group of prophets are attached to the king and royal functions as seen in Ahab's prophets prophesying for a war (1 Kings 22:5-6). Widely-known prophets in the Old Testament often come outside of this established system. For example, Amos, when confronted by the priest of Israel, claims no institutionalized prophetic legitimacy: 'I was neither a prophet nor a prophet's son, but I was a shepherd, and I also took care of sycamore-fig trees. But the Lord took me from tending the flock and said to me, 'Go, prophesy to my people Israel'' (Amos 7:14-15).

If we understand 'charismaticity' as God's direct and personal intervention in the election, equipping and giving of a leader, be it a king or a prophet, the call is an important part of this charismatic process. When an individual is sovereignly elected by God, in the middle of a 'negotiation' between God and the called, a sign plays an important role to authenticate the validity of the call. For example, when Saul was called, the royal office had not yet been introduced and established. When Saul was anointed in the presence of local leaders, it was a surprise both to Samuel and Saul, let alone all others who had to wonder: 'Is Saul one of the prophets?' (1 Sam. 10:12). Although it may not be recognized immediately, the presence of a divine sign is to authenticate a divine call placed upon the particular individual. The coming of the Spirit, often with prophesying serves this important purpose. In fact, Saul was instructed by Samuel to note the signs as he travelled to Gilead:

---

[10] Richard J. Sklba, ''Until the Spirit from on High Is Poured out on Us' (Isa 32:15): Reflections on the Role of the Spirit in the Exile', *Catholic Biblical Quarterly* 46 (1984), 1-17.

After that you will go to Gibeah of God, where there is a Philistine outpost. As you approach the town, you will meet a procession of prophets coming down from the high place with lyres, tambourines, flutes and harps being played before them, and they will be prophesying. The Spirit of the Lord will come upon you in power, and you will prophesy with them (1 Sam. 10:5-6a).

In the New Testament, on the Day of Pentecost, when the 120 experienced the coming of the Holy Spirit upon them, they spoke in tongues. Peter explained this as a sign of the Spirit's presence as prophesied by Joel (Acts 2:14-21). The sign throughout the Bible is tangible and presumably culturally conditioned. That is, in most cases, prophesying has served as the sign of the Spirit's presence, and this expectation must have been conditioned by cultural and religious expectations.[11]

From the beginning of the modern Pentecostal movement in the beginning of the twentieth century, among others, the belief in the baptism in the Holy Spirit distinguished this new group of Christians from others. They did not see this as a one-time event in the first century, but as an event expected for every believer throughout generations. The 'recovery' of this gift has been the constant claim of the Pentecostal movement. Speaking in tongues as a sign of the Spirit's presence is analogous to the Old Testament evidence, especially when most references to 'prophesying' as a result of the Spirit's presence suggests an ecstatic behaviour rather than an oral activity.[12] Intentionally or otherwise, the (particularly classical) Pentecostal movement has been best known for an emphasis on its belief in tongue-speaking as 'the initial and physical evidence' of the baptism in the Spirit.[13] The logic is, when one is filled with the Holy Spirit, especially with a tangible sign, this signifies a divine call for service to God, to his people and to the world.

The immediate consequence of the strong sense of call is found in unbelievable dedication to God's work, such as in mission. Further strengthened by the expectation of the imminent return of the Lord, within ten years of the outbreak of the movement in the Azusa Street Mission in 1906, 185 missionaries were already working in many countries, often with little or no training for the work.[14] Vinson Synan coined the term 'one-way ticket missionaries', some of whom were willing to break their marital engagements and set out to a mission

---

[11] Wonsuk Ma, '"If It Is a Sign": An Old Testament Reflection on the Initial Evidence Discussion', *AJPS* 2:2 (1999), 165.

[12] Robert R. Wilson, 'Prophecy and Ecstasy: A Reexamination', *Journal of Biblical Literature* 98 (1979), 321-37.

[13] General Council of the Assemblies of God, 'Our 16 Fundamental Truths' (http://ag.org/top/Beliefs/Statement_of_Fundamental_Truths/sft_short.cfm), accessed on 8 Feb, 2010.

[14] Gary B. McGee, 'Mission, Overseas (North American)', *Dictionary of Pentecostal and Charismatic Movements*, eds. Stanley M. Burgess, Gary B. McGee, and Patrick H. Alexander (Grand Rapids: Zondervan, 1988), 610-25.

field.[15] They were quite sure that they, as the 'last day saints', would never see their loved ones again in this side of heaven. Their passion and urgency was motivated by a keen sense of a divine calling to save souls and the immanent second coming of the Lord. In spite of an over simplistic approach to mission, their sheer commitment, in part, explains today's global spread of the 'full gospel' religion.

Experiencing God

The entire process of call and the endowment of the Spirit are characterized by a life-changing encounter with God. The exact nature of this experience can vary from a subtle inner impression to sensual and physical involvement. The coming of God's Spirit upon Othniel (Judges 3:10) is almost a matter-of-fact presentation, 'The Spirit of the Lord came upon him, so that he became Israel's judge and went to war'. On the other hand, Saul's experience with the Spirit is not only visible and tangible, but also public as well private. Through this experience, in fact, 'God changed Saul's hear' (1 Sam. 10:9), although the exact nature of it is not clearly known. Nonetheless, the drastic effect of the Spirit's coming and empowerment is no doubt clear in the case of Saul's attack against the dreadful threat of the Ammonites (1 Sam. 11:1-11). Equally significant is what is called prophetic ecstasy. Although the circumstance is rather untypical, as mentioned above, 'He [Saul] stripped off his robes and also prophesied in Samuel's presence. He lay that way all that day and night' under the influence of the Spirit (1 Sam. 19:24).

The tangibility of experiences with God is not limited only to people who have received the Spirit. In fact, at the heart of the biblical worldview are encounters with God. As discussed above, call narratives are but one example of such. Subjective as they may be, what distinguishes such 'experiences' from non-encounter religiosity is the unmistakable conviction of God's will for each person and community. The heroic life and ministry of Isaiah, for example, can naturally be attributed to his very first experience with God when he is called to the vocation (Isa. 6). The book of Acts again fills its pages with accounts of encounters that first Christians experienced as the early church brings the good news to the 'ends of the earth'.

Pentecostals from the beginning have been characterized by their high value placed on religious experiences. It is not unusual to hear unique expressions in a Pentecostal circle such as 'hearing the voice of God', 'touched by the Lord', or anointed by the Holy Spirit'. Such spiritual tradition also creates an environment where God is expected 'to show up' or 'to meet his people'. This leads to another hallmark of Pentecostal life: signs and wonders. Following the ministry pattern of Jesus, Pentecostals expect not only 'enlightening' but also exorcism, healings and miracles through the ministry of the Holy Spirit. They have argued that

---

[15] Vinson Synan, *The Spirit Said 'Grow': The Astounding Worldwide Expansion of Pentecostal and Charismatic Churches* (Monrovia, CA: MARC, 1992), 39-48.

various spiritual gifts, particularly the supernatural kind such as tongues, prophesy, healing and the like, have been fully restored for modern Christians. The stories found in the Gospels and the book of Acts are replicated, according to Pentecostal belief, in modern days particularly in mission settings. In the cultural and religious context where miracles and healings are regularly expected from their native deities and spirits, this belief and expectation hits the critical code of native religiosity. Often this aspect of Pentecostalism is believed to be the main reason for the phenomenal growth of Pentecostal churches.[16] The role of signs and wonders is also believed to have a restorationalist value, as often the western version of Christianity was carefully 'sanitized' or 'demythologized' to suit the rationalistic mindset. It is not only the careful 'explaining away' of any irrational account of the scripture, but more importantly a distortion of the biblical worldview, which in turn has been exported to the mission field. Ironically the 'pagan' lands proved to have worldviews much closer to the biblical one than the missionary's. This 'confession' and a subsequent 'conversion' to a more holistic worldview are popularly presented by recent Third Wave advocates.[17]

Empowerment

Supernatural and superhuman-divine equipping is at the core of the charismatic tradition. When leadership in general was not organised, especially in early periods of Israelite history, we often see leaders directly elected by God. It is natural for the chosen leaders to be equipped by God himself, and empowerment is exactly that.

For example, some judges are called specifically 'to judge' Israel. When Gideon is called, Israel is attacked by the combined force of eastern tribal army including Medidianites and Amalekites. When the Spirit of God 'clothes' him (Judges 6:34), he organizes an inter-tribal army. With a small elite group of 300, he destroys the vast combined troop. His wisdom, courage, military strategy, and the ability to hear God's voice can be attributed to the presence of the Spirit (Judges 6-7). In the same vein, Saul's exploit over the Ammonites is another fine example. Although he earlier experienced the coming of the Spirit when Samuel anointed him (1 Sam. 10:6, 10), this time, the nation was at the verge of annihilation. The Spirit called, empowered and deployed Saul for a hugely successful military campaign. The most prized presentation of the Spirit's empowerment, however, is beyond physical and military achievement: it is the persevering tenacity to eventually fulfil a God-given task in the middle of adverse forces, as well as introduced in the life of the Servant (Isa. 42:1-4).

---

[16] For example, Julie C. Ma, *When the Spirit Meets the Spirits: Pentecostal Ministry Among the Kankana-ey Tribe in the Philippines* (Frankfurt am Main: Peter Lang, 2000).
[17] For Peter Wagner's experience, see Chapter 4, 'Full-Circle Mission' in C. Peter Wagner, *On the Crest of the Wave: Becoming a World Christian* (Ventura, CA: Regal Books, 1983).

Pentecostal mission has been anchored in its unique belief in the baptism in the Holy Spirit, which is directly linked with mission, according to Acts 1:8. The principle purpose of the coming of the Holy Spirit, according to this belief, is to empower for witnessing. This explains the sheer commitment of missioners found in the Pentecostal movement. Unlike the stereotype image of Pentecostal ministry, most of them quietly ministered in proclamation and service among the destitute, while enduring extreme difficulties. Some one like Lillian Trasher (1887-1961) is a good case in point. She broke her engagement, when her call to mission in Egypt was not shared by her fiancé. She was only twenty-three years old when she left for Egypt. Her ministry once cared for 1,200 orphans, the blind and widows in Egypt. Her life-long ministry in translating the Christian message into tangible reality won her praise by a Muslim leader at her funeral: '[Even if] she is a woman and a Christian, God will take her directly to paradise'.[18] The strong sense of calling and empowerment has made the movement a global phenomenon today.

Having discussed this unique theological resource which is responsible for the movement's expansion, it is also honest to recognize that Pentecostalism has revealed the shadow side of power-orientation. Just as found among charismatic leaders of the old, such as Samson and Saul, some popular and some unknown 'stars' of Pentecostal/charismatic Christianity have fallen into moral sins. This is not limited to one geographical context, but the 'powerfulness' of Pentecostal Christianity frequently makes its leaders vulnerable to temptations. Sometimes organisational structures built around charismatic leaders makes the leaders more susceptible to such danger. For this reason, massive movements, rising and expanding exponentially and becoming increasingly popular, need to find ways to increase accountability to God and to the people they serve. Empowerment can be a double-edged sword: to significantly enhance God's work if it comes with an inner-working of the Spirit, or to accelerate one's downfall, if spiritual power is wielded without proper spiritual and organisational accountability. Power tends to corrupt, and this includes spiritual power. For this reason, it is critical to expand the concept of power to include weakness and humility as seen in the life and work of the Servant (Isa. 42). The bottom-line of 'charismaticity' is God acting through his vessel.

---

[18] S. Shemeth, 'Trasher, Lillian Hunt', *IDPCM*, 1153.

Chapter 4

Full Circle Mission:
A Possibility of Pentecostal Missiology

Introduction

In the early 1980s, Peter Wagner, a church growth specialist of Fuller Theological Seminary, wrote a book entitled *On the Crest of the Wave*.[1] Typical of Wagner, this is a practical and easy to read book, with each chapter concluding with a 'Do Something Now' list. This 'one of Wagner's casual writings' has proven to be an extremely helpful book, especially among Christians to whom 'mission' is a too familiar word to bother looking up in a dictionary, and yet precisely what it means, or what is not meant, is widely unknown. As an Asian Christian, I suppose this is more so among Asian churches. There are several critical and important concepts found in this book that all churches need to heed to.

This study is a reflection on one particular chapter of the book: 'Full Circle: Third-World Mission' (chapter 9), dialogue with the author, and a further application to Pentecostal mission. The thesis is that the Pentecostal mission has a good potential to reach the ideal pattern of Christian mission, which Wagner labels as a 'full circle mission'. The perspective for this paper is obviously Asian, and mission-field oriented.

Basic Considerations

Wagner rightly argues, as anyone would agree, that the Great Commission (Matt. 28:19-20) provides the basis for mission. I would like to interact in two areas: the goal of mission and the 'full circle mission' as Wagner advocates.

Goal of Mission

As the majority of NT commentators would argue, 'going, baptizing, and teaching', being participles, are means to accomplish the ultimate end, 'making

---

[1] C. Peter Wagner, *On the Crest of the Wave: Becoming a World Christian* (Ventura, CA: Regal Books, 1983). This typical interpretation is found in many commentaries.

disciples'.[2] However, observing the modern missionary movement, Wagner laments, '*In my judgement, the greatest error in contemporary strategy is the confusion of means and end in the understanding of the Great Commission*'.[3] In his view, missionaries often 'baptize' or plant local churches,[4] but fall short of the ultimate goal of mission, disciple-making.

In view of this, the precise definition of 'disciple' becomes crucial. According to Wagner, 'people are not disciples...even if they are church members',[5] although the basic New Testament meaning of the term is equivalent to 'a true, born-again Christian',[6] 'followers' of Jesus,[7] or more specifically 'a disciple is a responsible church member' based on the description in Acts 2:42.[8]

Now the question is: Is this definition sufficient and adequate? Wagner further argues that 'part of becoming a disciple is to be disposed to obey Jesus as Lord',[9] but nowhere does he include witnessing as an essential component of being a disciple. I am beginning to wonder if Matthew makes it clear that the highest task of the disciples is making disciples, or in other words, reproducing themselves. 'Following' has a definite purpose, and this passage indicates that the ultimate purpose of the calling for discipleship is the Great Commission. It is what the disciples were called for, and their ultimate task was to make nations disciples of Christ, ones who would in turn make others disciples. Then, the Great Commission is given to the disciples of Jesus, including those who would become disciples through this unending reproductive process. This is the utmost test of true discipleship.

'Full Circle Mission'

Wagner pointedly states a major weakness of the modern missionary movement. 'One of the problems is that we have tended to see missions as a straight line' with a starting point and the end.[10] The mission, in Wagner's view, should be a circular movement continuously 'turning around and around with no foreseeable end in sight'.[11] To make his point further, he presents four patterns of missionary work:

1) 90 degree mission: a missionary is sent and a church is planted.
2) 180 degree: the new church grows and matures but still under missionary control.

---

[2] Wagner, *On the Crest of the Wave*, 108. *OCW* henceforth.
[3] *OCW*, 109 (italics are not mine).
[4] *OCW*, 144.
[5] *OCW*, 110.
[6] *OCW*, 110.
[7] *OCW*, 146.
[8] *OCW*, 111.
[9] *OCW*, 110.
[10] *OCW*, 162.
[11] *OCW*, 163.

3) 270 degree: the church becomes autonomous and the missionary either remains as a partner or leaves for elsewhere.
4) 360 degree: the church becomes mission-minded and planting churches in other cultures.[12]

He also points out the fallacy of the indigenous church principle. Often self-supporting is the major goal, and the missionary goal is in truth bringing the church to the level to be 'capable of keeping itself alive'.[13] Thus, even if there are many 'indigenous *churches* and denominations', 'indigenous *missions*' is seldom part of the picture.[14]

As a third-world missionary, I concur with him entirely. In my formative Christian years, I never heard a sermon on missions except one delivered by a missionary. This implies that the goal of the mission in their mind was not to produce mission-minded churches, but only churches that can support themselves, so that missionaries could find other places to repeat the process. It is, therefore, the special grace of God that Korean churches began to catch the missionary burden in the late 1970s. But there is little evidence that this new movement was motivated by missionary calls issued by missionaries in Korea.

Wagner's observation may have come from practical observations. The assumed traditional goal of mission will perpetuate the need for missionaries, and mission will still be the 'white man's burden',[15] thus implicitly suggesting that mission can be done only by rich nations. However, the new goal of mission and the meaning of discipleship provide the theoretical foundation for this important argument. Mission theologians need to further develop this critical and yet less explored area of study.

The Role of the Holy Spirit

The shift of Wagner's understanding of the work and role of the Holy Spirit in ministry and mission is rather dramatic. Considering that this book was written in the early 80s, this may be the period around the time of his 'paradigm shift'.[16]

---

[12] *OCW*, 165-66.

[13] *OCW*, 165.

[14] *OCW*, 165. Italics are his.

[15] British poet Rudyard Kipling's poem 'White Man's Burden' written in 1899 as exhortation to American to annex the Philippines. For a full text, see Rudyard Kipling, 'The White Man's Burden', *McClure's Magazine* 12 (Feb 1899) also available at http://www.boondocksnet.com/ai/kipling/kipling.html (checked, April 13, 2002). For a critique, Jim Zwick, '"The White Man's Burden" and Its Critics', in Jim Zwick (ed.), *Anti-Imperialism in the United States, 1898-1935*, (http://www.boondocksnet.com/ai/kipling, checked, April 13, 2002).

[16] Although it is possible that Wagner had been going through serious assessment of missions practices, his paradigm shift was motivated by the controversial course, 'MC510 Signs, Wonders and Church Growth', taught by John Wimber at Fuller Theological

He correctly points out the limitation of the traditional thinking of the Holy Spirit's work, by quoting Harold Lindsell, 'We were taught that the power of the Holy Spirit was for living a holy life'.[17] Wagner also refers to C. Kraft, 'Illness is a matter of theological (not simply medical) understanding in virtually all cultures except those characterized by Western secularism'.[18] Wagner argues, like many Pentecostals, 'The power of the Spirit was not only for cleaning up the life but for witnessing and winning souls'.[19] However, so far the discussions have been centered around signs and wonders that are linked to the work of the Spirit.

However, the Holy Spirit has more to do with mission than miracles and healings, or even power-encounter. The New Testament makes clear that the mission of God is carried out through the empowerment of the Holy Spirit. Thus, there is a dire need for pneumatological missiology, or missiology which gives intentional attention to the role of the Holy Spirit, which traditional Evangelical theology has overlooked.[20] Pentecostal theology and experience can provide a viable model for pneumatological missiology.

Pentecostal Possibility: 'Charismatic' Theology

As Max Weber defines, 'charismatic' encompasses several components: 1) the supernatural endowment of a leader;[21] 2) a sacred or awesome property of groups, roles or objects;[22] 3) the personal qualities of a leader;[23] and 4) a social relationship between charismatic leaders and followers.[24] To these, one can add that the selection of a leader (or 'calling') itself is strictly a divine prerogative.

Seminary in 1982, as featured in *Christian Life*, October 1982. The full account is later reported C. Peter Wagner (ed.), *Signs and Wonders Today: The Story of Fuller Theological Seminary's Remarkable Course on Spiritual Power*, new expanded edition (Altamonte Springs, FL: Creation, 1987).

[17] *OCW*, 129.

[18] *OCW*, 129 quoting Charles H. Kraft, *Christianity in Culture: A Study in Dynamic Biblical Theologizing in Cross-Cultural Perspective* (Maryknoll, NY: Orbis, 1979), 305.

[19] *OCW*, 129.

[20] Paul A. Pomerville, *The Third Force in Missions: A Pentecostal Contribution to Contemporary Mission Theology* (Peabody, MA: Hendrickson, 1985), 79 argues that Pentecostal theology can be correctional to traditional Evangelical theology.

[21] For example, Max Weber, *Economy and Society*, 3 vols, eds. G. Roth and C. Wittich (1925 original, New York: Bedminster, 1968), 241-50, 1112-17. Weber's pagination is consecutive throughout the volumes.

[22] For example, M. E. Spencer, 'What is Charisma', *British Journal of Sociology* 24:3 (1973), 341-54.

[23] For example, Bryan Lindsay, 'Leadership giftedness: Developing a Profile', *Journal for the Education of the Gifted* 1:1 (1978), 63-69.

[24] For example, see Alan E. Bryman, *Charisma and Leadership in Organisations* (London: Sage, 1992), 22-69.

Pentecostal theology is characterized by this charismatic nature of the spiritual experience commonly called the baptism in the Holy Spirit, the unique foundational belief of the Pentecostals.[25] It is important to note that, unlike their Evangelical counterpart, Pentecostals believe that baptism in the Spirit is distinguished from the conversion experience. This experience is interpreted as enduement of power for service. This unique belief is often based on the accounts of the book of Acts, but this 'charismatic' nature of the Spirit's presence upon individuals is also found in the Old Testament.

Old Testament Roots of Pentecostal Charismatic Theology

There are at least seven Spirit traditions identifiable in the Old Testament.[26] Among them, two are classified as charismatic traditions: leadership Spirit and prophetic Spirit traditions. As several sample passages are surveyed, the key elements will be highlighted.

LEADERSHIP SPIRIT TRADITION

The Book of Judges and First Samuel provide this important Spirit tradition. In this tradition, the presence of the divine Spirit serves two functions.

The first is the authenticating function. Considering the unpredictable nature of the emergence of leadership, it became essential for God to authenticate his election of the new leader. A good example is the anointing of Saul by Samuel (1 Sam. 10). When the prophet anointed Saul, three signs were predicted by Samuel primarily to confirm the authenticity of God's election of Saul as the king of Israel. One of the three signs was the presence of the Spirit upon Saul, as he was to meet with the sons of the prophets (10:5-6, 10). Indeed, Saul met a group of prophets 'prophesying' as the Spirit of God was upon them. Soon the Spirit came upon Saul as well and he began to prophesy along with the prophets. Here 'prophesying' is the sign of the Spirit's presence, which in turn functioned as a sign for God's election of Saul.

---

[25] The 'charismatic' nature of Pentecostal theology was elaborated by Roger Stronstad, *Charismatic Theology of St. Luke* (Peabody, MA: Hendrickson, 1984). Several Pentecostals convincingly argue that the theology of the kingdom of God provides the theological foundation for Pentecostal mission, e.g., Pomerville, *The Third Force in Missions*, and Gordon D. Fee, 'The Kingdom of God and the Church's Global Mission', in *Called and Empowered: Global Mission in Pentecostal Perspective*, eds. Murray A. Dempster, Byron D. Klaus, and Douglas Petersen (Peabody, MA: Hendrickson, 1991), 7-21. However, this may be a more elaborate version of Evangelical theology championed by George E. Ladd, *A Theology of the New Testament*, rev. ed. (Grand Rapids: Eerdmans, 1993). For this evaluation, see Gary B. McGee, 'Mission, Overseas (North American)', *Dictionary of Pentecostal and Charismatic Movements*, eds. Stanley M. Burgess, Gary B. McGee, and Patrick H. Alexander (Grand Rapids: Zondervan, 1988), 610-25 (622).
[26] For more detailed discussion, see Wonsuk Ma, *Until the Spirit Comes: The Spirit of God in the Book of Isaiah* (Sheffield: Sheffield Academic Press, 1999), 29-32.

It is not difficult to think that the sign was for Saul himself. This also became a sign for Samuel. Even the people were prepared for the subsequent election of Saul (1 Sam. 10:17-24) with this sign. A similar function is found in the case of the seventy elders in the wilderness. When the Spirit was upon them, they all prophesied, thus publicly authenticating Moses' selection of them (Num. 11:16-25).[27]

The second function is empowering or equipping. This function is rather logical, as charismatic leaders are raised by God for a specific task. Well-known cases are three passages regarding Samson's experience. Every time the Spirit of God came upon Samson, except for the initial experience (Judges 13:25), he gained superhuman prowess to counter the impending dangers. He tore a young lion on his way to Timnah (14:6), killed 30 Philistines to secure 30 set of festal garments (14:19), and to break the rope around his hands and kill a thousand Philistines with the fresh jawbone of a donkey (14-15). Another good example is found in the second experience of Saul with the Spirit in 1 Samuel 11. Unlike the earlier reported experience after the anointing of Saul (1 Sam. 10), this time, the coming of the Spirit is directly related to the military campaign against the Ammonites. Upon hearing the gloomy threat of the Ammonites, the Spirit of God rushed upon Saul, filling him with rage (1 Sam. 11:6). He immediately mustered an intertribal army and undertook a sweeping victory. The coming of the Spirit in this case is clearly linked to the military campaign and its empowerment function is evident. At the same time, the empowerment itself can have an authenticating role as well.

Thirdly, although less obvious than the first two functions, the 'sending' dimension is also under the direction and presence of the Spirit of God. The military campaigns of the judges (e.g., Othniel in Judges 3:10; Gideon in Judges 6:33-35; and Jepthah in 11:29-33) and Saul (1 Sam. 11:6-11) imply the work of the Spirit beyond the 'coming' and 'empowering' aspects. The successful campaigns take the role of the Spirit for granted. A more explicit role of the Spirit in 'sending' is found at least in two passages for the future leaders. The Servant will go to the nations and coastlands to proclaim the justice and teaching of Yahweh (Isa. 42:1-4). The Spirit will enable him to persevere against obstacles and difficulties until he fulfils his task.[28] The other text is found in Isaiah 61:1-4, although the speaker's identity is divided between a prophet and a political leader (i.e., king). The presence of the Spirit is for a specific task ('to proclaim...'), and the 'sending' role of the Spirit is clear.

The last element of the charismatic Spirit is the double beneficiary. The election, empowerment, and sending of a leader for a specific task is ultimately not for the elected leader, but for a larger group of people, i.e., various tribes, in the case of the judges (Judges 3; 6; 11) and Saul (1 Sam. 11), the nations and coastland for the Servant (Isa. 42), the poor, blind, and captives for the

---

[27] For more detailed discussion, see W. Ma, 'If It Is a Sign', 163-175, esp. 166-67.
[28] W. Ma, *Until the Spirit Comes*, 29-32.

prophet-king figure (Isa. 61). This double feature of beneficiary becomes more evident when other Spirit traditions are examined, such as creation Spirit, Spirit as God's impersonal agent, or personal agent, etc.

In a similar way, the prophetic Spirit tradition exhibits several aspects of the presence of the Spirit. First, it authenticates a true prophet. Perhaps the best illustration is found in 1 Kings 22:19-25. As Micaiah, God's true prophet faces the four hundred prophets of Ahab, he discloses his experience of the heavenly court session. By arguing that the lying spirit is upon the four hundred prophets of Ahab, Micaiah certainly claims the presence of God's Spirit upon him. This is confirmed by Zedekiah's question, 'Which way did the Spirit of the Lord pass from me to speak to you?' (1 Sam. 22:24).[29] In the case of the prophet-king figure (Isa. 61), the anointing and the presence of the Spirit serves as the proof for his genuine calling. Even the pagan diviner Balaam has the Spirit of God as a proof of God's election, at least for the occasion (Num. 24:2).

The second is closely related to the first, the Spirit's role as the source of the prophetic message and experience. Although with no intention of becoming prophets, prophesying became the evidence of the Spirit's presence in the case of the seventy elders (Num. 11:25) and Saul (1 Sam. 10; 19). Micaiah's claim of the Spirit is also the claim of the Spirit as the source of his prophecy (1 Kings 22:24). The 'sons of the prophet' under Samuel 'prophesied' as the Spirit of God was upon them (1 Sam. 10:10; 19:20, 21). In the coming age, as the Spirit of God is poured upon God's people, they will have various prophetic experiences such as seeing visions, and dreaming dreams (Joel 2:28).

The third is the element of empowerment in the course of proclamation. This dimension is less explicit than the first two, and yet essential, partly due to the harsh and difficult setting in which the prophets are often commissioned to deliver a message. Perhaps the only explicit example is the prophet Micah's claim, 'I am filled with power, with the Spirit of the Lord' (Micah 3:8). Here, as he differentiates himself from other prophets to whom 'it shall be night...without vision and darkness...without revelation' (3:6), Micah boldly claims not only the Spirit of God as the source of his message, but also as the source of his strength and courage to unashamedly 'declare to Jacob his transgression and to Israel his sin' (3:8). Such an empowering effect is also seen in the Servant's calling (Isa. 42). He will persevere and persistently fulfil the God-given task (42:1-4), because the Spirit of God is upon him (42:1).

The fourth is the double-recipient nature of this tradition. It is obvious that a prophetic message is intended to a third party. However, it will be a little difficult to argue the same for the prophetic 'phenomenon' as we see in the 'sons' of the prophet. This 'third-party' orientation of the prophetic vocation is also found in

---

[29] For this chapter, scripture quotations are from *New Revised Standard Version*, unless stated otherwise.

the prophet-king figure(s) such as the Servant (Isa. 42:1-4) and the preacher (Isa. 61:1-4).

New Testament: Luke's Charismatic Role of the Spirit

Pentecostals have often been accused of majoring in Luke's writing over Paul's, when it comes to pneumatology. This criticism is certainly true. However, equally true is the Evangelical's bias against non-Pauline corpus. The 'quite revolution'[30] in biblical scholarship in the last century has opened a new door for narratives including Lukan literature to be treated as legitimate theological books.[31] This new appreciation of narratives is a significant theological contribution that the Pentecostal movement has brought into the theological world. Lukan pneumatology, among others, significantly emphasizes and further develops the leadership and the prophetic Spirit tradition of the Old Testament. Perhaps the most important passage for the Pentecostals in this aspect is Acts 1:8, 'But you will receive power when the Holy Spirit has come upon you; and you will be my witnesses in Jerusalem, in all Judea and Samaria, and to the ends of the earth'. There are two important features of Lukan theology for Pentecostal missiology.

CHARISMATIC THEOLOGY

The charismatic orientation of Lukan theology has long been assumed since the advent of the modern Pentecostal movement. However, the first serious academic attempt was made by Roger Stronstad in his *Charismatic Theology of St. Luke*.[32] This was followed by several others, including Robert Menzies.[33] Luke, when referring to Old Testament sources, most frequently uses the two charismatic Spirit traditions: the leadership and prophetic Spirit traditions. They are borrowed mostly from the Book of Isaiah.[34]

The charismatic feature of Lukan theology implies not only a drastic manifestation of God's power, such as healing and miracles,[35] but also persevering persistence to fulfil the calling. In fact, Luke seems to stress the

---

[30] William W. Menzies and Robert Menzies, *Spirit and Power: Foundations of Pentecostal Experience* (Grand Rapids, MI: Zondervan, 2000), 37-45.

[31] For instance, I. Howard Marshall, *Luke: Historian and Theologian* (Grand Rapids: Zondervan, 1970). This view is in contrast with the prevailing Evangelical attitude toward narratives, e.g., Gordon D. Fee and Douglas Steward, *How to Read the Bible for All Its Worth*, 2nd ed. (Grand Rapids: Zondervan, 1993), 94-112.

[32] Stronstad, *Charismatic Theology of St. Luke*.

[33] Robert Menzies, *Empowered for Witness: The Spirit in Luke-Acts*, JPTSS 6 (Sheffield: Sheffield Academic Press, 1994).

[34] See below for details.

[35] For a fine study on the nature of the 'power', see Manuel A. Bagalawis, '"Power' in Acts 1:8: Effective Witnessing through Signs and Wonders', *JAM* 3:1 (2001), 1-13.

latter equally, if not more emphatically, than the supernatural demonstration,[36] and this is natural considering the oppressive setting of the early church. This is also arguable from the Old Testament perspective. The earlier stage of the leadership Spirit tradition displays more of the physical and military effect of the charismatic endowment, as in the judges and King Saul. However, the later development emphasizes moral and spiritual aspects, as in the Servant. There is more perseverance and persistence than just the demonstration of supernatural power. Luke understands that the charismatic empowerment of the Spirit is to enable the disciples to go out in power and perseverance. Even this perseverance aspect of Luke in fulfilling the God-given task, is quite different from the Johannine idea of the indwelling presence of the Spirit.

The seemingly most highlighted individual in Acts, besides Paul and Peter, is Stephen. Acts 6–7 lists at least seven phrases indicating the fullness of the Spirit or its effect on the life of Stephen: 'full of the Spirit and wisdom' (6:3, for the deacons in general), 'full of faith and of the Holy Spirit' (6:5, specifically for Stephen alone), 'full of God's grace and power' (6:8), '[doing] great wonders and miraculous signs' (6:8), 'his wisdom or the Spirit by whom he [Stephen] spoke' (6:10), 'his face was like the face of an angel' (6:15), and 'full of the Holy Spirit' (7:54), in addition to his reference to the Holy Spirit in his long sermon (ch. 7). There are effects of the Spirit that are different from the astonishing demonstration of God's power. It is important to note that early Pentecostal spirituality shows this balance with practices such as 'praying through', 'tarrying', etc.

MISSION THEOLOGY

The two books of Luke were written not just to preserve the life and ministry of Jesus, but ultimately to convince 'most excellent Theophilus' (Luke 1:3, cf. Acts 1:1), presumably a high-ranking Roman official, of Christian faith. Thus, the books were written with a missionary purpose.[37] Here are several points that illustrate Luke's mission-oriented theology.

Luke's gospel presents the ministry of Jesus as initiated and empowered by the Holy Spirit. This is expressed not only in the descent of the Spirit upon Jesus in his baptism (Luke 3:22), but also in the public proclamation of his mission by quoting Isaiah 61 (Luke 4:18-19). The book also concludes with a shorter form of the Great Commission ('...repentance and forgiveness of sins is to be proclaimed in his name to all nations, beginning from Jerusalem. You are witnesses of these things', Luke 24:47-48) and his command for the disciples not to leave Jerusalem until they 'have been clothed with power from on high'

---

[36] Robert Menzies, 'A Pentecostal Perspective on "Signs and Wonders"', *Pneuma* 17:2 (1995), 265-78, esp. 272-73.

[37] E.g., John Michael Penney, *The Missionary Emphasis of Lukan Pneumatology* (Sheffield: Sheffield Academic Press, 1997), esp. 18-25.

(24:49). Here is a clear connection between the Great Commission and the role of the Holy Spirit.

In the Book of Acts, Luke connects the two books by repeating the concluding statement of the Gospel of Luke: '...he [Jesus] ordered them not to leave Jerusalem, but to wait there for the promise of the Father' (Acts 1:4). But here, Luke makes an interesting reinterpretation of the popular remark of John the Baptist: 'He [Jesus] will baptize you with the Holy Spirit (and fire)' (Mark 1:8; Matt. 3:11; Luke 3:16). In all the verses, the Holy Spirit (and fire) functions to cleanse people of sins. However, Luke, by placing the same statement right after Acts 1:4, Jesus' baptism in the Holy Spirit acquires an 'empowering' function.

Thus, in the Book of Acts, the mission of the disciples is initiated and empowered by the Holy Spirit (Acts 2:4). The Book of Acts almost duplicates the pattern of Jesus' ministry (initiated and empowered by the Spirit), but this time for the disciples. This apostolic transfer of mission and authority was introduced in Luke's account of seventy disciples. They were assured not only of God's provision for their needs (Luke 10:7), but also of supernatural authority to pronounce peace (vs. 5-6), heal the sick (v. 9), and cast out demons (vs. 17-19). This commissioning with the manifestation of God's power, however, reaches its climax in salvation (v. 20). The Book of Acts makes it clear that the mandate of Jesus was carried out by the disciples through the empowering presence of the Holy Spirit.

The Book of Acts is a record of the expansion of the church as promised in 1:8. It began in Jerusalem signalled by the coming of the Spirit, which also equipped the disciples for the task (Acts 2:2-4). Then the expansion of the Christian gospel to Samaria is also marked by the coming of the Spirit upon the disciples (8:17), and to Ephesus, the representative of the gentile world (19:6). The coming of the Spirit in Luke has its ultimate goal in the spreading the gospel.

The disciples through the empowerment of the Spirit became not only witnesses but also disciple-makers. Barnabas' discipling of Paul, and Paul's training of Timothy are typical examples. Also the life stories of the major figures in the book mostly follow the pattern established for the Servant in Isa 42:1-4: persevering persistence under the empowerment of the Spirit. Here, persistence is to fulfil the missionary task, and they include Peter, Paul, Barnabas, Stephen, etc.

Thus, one can call Luke's theology missiological pneumatology or pneumatic missiology. Without the 'witnessing' the presence of the Spirit has almost no meaning in Luke. One can say that the Holy Spirit is indeed the missionary Spirit.

Pentecostal Mission Practices

In its one-century history, Pentecostals have distinguished themselves in the area of mission. Before any attempt to form a denomination, except those that predated the Pentecostal movement, mission agencies appeared as early as

1909.[38] Even the formation of the Assemblies of God, U.S.A. had a distinct two-fold purpose: 'to promote missions, and to establish a Bible school for the training of ministers and missionaries'.[39] It is not an exaggeration to state, 'Mission for most Pentecostals has never been merely the dutiful fulfillment of an obligation. The missionary task for many came close to being their movement's organisational reason-for-being'.[40] By 1910, only ten years after the beginning of the Pentecostal movement, 185 missionaries from North American Pentecostal groups are reported to be in various mission fields.[41] However, Pentecostal mission has been carried out without much reflection. They were more acts of intuition, often 'led by the Spirit'. Several unique characteristics have emerged, primarily from stories from various mission fields.

Democratization of Ministry

Perhaps one of the most cherished Old Testament passages by Pentecostals must be Joel 2:28-29. This passage was quoted by Peter on the Day of Pentecost to explain the advent of the Spirit upon the 120 (Acts 2:17-18). The passage includes an explicit reference to the democratization of the Spirit in the last days. It is no longer a small chosen group of people to experience the Spirit, but 'sons' and 'daughters', old men and young men, and male and female slaves. This is not just the experience itself, but it implies God's calling upon them for service.

The experience of baptism in the Holy Spirit, for instance, in the Azusa Street Mission, was commonly understood as the empowerment for service. This had a profound implication in mobilizing every believer for ministry, especially for mission. The first observation was the 'empowerment' of laity, against the prevailing clergy-centred ministries among the mainline churches. *The Apostolic Faith*, the publication of the Azusa Street Mission, reports many accounts of ministry carried out by ordinary people. Also evident is the active mobilization of women in ministry.[42] V. Synan reports many women, often single, missionaries went to foreign fields, and they were called 'missionaries with the

---

[38] Stanley Horton, *Reflections of an Early American Pentecostal* (Baguio, Philippines: APTS Press, 2001), 53.

[39] Horton, *Reflections of an Early American Pentecostal*, 53.

[40] Everett A. Wilson, *Strategy of the Spirit: J. Philip Hogan and the Growth of the Assemblies of God Worldwide 1960-1990* (Oxford: Regnum, 1997), 15.

[41] McGee, 'Mission, Overseas (North American)', 612.

[42] One contemporary example is the mobilization of women for the cell structure in the Yoido Full Gospel Church, Seoul, Korea. David Yonggi Cho, 'The Secret Behind the World's Biggest Church', in L. Grant McClung, ed., *Azusa Street and Beyond: Pentecostal Missions and Church Growth in the Twentieth Century* (South Plainfield, NJ: Bridge Publishing, 1986), 104. This is particularly significant considering the traditional male dominant culture.

one way ticket'. [43] Although this trend has gradually declined, the active women's participation in mission among Pentecostal denominations continues on. One notable example is Youth With A Mission. Although not a Pentecostal mission by affiliation, its historical roots and its mission practice with successful mobilization of laity (mostly youth) presumes Pentecostal mission theories. [44] The 1860 revival in South India is also marked by the link between the Pentecostal gifts and evangelism. As a result of the revival, a new era began, that 'lay converts going forth without purse or scrip to preach the Gospel of Christ to their fellow country-men [*sic*], and that with a zeal and life we had hardly thought them capable of'. [45]

Strong Commitment

It is rightly argued that early Pentecostal mission was primarily motivated by the eschatological urgency. [46] Borrowing dispensationalistic theology, the advent of the Holy Spirit was interpreted as the 'latter rain' blessing immediately before the Second Coming of the Lord. Thus, the 'call for harvest' was heard in every Pentecostal gathering. Theological education, accordingly, was to quickly train more harvesters. Tent meetings and evangelistic trips were the norm. Early missions also had a strong eschatological urgency and this made them committed workers.

However, Pentecostal mission did not decline after, let's say, a generation. Their dissonant experience did not discourage the missionary zeal. This proves that Pentecostal mission is not motivated primarily by eschatological urgency. One possible answer is the 'empowerment' Pentecostal theology.

---

[43] This is the title of the chapter describing the early Pentecostal missionary impetus. H. Vinson Synan, *The Holiness Pentecostal Tradition: Charismatic Movements in the Twentieth Century*, 2nd ed. (Grand Rapids: Eerdmans, 1997), 129-42.

[44] Carsten Aust, 'The Pentecostal Missiological Root of Youth With A Mission' (an unpublished class paper, Asia Pacific Theological Seminary, Baguio, Philippines, 2000).

[45] Horton, *Reflections of an Early Pentecostal*, 45-48, esp. 47. Ashton Dibb appeared in *Church Mission Intelligencer* (Aug, 1860), 622 quoted by Gary B. McGee, 'Pentecostal Phenomena and Revivals in India: Implications for Indigenous Church Leadership' (a paper presented at the annual meeting of the Society for Pentecostal Studies, Wheaton, IL, Nov 10-12, 1994), 8.

[46] For example, L. Grant McClung, Jr., 'Introduction: Truth on Fire: Pentecostals and an Urgent Missiology', in L. Grant McClung, Jr. (ed.), *Azusa Street and Beyond: Pentecostal Missions and Church Growth in the Twentieth Century* (South Plainfield, NJ: Bridge Publishing, 1986), 47-54 (51-52); '"Try to Get People Saved": Revisiting the Paradigm of an Urgent Pentecostal Missiology', in Murry W. Dempster, Douglas P. Peersen, and Byron D. Klaus (eds.), *The Globalization of Pentecostalism: A Religion Made to Travel* (Oxford: Regnum Books, 1999), 30-51 (38-40). Also D. William Faupel, *The Everlasting Gospel: The Significance of Eschatology in the Development of Pentecostal Thought* (Sheffield: Sheffield Academic Press, 1996), 36-47.

As people were baptized in the Spirit, the burden for the lost became intense. Often unusual spiritual experiences enhanced such sensitivity. For instance, Elva Vanderbout, a widow missionary from California, received a missionary call while her husband was still alive. As she was struggling between the missionary call and her family life, the Lord revealed that her husband would no longer be a hindrance. Soon, her husband died and she left for the Philippines.[47] Although still debatable, her commitment to mission reflects her clear understanding of God's calling. She laboured among mountain tribes—some of them were known for headhunting—and, as a result of her work, Pentecostal ministry was born and countless communities in the northern Philippines have been changed.[48]

Expectation of Signs and Wonders

In early days, particularly by Charles Parham, tongue-speaking was understood as the ability to acquire a known language without learning it. This new generation of tongue-speaking missionaries was considered to be a drastic measure of the last harvest before the return of the Lord.[49] This shows a connection between Pentecostal experience of the supernatural and mission. In Pentecostal mission, healings and miracles are regularly reported. Even calling was experienced in supernatural ways such as dreams, visions, prophecy, etc.[50] In the non-western world, gods and spirits are expected to demonstrate their power in tangible ways. Often, the missionary message and practice brought the western worldview, causing a clash with the non-western worldview, of the mission fields. This often resulted in 'split-level Christianity'[51] or a syncretistic one.[52] In contrast, the Pentecostal worldview is much closer to the animistically oriented non-western worldview.[53] Thus, the Pentecostal message easily opens the minds of people and raises an expectation for God's miraculous work. Perhaps this may partially account for the success of the Pentecostal mission.[54]

---

[47] Inez Sturgeon, *Give Me This Mountain* (Oakland, CA: Hunter Advertising, 1960), 36-47. See also ch. 11.

[48] See J. Ma, *When the Spirit Meets the Spirits*, 74-86.

[49] James R. Goff, Jr., *Fields While unto Harvest: Chares F. Parham and the Missionary Origin of Pentecostalism* (Fayetteville, AK: University of Arkansas Press, 1988), 15-16, 72-75, 84.

[50] L. Grant McClung, Jr., 'Introduction: Explosion, Motivation, and Consolidation: The Historical Anatomy of a Missionary Movement', in *Azusa Street and Beyond*, 11.

[51] Leni Mendoza Strobel, 'On Becoming a Split Subject', *PATMOS* 9 (May 1993), 8-11, 19.

[52] For example, Rodney L. Henry, *Filipino Spirit World: A Challenge to the Church* (Manila: OMF Literature, 1986), 6-16.

[53] For instance, a comparison between the Pentecostal worldview and the tribal Kankana-ey worldview, see J. Ma, *When the Spirit Meets the Spirits*, 213-32.

[54] Although Pentecostal mission has advantages in this area, it is still open to syncretism. See, for example, Mathew S. Clark, 'The Challenge of Contextualization and Syncretism to Pentecostal Theology and Missions in Africa', *JAM* 3:1 (2001), 79-99. See also ch. 14.

Healing or the supernatural work of God causes a 'wow' effect in the mind, and it causes a 'crack' in their tight worldview reinforced by community life in a tribal setting. It is significantly heightened when a family faces a crisis, such as illness, and their traditional gods and spirits are unable to help them. A tangible experience of the power of God brings changes in numerous areas of personal, family and even community life.[55] Such a healing or miracle plays a decisive role in a mass conversion or people's movement. It is well known that the most effective element of Muslim evangelism is through the supernatural demonstration of God's power.[56]

Expansion of Pentecostal Churches

Perhaps the most convincing argument for Pentecostal mission theory and practice is the unprecedented growth of the Pentecostal churches worldwide. The latest statistics account for over half a billion Pentecostals/Charismatics (523,767,000) by mid-2000, more than all the Protestant Christians put together (342,035,000), only second to the Roman Catholics (1,056,920,000).[57] For instance, in Korea, ten of fifteen mega-churches are Pentecostal/Charismatic type.[58]

It is, of course, impossible to think that all this expansion is the work of missionaries. It should be credited, more correctly, to the work of nationals. It is known that Pentecostal missionaries began training schools in their early days on the mission field.[59] However, the real secret may not be just schools, but the

---

[55] See ch. 5. Also Wagner (ed.), *Signs and Wonders Today*. A good example of the role of signs and wonders in Asia is collected in Mel Tari with Cliff Dudley, *Like a Mighty Wind* (Carol Stream, IL: Creation, 1972).

[56] Christian DeWet, 'The Challenge of Signs and Wonders in World Mission for the Twentieth Century', in *Azusa Street and Beyond*, 161-65.

[57] David B. Barrett and Todd M. Johnson, 'Annual Statistical Table of Global Mission: 2000', *IBMR* 24:1 (Jan 2000), 24. For a comparison, the mid-2001 projected figures are: 533,581,000 Pentecostal/Charismatics; 346,650.000 Protestants; and 1,070,457,000 Roman Catholics, idem, 'Annual Statistical Table on Global Mission: 2001', *IBMR* 25:1 (Jan 2001), 24-25 (24). For observations of Pentecostal church growth, see, e.g., Donald A. McGavran, 'What Makes Pentecostals Grow?' in *Azusa Street and Beyond*, 121-23; C. Peter Wagner, 'Characteristics of Pentecostal Church Growth', in *Azusa Street and Beyond*, 125-32.

[58] Young-gi Hong, 'The Backgrounds and Characteristics of the Charismatic Mega-churches in Korea', *AJPS* 3:1 (2000), 99-138 (101, 104). According to his classification, a mega-church has over 10,000 Sunday attendants (p. 100 n. 4). For the Philippines, see George W. Harper, 'Philippine Tongues of Fire? Latin American Pentecostalism and the Future of Filipino Christianity', *JAM* 3:1 (2001), 225-59.

[59] Yeol-soo Eim, 'The Roots of Korean Pentecostalism' (A paper presented at the Theological Symposium for Asian Church Leaders at the 18th Pentecostal World Conference, Seoul, Korea, Sept. 1988), 48-49 observes that the Korean Assemblies of God began to grow notably only after the opening of its Bible school.

training itself. The 'empowerment' theology may have been the main force behind the explosive growth of Pentecostalism.

By Illustration

I would like to offer two examples, both taken from Pentecostal congregations. The first is rather a microscopic one representing a local development, while the other is macroscopic representing an international movement. The two are selected to illustrate that a global movement is possible only where there is a local movement. It is like the earth revolves itself, and this provides necessary energy for the earth to circle around the sun.

LOCAL REPRODUCTION

The Kankana-ey tribe dwells in the rugged mountains of the northern Philippines. Small villages are accessible only by hiking. The average life span is short, since little medical services are available. Often their traditional religious practices, such as sacrifices and funerals, worsen their lifestyle conditions. Buguias is a Kankana-ey municipality of the Benguet Province. Buguias borders with the neighbouring Ifugao Province, with the Kalango-ya tribe right behind the Pulag Mountain. Thus, often Kalango-yas trade with Kankana-eys and their children go to schools with Kankana-eys in Buguias. Naturally the Kankana-eys in Buguias have developed an affinity with the Kalango-yas, although traditionally the mountain tribes are known for their headhunting practices.

Balili is an old Kankana-ey 'mother church' in this area. As the church grew, members residing in a far distance wanted to have their own 'chapel', especially for the long rainy season. Thus, the Sebang Church was born. In Sebang Church, Miss Pynie Bacasen, a young Bible school graduate, naturally motivated several young people to pray for the Kalango-yas over the mountains. One summer, Pynie hiked through the Spanish Trail often infested by Communist guerrillas. When she reached Cocoy after a five-hour hike, she found children all over the mountain villages. She conducted a vacation Bible school, and soon a church was born in this strictly animistic community. Young people from Sebang made almost weekly journeys to Cocoy to strengthen the believers. Through prayer, people were healed, and others were delivered from ominous dreams. In spite of much opposition from the village priest, the church grew steadily. Within a year, the church building was dedicated through the joint work of Balili, Sebang and Cocoy.

At this time, the young people of Cocoy began to pray for another nearby village, Docucan, as all the Cocoy children go to school in this community. Pynie led young volunteers from Cocoy, as well as Sebang, in her weekly evangelistic journeys to Docucan. Again, during this time, the young people regularly prayed for healing and deliverance from various spiritual and physical problems. When the church was constructed, the joint workforce consisted of people from Babili, Sebang, Cocoy and Docucan. Before the Docucan building was completed, the newest church had already begun to send their young people regularly to a nearby village, Ambakbak. Already six families are worshipping the Lord. Now, four churches are 'daughtering' this village church and they began to construct the church building and expect to finish it very soon. The ultimate goal for this 'chain of daughter churches' is Tinuc, the most influential and sizeable Kalango-ya centre in the country. The good news is that already there has been a Bible study at the centre of this tribal region. Again, this is a joint ministry participated in by all the 'mother' and 'daughter' churches: Babili, Sebang, Cocoy, Docucan and now Ambakbak.

INTERNATIONAL REPRODUCTION[60]

International Charismatic Service (ICS) in Hong Kong is a multi-national and multi-cultural Pentecostal congregation. This became a home for many foreign employees in this bustling city. A significant ethnic group was Filipinos serving in various jobs. The predominant component of the Filipino congregation (later they had their own worship centre due to their large number) were women who worked as house helpers. Many of them had left their families and even children behind. Many found Christ in their lonely life in this city.

As a Pentecostal church, members have been deeply committed to missionary works, much interested in reaching Mainland China. In the early 1990s, the church noticed that Mongolia was about to be opened to the outside world. The church sent a 50-member evangelistic team in September, 1992. At least two of them were Filipina workers who gave their precious vacation time (normally spent visiting home and their children) to this missionary cause. The team conducted a one-week open air evangelistic crusade in Ulaanbaatar, the capital of this newly opened country. As a result, the Hope Church was established with a group of 300 new converts of the crusade.

The Hope Church is one of the largest (with around 600 Sunday attendance) and thriving churches. A Bible school in the church has produced many workers. As a mother church, the Hope Church is now beginning to reach many rural areas of Mongolia with the gospel.

SUMMARY

These are good examples of 'full-circle mission'. One can easily observe several unique features in this 'multi-generation' expansion of God's work within an eight-year span.

1) The churches have been naturally taking the missionary work as part of their Christian calling. This can be easily attributed to the exposure of the members to Pentecostal teaching.
2) In all cases, the major ministry force has been laity. In fact, Pynie is the only trained and licensed worker with the Philippine Assemblies of God

---

[60] Details of this example were furnished by Kay Fountain on Aug 20, 2002, Baguio, Philippines, and through an e-mail message of Jordan Abellano, 'Re: An Information' (icafm@vol.net) (Aug 22, 2002).

for the first example, while the majority of team members were laity for the Mongolian evangelistic crusade.

3) Their commitment is something noticeable, as during the six-month rainy season, they still continue to hike several hours through rugged and stiff mountain trails to minister to the people. Of course, sacrificing their yearly vacation for mission requires a great resolution and commitment.

4) Praying for healing is a regular part of their ministry. Often a story of God's supernatural work provides a breakthrough in evangelism.

There is no doubt that such 'empowerment mission' in micro levels can be easily expended into a global scope. And this potential makes the Pentecostal mission unique and promising.

Suggestions for Pentecostal Mission

The following suggestions are listed as several practical tips.

Theoretical Level

In this area, a serious attempt is necessary to articulate the significance of Pentecostal mission. This includes the theological foundations, historical records, and practical/strategic approaches of Pentecostal mission. This attempt should be done at various levels, including Sunday school materials, missionary training manuals, and textbooks for Bible colleges.

For this reason, a networking of Pentecostal missiologists is urgent. Such an international and interdenominational body of Pentecostal missiologists should be able to produce textbooks to be used widely, not only among Pentecostal schools but also Evangelical institutions. Also desirable is an academic journal solely dedicated to Pentecostal mission. Again, the body of Pentecostal missiologists can easily launch such a journal.

This will also require an inter-agency corporation among Pentecostal mission agencies, archives and schools. An interlink among Pentecostal archives will provide a rare resource immediately accessible by anyone interested in Pentecostal history and mission. The publication of historical materials, including life stories of missionaries, will provide a valuable primary source.

Also critical is the training of mission faculty members for Pentecostal schools. Schools and programs which provide training specifically from a Pentecostal perspective should be identified and actively utilized.

New Role for Western Churches

Pentecostal churches in North America and Europe have greatly contributed to the spread of the Spirit movement all over the world through their missionary work. Most Asian Pentecostal churches are a direct result of their missionary work.

However, as the western Pentecostal churches begin to lose their dynamic, especially due to the decline of their growth, this is particularly true for Pentecostal churches with a congregational polity, as the success or decline of their missionary work is directly linked to the growth or decline of their churches. Local churches need to provide missionary personnel, funds, and influence. Unfortunately, most of the classical Pentecostal churches in the West have either stopped growing or are even losing their members. The simple and best way to reverse this unfortunate trend is to make their churches grow. The challenge is when this growth does not happen, then is the time to find new constructive ways to 'continue' the Pentecostal mission heritage.

First, it is to 'mentor' the developing mission forces in the two-thirds world. The growth of the Pentecostal movement in the new century will continue to take place in the non-western world. It is also clear that some of these churches are already sending their missionaries to nearby countries, as Korean Pentecostal missionaries working in Asia, far away, as African missionaries in Asia, or even to the western world. As mentioned above, in most cases this missionary movement came about from a self-understanding of these churches, rather than an intentional training of western missionaries.[61] This is a time for the western churches to assist the two-thirds world churches to become effective and intentionally Pentecostal mission forces. Some areas can be institutional assistance such as mission structuring, recruitment, training, developing support systems, missionary education in local churches, etc., and while on the field, individual missionaries can mentor, train and partner with missionaries from emerging nations.

Second, the western churches should also train ethnic congregations in their own countries for mission. For instance, the U.S. Assemblies of God has various ethnic groups as part of its congregation. In fact, in the past several years, the net growth of the denomination is attributed to the growth of this sector, while the traditional white congregations have declined. Considering the local church based mission policy, it is imperative to bring the ethnic sector into the mainstream missionary movement.

The Role of Missionaries

The new role of western Pentecostal missionaries was mentioned briefly above. Pentecostal missionaries have excelled in evangelism, church planting, even in social services in some areas, and distinguished in the area of training. Training schools and programs have greatly contributed to the expansion of the Pentecostal movement in the non-western world.

Now, missionaries, regardless of their origin, and national leaders should work together to actively teach Pentecostal, or full-cycle, mission to local

---

[61] Perhaps this is shown among Korean Pentecostal missionaries now serving in various places whose theology and practice of mission is not different from their Evangelical colleagues.

churches. One effective way is to partner with national workers to engage in evangelism, church planting and training, so that national workers will be theoretically and practically oriented to unique Pentecostal mission. This will also require the missionaries to prepare themselves not only in missiology in general, but Pentecostal missiology in particular. In Asia, the educational level of national leaders has been rising steadily and now we are beginning to see many national workers better prepared in theological education than some missionaries. Often a good role model is the best way to teach and train others. With resources available to missionaries, they must actively partner with nationals or even with missionaries from other nations in training for future mission.

Global Networking

In order to achieve these new goals, it is critical to have a broader participation. How various national groups such as denominations can be helped by others was discussed earlier. In addition, regional mission associations such as Assemblies of God Asian Missions Association (AGAMA) should take an active role to network member churches. Also important is the role of regional schools. For instance, Asia Pacific Theological Seminary (APTS) in the Philippines has trained numerous top-quality Asian missionaries. What is important is that it provides a natural environment where students develop mission awareness and commitment. Some of the Asian students had almost no ideas about mission, when they first came to APTS. But in the course of their study they developed a strong mission's commitment and eventually became career missionaries and they are still active. However, true networking should take place at the grass roots level among individual missionaries, or between missionaries and nationals.

In closing, it appears that Pentecostal mission holds a unique key to full circle mission. In this aspect, history and theology of Pentecostal mission in the last century is too uniquely significant to be buried in a history book. There has not been sufficient reflection on the theology and strategies of Pentecostal mission. This requires a close working together in academic (reflection), institutional (strategic), and missionary (practical) levels. However, as history tells, perhaps because of human limitation, one particular group is not to continuously hold the tradition, but to mentor another. Here are different roles of Pentecostal churches worldwide. Could it be like a human? There is a time to grow and bear children, but then to nurture, grow and empower them, so that the tradition will continue.

Chapter 5

Signs and Wonders, and a Crack in Worldview

Introduction

In many parts of the world, Pentecostal ministries among tribal groups have produced an unprecedented success. Various elements are attributed to this, including the similarities between Pentecostal and tribal worldviews,[1] points of contact and conflicts[2]. Being a Pentecostal missionary within Asia, I intend to evaluate various attempts made by numerous Christian groups to preach the Gospel. Whether the communicator is conscious or not, contextualization is a procedure that every Christian communicator is employing. It is particularly of interest to consider how western missionaries have approached an animistic group of people.

Problems Observed

Throughout a personal missionary experience in an animistic region, it became evident that the implementation of the idealistic contextualization seldom takes place. Often, just as in any other human phenomena, contextualization happens before one carefully plans and orchestrates. The difficulty of ideal contextualization can be illustrated with Paul Hiebert's simple model. For him, the ideal model or 'critical contextualization', to use his term, will take place when a native form is reassigned with a new meaning and used to communicate the gospel message.[3] However, simplistic as it may sound, in reality, this seldom happens. Firstly, logically speaking, a subject (the old form) influences the object (the new meaning), but not vice versa. Secondly, the old meaning attached to the native form is the culmination of group interpretation involving the entire community as well as many generations in the past. The old meaning is the

---

[1] Julie C. Ma, 'A Comparison of Two Worldviews: Kankana-ey and Pentecostal', in Wonsuk Ma and Robert Menzies, eds., *Pentecostalism in Context: Essays in Honor of William W. Menzies* (Sheffield: Sheffield Academic Press, 1997), 265-90.

[2] Sunday Aigbe, 'Pentecostal Mission and Tribal People Groups', in Murray A. Dempster, Byron D. Klaus, and Douglas Petersen, eds., *Called and Empowered: Global Mission in Pentecostal Perspective* (Peabody, MA: Hendrickson, 1991), 172-75.

[3] Paul G. Hiebert, *Anthropological Reflections on Missiological Issues* (Grand Rapids: Baker Books, 1994), 64.

reflection of their culture, values and worldview. The new meaning has a chance to penetrate the old form only when their values and worldview are questioned, thus initiating changes. Thirdly, there is another element which makes the ideal, balanced critical contextualization more difficult. When one attempts to convey a religious message, as any missionary would do, the communicator will most likely choose a native religious form or symbol. The attachment of the meaning to the form is much stronger than purely 'cultural' forms. Culture is closely interwoven with religious beliefs and religion is a matter of life and death to them. Altering a religious meaning may be a taboo in the culture.

Thesis and Questions

The difficulty of the balance of contextualization is further illustrated below in its actuality. This fact leads to a conviction that the arbitrary assignment of a new meaning, from the receptor's viewpoint, to an old (religious) form can take place only when a serious and compelling persuasion is present. This also illustrates how critical the beginning of the whole process of contextualization is.

The scope of the present study is a microscopic investigation of the very beginning stage of the contextualization process. The thesis which I attempt to prove, therefore, is that an initial radical challenge to the old worldview and belief system is the key to a successful and balanced contextualization, and the radical challenge can be achieved through a power encounter.

There are a number of questions which I will constantly ask in order to explore how critical it is to crack the receptor's existing worldview.

1) Throughout the history of Christianity in an animistic society, what are various 'entry approaches' which Christian groups have applied?
2) What are the phenomenological consequences from the perspective of contextualization?
3) What is role of power encounter from various perspectives: spiritual, religious, sociological, communicational, and physiological levels?

Methods

This investigation is a case study limiting its record among northern Philippine mountain tribes. Some Pentecostal groups have been ministering to them for several decades. In order to probe the role of power encounter in the initial stage of a contextualization process, two approaches will be employed: observational and analytical. First, through observation, I will compare three distinct contextualization consequences evident in an Igorot tribe. Beginning with the end result, their initial approach of contextualization will be traced back to determine if there are any observable differences in the initial stage. Secondly, assuming that the element of power makes the difference, its role will be probed from various angles to determine its contribution to the contextualization initiation. Much discussion will be based on Kraft's communication theories.[4]

In the course of this discussion, there should be a word of caution. In many cases, generalization is unavoidable. It is particularly true when various church groups are discussed and compared. Often a local church's attitude toward pagan practices has much to do with the pastor's view. Hence, it is possible to find exceptions among local churches to the general descriptions of a given Christian group.

Definition of Terms

In this study, the term 'power encounter' is not used in an exclusive sense of an expressed confrontation between spiritual forces. Rather it takes on a broader meaning to include the personal experience of the divine element of power. This can take various forms. The expression, therefore, is used in contrast to a mere verbal proclamation of the gospel.

The exact definition of 'contextualization' is still a matter of scholarly debate.[5] The working definition of 'contextualization' is based on Bruce Nicholls' statement:

> ...the translation of the unchanging content of the Gospel of the Kingdom into verbal form meaningful to the peoples in their separate cultures and within their particular existential situation.[6]

However, in the present study, the communication takes place not only in its verbal expression, but also in action. Another clarification is that the recipient culture includes their entire world view including their religious practices.

There are a number of subgroups within the target people, the Igorots. Occupying five provinces of the northern Philippines, the inhabitants were first called Igorots by the Spaniards.[7] They are subdivided into seven major tribal groups. Kankana-ey is a tribe occupying the north-western part of Benguet Province and the south-western part of Mountain Province. The observations in

---

[4] Charles H. Kraft, *Communicate With Power: Jesus the Model for Contemporary Communication* (Manila: OMF Lit., 1991).

[5] Various proposed definitions are discussed by David J. Hesselgrave and Edward Rommen, *Contextualization: Meanings, Methods, and Models* (Grand Rapids: Baker Book, 1989), 33-35.

[6] Bruce J. Nicholls, 'Theological Education and Evangelization', in J.D. Douglas, ed., *Let the Earth Hear His Voice* (Minneapolis: World Wide, 1975), 647.

[7] William Henry Scott, *On the Cordillera: A Look at the Peoples and Cultures of the Mountain Province* (Manila: MSC, 1969), 154-74, a chapter under the heading, 'The Word *Igorot*'.

this chapter are primarily about the Municipality of Bakun, in Benguet Province. More specific historical material is found elsewhere.[8]

Current State of Contextualization among Igorots

The presence of the Roman Catholic Church traces back to the time of the Spanish colonization. Although their military attacks almost always failed to conquer the highland, the Catholic Church was able to establish various mission points. As the Americans replaced the Spanish rule at the turn of the last century, the northern highland region was left to the Anglicans to carry on the gospel work. More Protestant groups joined later.

Among Kankana-ey people in Benguet province, practically all three modes of contextualization are present: syncretism, rejection, and critical contextualization.[9] Of course, it is impossible to expect a perfect and ideal form of critical contextualization in reality. However, there is a relatively balanced form of contextualization present. In this study, terms such as context-priority contextualization, text-priority contextualization and 'power contextualization' will be used instead of Hiebert's terminology. These terms are selected in the belief that the amount of attention a group is giving to the existing religious context determines the mode of contextualization.

From a practical perspective, the three streams are easily recognized by how a church views native religious practices, especially *cañao*, the most elaborate form of sacrifice/celebration offered to a host of gods and spirits. Basically there are two reactions toward it: 1) accommodation as cultural elements; and 2) total rejection and consequential segregation from the community. The latter, however, can be divided into two vastly different consequential categories: one is a passive attitude toward the pagan religion and the other is a more active and even offensive attitude toward the surroundings.

Borrowing from exegetical discipline, the three groups can be described by text-or-context priority. The first group is more conscious of the (cultural) context, while the second and the third groups give their priority to the text, or Christian truth. The only difference between the second and the third is the presence of the divine power element in the presentation of the message

Context-Priority Approach

As pioneers of Christian mission in the region, Roman Catholics and Anglicans trod a similar path. The sheer primitive state of the Igorot life compelled them to concentrate on social work more than preaching the gospel. Schools and hospitals became powerful tools to reach out to the people and introduce new life styles as well as a new religion. They were successful in producing many

---

[8] For instance, Julie Ma, 'A History of Assemblies of God in the Northern Philippines' (unpublished tutorial paper, Fuller Theological Seminary, 1993).

[9] Hiebert, *Anthropological Reflections*, 88-92.

professionals among the tribal groups. This emphasis continues in other Christian groups such as the Lutherans and the United Church of Christ in the Philippines (UCCP). These groups normally maintain excellent dormitory facilities in Baguio, the main education centre from the mountain provinces.

Roman Catholics and Anglicans alike, in the beginning, insisted on the total abstention of their members from non-Christian pagan practices.[10] This initial 'text-priority' policy immediately created a divide between the church and the people. This also precluded many from attending their schools and receiving medical services. It is conceivable that some teachers were not qualified to remain in their schools.

As they became more lenient in theology toward the current situation, they finally reinterpreted the traditional religious rites as cultural elements. Today, often a minister is invited to bless the sacrificial food, which in fact is part of their pagan ritual. The minister is respected by the community elders as one of them, and therefore he receives the first batch of the *tapey*, sacrificial rice wine, and a choice portion of the sacrificial animal including the liver.

This approach has two distinctly tempting merits. One is that the gospel, or Christian religion, remains greatly approachable to the people. They do not have to denounce their old practices to embrace the new. It is apparent among Bontoc tribe in Mountain Province. Many communities are believed to be Christian. It is not uncommon to witness Anglican Bontoc immigrants in Baguio city celebrating pagan *cañao* in order to give thanks to their ancestor spirits for the church baptism. The other advantage is the formal recognition of the pastor as a social and religious leader. In some areas, people would visit the pastor for the interpretation of a dream or omen. This is the exact role a pagan priest would play.

In this case, their old world view and belief system are never confronted and questioned. Christianity does not create a crack or doubt in their paradigm, by considering that the 'cultural' traditions have no direct bearing on Christian life. As the Christian gospel fails to create a shock wave which creates a crack in their old world view, it also skips the crucial first step toward a balanced contextualization. The first button is in a wrong hole. Instead of the gospel going out to the community, the old pagan religion comes in to the church. Often, old folks would discuss the next *cañao* celebration right after the church service. Syncretism characterizes this form of contextualization.

Text-Priority Approach

This is a more cautious group, generally reflecting conservative Christianity. This camp includes Southern Baptist, Nazarene church, and probably New Tribe

---

[10] Renaldo Cadangen, personal interview with the author, 20 January 1991, Baguio City, Philippines.

Mission.[11] As far as the mode of contextualization is concerned, Seventh Day Adventist and Jehovah's Witness can be included.

The churches are relatively small in size and church growth is disappointingly slow. House churches can easily disappear. The most identifiable characteristic is the complete separation between Christians and the rest of the community.

Igorots do not celebrate any fixed festival, such as New Year's day or Christmas. Family ritual, especially the more elaborate *cañao*, plays a critical social role in the community. In this society, therefore, a family ritual is always celebrated or observed as a community occasion. The separation, therefore, is a painful experience to the Christians. It is particularly so in two ways.

Firstly, a village is practically an extended family. Almost everyone in it is related to one another. Marginalization entails an unbearable burden in emotional and practical aspects. Secondly, their life is characterized by reciprocity. If I work one day for you, you do the same for me another day. If I attend your ritual, whether it is wedding or funeral, you are expected to be part of mine. The total separation practically makes Christians an island within the society (extended family society).

The Christians' major approach is teaching. Introduction of new truth is the main emphasis or truth encounter in Kraft's term. Sunday school, Bible study, attending group seminars are all part of the much emphasized Christian education program. The members become knowledgeable in the Bible. This work encourages a limited success.

This does not preclude occasional, but serious attempts of contextualization. Once there was a courageous experiment by New Tribe Mission. In evaluating various cultural and religious forms and symbols, they chose *tapey*. This was served in their communion service, to replace grape juice or wine. Considering that *tapey* is a religious element to invite the spirits, this was a brilliant idea.

However, not many participants were able to replace the old meaning attached to the object and assume the new. For the Igorots, the rice wine is sacred in their perception. Only a priest or village elders have authority to open the sealing of a jar. Once opened, they are to prepare a ritual with an animal(s) to offer to the spirits. Opening the jar is a formal invitation issued to the spirit. The spirits will smell the aroma of *tapey* and travel to expect a feast. If this anticipation is not met, a serious retaliation would follow.

The participants were simply not willing to ignore this rich and relevant significance by a simple instruction. One may say that the instruction was not enough. This could be the case. However, even with much instruction, the best one could expect was that the new meaning would become 'attached' to the old, without replacing it. Undoing is never easy. It takes either a lapse of a generation or a radical paradigm shift. As long as there is no crack in their allegiance to their

---

[11] An Evangelical interdenominational missions agency, particularly participating in church planting in the mountains of the northern Philippines.

old spiritual forces, a total elimination of the old meaning will not take place. It will take much more than teaching.

Their non-participatory attitude keeps their Christian gospel uncontaminated or uncompromised. At the same time, this makes the Christian truth unapproachable to the rest of the community. If the ultimate goal of the church is to win the entire community to the Lord, this approach appears to be equally unsuccessful. However, this still leave a potential of balance contextualization open.

'Power Contextualization'

This term is used in the same way that John Wimber uses 'power evangelism'.[12] This camp includes mostly Pentecostal groups such as Assemblies of God, Youth with Mission, and smaller native Pentecostal groups including Taneg, and Bethel Church which were separated from the Assemblies of God.

Their attitude toward the pagan religious practices is identical to that of the conservative group. They view the native religion at least as un-Christian, if not anti-Christian. As a consequence, just as in the conservative groups, there is a total separation between the church and the rest of the community. Christians are instructed not to take part in any traditional religious rites.

However, the similarity ends here. This group normally expects the demonstration of God's power, whereas the second group emphasizes teaching. Power demonstrations normally take two forms. One is an active initiation in power manifestation in the form of healing, stopping recurring bad dreams, or sometimes preventing an impending natural disaster. The other is a deliberate non-compliance to taboos. Tippet's illustration of eating a sacred turtle is an example.

This group has a better survival rate than the under-contextualization group, and often, after years' of persistence, the entire community becomes Christianized. They are characterized by an apparent conviction of God's reality and power. Although it may be far from perfection, the last case seems to produce by far the most desirable result.

Power Encounter in Contextualization

In this section, the role of the power manifestation will be examined from various perspectives. It is to determine the role of the power manifestation in the initial stages of the contextualization process.

---

[12] John Wimber, 'Power Evangelism: Definitions and Directions', in C. Peter Wagner and F. Douglas Pennoyer, eds., *Wrestling With Dark Angeles: Toward a Deeper Understanding of the Supernatural Forces in Spiritual Warfare* (Ventura: Regal Books, 1990), 13-14.

Spiritual Aspect

The presence of a Christian communicator in a non-Christian community creates immediate spiritual tension. As a never-challenged stronghold of spirits faces an invasion from a higher spiritual power, the existing spirits issue a 'red alert'. When the new religion sets out to 'replace' the old, instead of acting as an addition to the old belief system, the threat becomes critical. The existing spiritual forces would mobilize every power and strategy. They would do it for two reasons: 1) to keep the communicator from proclaiming the Christian God; and 2) to keep receptors from accepting the message. This encounter in the spiritual world will have a significant bearing to the success/failure of evangelism.

It is, therefore, not unusual to see that initial spiritual victory signals that the 'territorial spiritual forces' have begun to experience their defeat. As a consequence, the gospel work experiences a breakthrough. Yonggi Cho's early experience is typical.

> When I first pioneered my church ... there was great demonic oppression over the village. The key to breaking that bondage was the casting out of a demon from a woman... our church exploded with growth. The sky above the village was broken open and the blessing of God began pouring down. [13]

Often the critical point is not that Christians have incomparable spiritual power, but that the majority of Christians do not know this fact and consequently do not know how to use the spiritual power. [14] Therefore, a Christian communicator who knows how to use the spiritual power poses a great threat, especially when he or she comes to challenge and break the stronghold of the enemy. [15] The presence of such a communicator is, in fact, a declaration of spiritual war.

Among the Igorots, the traditional spiritual forces are symbolized by a sign post on which the jaw bones of sacrificial animals are hung. In the confrontation, the communicator would experience a great resistance by harassing, intimidating, etc. to the gospel 'invaders'. One does not have to believe in territorial spirits. The fact that the spirits have single-handedly controlled the people without facing any challenge to their authority undermines the significance of the spiritual struggle.

---

[13] Paul Yonggi Cho, 'City Taking in Korea', in Peter Wagner, ed., *Engaging the Enemy: How to Fight and Defeat Territorial Spirits* (Ventura: Regal Books, 1991), 117-20 (117-18).
[14] Charles H. Kraft, *Defeating Dark Angels: Breaking Demonic Oppression in the Believer's Life* (Ann Arbor, MI: Servant, 1992), 85.
[15] Kraft, *Defeating Dark Angels*, 85.

Pentecostals take the hard realities of the spirit world seriously, and consequently the power confrontation.[16] As the communicator is well aware of the spiritual reality and the delegated spiritual authority, often, the Holy Spirit breaks the enemy's grip in an individual. As the individual eventually affects his or her family and soon the extended family, the defeat of the enemy begins.

Religious Aspect

The religious area greatly overlaps with the spiritual area. Basically Igorot religion, in common with any animism, centres around the manifestation of spiritual power.[17] Often this determines one's religious allegiance. In this power-oriented religious mentality, spiritual beings are either feared for their powerful retaliation or exploited for human interests. For this reason, taboos are strictly observed. When one changes allegiance, retaliation is expected, unless the movement is from one god to another more powerful than the former. In this way, the worshipper is protected. In this religious area, as in the confrontation between Moses and Pharaoh's magicians in Exodus, a god which cannot demonstrate the power which it claims to have, does not have power. Here is the limitation of a mere verbal proclamation of the Christian message.

A power demonstration, first of all, proves the supremacy of the new God over their traditional sprits and deities. Their religious orientation readily accepts that the new God is more powerful, especially when some one is healed who has previously received native religious healing rites to no avail. With a proper orientation that the power demonstration is an expression of God's love, the Igorots not only contrast the new God with their old deities, but also seek the protection of the new God. Then their allegiance shift becomes a strong possibility.

This will also prepare a willing heart to listen to the presentation of the gospel, which leads to a meaningful paradigm shift or a change in allegiance. Only with this basis established, can a new meaning replace the old in a native form, minimizing a chance for syncretism.

Sociological Aspect

The receptor of a communication always has his or her sociological context: that is, in Kraft's word, part of reference groups. This social context becomes extremely serious for two reasons: 1) the communication purports to bring about change, eventually, within the whole community; and 2) the receptor lives in a highly concentrated kinship environment. Hence, the receptor will take into a serious consideration how the people in the social context would think.[18]

---

[16] Arthur Glasser and Donald McGavran, *Contemporary Theories of Mission* (Grand Rapids: Baker, 1983), 120.

[17] Alan R. Tippet, *People Movement in Southern Polynesia* (Chicago: Moody Press, 1971), 80-82.

[18] Kraft, *Communicate With Power*, 64.

As in any tribal society, Kankana-eys consider conformity an important merit in achieving harmonious community living. Rituals such as *cañao* often play significant social functions. It promotes solidarity among the members of a community. By sharing a common meal in the presence of the spirits and gods, the goodwill of the people and the spirits are secured. It also confirms the social hierarchy which has existed in the community. As the outside communicator poses a disturbance to the basic values, allegiance, and beliefs on which the tribal animistic life is built, the communicator may find a hostile audience, if there is one.[19]

Under heavy social pressure, the communicator is suspected of destroying their traditions. However, severe difficulty remains with those members of the community who have accepted the new message. Often the community penalizes new members by disowning and ostracizing them from the community. Only a deep conviction in the new found God will sustain their new allegiance. A power encounter provides such a foundation, not only for the members, but also for the neighbours who will eventually turn to the ostracized members in time of needs.

Communicational Aspect

Communication for contextualization is a receptor-oriented communication. Even in any communication, the importance of the receptor cannot be overemphasized, since the receiver of communication has the final say.[20] Communication is never a one-way traffic. The receptor undergoes a negotiation process to perceive a meaning.[21] The form presented by the communicator is constantly negotiated to determine the receptor's determined meaning. A major problem to the communicator is that the 'receptors are not compelled to interpret according to the desire of the initiator of the communication process'.[22] It is particularly true when the initiator is an outside of the culture and religion. Their defense mechanism is instantly activated.

To overcome this, Kraft suggests building a trusting relationship.[23] The maxim proves true, 'No relationship, no communication'. A cross-cultural communicator, especially one coming from the West where a preacher always finds a gathered audience, should realize that the audience is not there. If people are there, then they are not willing to hear, if not antagonistic against, the communicator and his or her message. This requires a long-term contact with

---

[19] Kraft, *Communicate With Power*, 65.
[20] Kraft, *Communicate With Power*, 62. Del Tarr, 'Preaching the Word in the Power of the Spirit: A Cross-cultural Analysis', in Byron D. Klaus and Douglas Petersen, eds., *Called and Empowered: Global Mission in Pentecostal Perspective* (Peabody, MA: Hendrickson, 1991), 127 goes as far as to arguing, '...words do not mean at all! Only people mean...'.
[21] Kraft, *Communicate With Power*, 63.
[22] Kraft, *Communicate With Power*, 63.
[23] Kraft, *Communicate With Power*, 63.

genuine love. Often, a native Christian can accompany the outsider to bridge the emotional gap.

The other way to overcome this obstacle is through a power encounter. Elliston correctly argues that a power encounter provides 'events that gained a hearing for the message of the gospel'.[24] To the individual who experiences the power encounter, the event will provide an opportunity to re-evaluate his or her own existing world view. The individual will go through a simple comparison process between the old and the new set of world views that have just been introduced through the incident. If this does not provide a revolution of the existing world view, it will certainly create a 'crack' in the tight old belief system and world view. The primary beneficiaries, including the individual and his or her family, will be an instant enthusiastic audience. The occasion will also attract the interest of others.

Practical Aspect

In this severely depressed society, meeting felt needs always attract close attention.[25] Because of self-interest, they are more open to changes.[26] Many groups, Christian as well as non-Christian, have endeavoured to meet these needs. The Roman Catholic Church as well as the Anglicans took this approach. There are many schools and hospitals now standing and serving the crucial needs of the people: medical and educational. This approach, however, sets the wrong priority in the people's mind. The social services did not evolve into evangelism in its true sense. Many virtually remain as Christo-pagans, or 'rice Christians' to use the local expression.

Animism maintains its effective grip with the element of fear. When ritual requirements are not properly met, the people naturally expect signs and communications from the spiritual world. Often this takes the form of mysterious sickness, disturbing and repeating bad dreams, the failure of crops, or bad luck in the household.

Combined with the lack of medical services, illness is often an immediately felt need. The infant mortality rate in the mountains is much higher than the national rate of 40%, which is already considered far higher than the neighbouring nations. They often resort to the healing rituals which are known to be effective. However, this requires careful counselling from a pagan priest. This

---

[24] Edgar J. Elliston, 'Response to "Power Evangelism in Pioneer Mission Strategy"', in C. Peter Wagner and F. Douglas Pennoyer, eds., *Wrestling with Dark Angels: Toward a Deeper Understanding of the Supernatural Forces in Spiritual Warfare* (Ventura, CA: Regal Books, 1990), 297.

[25] For instance, in Bakun Municipality of Benguet Province, most *barangays* (the smallest administrative unit, often consisting of three to four *sitos*, each of which may have from fifteen to forty families) do not have electricity, roads, medical facilities, or a communication system. Even a postal service is not available.

[26] Kraft, *Communicate With Power*, 67.

also entails a heavy economic burden. The Ibalois, a neighbouring tribe to the Kankana-eys, considers that a family is preparing a ritual, if the ownership of a rice pad changes.

The manifestation of God's power through healing is a common path for the Christian gospel to take root in a community. The family often consents on a 'give-it-a-try' basis. Lamew Assembly of God was established through the healing of an infant, when the pastor of a neighbouring village visited and preached the gospel. Their commitment to the old religion still remains in effect.

Concluding Observations

Having hailed all the fascinating roles of the power encounter, history clearly suggests that there are several areas where this approach can be vulnerable. Firstly, the necessity of proper biblical and theological instruction is essential in order to cultivate the fruit of evangelism initiated through a power encounter. Without a serious follow-up, this experience can create a religion which seeks a power encounter by any means. In the northern Philippines, Santoala is such a group. This is another form of syncretism: Pentecostal syncretism.

Secondly, a power encounter should be sought not as an end, but as a means to advance God's kingdom. For this reason, Tippet believes that a power encounter is only for the beginning of evangelism.[27] Its role is to create a crack in the old world views and its effect can be compared to that of an air raid which prepares the people for a subsequent real combat. Due to the lack of proper follow-up, in some Igorot tribes, Pentecostals have minimal presence, in spite of the success among the Kankana-eys. However, this should not mean that the power encounter is limited to the initial stage, or only for the 'good old days'. The power encounter should be continually practiced to liberate people from the enemy's control and to affirm God's power and love. Probably that is a mistake some Classical Pentecostal churches have made in the past.

Thirdly, the Pentecostals need to be aware that every church is called by God to be the light and salt to the darkened pagan world, no matter how ineffective some appear to be. Spiritual pride is something to guard them from. In truth, for instance, healing does not always take place every time someone is prayed for. The power encounter is manifested within the sovereignty of the Lord. This necessitates that other groups should concentrate on social works. The Pentecostals should be aware that every Christian or group works uniquely in the kingdom of God. Furthermore, they should also exert their efforts to expressing God's love and Christian concern through social services.

In spite of the foregoing cautions, one should never underestimate the critical role of, and contribution to, contextualization. John Wimber illustrates this in Paul's ministry.[28] In Athens (Acts 17:16-34) he acted like a good Evangelical

---

[27] Tippet, *People Movements in Southern Polynesia*, 322.
[28] Wimber, 'Power Evangelism', 26.

preacher. He probably employed state-of-the art techniques in communication including debate and eloquent logic. In other words, he faced them with wisdom. As a consequence, only a few became disciples (17:34). However, in Corinth (1 Cor. 2:1, 4, 5), he ministered with the power of God. The exact nature of the power is not specified, hence it is debatable. In Paul's language, the *teram* is used to refer more than to power encounter (e.g., Rom. 1: 16). It is, however, reasonable to assume that Paul presented with the combination of proclamation and power demonstration.[29] The result is the establishment of a powerful Charismatic church.

Although the second and third groups appear similar, the long-term consequences differ radically. There are several communities which are completely evangelized. Each of them has a Pentecostal church. And all of them began the history of the church with a series of power encounters. It is like putting the first button in the right hole. The consequence is encouragingly different.

---

[29] Wimber, 'Power Evangelism', 26.

Chapter 6

Social Context of Pentecostal Mission:
An Asian Case

Introduction

Asia is a vast and diverse phenomenon and one cannot justify placing Mongolia and Singapore together and treating them equally. Each country is unique from the rest in its social, cultural, political, economic, and religious experiences and orientations. As this paper deals with East and Southeast Asian countries and their people, over-generalization is unavoidable, although utmost care will be exercised to be fair to each people group in the region. In my mind, the region stretches from Mongolia and northern China in the north to Indonesia in the south and from Japan in the east to Myanmar in the west.

Oppression and deprivation still exist in the countries of East and Southeast Asia. An apparent lack of equal distribution causes the poor to become poorer and the rich to become richer. However, the countries have been experiencing rapid changes in their various economic, political, and social scenes. Rapid economic growth among many countries affects the social environment and life patterns of the people. Advanced technology fuels economic growth, bringing affluence. As a result, people tend to become strongly materialistic and secularistic. Sexual promiscuity, communication evolution, and urbanization are now a common sight in the region. These rapid changes are evident not only in everyday activities, but also in internal worldviews. The mindset of the people has experienced a major shift from group-oriented to individualistic and task-oriented; old traditional ethics are gradually breaking down. For instance, in many societies affectionate expressions between the opposite sexes, once considered taboo in public, are no longer true today.

At the same time, many societies have recently opened to the outside world. They are marked by economic poverty as well as drastic political and social changes. Even among the 'open countries', a major portion of the population live in tribal environments. They have not benefited from so-called 'civilization'. Often they are deprived of their resources and territories for the sake of the more modernized world. Social infrastructures such as roads, electricity, medical services, communication services, and educational facilities do not exist. Often, we hear news of the violation of human rights from this segment of the region.

The Pentecostal movement in these countries has had a varying impact over the last few decades. In places like Korea, Indonesia, Malaysia, Singapore, Philippines, and Myanmar, the Pentecostal impact has been rather significant. Churches grew by the distinctive message (power) of Pentecostals and its manifestation. The Pentecostal message of hope and power has made a strong appeal to people in the low social strata.

The success story of Yoido Full Gospel Church (Rev. David Yonggi Cho) is classic. His initial members were poor farmers, widows, and Shamans. As the people were desperate to find hope for their lives, especially at the end of the Korean War, the powerful message of God as healer and blesser made an unprecedented impact upon them. The poor social environment facilitated a place for the gospel to be shared and wounded hearts and sick people were receptive to the healing touch of the Holy Spirit and the Word of God. Today, in Korea, the common message of Pentecostalism is often heard in churches across the denominational border. China is another example. Before Communism took over, Chinese Christians were Pentecostal in nature, and Pentecostals have reaped a great harvest in the last few decades. However, not every nation has been receptive to the Pentecostal message. Countries like Japan, Taiwan and Thailand are fundamentally resistant to the Christian message. Their strong religions and cultures are often blamed. Recent reports of a phenomenal growth among some Pentecostal churches in Japan, however, seem to indicate that the Pentecostals have potential to make a difference, even in a difficult environment.

There is yet another group of nations in the region which are going through a dramatic change from a closed, socialistic system to a more open system, at least economically. Vietnam, Laos, Cambodia, Tibet, Nepal, Mongolia and China belong to this last group. Although some countries such as China had a strong Christian presence prior to the socialist regime, decades of a controlled political system did not allow any missionary presence and all religious activities were banned. Although they had once been practically the majority of Chinese Christians, the Pentecostal churches had to start all over again. This region still has one country which has not yet opened its doors to the outside world: North Korea.

In all these countries, the effect and impact of the Pentecostal movement differs significantly from one to the other. Even in the countries where Pentecostal churches once experienced unprecedented dynamism, the movement now does not seem to exhibit the same intensity as it used to have. The rate of church growth has either stopped or declined. In this respect, the Pentecostal movement should be evaluated and revolutionized in order to fulfil its task in the forthcoming era.

This chapter is a moderate attempt to offer a brief description of the environment into which the Pentecostal effort has been made. Some issues in the past which East and Southeast Asian countries have generally faced are formidable. Secondly, the present and future state of the society in this region is characterized by the word 'change'. This will also pose a challenge to the

Pentecostal churches in the coming years. Thirdly, I will examine the impact of the Pentecostal churches in the past, and suggest some tasks the Pentecostal church is going to face in the future.

Context

Issues

OPPRESSION AND DEPRIVATION

In this present century, the majority of the countries in the region were under colonial rule. Political power did not work for the interests of the people, but for those who held power. Unfortunately, even after liberation from foreign oppressive rule, many countries suffered under a dictatorial military rule.

In such political structures, force is often used to suppress any demand for political rights, human rights, and freedom of speech. Laborers and peasants become a suffering majority. Liberty is not allowed to practice in such a political environment. The government had absolute power to throw people into prison, thus resulting in an increasing number of political prisoners. Many were not given a fair trial, and some were even 'salvaged'.[1] Injustice was done openly with only fair attention from the media, which was closely watched by the authorities. Often people were caught in the cross-fire between the government troops and anti-government forces. They also became double victims of injustices done by the opposing parties. People in the mountain regions of the Philippines were afraid, not only of the New People's Army communist guerrillas, but also of the national military. A similar case can be made in the East Timor region in Indonesia, the Moslem militant separatist group in Mindanao of the Philippines, and the independent movement in the mountain area of Myanmar.

Power tends to corrupt, especially when taken by force. To maintain the illegitimately-owned power, much money was needed to coerce the people. Two former military Korean presidents were arrested for taking huge amounts of money from large conglomerates. In turn, the business sector received 'favours' from the government. When Marcos fled the Philippines, his 'colonies' accompanied him. Once the top is corrupt, the entire system is corrupted. In some countries of this region, 'there is nothing that will be done without money, but there is nothing that cannot be done with money'.

War has been another cruel element that has destroyed thousands of lives in this region. Since World War II, war has not disappeared from this region. The Korean War cost millions and the Vietnam War destroyed countless people.

---

[1] This term was popularly used to describe abducted and consequently vanished victims under the Marcos' rule in the Philippines.

Racial conflicts in Malaysia, the Sino-Communist struggle in Indonesia, and the Cambodian 'Killing Field' are just a few worth mentioning.

In this oppressive political climate, women are double victims: by the social system and by culturally male-dominant values. Women have been rendered speechless, since they can hardly find their identity in the male-dominated societies. They do not have an opportunity to express their opinion in politics, economics, or religion. At the political level, women are aware of the political situation in their countries, but their competence and activity are greatly stifled. It is obvious that women in Asia have been victims of the structure of the domination of exploitation. This situation is worse in the poorer classes of society.

A male-dominated society decreases wages for the labours of women and limits a woman's participation in production. Women in such societies are vulnerable, both sexually and intellectually, where an interaction of traditional and modern forces constrain them to compromise with the consumeristic values of a capitalist society. On the other hand, in the rural areas, women not only raise children and are homemakers, but also do most of the domestic work.

POVERTY

Poverty is a complex problem, but it is principally an economic situation. Economic progress in these regions was hailed by the entire world, yet poverty continues to be a big challenge. For instance, over 70% of the entire Filipino population is below the poverty line. Traditionally having colonial experience, countries have mostly neocolonial economies, structurally and materially controlled and manipulated by the economic superpowers. The result is an economic debt crisis, export-oriented production, unemployment, and migration of workers.

Many East Asian countries often face the problem of industry absorbed by the national elite and the big companies. Industry has put together an export economy that does not meet the needs of the local population. It tends to depend largely on foreign capital and technology. International banks and transitional corporations have become domesticated by Asia's politics and economics.

The rural districts have stayed static. Uncultivated reforms did not change disparate social relations of production in the rural areas. Only the middle and upper-class landowners who could afford technology tended to benefit. Large numbers of peasants were herded off the land in the process, resulting in the slum areas of the cities. On the other hand, the rural surplus amassed was often reinvested in crops for export or funnelled into urban industries, preventing the growth of food production. The countries then had to import food from other countries, the amount rising at an alarming rate. The countries had to encounter hunger and poverty and will for many years to come.[2]

Poverty abounds in East Asia. Over the centuries, Colonialism and neo-colonialism left cultural marginalization and distortion. Cities became woeful slums and peasants were driven away from the land. The rich became extremely rich, some beyond human description. There are enormous disproportionate and egregiously unequal distributions of wealth and power in Asia. Broadening the gap between the rich and the poor has consequences that impact the economic and political life of the countries. Capitalist domination is practically overwhelming. Decisions about what should be produced, how it is to be produced, and for whom it is to be produced are made by transnational corporations, together with the national elites, with the support of the political and military forces.[3] The majority of East Asian countries are continually controlled with the structure and materials of imperialist powers through the operation of transnational financial capital and multinational corporations.

Contribution of the socialists needs to be mentioned in terms of alleviating the struggle of the poor. Asian people in the rural and urban areas were lifted up by the socio-political powers who promised their right to take their lives into their own hands. This engagement further determined both the social and economic conditions that controlled their well-being. After long struggles, such movements brought about a succeeding establishment of social order in a large part of Asia. Although the socialists have made benefaction in accomplishing social order, these countries are not yet complete and must continually liberate themselves from all distortions by an ongoing self-criticism.

In direct reference to East Asia, we can verbalize that in the midst of the continuing structures of economic poverty and dependence, lopsided development among the divergent countries, political instability and dominance, and ideological disharmony, movements of social alteration and political swap have grown in differing proportions. The Socio-political structure should continue to transform by its awareness. In this situation, coupled with the male-domineering cultural practices, women again become easy victims. They are driven to work away from home and are even compelled to do prostitution. Yet, instead of addressing the system which coerces women into prostitution, the women are condemned by the men who exploit them.[4] Today there are significant movements of social renewal and political and cultural change. It is expected that critical cultural action will destroy old myths and create new symbols in continuity with the cultural treasures of the past.

---

[2] Asian Conference of Third World Theologians, 'Asia's Struggle for Full Humanity: Toward a Relevant Theology', in *Asian Christian Theology*, ed. by Douglas J. Elwood (Philadelphia: Westminster, 1980), 100-109.

[3] 'Asia's Struggle for Full Humanity', 101.

[4] 'Asia's Struggle for Full Humanity', 103.

CHILD PROSTITUTION

This is just one specific symptom of rapidly eroding traditional ethical values. Child prostitution is a complex matter, having to do with the destruction of traditional values, the materialistic desires of adults, and a pleasure-seeking corrupted mind. Child prostitution has been rising rapidly over the past several years. According to some estimates, in 1985 Metro-Manila alone had about 60,000 street children either involved in prostitution or in peril of falling prey. Angeles City and Olongapo, near the former U.S. bases, are drenched with 'funhouses' and massage parlors. A similar phenomenon has been occurring in Bangkok's Patpong red-light district. There are an estimated 200,000 or 300,000 children in prostitution in Thailand.[5] It is reported that the customers of child prostitutes are mainly Australian and Japanese tourists. They carry photographs of Filipino boys in the nude or fulfilling sexual acts. Each picture has the name of a person who can be contacted to engage in child prostitution. Since 1984, authorities have arrested 95 foreigners suspected of the crime. Sixty-two have been deported and 27 are awaiting prosecution or further investigation. But the problem facing the law is how to deal with such foreigners.[6] The country that is attempting to control child prostitution still depends on the income which breeds it. Such activity, in a sense, becomes a means to surviving and supporting their families.

SEXUAL PROMISCUITY AND FAMILY VALUES.

A cultural debate is raging in the Eastern Asia countries throughout the region. The issue is sexual liberty versus traditional values, and the press for change and steady growth. People in China are more inquisitive about sex and sexual techniques. China is undergoing a 'great sexual leap forward'. Along with sexual aids, it dispenses open advice on problems that were formerly strictly taboo. Discussing sexual issues was not freely done because of traditional practices. At present, though college students are engaging in free love, there is no care for private life.[7] Unlike before, homosexuality is no longer a crime in China, but anecdotal evidence suggests that homosexuals are still subject to criminal treatment.

Even in conservative Malaysia, traditional attitudes appear to be relinquishing ground, particularly when it comes to premarital sex. Young Malaysian couples who engage in sex before marriage are no longer ostracized. In the past, parents were strict, forcing their son to ask if his fiancée was intact or not. Such demands

---

[5] http://www.ips.fi/koulut/199742/6.htm: 'Philippines-Children: Scourge of Child Prostitution' by Sol F. Juvida, 1997. See also http://www.jubileeaction.co.uk/reports/GA%20THAILAND%20briefing.pdf: 'Guardian Angel: Jubilee Campaign', 20 June 2007.

[6] http://www.ips.fi/koulut/199742/6.htm.

[7] 'Sex in Asia', *Asiaweek*, June 23, 1995, 36, 40.

are no longer currently practiced.[8] One matter of concern is that young people who are idle may get into a lifestyle of casual sex and create sexual problems within the society.

In Tokyo, some young women were exposed to a new outlet for their erotic fantasies: sex tours to Southeast Asia. Their favourite destination is Bali where there are good clients of tough-looking Indonesian call-boys. No accurate information is available as to how widespread this practice has become, but the phenomenon is the new trend in Japan: young and rich women beginning to assert their sexual independence.[9]

In Japan, observers point to the rising popularity of a new type of *manga* (comics) pitched at women. Printed on cheap paper and drawn in the thin, quick style of other popular *manga*, they are more romantic than the erotic comics are for men. More sophisticated is *Kirei*, a glossy monthly magazine filled with photographs of nude young men and erotic prose. The editors are women and much of the content is sent to women.[10] In a Tokyo sex shop for women, sales assistants show off notebooks with messages from female customers describing erotic experiences and those who are looking for sexual partners. Male strip shows are almost a part of the mainstream entertainment.

An extraordinary increase in divorce among Japanese couples married for more than 20 years is responsible for the so-called 'retired husband syndrome'. Many Japanese salaried men spend years, living mostly separate from their families, committed to their jobs. Surprisingly, some couples have become aware of the fact that they barely know each other, and marriage counsellors are cautioning newly retired couples not to spend extended amounts of time together.[11] The divorce rate in Japan has increased 26.5% in 10 years, as reported by the health ministry, and according to International Herald Tribune, it is much higher at 38.3%.[12]

Relationship experts have figured out that festive cruises or extended holidays can cause a demoralizing effect on many marriages. Disagreements between spouses often grow deeper when they spend a lot of time together in an unfamiliar place. The BBC's Jonathan Head in Tokyo says numerous wives increasingly hate the small amount of time their husbands give to home life and they are in search of divorce when, after retirement, the men demonstrate no sign of altering their habits. Japanese tend to live longer, so when a man retires at 65, the wife may be thinking: 'I still have 20 or 30 more years with this person'.[13]

[8] 'Sex in Asia', *Asiaweek*, June 23, 1995, 36.

[9] 'Sex in Asia', *Asiaweek*, June 23, 1995, 40.

[10] 'Sex in Asia', *Asiaweek*, June 23, 1995, 39.

[11] http://news.bbc.co.uk/2/hi/asia-pacific/4741018.stm: *Japan Divorce Rate Soar*, 22 February 2006.

[12] 'To have and to hold...all the cash I can', *International Herald Tribune*, Saturday-Sunday, February 10-11, 2007.

[13] http://news.bbc.co.uk/2/hi/asia-pacific/4741018.stm: *Japan Divorce Rate Soars*,

Young people are also physically maturing earlier. They are making more social contacts at a younger age and are exposed to more sexually explicit material on TV, in movies and in magazines. People have more money, more time and more energy to invest in their private lives. They watch Western TV shows and movies, and often have the luxury of their own bedrooms. Not long ago, three generations slept in the same room, sometimes in the same large bed.

Many people are lamenting about the crumbling of the Korean value system found in Confucianism. Traditional marriage values have been so corrupted that the divorce rate is ranked seventh in the world, 47.4% according to a report in the *International Herald Tribune*.[14] Twilight divorce and honeymoon divorce are rapidly increasing.

Among the primary Western concerns that are rapidly becoming common in Asian societies, are the increasing teenage pregnancy rates, single-parent families, rising divorce rates, and the undermining of the traditional value system. Sexual promiscuity leaves behind it an incurable disease: AIDS. However, there is not adequate information about AIDS and its prevention and some AIDS' messages are rendered ineffective by the absence of explicit wording. AIDS is obviously becoming a serious problem in the regions of Eastern Asia.

The drive to procreate and the need for a nurturing family are fundamental human attributes. In reconciling the two, Asians still attempt to put family first, as a family-oriented mindset still exists among the people. However, it is fading due to the influence of 'individualism' from the West. The desires of the individual are gaining ground. Obtaining sexual freedom indicates the aim for individual pleasure in society and concern for the family is no longer an important issue among young people.

TRIBAL GROUPS

While speaking of the rapid urbanization and 'civilization', we should not forget that a substantial number of people are still living in rather secluded areas, maintaining their old tribal identities and lifestyles. They easily fall into the 'poor' group and many of them are so-called 'unreached' groups. Their animistic orientation is a ground where Pentecostals have found themselves greatly successful in many cases.[15] However, the challenge the Church faces toward them is often different from the challenges other poor people present to the Church.

The tribal people suffer multiple hardships and enjoy very little of what modern civilization can offer. Their regions lack basic infrastructure such as

---

Wednesday, 22 February 2006.

[14] *International Herald Tribune*, Saturday-Sunday, February 10-11, 2007. See also http://aids.hallym.ac.kr/d/svk/asv05.html: 'Divorce Rate in Korea', August 29, 1999, reported by Cheng Sea Ling.

[15] J. Ma, *When the Spirit Meets the Spirits*, 45.

roads, electrical power and communication systems. This situation naturally leads to the lack of basic social services such as medical and educational services. Religiously, their pagan practices often result in an unbearable economic burden. For instance, if there is a burial among the Igorots of the northern Philippines, the entire community expects to eat and drink until the entire herd of livestock of the family has been butchered and 'offered' to the deceased love one, so that he or she has something to give to the formerly deceased ancestors. In truth, the family has to feed the entire village sometimes for two weeks, and they are forced to borrow money to buy more animals.

The tribal people have often been exploited for their property rights. They traditionally regard land as 'community ownership'. Their natural resources, such as minerals, lumber, and hydro-energy are developed for the benefit of the urban people at the cost of relocation and environmental destruction of the tribal groups. The recent environmental issues caused by environmental groups in East Malaysia are not much different. They also suffer from typical low self-esteem. As countries are spending more time and money for their cultural heritage, the tribal groups are 'show cased' and become a source for tourist attraction. A wrong mixture of the old lifestyle and modern materialistic interests degenerate their morale and very often their existence. The mountain tribal people in Taiwan have suffered a similar fate.

Changes

INDUSTRIALIZATION

It has been well publicized that some countries in this region have experienced tremendous economic achievement in only a few decades. 'The Four Dragons', referring to Korea, Taiwan, Hong Kong and Singapore, have moved from an under-developed to a developed status, while other 'Tigers', such as Malaysia and Thailand, are rapidly expanding their economy. China is emerging as a huge economic power after adopting the market economy system.

Korea represents the emerging successful group. South Korea suffered many painful experiences during the Japanese occupation and the communist invasion from North Korea. After liberation from colonization in 1945, South Koreans encountered war between the North and the South (1945) which left the country in ashes. Since then, South Korea has had to build its economy up from the bottom, with meagre resources. The former president Park Jung Hee made a strong effort to re-establish the economy. His strong military background assisted him in being a tyrannical leader, which, in a sense, directed the country's economy towards great improvement. From a mere $200 GNP in the 60s, the country has now risen to an impressive $10,000 GNP mark. However, this was achieved at the expense of many private and public sectors. From the beginning, the economy was export-oriented. In 1995, the country acquired an estimated $115 billion from exports, up 22.6% from 1994. This was more than Mexico and Australia combined. In 1996 it increased to $15.7 billion, as much as Iran exports. Sales of cars and microchips have grown at a pace of 45% a year. The managing director at Daewoo Research Institute, Shim Gon Sub, argues that 'Without their (conglomerates') exports, Korea would struggle'.[16]

Samsung Reports Exports, Particularly in America,

> Samsung became America's choice for digital TVs in 2006, with a total Digital TV unit share of 20.0 percent, which is a significant lead over the competition. In addition, Samsung demonstrated strong category leadership in Flat Panel TVs with a number one unit share of 21.5 percent and number one dollar share of 25.1 percent; Samsung grew its LCD market share (10' and larger) to the number one position in 2006 (from the number four position in 2005), with a market share of 14.1 percent; and its SlimFit line of flat tube CRT TVs claimed an overwhelming 46.1 percent unit share and a 43.7 percent dollar share in 2006, according NPD data.[17]

Still Seoul is pressuring the giants to yield some ground to small and mid-sized businesses at home. It is also taking aim at monolithic governing by the founding families. The 30 biggest *chaebol* must begin diminishing 'insider holdings'. These must be cut to a maximum of 25% of justice, down from the current 40%. The government will abolish controls on investments by the top ten *chaebol*. If they cut insider holdings to 20%, Seoul would elevate its restrictions on capacity growth.[18]

Similar economic problems are found among the 'developing' countries. However, more acute problems lie beyond the economic boundaries. The drive for economic growth permanently altered the basic social structure, work ethics, and fundamental mindset of the people. The success-oriented work environment destroyed the culturally relationship-oriented behaviour. The elderly were no longer respected, and were often deserted. In spite of the affluence, the crime rate is constantly rising and drugs have become a household item. People can now afford sex tours to poorer countries of the region.

Whether successful or not, every country in this region is working hard towards industrialization. Countries who have just opened toward the market economy, from their old socialistic closed system, are struggling to separate political ideologies, which they would like to maintain, from the new Western-style economic system. China is trying, while other countries such as North Korea are nervously watching. However, as seen in many countries, the

---

[16] 'The Global Chaebol', *Asiaweek*, April 7, 1995, 40.

[17] http://www.samsung.com/PressCenter/PressRelease/PressRelease.asp?seq=20070126_0000316052: American's Choice: Samsung Emerges as 2006 Market Leader, Selling the Most Digital TVs of Any Manufacturer in the U.S. For the first time, Samsung captures the number one unit and dollar share for Flat Panel TVs; number one unit share for LCD TV; number one unit and dollar share for Flat CRT. Reported by Ridgefield Park, N.J., Jan. 25, 2007.

[18] 'The Global Chaebol', *Asiaweek*.

gap between the 'haves' and the 'have-nots' is widening. Also the economic gap between urban and rural areas is increasing. Soon, only the aged population will remain to continue rural agricultural activities, while the young work-force will be in urban industrial centres. As the industrialization continues, society and families will continue to feel the pressure to find alternative values rather than maintain the old.

ETHOS AND VALUE CHANGES

Individualism

As is commonly known, Asians are group or family-oriented people. In Japan, people get their identity from their groups. Because they are involved in different groups, they have different 'faces'. In such situations, maintaining 'dignity', 'respect', 'honor', and 'harmonious relationships' are highly important. The most valued human qualities are those which help preserve group loyalties and which maintain congenial social relationships. Asians, in general, build group blocks to society, not as individual people. People do not see themselves as autonomous, but as members of the groups to which they belong. However, as industrialization continues, such tradition is falling apart. People become individualistic and individualism particularly affects the family system, from the extended family to the nuclear family. The view of fostering parents is changing. The responsibility of children for the parents is no longer the way it used to be. Young people want to live separately from their parents, because they do not want to limit their freedom and further carry the burden for them. Caring for their parents is seen through certain expressions, such as giving money or buying gifts. Perhaps both husband and wife are working which was unlikely before, since wives were confined at home to doing house chores. Such a new family system brings a gap between children and their parents.

Another factor is the compartmentalization of life. In many developing or developed urban areas such as Hong Kong, Korea and Singapore, the dense population is put into a limited land area. The majority of the people can only have their own dwelling place in the midst of high-rise concrete walls. Often people don't even know who their neighbours are and what happens in their lives. There is no communication or fellowship among them. Their lives easily get into a routine, from home to work and vice-versa. Such a lifestyle in urban cities automatically causes people to become individualistic.

Children grow up in a more selfish environment, which is partly created by society and also by a smaller family size. Unlike former generations, who had anywhere from five to fifteen children, the average family today may have only one or two children. There are a number of factors which contribute to this trend: the high cost of education is one and the changing role of women is another. Women no longer stay home as home-makers, rather they are career, working women. Children are often taken to child care centres, and they have less contact with their parents than a generation ago. This further makes the future society more individualistic.

Task Orientation

Asians are people-oriented. Their emphasis is on building a relationship with people. They find satisfaction in interaction with others. Their high priority is to establish and maintain personal relationships. But this worldview is being altered as the economy grows rapidly. People are becoming work-oriented. They tend to have the notion that self-worth comes from accomplishment and success. People want to be competent in order to be recognized in an area where they work. People also desire to have an affluent lifestyle. Particularly, people in Hong Kong, Singapore, Japan, and Korea are working harder as their countries rapidly industrialize. In a factory, if there is work to be accomplished within a limited time period, employees are requested to work overnight with the promise of double pay. One can prove him/herself by accomplishing the work, and successful task completion promises one a promotion in the company. And, long hours of hard work can help one establish a business of his own, as some people believe that with material goods, they can not only live a luxurious lifestyle, but can also accomplish their dreams.

Poverty, in a sense, brings the effect to Asian people of craving material goods to improve their lifestyle and therefore competition is high. Coupled with individualism, the spirit of competition is everywhere, including the churches. This makes everyone a competitor, rather than a co-worker. Hard work, severe competition, and the acute pain of loneliness drive the people to drugs, sex, and unhealthy entertainment. Alcohol consumption is rising and the tobacco consumption in this region is dangerously growing. Some cities such as Bangkok have become a favourite sex-tourism destination. When a huge department store in Seoul collapsed and killed hundreds of people, the owner made a statement which angered the entire nation. The content is basically: 'You think you lost your loved ones. Look, I lost everything I accumulated in my lifetime'. It seems that human life is simply a means for material gain. This represents the sick minds of many in modern humanity.

INFORMATION AND COMMUNICATION REVOLUTION.

It has often been said that Asia evolved its writing technology from handwriting to the computer age, while practically skipping the typewriter. Of course, the complexity of characters was one of the major reasons why typewriters were not popularly used. In this sense, the computer age has suddenly dawned on Asian societies. In fact, Taiwan, in this region, became a world famous supplier of many computer components.

Multi-media, which the communications industry hopes will be epitomized, are probably the apex of computer technology these days. It is simply the expertise to transport data, video, text, and image information over some kind of communication line. The computer, as well as today's other high technology, promises a more perfect union, combining graphics, video, audio, photos and text. This mix has one other crucial element: the capability to let the user interact or shape the material presented. This technology has improved enough so that one line may be run into homes, providing access to all sorts of services.

At the Hong Kong Industrial Technology Centre, computer jockeys manipulate video and tweak graphics to produce high-tech commercial work. Another software whiz combines, frame by frame, the film of a 1950s Hong Kong street scene with a contemporary sequence of two people on a bus. There is great power with the computer to compose images and to blend images with sound interactively.[19] A killer, who killed numerous students in a Technology School in Virginia Beach, used Interactive Graphics for perfect completion of his plan.[20]

CD-ROMs are the most popular and most public multi-media product, and some types include Compote's interactive encyclopaedia, exploring ancient cities, libraries of the future, and games. While most CD-ROMs are from two genres, education or entertainment, others are hybrids of both, called 'education'. They can contain a virtual art auction, take people on a simulated tour of exotic locales, help people design new houses and keep track of their investments. Russell Yeah, a Director of Retail Stores, Hong Kong's number one software retailer, says global monthly sales of CD-ROMs have shot up 50% from 1994. Next year, CD-ROM sales worldwide are expected to top 30 million, almost five times the number sold two years ago.[21] However, this mass storage system is being exploited by the pornographic industry. China, in particular, has been known for its mass production of CD-pornography for the world-wide market.

The internet connection has revolutionized the information delivery system in the region. Unlimited amounts of information are now available at one's fingertip. Also striking is the availability of typical Hollywood entertainment through cable TVs. The day when a government could decide which material was suitable for its people has passed. MTV is seen in remote places in the Philippines through a battery-operated TV. This TV has become the sole entertainment 'box' in the community. Tribal men still wearing G-strings, standing in bare feet, are in front of this foreign entertainment. The erosion of traditional values is inevitable.

Once virtually non-existent, the availability of the cellular communication system is welcomed in many rural areas of Asia. For economic reasons, the traditional land-line communication system was not attainable. However, the appearance of this wireless communication technology has revolutionized lifestyles in remote rural areas in East and Southeast Asian countries. In urban cities in the region, especially in Singapore, Seoul, Manila, Hong Kong, Taipei,

---

[19] 'A Multimedia Magic Act', *Asiaweek*, May 12, 1995, 42-43.

[20] 'Multimedia', *Newsweek*, May 11, 2007, 11.

[21] A Multimedia Magic Act', 43.

Kuala Lumpur, and others, pagers and cellular phones are everyday commodities. Travelling around several countries and still being connected through e-mail systems is an unbelievable convenience which modern communication technology makes possible. The change becomes breathtaking as one Asian country launches the world's first commercial digital cellular system.

POLITICAL CHANGES

Truly significant is the change in the political systems of this region. After World War II, the region was divided into two major blocks: democratic and Communist countries. This struggle left three countries divided into two parts: China, Korea and Vietnam, and two of them had destructive wars against their own people. Also prominent are other regional conflicts, particularly racial conflicts. These include the Malay-Chinese conflict in Malaysia, East Timor independence movement in Indonesia, Mindanao's Muslim separatist movement in the Philippines, and the Tibetan struggle against Chinese rule. The Tiananmen Square massacre in China is just another example. The rebel activities of the New People's Army in the Philippines are in part attributed to the corrupt and oppressive rule of Marcos. The less known Kwangju revolt in Korea and the bloody suppression by the military government has left hundreds dead and missing.

However, change in the last decade has simply been drastic. The late presidents Chun and Roh were arrested, in part, for their responsibility in the bloody suppression of the Kwangju democratic struggle. Former Communist countries have, at least in practice, abandoned their old Marxist ideology. As they are more attracted to the capitalist market economy, political changes are seen as inevitable in China. The Philippines and Korea have ended military rules; yet, there are some pockets of political landmines which threaten stability and peace in the region.

North Korea remains probably the only Communist state in the region that has resisted the call for change. The activities of the younger Kim, the little known successor of the late president, have created an acute food shortage and a cry for reform. Though he has limited military experience, he is in charge of a 1.2 million-man army.[22] Recently a critical publication notes, 'There's an allusion to the September, 2005 statement in which North Korea agrees to eliminate its nuclear capabilities, and the United States points to that as an indication that this agreement will eventually lead to nuclear disarmament. But the North Koreans certainly believe they're going to hang on to their existing nuclear weapons for the foreseeable future'.[23]

---

[22] 'Kim Loses a Friend', *Asiaweek,* March 10, 1995, 29.
[23] Gary Samore: 'First Phase of Nuclear Accord with N. Korea Likely to Proceed', interview with Bernard Gwertzmen, Feb. 13, 2007.

There are also transitions in Indonesian politics. In 1958, army chief Abdul Haris Nasution attempted to perpetuate the military's role in the nation's government. The concept was not well received, as the army's authority was under attack from political forces.[24] Nevertheless, that concept became the foundation stone for political life years later. The military was given a dual function, involved in operating in social and political arenas, as well as its security role. The military has had a hand in almost every phase of national affairs. The military officers serve in the government, provincial administrations and state-owned companies. The military, by right, gets 20% of the seats in parliament, and two military intelligence units, BIA and BAKIN, the social-political unit, examine potential candidates for links to leftist or rightist groups. Troops spend time in the villages performing tasks such as building bridges and roads.[25]

The armed force has been criticized for feudalistic abuses of power. More often, however, Indonesians see their presence as important and effective. Often, during labour riots, the military is quick to move tanks into the streets. Dual functions of the military may continue so long as the rule exists to support it and the roles are accepted.

In Thailand, the Parliament has passed constitutional amendments (January, 1995) which will increase personal liberty and citizen's rights. The measures will also whip the powers of the military-governed Senate, a holdover body from Thailand's days as Asia's most coup-exposed nation. Only five years ago, proposals for tampering with the army's duty in government caused immediate warnings that the tanks would roll into the streets. But then came 1991, when Thailand's most current putsch turned into a nightmare for the military. Its bloody repression of pro-democracy demonstrators in May, 1992 led to the junta's downfall and deep public anger.[26]

Philippine President Ferdinand Marcos decreed martial law in 1972, though ensuring that the military deferred to civilian authority. In the latter years of his rule, however, he depended more and more on loyalist generals in the military. Chief of Staff General Ramos and Defence minister Juan Ponce Enrile rebelled against the Marcos' rule. They played a key role in bringing about the 'People Power' revolution in 1986. Aquino's weak administration though encountered seven coup trials between 1986 and 1990. After Ramos won the election in 1992, he began to make moves toward peace with renegade army officers, as well as communist insurgents and Muslim rebels.[27] Ramos continued to focus on military reform creating a slim chance for a coup. The people at the helm of the

---

[24] 'Indonesia's Coming Test', *Asiaweek*, March 10, 1995, 20.

[25] 'Indonesia's Coming Test', *Asiaweek*, March 10, 1995, 20.

[26] 'Has the Coup Had Its Day?' *Asiaweek*, January 20, 1995, 26. See also more of arising political issues in http://www.cfr.org/region/300/thailand.html reported by Carin Zissis, Feb.1, 2007, 2.

[27] 'Has the Coup Had Its Day?' 28.

military were then respected and trusted. One newspaper reported about the current president: 'Current president Gloria Macapagal-Arroyo was nearly impeached twice over allegations of election rigging in 2004. Julkipli Wadi, a political science professor at the University of the Philippines says Filipino voters are 'jaded' because political expediency has long buried principles in politics in this country. '[28]

South Korean president, Kim Young Sam moved quickly to decrease the military's influence. He dismissed generals and other officers from civilian posts and appointed the professional soldier general Kim Dong Jin as army chief of staff. 'This is going to be the initial year of the development of a military of the people and for the people', the president declared in 1993.[29] So far, the armed forces have been relinquished to their new role. A grave change has been seen in the support of civilians for the military. The Korean people simply do not want a coup to be involved in the social and political affairs or to be associated with government.

Myanmar's military rule has remained a target of human rights activists. Aung San Su Kyi, once elected the president in a popular election, was under house arrest for many years. Cambodia is still reaping its past acts of war. Every day, many people lose their lives or are maimed by landmines. Many of them are children. Vietnam, a former Communist country, is applying for membership in ASEAN. Months ago, China staged a military demonstration near the border, which could have triggered another war. Political change is a constant scene in this region. As the economic standards rise, a demand for more political freedom is inevitable. This means a social struggle which often costs human lives.

Religiosity and Religious Plurality

Religions have played, and continue to play, a critical role. People are deeply religious and many countries have their own state religions. It is also true that several world religions came out of Asia. Islam practically controls millions of lives in Indonesia, Malaysia, Brunei, parts of the Philippines and China. Buddhism, or a variation of it, rules the populations of Tibet, Nepal, Thailand, Myanmar, and many in China. Hinduism is another major religion in this part of the world. In addition to these 'high religions', many sects and folk religions, including animism, greatly influence the region. The following are some examples of recent religious movements.

CULTIC MOVEMENTS IN JAPAN

The Japanese religious concern was derived from ancient Shintoism, which has an analogous meta-cosmic orientation attributing sacred power to natural objects or people so long as they share in the force (or in *kami*) that comes from above.

---

[28] *Davao Daily News*, May 14, 2007. See also *Filipino Reporter Daily News*, May 18, 2007, 3.

[29] Has the Coup Had Its Day?' *Asiaweek*, January 20, 1995, 30.

Such was altered by the introduction of Buddhism in the sixth century A.D.[30] The Japanese, however, are interested in exposure to other religious practices, as a majority of the Japanese no longer seem attached to their traditional religion. The government tends to give special care to religious organisations with strong constitutional warrants of religious freedom. No cult has ever been dissolved, even though many have been accused of corruption.

On March 20, 1996, the *Aum* cultists attacked civilians with gas in a Tokyo subway. This attack killed twelve and left 5,000 injured. Nearly two-thirds of Tokyo's residents ride the railway and subway lines each day. It was indeed a life-threatening experience for the people. Initially, these cultists strongly denied their involvement in the gas attack. Many cult adherents have flooded the national Nifty-Serve computer network with messages protesting their innocence.

Police reported that an Osaka university-trained astrophysicist designed the cult's complex chemical laboratory in Kamikuishiki Village at the base of Mount Fuji.[31] A cult temple was discovered with the lab behind it, in a three-story building. The report said that in spite of such a chaotic situation, the cult members continued to undergo a daily routine of worship, chanting *sutras* and reading the works of their supreme leader, whose image, dressed in a purple tunic, is still prominently displayed on the walls.

Maria Romandina, a Russian, had been fascinated with the *Aum Shinrikyo* cult after an opportunity to study Buddhism and yoga. On entering the sect, her brainwashing began immediately. She soon believed the universe was dark and that only *Aum* could do what was good for her. She was pressured to donate money and property and was subjected to fasts and other ascetic rituals. Not only her, but other cult members were forced to bestow their property to the sect. An *Aum* official claimed that the sect possessed assets worth about 1.2 billion dollars. *Aum* claims to have won more than 30,000 Russian converts. In 1992 *Aum*'s leader, Asahara Shokou, preached to 19,000 at Moscow's Olympic stadium.[32]

It is certainly an unusual religious phenomenology which challenges these traditional religious people. Scientism is no longer the religion for the Japanese. Obviously the Japanese are getting a chance to be exposed to more religious plurality and more challenging religions are invading their lives.

INFLUENCE OF BUDDHISM IN CONTEMPORARY THAILAND

Buddhism has been influencing the socio-political fabric of the nation and its modernization. The government of Thailand embraced the involvement and contribution of Buddhism, from the time of the great kings of the 19th century

---

[30] William Dyrness, *Learning About Theology From the Third World* (Grand Rapids: Zondervan, 1990), 142.

[31] 'Closing in on the Cult'. *Asiaweek*, May 5, 1995, 37.

[32] 'Closing in on the Cult'. *Asiaweek*, May 5, 1995, 38.

(Mongkut and Chulalongkorn) through the numerous post-1932 constitutional military regimes, and up to the present. There has been a remarkable firmness and continuation of the political process, and an evenly marked absence of social upheaval or demonstration. For such reasons, the Thai government has been said by many onlookers to have 'managed' modernization well.[33]

People in the Thai society are commonly in agreement that Buddhism is the key to bringing stability and continuity to the political process during the present time period in institutional change. The traditional role of Thai Buddhism in Thai society is not just for the future of Thai religious institutions, but also for the balance between the national religion and socio-political processes. The implication is that there is a relationship between Thai Buddhism and the stability of the national political processes.

It is noted that Buddhist cosmology has been seen as highly (or uniquely) consonant with a socio-political order manifesting in noticeable status inequality, a degree of openness of status and positional change, that is a non-democratic basis for authority. However, it is apparent that although some Buddhist doctrines (*Kamma*) may help to legitimize a certain type of regime, only in certain cultural contexts will it specifically help a specific government or ruler.[34]

Buddhism is regarded as a source of moral authority which may support a particular government, or series of governments in one national tradition. Its legitimacy is enhanced by attaching its imprimatur to the specific government or governments. In this way, religion may contribute directly to the stability and continuity of political processes, not simply to the legitimacy of a certain type of socio-political order, within which instability and discontinuity may or may not occur.[35]

Thai Buddhism has contributed to the socio-political stability in the post-1932 period. Thai Buddhism has been ready publicly to bear with all the post-1932 governments as legitimate custodians of Thai national symbols and traditions, as well as protectors and patrons of Thai Buddhism itself. Thai Buddhism has authority to confer legitimacy upon specific governments because its leading practitioners, Buddhist monks, are highly respected. The ability of the national religion to grant legitimacy to governments, and thereby to contribute to the stability and continuity of political processes, has popularized the veneration of institutional Buddhism.

ROMAN CATHOLICISM IN THE PHILIPPINES

The majority of Filipino Roman Catholics believe that salvation can be had through performing religious rituals, fulfilling devotions or offering sacrifices.

---

[33] Steven Piker, 'Buddhism and Modernization in Contemporary Thailand', *Contributions to Asian Studies* IV (1973), 51-67.

[34] Piker, 'Buddhism and Modernization in Contemporary Thailand', 64-65.

[35] Piker, 'Buddhism and Modernization in Contemporary Thailand', 64-65.

They believe that they receive Christ every time they partake of the bread and wine of Holy Communion. They recount to God every aspect of life and experience through religious rituals. They think of God as distant and unapproachable. In order to approach him, they have to resort to intermediaries through which they can reach him. This concept of God is similar with that of traditional gods, *Kabuyan, Anito*.

The chief images of Christ to the Filipinos are the *Santo Nino* (Holy Child) and the *Santo Entierro* (Entombed Christ).[36] The one depicts the weak, innocent child and the other represents the victim of suffering and death. These images coincide with the Filipino's sense of weakness and experiences of suffering under colonial rule for years.

These two concepts of Christ represent deficient views. The child Jesus never grows up to manhood. This idea neglects the man Jesus, the Son of Man and the Son of God in the gospel, who preached the goodness of God to the poor, condemned the hypocrites, and drove away the money changers from the temple. On the other hand, the horizontal Christ who lies in state is not the Christ of Easter Sunday. He is not the risen, glorious, awesome Christ.[37] Thus, the Filipinos are not able to obtain faith in Christ through such notions. Further, their life pattern and worldview remains as it was.

The Filipino culture is a shame-based culture, so that the concern to let one's sin be revealed never happens, due to the fact that they elude from sin ever being exposed. Their sense of guilt does not appear to be strong. Rather, it is justified in the statement, 'because we are only human'.[38] This implies that since nobody is flawless, we should not be firm with those who fall into sin! Failings and shortcomings are natural. It seems that the Filipino's behaviour is governed more by the group around him or her, than by inner conviction, showing no desire for internalizing moral standards and standing up for them.

The Filipino Roman Catholic needs to understand Christ through biblical knowledge, and wrong comprehension about Christ should be corrected. They need adequate teaching that the God they worship is holy and righteous and never compromises with sin. These so-called Christians have to learn to renounce and confront sin. A profound sense of individual moral responsibility should affect a feeling of true repentance for sin, not just shame. They truly need to be transformed in the light of truth.

---

[36] Douglas Elwood and Patricia Magdamo, *In Christ in Philippine Context* (Quezon City, Philippines: New Day Publishers, 1971), 18.

[37] Rodrigo D. Tano, 'Theological Issues in the Philippine Context', *Evangelical Review of Theology* 19 (1995), 360.

[38] Leonardo N. Mercado, *Elements of Filipino Theology* (Tacloban City, Philippines: Divine Word University, 1975), 77-84.

Minjung is inferred as a political notion, which emerged in the 1970s. In history, the condition of the *Minjung* is resolute by the total framework of the ruling power and by the *Minjung*'s struggle. The *Minjung*'s history is clarified by their social life, the story of the people, and their socio-economic history. *Minjung* theology approaches the actuality of the people in the structure of their social biography and socio-economic history.

The *Minjung* have their own theological stance based on Deuteronomic and Covenant code.[39] It advocates for the rights of the poor people in the light of their socio-economic historical background. They argue that the prophets are the spokesmen for the poor and the psalms are the joyful songs of the poor people.

Ahn Byung Mu, a professor in a theological seminary, made an important interpretation based on the Gospel of Mark, where he discovered the true context of Jesus' message in Jesus' relationship with the *ochlos* (*Minjung*). Ahn used broad socio-economic historical materials to discover Jesus' message to the people (*Minjung*). It is one of his arguments that the writer of the Gospel of Mark protests the Pauline kerygmatization of Jesus' message and recovers the historical message of Jesus to the *ochlos*.[40]

The most significant aspect of *Minjung* theology is liberation, that is, liberation of people who are under oppression and struggle. They take not only the revolts and rebellions of the people seriously, but particularly the literary and artistic expressions of the *Minjung*'s struggle and aspirations. The literary works of poet Kim Chi Ha and other writers give prominent inspiration. '*Han of Minjung*' (righteous rage of the people under oppression) has emerged as one of the most important points of the social life of the *Minjung*, and is reflected in Korean theological circles.

Professor Hyun Young Hak has been working on theological thoughts regarding the Korean traditional Mask Dance. He catches the scenarios styles and languages of the *Talchum* (Mask Dance) and the dynamics of social transcendence among the oppressed people.[41] Thus, *Minjung* theology attempts to recount the gospel message to the struggle and aspiration of Korean people in their current conditions. Its position is on the side of the people; it searches for freedom in real life, beyond the philosophical and ideological frameworks.

[39] Yong Bock Kim, 'Doing Theology in Asia Today: A Korean Perspective', in *Asian Christian Theology* (Philadelphia: Westminster, 1980), 317.
[40] Kim, 'Doing Theology in Asia Today: A Korean Perspective', 318.
[41] Kim, 'Doing Theology in Asia Today: A Korean Perspective', 318.

Impact of Pentecostalism

In the Past

Throughout several decades, the Pentecostal movement in Eastern Asia was eminent. Pentecostals certainly contributed significant impact with their unique message in the Asian cultural, social and religious plural settings. The following section will probe the various aspects of the Pentecostal movement and its establishment in the region of East Asia.

AMONG ANIMISTS

In spite of the process of modernization and the advances in science and technology, Asians are relatively animistic and superstitious, whereas Westerners are materialistic and scientific. People in Asia, in general, are more person-oriented than Western people. They tend to look at the universe and natural phenomenon, like storms and typhoons, as personal. Asian people frequently look for spiritual power to control their environment. Thus, they give their attention to spirits to keep themselves from being impaired or harmed. They believe that accidents, sudden death, and bad luck are caused by malevolent spirits. Filipinos tend to be under the grip of fear by such beliefs. They view the spirit beings as inhabiting in, and having control over, nature. The spirit beings also cause sickness, volcanic eruptions, and success or failure. Often the spirits are vengeful and capricious. An appropriate means of soothing the spirits is offering animal sacrifices. Through receiving the ritual, the anger of the spirit is appeased. Their perception of deities has much to do with the spirits' power to bless or curse.

The Pentecostal's effectiveness is best found among the animistic people. As their religion is centred on the concept of power, the Pentecostal message not only proclaims a right message, but also demonstrates God's supremacy over their deities through the demonstration of power. One tangible form often taking place is healing. Pentecostals largely engage their ministry with the power of physical healing and exorcism. Their effectiveness is exceptional in an environment where medical service is not available. Early Pentecostal ministry (the Assemblies of God) in the tribal northern Philippines is a good example. God's power was demonstrated among various sick people and this healing ministry became a catalyst to bring the animistic people to Christ. The Kankana-ey tribal people whom the Assemblies of God workers and missionaries have ministered to are animistic and ancestral worshipers. Once a week, ministry team members preached the gospel in open-air services in mountain areas during the early stage of the ministry. They boldly proclaimed the healing power of God, based on Mark 16:15-18, 'They shall lay hands on the sick and they shall recover'. They saw the needs of these people and with simple faith in the Word of God, called on their ministry team members to pray for the sick.[42]

Bible study groups were added and eventually a church was erected. This was the pattern of Pentecostal evangelism in many rural parts of the region. As a result, the Pentecostals penetrated rural areas fairly well, often shying away from urban centres.

SPIRITUAL DYNAMIC AND CHURCH GROWTH

Phenomenal church growth in some countries is often attributed to a spiritual dynamic, brought in through Pentecostal churches or Pentecostal types of worship. Church growth in Korea is one such example.

Korean churches, regardless of whether Pentecostal or non-Pentecostal, have grown so rapidly that there are a number of the largest churches in the world in Korea. In fact, among the 50 mega churches in the world today, 23 are in Korea. Ten local churches in Seoul alone have a membership of over 30,000 each. There are hundreds of other churches with members of between 500 and 1,000. The explosive church growth from 1980-1990 was remarkable and in the capital city of Seoul, there are more than 6,533 churches. In the 100-year history of the Korean church, four chief periods of very rapid church growth are marked: 1905-1910, 1919-1931, 1945-1960, and 1980-1990. According to information, there were over 12.2 million Protestant Christians, 36,832 churches, and 67,008 pastors and evangelists in South Korea.[43]

In his recent article, Bong Rin Ro[44] lists several key contributing factors to church growth: 1) the dedication of pastors to ministry and their dynamic leadership; 2) prayer, especially in time of national crises; 3) emphasis on evangelism and missions, especially among lay people. Often 'power evangelism' is employed by both Pentecostal and non-Pentecostal Evangelical churches; 4) the cell group system which nurtures personal growth and provides time for intercessory prayer; [45] and 5) ample supply of highly trained workers from seminaries.[46] Pentecostal practices such as the baptism in the Holy Spirit, speaking in tongues, and prayer for healing are commonly held in most Evangelical churches, especially during revival meetings.

---

[42] Inez Sturgeon, *Give Me This Mountain* (Oakland, CA: Hunter Advertising, 1960), 95.

[43] Bong Rin Ro, 'The Korean Church: Growing or Declining?' *Evangelical Review of Theology* 19 (1995), 344-345.

[44] Ro, 'The Korean Church: Growing or Declining?'

[45] He points out Yoido Full Gospel Church in Seoul, Korea as a typical example. It has systematically organized about 52,000 cell groups for 706,000 members throughout Seoul for Bible study and prayer. Yonggi Cho claims that the basic strength of his church lies in the cell-group ministry, ibid., 346.

[46] There are 290 Bible colleges and theological seminaries, including Pentecostals and non-Pentecostals, which yearly produce more than 9,000 graduates. These young and old workers go out and plant a new church in different cities and provinces and go out oversees for mission work.

The Pentecostal impact is not limited to rural areas. The growth of indigenous Pentecostal churches in Indonesia is particularly notable. In the Philippines, the sudden surge of independent Pentecostal/Charismatic groups, as well as traditional Pentecostal denominations, receive much attention. For instance, a study of the ten fastest growing churches in Metro Manila was undertaken recently, and eight to nine of them are strong Pentecostal/Charismatic churches. [47] The growth of Pentecostal/Charismatic churches is especially significant in Singapore. We see not only classical Pentecostals, such as Assemblies of God, but also Anglican and Baptist Charismatic churches, as well as other independent churches. They are meagre churches, though making a significant impact on the society. Malaysia has also seen substantial growth among the Pentecostal churches. Even in Japan recently, several Pentecostal churches recorded an unprecedented growth making many mission watchers see possibilities to penetrate Japanese hearts with the Christian gospel. Pentecostal contribution to church growth is unquestionable.

INFLUENCES TO BROAD CHRISTIANITY

Pentecostalism was an object of suspicion in many places. Its emphasis on experiential dimension drew criticisms from mainline denominations. For instance, up until recent days, David Yonggi Cho was officially branded as having questionable doctrinal stands by a major Korean Presbyterian group. However, typical Pentecostal experiences were sought by pastors across the denominations. Prayer mountains are popular places where pastors of Pentecostal, as well as non-Pentecostal, groups come to spend secluded time to receive 'grace'. This refers to a personal encounter with God and often this means, in truth, a typical Pentecostal experience, including the baptism in the Holy Spirit with speaking in tongues, healing, 'receiving messages' and the like. Pentecostals have added a definite dimension to the traditional Christian life.

Also significant is the imminent picture of God the Pentecostals stress. The Word of God is preached in a dynamic movement of the Holy Spirit. When they preach and pray, they expect a response from the Lord. This is particularly significant for Asians whose religions have a direct bearing on people's felt-needs.

Missionary zeal and commitment is also significant to the Pentecostal movement. In the very beginning, the outpouring of the Spirit was understood as a signal for the last days. Early Pentecostals clearly perceived missions as their divine calling. Although it is not generally true, some Pentecostal churches have been leaders in missions movements. Big Pentecostal churches in Singapore and Malaysia initiated missionary endeavours to neighbouring countries, and this quickly spread to other churches in the region.

---

[47] Oscar C. Baldemor, 'The Spread of Fire: A Study of Ten Growing Churches in Metro-Manila' (Th. M. thesis, Fuller Theological Seminary, 1990), 54.

Pentecostalism has remained a strong impact within the church. This means that the movement did not pay much attention to the world outside the church. The Pentecostals, like their Evangelical counterparts, remained silent to the oppressive political issues. The Pentecostal churches chose to concentrate their attention on 'religious matters' only. Often silence was used by the dictatorial powers as an endorsement, while the so-called liberal wing fought hard for social and political issues. They were frequently questioned about their spirituality and commitment to God's work. Some Evangelicals, including Pentecostal leaders, were instead proud of being invited by the authority to bless them. For this, the Pentecostals neglected God's prophetic mission of the church to the world.

It is no wonder that the Roman Catholic Church grew significantly, while the Evangelical, including Pentecostal, churches recorded a minus growth right after the dictatorship fell in Korea. In Myanmar, it was the Buddhists and Baptists who have been 'politically' involved. Although Pentecostals may not have followed the same methods others have used, their concern and sympathy should be expressed toward the unjustly suffering masses.

Pentecostals have also remained silent to economic injustices. When labour struggles marred the entire Korean society, it was the Roman Catholics and the 'liberal' Christianity who raised their voices. They courageously engaged in a David-and-Goliath battle against mega-conglomerates and the government. From the poverty side, the Pentecostals may have done better. From the very beginning, the Pentecostal movement has been surrounded by the poor and underprivileged, and with the message of God's power and miracles, people are constantly nurtured with the spirit of hope. Many 'success' stories shared in Pentecostal churches can be attributed to the untiring proclamation of God-given hope. Many can testify even today of how God turned their lives around through healings and miracles.

In this area of social issues, some Pentecostals have taken a rather active role. In Singapore, Teen Challenge, Pentecostal program helping drug users, has helped many cases. In Malaysia, local churches operate successful rehabilitation programs. Many big Pentecostal/Charismatic churches in Metro Manila are ministering to street children and prostitutes. A Pentecostal seminary in the Philippines and radio ministry group produced a simple, but effective comic booklet to be used for AIDS education. They have also conducted awareness seminars among the youth of the Philippines. A well-known Korean Pentecostal church started a daily newspaper several years ago and its daily distribution runs more than a million copies. It creates and shares powerful Christian opinions and makes a significant impact on the society. Recently, another Korean Pentecostal church opened a 2.5 million US dollar facility for women in the community. This same church is also building an impressive multi-million dollar complex for urban youth, for both Christian and non-Christian. Another big Pentecostal church has developed an extensive feeding program in the Philippines. It was wonderful to see that prayer for the fragile environment was one of several key prayers offered during the First World Assemblies of God Prayer Congress in Seoul, in 1994. The final rally drew close to a million Pentecostals. In Vietnam, Laos and Cambodia, a US Pentecostal body was invited to operate the social services program, such as orphanages and English instruction. Lately, a plan is underway to begin a clinic in the underdeveloped region of China. They all appear impressive and rightly so. However, most of these are not concerted programs; they all depend upon the ministerial philosophy of a pastor, who often fails to point to the root cause and rather deals with the consequences.

Future Tasks

The following discussion is a moderate reflection on the future role of the Pentecostal churches in the region.

MAINTAINING ITS DISTINCTIVENESS AND THEOLOGICAL REFLECTION

The Pentecostal Movement has been a spiritual movement. Although much was said about its social involvement, or lack thereof, Pentecostals need to recognize, nurture and maximize their spiritual dynamic in encountering political, social, economic, and religious challenges. Power evangelism is what the Pentecostals are known for; signs and wonders are revealed through the power of the Holy Spirit and Pentecostals take this as a Biblical pattern (e.g., Acts 3:1; 16:14 Rom. 1:16; 1 Cor. 2:1, 4, 5). Pentecostals should not pursue conformity to their established and well-recognized Evangelical neighbours. Rather, Pentecostals must remain faithful to their distinctiveness in order to be effective in their mission and calling.

As the Pentecostal churches mature, we expect serious theological reflections within their own context. [48] The traditional anti-intellectualism among the Pentecostals has changed in Asia. Because of a high value given to education itself, Asian Pentecostal leaders are now eager to obtain higher educations. In the Asia Pacific region, not including India, the Assemblies of God alone has more than 150 Bible schools and there are at least five schools offering master's programs. Hence, it is not inconceivable to have some creative theological works among Asian Pentecostal thinkers in the near future.

MISSIONARY AND CHURCH GROWTH MOVEMENT

Pentecostal identity has much to do with a missionary call. Empowerment is perceived specifically for the spreading of the good news of the gospel. Faithfulness to the word and faith in God's power will make Pentecostal missionary work profound and effective. For instance, among Muslims, the only

---

[48] For instance, Simon Chan, *Spiritual Theology: A Systematic Study of Christian Life* (Downers Grove, IL: InterVarsity Press, 198).

effective way of evangelism is through power encounters of God. The same can be said for tribal evangelism. As long as Pentecostal churches maintain a high priority to mission, the Holy Spirit will continue to bless and use them. Social involvement should be explored within this context.

The Pentecostal churches are also expected to lead the church growth trend. It is true that the context is rapidly changing. Yet, the Pentecostal churches have proven that they can turn the seeming hindrances into a springboard for growth. The rapid church growth of Yoido Full Gospel Church is a fine example. This church has contributed to the worldwide church growth movement through its Church Growth International. Even in the midst of a seeming cessation of church growth, the Pentecostal church seems to have a solution. Very recently, about ten Korean mega-Pentecostal churches, including Yoido, started a fresh prayer movement. Every night, Gethsemane Prayer was held asking for God's touch in the lives of individuals, family, business, church, nation and the world. The churches began to reap immediate results. The churches were gaining their spiritual dynamics back. Many testimonies of God's work spread and daily prayer became a popular place, not only for church members, but also for Christians of other churches. This was sometimes accused as being 'sheep stealing'. However, the point is that church growth can be achieved primarily through a spiritual movement, and Pentecostal churches in Korea are leading this.

As already mentioned, Japanese Pentecostal churches have recently proven that Japan is not impossible, although it may be difficult, to accept Jesus. We also pray that the social work which the Pentecostals were invited to establish in former socialist countries will gradually open doors for full Pentecostal evangelism. China is another place we need to reclaim for a Pentecostal revival.

ECUMENICITY AND INTER-RELIGIOUS CONCERNS

Considering the religiously pluralistic nature, Pentecostals often find familiar supernatural works in other religions. This sets a limit to power encounter. It is not the demonstration of power, but the revelation of truth which will ultimately determine which religion is true. As other religions, including Roman Catholicism, fall into the trap of syncretism with folk religions, there is a strong possibility for 'folk Pentecostalism'. This is a theological concern.

On the other hand, Pentecostals should develop an ecumenical sense among Christian groups in working together for the expansion of God's kingdom. At the local level, there are endless things Pentecostals can do with other Christian groups. For example, in the northern Philippines, churches are using an Ilocano song book which was compiled by Philippine Assemblies of God. There is a good chance that various other Christian groups will join together to revise and eventually come up with a hymn book which will be 'universally' used among Ilocano-speaking Christians. This 'ecumenical' cooperation can expand to social, educational, and economic areas, in addition to the 'religious' works.

Concluding Remarks

This study began with a rather gloomy picture of the present and the future of the East and Southeast Asian region. As already mentioned, this picture may not accurately describe every nation. Yet, the challenge is formidable for Christianity, including the Pentecostals. The issues which various societies are facing are very difficult. Often governmental control is not as effective as before and the region is part of a larger move toward globalization. Even more difficult is that the situation is rapidly changing. This includes almost everything, from how to operate a business to how to learn to live and think. Besides, the region is religiously fertile; high as well as low religions are very active in people's lives.

Although the challenge is great, so is the task for the Pentecostal churches in the coming years. The past record of its impact within the Christian community, and its unique message, has a strong potential to play a significant role, not only for Christianity, but also for society. The true challenge seems to lie within the Pentecostal churches: self-realization and a sense of its call. Just like any Christian revival movement such as Methodism, the Pentecostal movement has a strong possibility of following the degeneration path and ending up with a sophisticated institution. Yet, the movement is more than a revival movement. As the early Pentecostals perceived, God has poured his 'latter rain' on us for the final harvest. This sense of a unique call will cause the Pentecostals to remain as Pentecostal as possible. This will be a powerful weapon to fight against rising secularism and materialism. Pentecostalism will not be able to defend the traditional Oriental lifestyles and values. It was not called to do that; but, it will stand in the forefront to show our loving and powerful God.

However, it will take more than the simple message of God's power to win billions of Asians for the Lord. Pentecostals have three kinds of front-line: 1) Pentecostal works in an infant stage in countries such as Mongolia, Cambodia, Vietnam, Laos, Tibet, Nepal, China, and hopefully North Korea; 2) struggling areas which need a fresh breakthrough, such as Japan, Thailand and Taiwan; and 3) countries where the Pentecostal churches have enjoyed significant success in the past and are now facing new challenges. This group may include nations like Korea, Singapore, Malaysia, Philippines and Indonesia.

To be at the forefront of God's move in this region, the Pentecostal churches will need to raise workers in every field: pastoral, evangelism, missions, Christian education, theological reflection, and social work. We need to guard and keep the word 'post-Pentecostalism' from entering into a dictionary. The Holy Spirit means to work powerfully among His people until the return of the King.

Chapter 7

Religious Worldviews in Asia

Introduction

One distinctive belief of dynamic Christianity is in God's unrestricted power to meet various daily human needs. This theological belief gives committed Christians a unique opportunity to relate to animists and other religious groups. In Asia, some of the major religions are Buddhism, Hinduism and Confucianism. Although Asian societies are rapidly changing due to the influence of secularism and materialism, they are still deeply connected to their own distinct religious beliefs. In fact, the greater their exposure to materialism, the more they seek blessings from their spirits. Thus, it is critical for those who are involved in missionary work in Asia to understand the worldview of these religions. A lack of understanding could cause the gospel message to be unclear, and could also result in fatal errors being made.

In this chapter I will discuss the worldview of several Asian religions, including animism. I will use the worldview of the Kankana-ey tribe of the northern Philippines as an example of animism.[1] In spite of the differences in beliefs and practices among various animistic groups, I believe that there is a fundamental belief common to all animists: the spirits exist and they animate the world.

A worldview consists of assumptions, perceptions, interpretations and values. It does not exist by itself, but rather it co-exists with culture, as culture is on the surface (thus, visible), whereas the worldview is under the surface (thus, invisible). In other words, the way people behave is connected to their culture, while what people think is related to their worldview. To demonstrate the inter-influential nature of the two, a simple illustration may be of help. When a big piece of wood (culture) is thrown into the river, the river water splashes back (worldview) to the surface of the water in and around the area of the wood. These two elements are always side by side.[2] The following are characteristics of the worldview.

---

[1] One of fifteen major tribes in the mountains of Northern Luzon who frequently perform rituals for blessing and healing.

[2] Charles Kraft, *Anthropology for Christian Witness* (Maryknoll, NY: Orbis, 1996), 52.

Assumptions

One's underlying assumptions are unquestionable, particularly for many Asians, because their religious beliefs have deeply influenced their assumptions. For example, a tribal group called Hae Enga in India believes, like any animist, that their ancestor spirits are deeply involved in their daily affairs. In one case, a boy became ill and his symptoms suggested pneumonia. The father believed that the disease came from the ghost of his mother. And people in the village assumed that his mother wanted pork, but the father did not want to offer a pig. A few days later the son died. The family, as well as the villagers, believed that the boy's grandmother took his life, not because he had done anything wrong, but because the spirit needed pork. This was their assumption, and whether this was right or wrong it was never questioned, because they automatically believed that this is what the spirit did.[3]

The assumption lies in the fact that the mother liked pork while living; thus, her spirit craved pork even after her death. It is also possible that the Hae Enga place a high value on pigs and this may have led them to form an assumption that the spirits prefer pigs over other animals.

By and large, most Asian cultures believe in the spirit world and the spirits' activities in both their individual and community life. Often they tend to have constant fear of attacks from spirits; and in order to prevent such attacks by deceased spirits, sacrificial offerings are made. Such 'primitive' assumptions do not easily disappear, even in the midst of rapid social changes with strong materialistic and secular influences.

Values

Values are mental concepts. In Chinese culture, husbands are viewed as the sky and wives as the earth. In the male dominated environments throughout Asia, the sayings of men are considered more valuable than those of women. This value system is often traced to the influence of Confucianistic teachings. A value is heavily weighted with emotional feelings. It is a concept which refers to a desirable or undesirable state of affairs. The desirable or undesirable position of problems refers to the values or what their values ought to be.[4]

As an illustration of the desirable and undesirable state, the Hae Enga tribe believes that a husband and his wife should not sleep in the same house, and a woman should not enter a man's house where he is sleeping. The strong concept that men and women should sleep in separate houses leads to a value system where men are regarded as being superior to women. On the other hand, when values are violated, in this case by a man sleeping in the same house as his wife,

---

[3] James Spradley, 'Worldview and Values' (A reader used in Worldview and Worldview Change class, School of World Mission, Fuller Theological Seminary, 1994), 156. See also Michael Kearney, *World View* (Novato, CA: Chandler & Sharp, 1984), 68-74.

[4] Spradley, 'Worldview and Values', 157. See also Paul G. Hiebert, *Anthropological Insights for Missionaries* (Grand Rapids, MI: Baker, 1991), 30-34.

mother or sisters, which seldom goes unnoticed, it becomes an undesirable state of affairs. In such a case, an attempt to make a justified exception, for example, because he is old or poor, reflects another value of the community toward the aged or destitute.[5]

There are ways to learn the values of people, and observing their behaviour is one such way. As an outsider, I could make a judgment about the Hae Enga tribe by observing that, for them, offering a pig is more valuable than selling it. However, it is possible that urban dwellers would consider selling the pig to be more valuable than offering it to the spirits. Although they may belong to the same tribe, individual lifestyle and environment affects their values.

Observing how one teaches is another important way to learn a particular set of values. In Asia, parents teach their children proper behaviour. For example, bowing one's head to the elderly shows respect; thus, it is a proper way of greeting, particularly for Koreans and Japanese. In contrast, waving to the elderly is considered improper.

Observing behaviour and also exploring how these values are taught to the next generation, reveals the hierarchy of values. A value is associated with people's feelings and with the concept of a desirable and undesirable condition of problems.

Worldviews of Asian Religions

Buddhism

In order to understand Buddhism better, it is worth briefly reviewing Siddharta Gautama's personal background. Siddharta Gautama was perceived as Buddha, the founder of Buddhism, who lived in the sixth century, B.C. His parents named him to mean 'he who has reached his goal', and his life story is shrouded with myths. He was born in about 560 B.C. in a village called Lumbini near the border between India and Nepal, and later died at the age of eighty.

One night Maya, the mother of Buddha, had a dream about a white elephant entering her womb. She gave birth to a son, but sadly died seven days later. The little child was brought up by his mother's sister in affluent and splendorous circumstances. Although he was highly educated in the arts and science, he found that his life did not give him any satisfaction and he determined to leave that lifestyle and become homeless. He fasted to the point that he lost his hair. The crucial turning-point prior to his enlightenment was his awareness of the spiritual and moral vainness of human life and his acceptance of the use of meditation and faith. He taught the public and people followed him.[6]

---

[5] Spradley, 'Worldview and Values', 157.
[6] Wulf Metz, 'The Enlightened One: Buddhism', in Pat Alexander, et al. (eds.), *Eerdman's Handbook to the World's Religions* (Grand Rapids, MI: Eerdmans, 1994), 224.

Siddharta Gautama was greatly influenced by the teachings of Hinduism. Therefore, Buddha was a reformer of Hinduism, just as Luther was of Roman Catholicism. He wrestled with the question of how to be liberated from the grief of unceasing rebirths. Buddha's original desire was simply to re-establish Hinduism in its original form. His teaching, therefore, presents major ideas of the traditional Indian religion, namely the doctrine of rebirth and the law of karma.[7]

SELF-LEARNING KNOWLEDGE AND SPIRIT-RELATED PRACTICE

Buddha's understanding of knowledge is different from the western intellectual understanding of the term. Buddha interpreted knowledge far beyond the restrictions of reason and intellect. His understanding of knowledge did not come from the study of related books or revelations from a spirit. Buddhism has sometimes been called an 'atheistic religion'. Miracles have little significance, and Buddha himself is simply a human being who awoke from the gloom of blunder to live in freedom from self-centeredness and self-indulgence.[8]

Therefore, it is quite obvious that Buddhism did not originate from a god, since there is no relationship with the spirit world. Rather, the majority of Buddhists evoke the spirit of Buddha by bowing before his statue over a hundred times each day, in order to have their wishes granted through the incomprehensible power of his spirit. Some Buddhists wake up at dawn and spend a sacrificial amount of time in meditation in front of a small image of Buddha. The followers believe that Buddha is a spirit being who obtained almighty power and this can, in turn, be released when a ritual requirement is adequately met. Over the course of Buddhism's development in various Asian nations, it has become obvious that many non-Buddhist beliefs and practices have been added from other spirit-related religions such as shamanism and animism; thus, it is often extremely syncretised. This view is from my own personal observations and experiences as a former Buddhist.

PERCEPTION OF HUMAN SUFFERING

Buddha found important truths of his own, which represent the crucial points of Buddhist philosophy. The first is the knowledge of suffering; that all individual existence is hopeless and full of pain. This teaching makes human suffering during birth, aging, sickness, anxiety, pain, agony and hardship a negative element of life.

The second truth regards the cause of suffering. Suffering of all beings, including humans, has its source in desire and unawareness. It is the desire which

---

[7] Metz, 'The Enlightened One', 224.

[8] Metz, 'The Enlightened One', 224. C.K. Yang, *Religion in Chinese Society* (Berkley: University of California Press, 1967), 117-18, argues that for the first two or three centuries after its arrival in China, Buddhism spread in its Hinayana form, which 'emphasized attainment of magical power to ward off demonic influences which wrought misery in the human world'.

takes place when one is re-birthed and the desire, bound up with waiting and greediness, which draws itself into different situations to become great, whilst at the same time threatening individual destruction.[9]

The third truth concerns the alleviation of suffering. The ultimate teaching of Buddhism gives humans eternal deliverance from suffering. One should become liberated from the unceasing cycle of rebirth (*samsara*) and enter the blessed condition of nirvana. It is a radically 'other' state to that of the material world; the eternal realm, the utterly dependable, the true refuge.

The fourth truth presents the way to the eradication of suffering: the noble eight-fold ways. 'Essentially it is concerned with three things: with morality (right speech, right action, right occupation); with spiritual discipline (right effort, right mindfulness, right composure); and with insight (right knowledge, right attitude)'.[10]

The philosophical teaching has been one of the attractive points that draws people to Buddhism. If one is not fully committed to his or her own religion, it is easy to be 'converted' to another religion, which may present more noble teachings and beliefs, with practical benefits. The matter of eternal life may not be the primary focus in this process. As mentioned briefly, throughout its long history of evolution, Buddhism has incorporated many native spirit-believing religions to the extent that the original teachings of Buddha are no longer clear in the common mind. In fact, many gods and spirits were created or added for the convenience of believers who wanted to fulfil their wishes through the spirits' trans-empirical power.

The film *An Initiation of Shaman*, for instance, clearly shows the convergence of Buddhism and shamanism.[11] This is the story of a woman who was forced to become a shaman not through her own volition, but through the desire of the spirits. She went through a process of resistance and struggle with the spirits and this made her life full of misery, as she had no desire to become a shaman. However, she could no longer resist and finally surrendered herself to the spirit. One scene in the movie shows the initiation process of her shamanhood. The spirits in the room were depicted as Buddha, the same Buddha, but with different faces and looks. The depictions of Buddha were quite different from the ones that I had seen in a Buddhist temple. I immediately noticed a confluence of two religious systems: Buddhism and shamanism. I regularly include this video presentation in my Folk Religion class to illustrate the point of syncretism, as well as the world of the spirits.

---

[9] Metz, 'The Enlightened One', 231-32; E. Zurcher, *The Buddhist Conquest of China: The Spread and Adaptation of Buddhism in Early Medieval China* (Leiden: Brill, 1972), 71.
[10] Metz, 'The Enlightened One', 231-32.
[11] Diana S. Lee and Laurel Kendall, *An Initiation of Kut for a Korean Shaman* (videotape; Honolulu: University of Hawaii Press, 1991). See also Ralph R. Covell, *Confucius, the Buddha, and Christ: A History of the Gospel in Chinese* (Maryknoll, NY: Orbis, 1986), 137.

Among average Korean Buddhists, it is perfectly acceptable to look to a shaman or other religious practitioner for help. In fact, they regularly seek the help of spirits through mediums (or shamans) in order, for instance, to know about the future. My own mother serves as a typical example. She was a devoted Buddhist who always visited a Buddhist temple on special occasions and festivals, taking her children with her. She was strongly influenced by her own mother, my grandmother, who was equally committed to Buddhism. However, she also served as a shaman, functioning as a medium who could communicate with deceased spirits on behalf of living members of the family. When my mother encountered a problem, such as sickness in the family, she went to a village shaman for his or her help. Often the shaman would come to our house to cast out the evil spirit that was believed to have caused the trouble. She (often it was a female shaman) would dance up and down, while someone played a gong. After that, she ate food prepared by my mother, which had been initially offered to the spirit. I believe the shaman was also a Buddhist who regularly attended the local temple more often than average members did. And yet, in their daily lives they were more conscious of the spirit world.

It is worth noting that Asians had already been fully exposed to the spirit world by the time Buddhism reached the various nations in Asia. Since the basic teachings of Buddhism do not include the role of the spirits in daily life, the powerful influence of animism on Buddhism is not a surprise at all.

Confucianism

Korean, Chinese (including overseas nationalities such as the Singaporeans and Malaysians) and some elements of Japanese culture were shaped by Confucian philosophy. Confucianism looks for perfect human beings within the planet world. Confucianism is a Latinized name, and is presumably from the seventeenth century Jesuit missionaries. *Fu*, the Chinese term for Confucianism, literally means scholars with the special meaning of Confucian from the T'ang dynasty which encompasses its wider character and intellectual culture. It is commonly considered as philosophy (*chia*) and refers to the elements of worship, ritual and sacrifice which are part of religious teachings.[12] However, philosophical teaching, which is related to morality, is considered far greater than any of the other aspects.

Confucianism is best known for its moral philosophy, which is closely associated with Confucius (551-479 BC), Mencius (371-289 BC) and Hsun-tzu (298-238 BC).[13] 'Nonetheless, Confucianism gives primary emphasis to the ethical meaning of human relationships, finding and grounding the moral in the divine transcendence'. The best example of this is Confucius himself. He was

---

[12] Raymond Hammer, 'Concepts of Hinduism', in *Eerdman's Handbook to the World's Religions*, 185.

[13] John Berthrong, 'Sages and Immortals: Chinese Religions', in *Eerdman's Handbook of World's Religions*, 248.

regarded as a great teacher, and the basis of his teaching was the notion of humanity (*jen*). In the same way that Buddhists underscore the importance of compassion and Christians emphasize love, *jen* is the ultimate goal of 'self-transformation' for the Confucian. Confucius stressed the ethical dimension of humanity. He made it clear that it was Heaven itself which protected him and gave him his message: 'Heaven is the author of the virtue that is in me'.[14]

However, Confucianism is also characterised by elements of mysticism:

> It is clearly grounded in religion - the inherited religion of the Lord-on-high, or Heaven. Even the great rationalist Hsun-tzu sees society founded on the penetrating insight of the sagely mind. And though Confucianism is less known for its mysticism, the *Book of Mencius*, as well as other works cannot be fully understood except in the light of mysticism. The *Chung-yung*, one of the 'Four Books' which became the basis for Confucian self-cultivation in the Southern Sung (1126-1279 CE), explicitly states that the sage, having realized true integrity (*ch'eng*), becomes one with Heaven and Earth. Confucian moral metaphysics reaches over into the religious quest for unity with the ground of being.[15]

Confucius taught ethical teachings based on his religious consciousness, although he avoided discussing the relationship between human nature and the 'Way of Heaven'. However, Mencius constructed his whole system of thought around these two concepts. He attempted to demonstrate how the very core of the 'Way of Heaven', the heavenly power of the cosmos, became human nature. He believed that if human nature could be suitably refined and nurtured, even the common person could become wise.[16]

Confucianism stresses the importance of relationships. The vertical relationship includes, first of all, filial piety, the greatest of all virtues and the basis of all good works. The right performance of filial piety is the source and basis of the five cardinal relations: between ruler and subjects, there should be respect for rulers; between father and son, the father should be respected and honoured; between husband and wife, the husband should be obeyed; between brothers, elders should be honoured; and between friends there should be affection, loyalty and trust. Confucianism teaches ethics in relationships with different levels and groups of people.

In this system, there is no concept of a horizontal relationship with spirit beings. Confucius and Mencius neither acknowledged nor denied the existence of G/god or the immortality of the soul. They were humanist teachers of morality

---

[14] Berthrong, 'Sages and Immortals', 246; John D. Young, *East-West Synthesis: Matteo Ricci and Confucianism* (Hong Kong: Hong Kong Centre of Asian Studies, University of Hong Kong, 1980), 39.

[15] Berthrong, 'Sages and Immortals', 246. See also Covell, *Confucius, the Buddha, and Christ*, 46-48.

[16] Berthrong, 'Sages and Immortals', 248.

and ethics. They spoke about Heaven (*Tien*) and enjoyed its protection. However, Neo-confucianists later cultivated the atheistic idea of *Tai-Chi* (Supreme Ultimate) and *Wu-Chi* (Supreme Ultimateless).

People may question if Confucianism is a religion, because there are no deities to worship or honour. However, on the other hand, it does have religious elements: ancestor worship and rituals, although these are not a matter of beliefs but ethics. It is noted that:

> Ancestral worship was first introduced to China at the beginning of the Chou dynasty (1122-325 BCE). It was Confucius (551-479 BCE) who popularized this practice by his teaching on filial piety, decreeing that parents and elders are to be honoured and respected while they are alive. This sense of reverence continues after their deaths. The Chinese believe that at death the soul of the deceased ancestor resides in three places. One part goes to heaven, the second remains in the grave to receive sacrifices and the third is localized in the ancestral tablet or shine. The soul has to be assisted as it journeys to heaven. Hence, at Chinese funerals, elaborate rituals are meticulously carried out to ensure that the soul is amply provided for on its course. [17]

Children are responsible for the well-being of their parents' spirits. The ancestor spirits play an extremely important role in the living family, according to Confucian teaching. They are a source of help and protection, and they lead their descendents through an uncertain future with guidance and protection. Such beliefs reinforce the teaching of filial piety, as they rely on the spirits of ancestors for their well-being. Although Confucianism deals with various relationships, the foundational one is the relationship between father and son. This teaching, eagerly incorporated by other religious groups in Asia, has become a part of their religious traditions.

Hinduism

In the concept of the absolute, Brahman is the origin, cause and foundation of all existence. It is neutral and impersonal. Indians see several attributes or functions of divinity manifested in a multiplicity of forms. In the Vedic hymns, a god is not fully seen in human terms. The gods are the manifestations of nature or cosmic forces. Divine names may be countless, but they are all understood as the expressions of Brahman. Even if it may have limitless forms, it is still regarded as one in essence. [18]

In relation to Hindu ethics, Raymond Hammer states that:

---

[17] Wee Hian Chua, 'The Worship of Ancestors', in *Eerdman's Handbook of World Religions*, 247.

[18] Raymond Hammer, 'Approaches to Truth: The Great Interpreters', in *Eerdman's Handbook of World's Religions*, 183.

In classical Hinduism actions (*karma*) and duty (*dharma*) were the dominant concepts. *Karma,* as the accumulation of good and bad acts, would influence a person's destiny, but there was no one way to acquire good *karma.* Early in the Veda there had been the notion of an overriding moral law (*rita*), of which Mitra and Varuna were the guardians. Humanity had to recognize a divine imperative, and prayer and sacrifice were necessary to maintain a right relationship between the divine and the human. Sin, however, could be either moral or ritual.[19]

The only complete ethic was connected to the freedom of individuals from the cycle of rebirth. This is what the 'ascetic' emphasis of Hinduism is aiming for, as a practice to seek for 'salvation'. They are to keep fundamental morality, 'refraining from killing, stealing, sexual impurity, or the consumption of intoxicants'. Otherwise, they are not able to achieve the essential purity necessary to bring them further on the path of *moksha* ('release').[20]

In addition to the ethical obligation, their commitment to devotion to God is also required. According to Hindu teaching, obtaining *moksha* depends completely upon God. In other words, 'grace alone' enables the follower to attain *moksha*. It appears that the Christian theology of God's grace finds an excellent contact point in Hindu thought.[21] However, the balance between the human role and the divine in this process is rather delicate:

> Two theories of the operation of grace were put forward: the 'kitten' and the 'monkey' approach. A she-cat seizes the kitten and carries it where she wills. This involves a total passivity on the part of the kitten, and there were those who stated that God's grace operates in the same way. All is effected by God, and humans do nothing to achieve *moksha.* By contrast, the baby monkey clings to its mother. The mother monkey is responsible for the baby monkey's continuance of life and movement, yet there is not total passivity. Most Hindu teachers within the *bhakti* tradition took this standpoint. We cling to God, and God effects our salvation.[22]

Human effort, therefore, is essential in bringing the ultimate goal, *moksha*. However, there must be grace from deity to make this complete.

Animism

The discussion in this section comes from my personal experiences and research in the Kankana-ey tribe of the northern Philippines.

Animism is defined as:

---

[19] Raymond Hammer, 'Karma and Dharma: Hindu Ethics', in *Eerdman's Handbook of World's Religions*, 190.

[20] Hammer, 'Karma and Dharma', 190. Also Sunil H. Stephens, 'Doing Theology in a Hindu Context', *JAM* 1:2 (Jan 1999), 185.

[21] Hammer, 'Concepts of Hinduism', 185. H.L. Richard, 'Evangelical Approaches to Hindus', *Missiology: An International Review* 29 (July 2001), 312-13.

[22] Hammer, 'Concepts of Hinduism', 189.

[A] belief in personal spirits and impersonal spiritual forces. Animists also perceive that the spirits and forces have power over human affairs. People who have experienced such spiritual power and influence constantly seek its help to meet various daily human needs such as healing, success, and decisions for the future. They attempt to manipulate the power of the spirits for the favourable future.[23]

Animistic believers include organic spirit beings such as gods, ancestor spirits, ghosts, nature spirits, and demons in their understanding of the world. The spiritual forces are impersonal powers which can be revealed in various ways, for example through magic, astrology, witchcraft, the evil eye, and sorcerers. According to their beliefs, both living, as well as non-living beings interact with people in their daily lives. The power of the spirits and the forces can convey evil as well as good.[24]

The Kankana-eys think that countless spirits are above and below the earth. They trust that all living beings have their spirits, and they unite with other spirits after death. These spirits closely relate with people, intermingling with their lives as though they were living.

It is stated that human beings are associated not only with the creatures of the natural world, but also with the beings of the supernatural world. This inter-relationship inevitably compels the animists to get closer to these beings, and this explains the mysteries of human life, such as pregnancy, illness and death.[25]

The Kankana-eys keep the faith that these spirits communicate with humans through dreams and omens. Religious specialists such as priests look for a means to communicate with the spirits through rituals, often involving sacrificial offerings. Through many generations, the Kankana-eys have cultivated these beliefs and practices as part of their lives.

CONCEPT OF DEITY

The Kankana-eys classify the spirit beings in ranks. Deities in each rank, according to their beliefs, play different roles and release their powers for diverse occasions. This section briefly discusses various deities in Kankana-ey belief.

According to D.W. Sacla, Adika-ila is the highest spirit, who created the sun, the stars, the moon, the earth, and all creatures. This supreme spirit is the creator of the universe. The Kankana-eys believe that all other spirits, including the

---

[23] Julie C. Ma, 'Animism and Pentecostalism', in Stanley M. Burgess (ed.), *The Encyclopedia of Pentecostal and Charismatic Christianity* (New York: Routledge, 2006), 26-27.

[24] Julie Ma, 'Animism and Pentecostalism: A Case Study', in Stanley M. Burgess and Eduard M. van der Mass (eds.), *NIDPCM* (Grand Rapids, MI: Zondervan, 2002), 315.

[25] Norma Lua, *Fiction in the Traditional Kankanay Society* (Baguio, Philippines: Cordillera Studies Centre, 1984), 15.

human spirit, are under the dominion of this spirit.[26] A priest prays to Adika-ila for wisdom, knowledge and justice in making decisions on any public dispute within the tribal community. The priest also asks the arguing parties to seek the help of Adika-ila for justice and fairness. The Kankana-eys believe this spirit is able to intervene by revealing hidden truths, such as the identification of a thief who has stolen a cow, and the guilty party in cases of fraud or land disputes.[27] Adika-ila is believed to be the protector of justice and righteousness.

The Kabunyan (gods/goddesses) are spirits with supernatural powers and they rank next to Adika-ila. The Kankana-eys believe the Kabunyan live in the sky world, and had limited power in the creation of the universe. There are twelve Kabunyan gods and twelve goddesses. According to legend, the gods are good-looking, and the goddesses are beautiful. If humans were to see them, they would not even be able to close their eyes and might even forget their spouses.[28] Among the tribal groups in Luzon, the understanding of Kabunyan differs. For instance, the Ifugao tribe believes that there is only one Kabunyan as the nature/sky god, while the Ibalois and Kankana-eys acknowledge twenty-four deities and the different important role that they have.[29]

The spirits of people who have long been dead are cooperatively called Ap-apo. The Kankana-eys think that these spirits dwell together with other deities. They make trips from the sky world to the earth, to the underworld and back. The Ap-apos, while in the sky, are effortlessly awakened by the sweet aroma of *tapey* (sacrificial rice wine) and the noise of gongs. In a ritual, the celebrating family invites the Ap-apos, and in response, they descend down to the earth, and bring good luck to the family.[30] A divine message is conveyed by way of omens and signs. Often the priest cautiously observes the intestines of the sacrificial animals for a sign of blessing. An example of a positive omen is the well-filled bile of an offered ritual pig, suggesting that the family will have long life, will earn plenty of money and have herds of animals. The Ap-apos can also heal family members suffering from sickness caused by other spirits of the underworld.

The spirits of the underworld are collectively called Anito. The Anito includes several groups, and the Kankana-eys believe that the Anitos live everywhere in the earth.[31] The Kankana-eys worship different spirits, including ancestral spirits, to bring their needs through rituals. They are, therefore, intimately related

---

[26] D. Wasing Sacla, *Treasury of Beliefs and Home Rituals of Benguet* (Baguio, Philippines: BCF Printing, 1987), 10-11.

[27] Sacla, *Treasury of Beliefs*, 11, 15.

[28] Sacla, *Treasury of Beliefs*, 16-17.

[29] William H. Scott, 'Cultural Changes Among Igorots in Mining Companies', *Church and Community*, Jan.-Feb., 1967, 27-30.

[30] Sacla, *Treasury of Beliefs*, 18.

[31] A. Bagamasped and Z. Hamada-Pawid, *A People's History of Benguet* (Baguio, Philippines: Baguio Printing, 1985), 103.

to the spirits and fully aware of their abilities and demands. It is particularly true of the ancestor spirits, who they believe are deeply involved in the day-to-day lives of their descendants. The Kankana-eys take comfort and encouragement from the spirits, especially during difficult times in their lives.

RITUAL PERFORMANCE

Among the Kankana-eys, there are two major rituals: thanksgiving and healing. A thanksgiving ritual is performed on various occasions to express gratitude, and healing rituals are practiced for those who are sick, with the expectation that they will be healed through the spirit's help. Ritual performance is a very important activity in the Kankana-eys' lives. In addition to the religious significance, the rituals also legitimize existing institutions (community leadership), initiate new relationships (marriage), mark agricultural activities (rice planting rites), and so on.[32] Daniel Shaw states that the ritual, in a sense, is understood as a total world, and this applies to the Kankana-eys.[33] The rituals bring order to their society and open the way to supernatural powers.[34]

Thanksgiving rituals are practiced for various occasions. *Dasadas* is offered when a family dedicates their newly built house to gods and ancestors. The celebration begins with the *manbunong* (priest) carrying a mother hen and a cup of rice wine. He gazes on the eastern sky towards the sun to call for the living spirits of the owners of the house (the couple) to come and live in the new house. This invocation is followed by the sacrifice of a pig to the ancestor spirits, and an appeal to them to visit on this special occasion. The *manbunong*, in his *bunong* (prayer), also makes a vow that the owner of the new house will bring even greater sacrifices to please their ancestors and the Kabunyan, if they become affluent. Then, a pig is killed and the intestines of the pig are examined for signs. The boiled meat and wine are served to the Anitos, the spirits of deceased ancestors. People who are present are then served food; and the elders will stay until the evening, drinking wine and passing the time by singing native ritual songs, called *bal-iw*, to plead for the assistance and blessing of the Anitos.

Liyaw is a group of rites which follow every phase of the agricultural calendar of the mountain people: from preparing the rice seedbeds and sowing the seeds to the transplantation of seedlings, peril from worms and drought, and harvesting and storing the yields in the granary.[35] It is thought that the ancestor spirits affect rain, planting, seed time, first fruits, and other matters.[36]

The healing rituals are also important. *Dipat* is a ritual which is meant to soothe an ancestor spirit that has caused sickness. It is believed that suffering is

---

[32] Flora Tabora, 'Some Folk Beliefs and Practices Among the Mountain People of Northern Luzon', *SLU Research Journal* 9:3-4 (1978), 494-515.
[33] Daniel R. Shaw, *Kandila* (Ann Arbor, MI: University of Michigan Press, 1990), 132.
[34] Paul Hiebert, *Konduru* (Minneapolis, MN: University of Minnesota Press, 1974), 146.
[35] William H. Scott, *On the Cordillera* (Manila: MCS Enterprises, 1969), 145.
[36] M. Steyne, *Gods of Power* (Houston, TX: Touch, 1992), 84.

often caused if an inappropriate ritual has been performed in the past. In particular, offering only one animal is regarded as a serious offence, as many rituals require animals in pairs (male and female). The Kankana-eys believe that the animals continue to multiply in the sky world. To correct the mistake, another ritual is performed.

Bosal-lan is a ritual for any person who has abruptly lost his or her sense of hearing without any obvious cause. Understandably, the elders of the community attribute this deafness to a spirit. Instantly, a *bosal-lan* is prescribed. In this ritual, first of all, the *manbunong* make a replica of a tiny hut, about one foot wide and a foot high, in the vicinity of the victim's parents' house. Then the priest, believed to have power imparted by the spirits, performs the ritual near the small hut by offering a chicken to comfort the spirit which has caused the deafness.[37] The *manbunong* asks the spirit to leave the ears and to move to the newly constructed hut by persuading the spirit that it is a better place to live. As the *manbunong* offers the prayer, the deaf person plucks wing feathers out of the chicken and puts them inside the hut, so that the spirit will come in.[38] Then the chicken is singed, sliced, cooked and eaten.

Missiological Implications

My immediate question after discussing the religious worldviews is: 'How can missionaries effectively approach Asians with God's message?' It is my firm conviction that an adequate comprehension of the worldview of a target people is essential, as it affects their thoughts, minds, and behaviour. The following sections outline several implications for mission.

Spirit-Consciousness

Many Asian religions (and ultimately animism, which has profoundly influenced all the religions in Asia), believe that the world is filled with spirits. They are everywhere: in trees, rocks, houses, hills and farms. As noted above, no religion was able to repel the powerful influence of animism (or shamanism as its counterpart in north eastern Asia). In fact, animism often supplements the religions which do not have an adequate answer to life's questions by presenting the belief in the world and power of the spirits. Thus, in most religions, at least at the grassroots level, the cause of sickness is naturally attributed to spirits. It follows that the spirits have to be evoked for healing and intervention. Regardless of religious beliefs, there is a strong assumption that invisible beings

---

[37] Melanie Wiber, 'The Canayao Imperative: Changes in Resource Control, Stratification and the Economy of Ritual Among the Ibaloi of Northern Luzon', in Susan Russell and E.C. Clark (eds.), *Changing Lives Changing Rites: Ritual and Social Dynamics in Philippines and Indonesian Up-lands* (Ann Arbor, MI: University of Michigan, 1988), 58.
[38] Lolito Igualdo, 'The Social World of the Kankana-eys' (Ed.D. dissertation, Baguio Central University, 1988), 231.

are closely associated with visible beings and realities in the world. Although many Asian societies have rapidly become modernized and urbanized, the underlying belief in the spirits has persisted. In fact, this belief has creatively adapted itself to modern development, as seen in the burning of paper credit cards or a paper Mercedes Benz in Singapore during funeral rites. In fact, with the complexities of life and society, people tend to seek more power and blessing on their families and businesses.

How do cross-cultural Christian workers deal with spirit-believing people? What elements of the gospel do we present? This work will inevitably require more than an intellectual version of Christianity. Only the message of the Supreme God, whose power surpasses not only natural forces, but also unseen and yet real, spiritual powers, will prevail. The message of the power of the Holy Spirit upon believers will be a powerful and attractive aspect of the Christian gospel message. The key in this presentation is the experiential dimension of God's power, be it healing, miracle, or even the powerful transformation one experiences through conversion. Such concrete experiences enable people to understand the extent of God's power over the spiritual world. Christians who have an adequate understanding of such beliefs have a unique edge in this process.

Power-Associated and Ancestor Worship

The underlying assumption of ancestral worshippers is that the spirits, especially those of deceased ancestors, have knowledge that is not known to humans which includes the ability to predict the future of the descendents and to influence the course of the future, for example by granting victory over a tribal enemy. Some of the mountain tribes practiced head-hunting, often to revenge a victim from their village who had been harmed and often killed, by a member of another village. This often resulted in a tribal war involving an endless cycle of revenge. Prior to a head-hunting expedition, they would plead, through a ritual, to their ancestor spirits for protection and success. A record reveals that in one night over four hundred people lost their heads in a bloody war. Therefore, their religious life concerns not only petty wishes and the problems of life, but also the very existence of a community.

Understandably then, ancestor worship reinforces the solidarity between the family and the extended kin group, and between ancestors and their descendants. Any ritual, such as a wedding or a funeral, has this important social function. Therefore, in a ritual, all the family members of both the mother and father (if possible), and close friends, are expected to attend the entire course of the ritual, after which they join in the dining and fellowship. It is indeed time-consuming, ranging from a whole day to several days.

This worldview and practice poses several important missiological and pastoral challenges. One is to present the Christian message with a functional substitute for the 'powerful' ancestor spirits. Often Evangelical Christianity presents the message without this critical and existential quest for spiritual 'power', and fails to bring about a complete shift in their spiritual allegiance to God. The 'split-level' Christians abound among tribal groups, when Christianity fails to meet the needs of their 'power-oriented' worldview. This explains why missionary works, particularly by Pentecostal believers, have more success, as the worldview presented by them is much closer to the tribal view than the traditional Christian worldview.

From a pastoral viewpoint, new converts should be taught the solid scriptures so that God will completely replace their ancestors in their allegiance. Secondly, it is critically important to help facilitate them to experience God's power of protection, especially from their 'ancestor spirits' (and by now they should know that there is no such thing as 'ancestor spirits', but only demons pretending to be the ancestor spirits). They should be helped, not only to understand that God's power is above all other powers, but also to experience God's power in protection, provision and guidance.

One persistent argument is that honouring ancestors is not necessarily 'worshipping' them, thus this is not religious but cultural. To further complicate the matter, in some societies, it is argued that such practices fulfil the fifth commandment, 'to honour your father and your mother'. If worship is defined as putting somebody else in the place of God for veneration as a deity, then it is obvious that most, if not all, such practices are worshipping, and thus are religious. It would be advisable, however, for the church to provide culturally acceptable and theologically correct ways to express respect for ancestors, whether living or deceased.

Relation-Orientation: Horizontal and Vertical

Ethical teachings of Confucianism also presuppose the existence of deities, particularly the spirits of the deceased. Even if this aspect is not fully developed or emphasized, it has implications for ancestor worship/veneration. The extremely strong emphasis on relationships in human society reinforces the holistic and community-oriented value. In this way, vertical generational solidarity is achieved and this can be traced all the way to the spirit world. Due to globalization and urbanization, Western lifestyles and worldviews have begun to affect the newer generations, seriously undermining the traditional values and cultures. Nonetheless, there is a growing appreciation for the traditional holistic and community-oriented values.

Missionaries, coming from more pragmatic and goal-oriented cultures, have experienced serious cultural crashes and often have to make a significant adjustment to the receiving culture. Often the hasty construction of physical structures may reflect this kind of problem. Buildings should be secondary to relationship-building. If a missionary does not build a good relationship with the local people first, people will not open their hearts and may even become resistant to the word of God. Therefore, understanding and adopting the relationship-oriented values and practice becomes critical in carrying out the successful work of God's mission.

Belief in the Unseen World

For the Kankana-ey tribe, death is understood to be a transfer from this world to the unseen world, and as the beginning of a new life in the invisible and mysterious world. This is based on their belief in the immortality of human souls. This belief can be compared to the Christian belief in eternal life in heaven. Christian workers should take full advantage of this area of common belief. It is, therefore, against the purpose of such work to see Christians whose commitment to spiritual living is questionable, and whose lifestyles are characterized by pursuit of worldly pleasures and material gain. Even among some dynamic Christian sectors, the power of the 'health and wealth' belief has become alarming. In the context of poverty where basic daily needs are not adequately met, this message of God's blessing is perfectly legitimate and even desirable. However, history informs us only too well that human greed does not know its limit. We have to remember that our eternal home is in heaven, which is the ultimate goal of our spiritual journey in this world. Thus, teaching about an unseen world is in accordance with people's previous beliefs.

Conclusion

Different religions - Buddhism, Hinduism, Confucianism and animism - present their own unique teachings and religious philosophies. It is obvious that there are many commonalities between the teachings of Buddhism and Hinduism, primarily because Buddhism was greatly influenced by Hindu teaching and philosophy. Many Buddhists visit temples regularly to make their wishes known to Buddha and the spirits. The ethical teachings of Confucianism are deeply imbedded in the lives of the people and are handed down from one generation to another. The core of the teachings is filial piety and ancestor veneration. No matter how rapidly a society changes, this practice continues without questioning. As discussed above, all religions are associated with the spirits to varying degrees, particularly with the strong animistic influence.

The study of the worldview of a given people group - be it religious or cultural - is crucial for every Christian worker in order for them to be effective in mission work. If the mission worker can grasp the community's mindset they will be able to understand why people behave as they do. Once they are able to comprehend certain behaviours, then they are able to understand what is underneath the community members' actions. For example, if an individual believes in the existence of spirits, he or she will worship the spirits by bringing a sacrifice, as behaviour is determined by a belief or an assumption. Unfortunately, missionaries frequently ignore the importance of this kind of study. This ignorance, in turn, results in inappropriate attitudes and statements toward the religions. Needless to say, understanding necessitates knowing and learning who their target people are and what they think. Missionaries work with a great desire to excel in fulfilling God's calling, and this desire should be coupled with a full knowledge of their target people and in particular their worldview.

PART TWO

On the Frontline

Chapter 8

Church Planting

Introduction

Evangelism and church planting are two distinct features of Pentecostal mission from the early stages of its mission movement. As a rule, evangelism inevitably led to the establishment of local congregations, and thus, one might say that church planting is one distinct strategy of Pentecostal mission. History shows that church planting in turn became a great means of bringing myriad souls to Christ. Needless to say, this thrust, which has continued through generations, has caused the phenomenal growth of Pentecostal churches throughout the world.

Paul planted churches wherever he went. The church planting in Acts most likely refers to a gathering of people in a house for worship. It does not therefore refer to any identifiable physical structure. It was only some time later, and, it is assumed, as a result of necessity, that the church building became an added element.

Our missionary experience over two decades has informed us that there is an established pattern to a church's life. It is often our experience that a new congregation is born as a result of evangelistic activities. As a rule, the believers gather in a house for worship, fellowship and teaching. As the congregation grows in number the 'church' outgrows the space. As a natural consequence, the erection of a church building becomes a necessity. Then, at least in our case, a strong emphasis is placed upon the young church to reproduce itself, often in cooperation with other neighbouring congregations, to establish an outreach through evangelism. This seems to be a watershed locus where the future of a local church is radically determined. The churches which tend to be content with their own church's growth set a goal of 'mega-church', while those which reproduce themselves will become strong missionary churches. There is no doubt that both models can make a unique contribution to the expansion of God's kingdom, in small communities where a mega-church is not a reality; the latter 'reproduction' model appears to be the right strategy for mission.

In this chapter, specific factors and strategies for church planting will be discussed on the basis of personal and practical experiences of church planting in smaller tribal communities. In the course of discussion, I hope to be able to detect and elaborate components that are unique to Pentecostal mission.

Church Planting Basics

Why Church Planting?

Some people may ask questions such as: 'Why do we have to plant churches?' 'Is it not enough to have one large church?'. They may think that planting and growing a sizeable church with a good number of believers is sufficient. However, this notion is neither fully biblical nor true to the teaching of Christ. His Great Commission is for his followers to go as far as the ends of the earth to preach the gospel and make disciples. Theologically this is the building of the body of Christ, the Church, establishes local churches, that is, groups of believers who then gather in his name to worship him and fulfil his mission. Therefore, establishing many local churches presumes the birth of many new lives into the kingdom, and this is achieved through bringing people into the knowledge of Jesus Christ (Mt. 28:18-20; Mk. 13:10; Lk. 24:46-48; Acts 1:8). The word of God makes it clear that the heart of God's mission in the New Testament is the planting of local churches where there is no gospel witness (Mt. 16:18; Acts 2:41-47; 13:1-3; 1 Tim. 3:15).[1]

Ralph Winter, through various symbols of evangelism and church planting, argues that church planting is a crucial means toward the fulfilment of God's mission:

> E-0 is conversion growth of nominal Christians within the Church, internal growth. E-1 is expansion growth: biological; transfer; and conversion of unsaved community members. It is also E-1 when established churches plant new churches in that same culture, extension growth. Cross-cultural evangelism and church planting are E-2 and E-3, bridging growth, the classical missionary task.[2]

As the scope of our discussion is the multiplication of believers through evangelism and church planting, we try to maximize the effect of E-1 in Winter's definition.

Where to Plant Churches?

First of all, a new church is planted in a community where people are culturally and religiously homogeneous, and of course, where they speak the same language. This, first of all, minimizes communication problems. Also potential socio-cultural homogeneity makes the initial stage of church life smooth. However, this homogeneity principle is applied only in the beginning and, to be a true biblical church, this 'utilitarian' principle must be overcome as soon as possible.

---

[1] Matao Okamura, *Missions and Local Church in World Missions: The Asian Challenge*, ed. by Met Castillo, (n. p.: A Compendium of the Asia Missions Congress'90, 1991), 254.

[2] Ralph Winter, *Crucial Dimensions in World Evangelism* (Pasadena, CA: William Carey Library, 1976), 100.

The mountains in Northern Luzon, in the Philippines are divided into seven provinces where thirteen major tribes live, with countless numbers of minor tribes under them. Interestingly, all the tribes, both major and minor, speak their own dialects and maintain their own distinctive customs. For instance, Benguet Province is inhabited by two major tribes, the Ibaloi and the Kankana-eys.[3] Besides these two major tribes, two other small tribes are also found: the Iwak and the Karao. Inevitably, any church planting effort is made by a tribe where they can freely associate among themselves speaking their own dialect. If there is an established church in the neighbouring village, but it is used by a different tribe, planting a new church for the other tribe is essential.

However, the church should be taught from the beginning that the gospel needs to cross geographical and cultural boundaries to reach people who use different dialects and languages. Thus, the missionary mandate is taught from the beginning. In this process, the lead of the Holy Spirit is very important particularly in selecting a community for church planting. In fact, the Holy Spirit should choose both the community and the gathering place (Acts 16:1-15). Our primary task is to look for his direction and guidance through prayer. Frequently the Spirit guides us as we pray about such matters as receptivity, the strategic nature of the location, and evangelistic strategy. The Holy Spirit's guidance in Paul's vision for Macedonia is a good biblical example (Acts 16:9).

From a more practical angle, I have often noticed many churches in the same places while neighbouring communities have not even a single church. In order for us to avoid such duplication and disparity, it is necessary to do field research on the candidate communities. We regularly include demographic data such as the size of a community, the existence of churches, along with cultural and religious surveys.

Who Empowers Church Planting?

Before Jesus ascended to heaven, he promised his disciples the empowering presence of the Holy Spirit. Christ's command, therefore, was not to leave Jerusalem until they were clothed with the Holy Spirit (Acts 1:8). This clearly implies that mission from the outset is possible only through the empowerment of the Holy Spirit. This also means that a human agent is only secondary to the role of the Spirit. As we are convinced that church planting is a great tool to win souls, we should seek the help of the Spirit.

When the disciples spread the gospel, they were full of the Holy Spirit. They met every day to pray and praise and experienced further signs and wonders (Acts 5:12-16). This example portrays an ideal relationship between the Holy Spirit and his human agents in fulfilling God's mission. Even though early

---

[3] Benguet province is one of seven major provinces in the mountains in Northern Luzon, Philippines. The Assemblies of God concentrated its mission in this province in the early stage through church planting and evangelism. The church planting continues to expand even at the current time.

Christians were socially powerless, the Book of Acts shows the explosive geographic expansion of the church from Jerusalem to Rome. As they set foot in a community, they also witnessed the good news of Jesus, and in many places, believing communities were established in the form of house churches. Perhaps it would be more appropriate to call them fellowship groups in the beginning, with little organisational structure. One obvious fact is that the gospel bearers in Acts were always accompanied by the Spirit whether in their preaching, teaching, healing, or casting out of evil spirits. This makes the mission of God's people indeed the mission of the Holy Spirit, *missio Spirito*.

Such total reliance on the Holy Spirit in guidance and ministry is a hallmark of Pentecostal mission, although we also have seen equally tragic fallouts of powerful Pentecostal preachers. The dependence on the Spirit, when coupled with careful nurturing in an appropriate organisation, ensures a great success in Pentecostal mission.[4] We have to remember that we do not do the mission, but rather we have been graciously invited to be partners of God in labouring for his kingdom. It is God's Spirit who empowers human agents in this endeavour.

Proclamation

It is not adequate for a farmer to just select the right area to plant his or her grain. The person needs to choose good seeds and plant them in the right way. If a farmer does not do this, even the golden soil will not produce a good harvest.

In church planting, the message is like good seed and the method is like planting them in the right place. An effective evangelism strategy must have both the right message and the right method. Church planters and their team need to be concerned in both areas. The evangelistic message may be in the structure of preaching, a Bible study or a personal witness.[5]

The message must be on the basis of the Word of God. It is the 'sword which the Spirit gives you' (Eph. 6:17) that is 'sharper than any double-edged sword. It cuts all the way through, to where soul and spirit meet, to where joints and marrow come together. It judges the desires and thoughts of man's heart' (Heb. 4:12). Some preachers deliver a message that is not based on the scriptures but rather on human knowledge and experience. This can be useful, but only as a supplement to the former. The book of Acts records that Stephen (ch. 7), Peter (ch. 2), and Paul (ch. 13) preached the gospel from the solid divine Word. Romans 1:16 says, 'It (the good news) is God's power to save all who believe'. This implies that God's power to save cannot be disassociated from the gospel. Thus, the preachers must share the 'good news' if we want to see authentic conversions.

---

[4] For example, Melvin Hodges, *A Guide to Church Planting* (Chicago, Moody Press, 1973), 23.

[5] Albert W. Gammage, Jr, *How to Plant a Church* (Makati, Philippines: Church Strengthening Ministry, 1995), 29.

One area that preachers need to be concerned about is the use of language. If the audience has a low educational background, a message with difficult expressions and flowery words will not affect the hearts of the listeners. The message should rather be simple and straightforward for the hearers to be able to comprehend and feel the divine presence.

The solid Word of God should be accompanied with the right illustrations from the common life of the people. This is what Jesus did with his parables. In the Philippines, because of the strong Roman Catholic influence, for instance, a message of salvation by faith is difficult for some people to understand. 'Faith, to most Roman Catholics means to accept...the teachings of the church and to obey the rules of the church'.[6] The gospel bearers must have a good example to delineate the faith in Christ, which means personal trust in him as the Saviour and giving our life to him who is our Lord. Thus, it is necessary to explain the meaning of a public decision to confess Christ as Saviour. Jesus explained it to the crowd who promised to follow him (Lk. 9:57-62). Gammage notes:

> People with a Roman Catholic background may think that going forward during an evangelistic invitation is like going forward to receive communion in the mass. In other words, they may think that going forward brings a person God's grace. Some people may make a public decision only because their feelings are stirred up, not because they are really accepting Jesus as Saviour (Mt. 13:20-21). We can call these 'cogon grass fire' (ningas cogon) decisions because they don't last long. Remember that our goal in evangelism is not just to get decisions but real conversions.[7]

Mass and individual conversions need solid follow ups in order to make real disciples of Jesus Christ. The great number of converts presented by evangelists is overwhelming and exciting in terms of the growth of the Kingdom family but there is a question at the back of my mind: 'Was there an adequate follow up?' or 'Were they all genuine converts?'

Power Evangelism

The manifestation of God's power in evangelism is a great way to draw unbelievers to Christ. Such supernatural phenomena are also vivid evidence of God's power. From the very beginning of the Pentecostal movement, the divine power was revealed in diverse aspects: healing, casting out demons, and others. The tribal groups in the mountains in northern Luzon of the Philippines were not an exception. Radical testimonies of divine manifestation are well recorded from the earliest period of the Pentecostal movement in this region. One of the pioneers was a female, widow missionary named Elva Vanderbout who ministered in mountain communities with power evangelism.

---

[6] Gammage, *How to Plant a Church*, 32.
[7] Gammage, *How to Plant a Church*, 30, 77.

The grandmother of the household in the mountain village had seen her deceased ancestor in her dreams for three days in a row. According to the common belief, this is a sure sign that the ancestor was now 'claiming' her life; that is, her death was sure and imminent. This was almost a self-fulfilling prophecy, because she had stopped eating, drinking and sleeping. The whole family and village were just waiting for her death. The village priest and elders had prescribed details of burial rituals, including a specific number of animals that she needed to take to her ancestors. Tito Inio, the mountain pastor arrived in this house on his weekly 'godly' day, and only the dogs welcomed him, as the house was virtually empty. Only when he was about to move on to the next house, he heard a sigh from inside the house. The lady, who had been left to die, told him her story with emotions mixed with anxiety, sadness, fear, and quiet surrender. Tito spoke to her about a God who had dealt a blow to death. He then laid his hand on her head and began to pray for the restoration of her life. She recovered very quickly and a Christian gathering was born in her house.[8]

The divine convincing power worked in the hearts and assisted them to build a true and solid faith. God's power is displayed always to convince people of God's power and love. The power evangelism, which was very effective in spreading the Kingdom of God in the early church, has continued even until today. Power evangelism is not only efficient among the tribal groups but also among urban people, regardless of their religious orientation.

All religions including Islam have an animistic character and practice including their beliefs in supernatural power. Gailyn Van Rheenen elaborates the point:

> According to Timothy Kamps's interpretation of the data of Ralph Winter and D. Bruce Graham (1982), most of the world's 'unreached peoples' are animistic: 'Among the 88 percent of those classified as unreached peoples, it is estimated that 135 million are tribal animists and 1.9 billion are involved in a world religion based in animism' (Kamps 1986, 6). Thus Timothy Warner is correct when he says, 'The unreached world as a whole is animistic at its base' (1988a).[9]

Phil Parshall estimates that 70% of Islamic believers are folk Muslims and only 30% are conventional. Animism and Islam are often interestingly mixed resulting in 'theism and paganism' existing 'side by side'.[10] An affluent and educated Brazilian Christian once confessed, 'My religion is Catholicism but my

---

[8] Die Dynamik in der heutigen Missionsbewegung, *Mission Erfullt?* (Hamburg: Missionshilfe Verlag, 2009), 128-142.

[9] Gailyn Van Rheenen, *Communicating Christ in Animistic Contexts* (Grand Rapids: Baker, 1991), 25. See also Stephen C. Neill, *Christian Faith and Other Faiths* (New York: Oxford, 1970); Timothy J. Kamps, 'The Biblical Forms and Elements of Power Encounter' (M.A. thesis, Columbia Graduate School of Bible and Missions, Columbia, SC, 1986).

[10] Phil Parshall, *Bridges to Islam* (Grand Rapids: Baker, 1983), 16.

philosophy of life is spiritism'.[11] Such an animistic worldview, predominantly found in the tribal areas, contains a strong religious orientation. They believe in the existence of the spirits and their lively interference in human daily life. Thus, it is hard to abandon their well-preserved religion to convert to an unknown and foreign religion. However, to our astonishment they come to the gathering to hear the good news primarily because of the power manifestation. It is a fine collaborative work between the Holy Spirit and the human agent for the Kingdom.

The demonstration of God's power is strategically important in the evangelism of different religious groups who are animistically oriented. Often through healing or supernatural experiences, new congregations were born, often as house churches. We, as Pentecostals, need to continue to emphasize, and develop strategies of power evangelism.

Leadership Development

We maximize the application of the indigenous principles: self-support, self-governing, and self-propagation. The second point is the most critical area for the success of the local congregation.[12] A new pioneering work never begins without leadership in place. Indeed, we prefer to identify dedicated workers who are already initiating various evangelistic activities such as Bible studies and vacation Bible schools. Even if they have never received ministerial training, we help them to lead a group of new believers. Sometimes, a 'mother' church provides initial leadership until ideally someone from the congregation emerges as a candidate leader. Then the mother church, district, and the missionary provide a training program, often informal ones, for the new workers. However, in our experience, several were assisted to go to a Bible school for formal training. These home-grown leaders have proved to be the most effective pastors, and many lead the church in a successful way. The establishment of qualified and visionary leadership is essential for both internal maturity and the external growth of the church.

However, the overall development of the leadership requires more than the 'on-the-job' practical training'.[13] They also need to acquire a strong biblical and theological foundation for ministry. Jesus not only exposed his disciples to various aspects of ministry by example, but also provided them with a strong biblical foundation through his teaching. Often our experience seems to show that those who have received formal theological training in local Bible colleges

---

[11] Dan Coker, 'New Mission Opportunities in Communist Countries-Latin America' (Lectures delivered at Abilene Christian University Lectureship, 20 Feb. 2002, Abilene, TX).

[12] Lorenzo C. Bautista, 'The Church in the Philippines', in *Church in Asia Today: Challenges and Opportunities,* ed. by Saphir Athyal, (Singapore: The Asia Lausanne Committee for World Evangelization, 1996), 175-202.

[13] Bautista, 'The Church in the Philippines', 175-202.

do not perform better than those who have not. Perhaps their 'profound' theoretical knowledge is not properly applied in a real ministerial setting. Thus, our 'on-the-job' training sometimes supplements the formal training.

Often pastoral leaders are grown from the laity. Normally mature and committed leaders (often already exercising their leadership in the communities) emerge in the local churches, and the role of the missionary and the national work is to identify them and develop their gifts of leadership. It is also important to identify and develop low level leadership for children's ministry, outreach and others. Jesus not only commissioned the great twelve but also 'other disciples' such as the seventy in Luke 10. The deacons in Acts were mightily used for the expansion of the church. Stephen is an outstanding deacon who was willing to sacrifice his own life for the sake of the gospel.

Commitment in Church Planting

Commitment is one of the core elements for service in the Kingdom of God. Likewise in church planting, planters' solid undertaking appears very significant. As a known fact, the Pentecostal missionaries from the beginning were involved in church planting a great deal. One of the definitions about missions given by Keith Minus is,

> A group of Christian missionaries from various churches committed to their Lord Jesus Christ and to His command to go into all the world to preach the gospel of salvation to all mankind, and to plant his church. [14]

I agree with his definition of missions, particularly 'planting his church'. I believe the majority of missionaries in different countries are directly or indirectly involved in this activity as a mission tool.

On the missionary's part, the commitment consists of two aspects: balanced partnership with local pastors and steady fund-raising. These two are so far the crucial elements, which require planters' commitment.

National Pastor

In any missionary work, the role of a national partner is crucial to the success of ministry. The concept of working together as a team is a requirement for almost all missionary work. Even if a missionary has a burning desire and sufficient funds, it will require a committed national worker who knows the place, people and culture. Thus, a good outreach plan ideally designed and tested by the national worker is very necessary. It is advisable not to open a house church in a site where someone has already started.

---

[14] Keith Minus, *Missions and Indigenisation in World Missions: The Asian Challenge*, ed. by Met Castillo, (n. p.: A Compendium of the Asia Missions Congress '90, 1991), 260-65.

Our very first experience of this ministry began with the Kankana-ey tribe. We discovered that this tribal group in the remote mountainous communities has almost no cash income and their means of survival is only through farming and mining. This life leads them into poverty and destitution. Desperate for divine blessing, they perform rituals to various spirits as frequently as they can. Thus, another root for acute poverty is the ever increasing debt to buy expensive sacrificial animals for recurring sacrifices. The Lord led us to meet with several key national pastors who were deeply committed to bringing God's freedom and salvation to their fellow Kankana-eys. Upon learning this fact, we became more active in evangelism with them. In many ways, the truth freed them from this bondage. Divine intervention was regularly expected in this human labour in winning souls. The extent of church planting gradually expanded to include other tribal groups including the Bontoc tribe in Mountain Province, the Kalanguya tribe in Kalinga, the Ibalois in Benguet and the Southern Ilocos Region in the low land. Again, in each location, committed national workers became our partners. We made each ministry from the beginnings of the ministry of the national leaders. The practical experiences and lessons we learned are that God opens the doors in the form of national partners when we continually look for places and people to reach out to.

Fund-Raising

The work of church planting requires a constant flow of financial assistance. Missionaries raise funds through contacts with churches in various locations. For instance, throughout the years we have raised a substantial amount of funds from Korea. As Korean missionaries it was natural to draw money from our own churches in our country. However, we also turned our focus to other countries, instead of limiting our attention to one nation alone. There are quite a few Korean churches in the United States which have begun to send large amounts of money for church buildings. Over the years, more individuals have sent funds than churches. Through the mobilization of individuals, one Korean congregation in the Boston area assisted ten church buildings in the Northern Luzon region of the Philippines. This is not the only case: there are a few other instances such as this. My husband and I have never considered ourselves to be effective fund-raisers nor did we aggressively attempt to raise funds. However, during our deputations, we share our involvement in the church planting ministry and its effective role in spreading the gospel.

Often a visible church standing in a village directly speaks of God's presence. The tribal people tend to connect a physical church building with the divine presence, just as they have a notion that an idol, *Badda*, is a spirit in itself. Obviously their animistic orientation influences their interpretation. Surprisingly, our story, shared not only from the pulpit but also over coffee or a meal, attracted their interest in this ministry. Often individuals, after being convinced by the Holy Spirit, become willing to make a sacrificial donation toward this ministry. They also persuade other fellow members and neighbouring church people to join in this type of missionary involvement.

Providing a continually updated report of our work to supporters and friends has also encouraged potential donors. The commitment to this ministry requires a continual effort to identify and encourage committed Christians to become involved. To our surprise, we often receive overseas phone calls and email messages expressing interest in being part of this church planting and building ministry. They regularly tell us that while reading our newsletter, they have felt the Holy Spirit encouraging them to partner this ministry. Such unexpected participation also serves as God's affirming sign that this ministry brings delight to the Lord. Sometimes people whom we have never met before come to know of this ministry through their friends and eventually became our ministry partners.

Frequently, we have groups of short-term missionary training programs and participants of short-term mission are exposed to trips from various nations and churches. Regardless of their age, they could face a challenging environment, often without running water and electricity, deep in the mountains. In addition, they often hike rugged mountain trails for many hours to move from one village to another. Such intensive trips may initially generate discomforts and inconveniences, but soon they become well aware of the importance of mission involvement. They also become aware of the significant value of erecting a church building as a symbol of God's existence in an animistic village. Some of these mission visitors, after returning their home, become partners for our ministry, particularly in the church building program.

Teaching Church Planting

It is necessary to provide a program for church planting. Many church members, unless stimulated or taught, are not aware of the importance of this activity. This section presents several elements in teaching church planting.

Prayer

Prayer is the key to the success of every Christian ministry. Unfortunately, church leaders often fail to include a prayer time for their church and future churches to be planted. A long prayer list includes a variety of prayer requests for individual and church life, but seldom is church planting included in the prayer list.[15] The members should be encouraged to pray for church planting regularly in their daily prayer time and also at the regular weekly prayer meeting of their church. The prayer should include several specific related topics such as church planters, finance and the growth of the church. It is also important that ministers regularly highlight this prayer in their homilies and teaching, because church planting is perhaps the best way to reach the lost.

---

[15] Gammage, *How to Plant a Church*, 29.

Financial Support

The members should be taught that besides praying, they also need to participate in this ministry through financial support. Committing financial resources is essential both in a practical and a spiritual sense. Church planting requires financial resources. Also through actual giving, the giver's faith is stretched and strengthened. Unless they are taught to give toward ministry, people may think that it is someone else's job, like a missionary's. In fact, sharing is one of three foundational areas, along with praying and going, for the church to fulfill its mission. [16] Occasionally, an emphasis on giving must be brought to their attention through teaching and preaching, and also through special programs such as mission dinners. Making a monthly or yearly pledge is another way to encourage people to give. This has proven to be effective in many places.

Raising Church Planters

Of course not every member can be a church planter. Each member serves the church according to his or her gift and call. Church planting involves commitment of time, a space (often in his or her own house) for initial gatherings, leadership to lead the people in faith and spiritual growth, and eventually preparing the congregation for a church building process. Some lay people have amazing zeal and passion for this ministry. However, having a gift is one thing, encouraging and mobilizing people for actual ministry is another. Here is an example. Some mountain church pastors have never received any formal ministerial training. In fact, about 60% of pastors in the Philippines have never received any formal training. Perhaps their zeal for God's work, devoted prayer life and regular readings of the word of God has equipped them adequately enough to plant churches and later provide pastoral leadership in local churches. Many of them later participate in short-term pastoral training. To my amazement, the lay leaders' capability is far beyond what is normally anticipated from them. Sometimes they are better than those who have received a formal ministerial training in this given context. They are energetic in their efforts to reach out to other villages which do not have a church. Some churches, such as Lamut, Ambiong, and Beckel in Benguet Province were initiated by lay volunteers. These churches grew steadily and many laity assumed pastoral leadership.

Reproduction

Many churches become self-serving or inward thinking after the development of their own organisational structure and physical church building has been accomplished. Why is this the case? It is possible that during the long and rigorous process of self-development, they unknowingly developed a

---

[16] William V. Layda, Mobilizing the Church for Missions in *Into the 21st Century Asian Churches in Mission: A Compendium of the Asia Missions Congress II*, eds. Met Castillo and Katie Sisco, (n. p.: Evangelical Fellowship of Asia), 115-117.

self-centered and self-serving mentality. Obviously, this is a theological crisis. It is also plausible that the 'development' of the church began to serve as their model for every church, thus, they become unwilling to commit vast resources to another church. In many cases, the maintenance of the 'developed' church demands more resources, leaving little for the cycle of reproducing themselves. Often, this critical shift takes place after the completion of their own church building. Therefore, it is so important to teach the church from the very beginning that they need to make a serious commitment to reproduction. Also the function and nature of the church building should be placed in its proper theological perspective: as a place for worship, teaching and fellowship: a place where the reproduction mandate is prepared and executed.

What was the role of the baptism in the Spirit? The biblical pattern is for everyone to be empowered for witness (Act 1:8). They preached the gospel, gathered new believers in houses, and reproduced witnesses through prayer and teaching. This has become a never-ending cycle which has multiplied churches and witnesses for God's kingdom. Some people travelled as far as Antioch in Syria and won converts among the Gentiles as well as the Jews. Barnabas and Paul were key players in this cycle of church planting (Acts 11:19-26). The gospel bearers in Acts never ceased to plant house churches. Churches that are fully committed to church planting, therefore, are biblical churches.

Partnership

In order to be good partners, there are a few important and basic components that are essential: mutual understanding, trust, equal responsibility, and shared ministry between missionaries and local church leaders. Through keeping these over a long period, a good working relationship is established and maintained. Lewis comments:

> From 1910 to World War II, the most notable development of strategy was increasingly putting the national church in the central place, giving it full independence and authority, and developing partnership between the Western churches and the young churches. The indigenous church and partnership in obedience were watch-words which expressed the thrust of prevailing strategy.[17]

Mutual Understanding

When the missionary and the local leaders work together as partners, mutual understanding is an essential element in forging and maintaining a smooth working relationship. General ministry philosophy, specific goals of ministry, cultural orientation, personal strengths and weaknesses and others are not only

---

[17] Jonathan Lewis, *World Mission: An Analysis of the World Christian Movement, Part 2: Strategic Dimension* (Pasadena CA,: William Carey Library, 1987), 22.

understood but also appreciated. For this, clear communication, although it may take various forms, is also essential. Sometimes it may be necessary to clearly lay out foundational values and goals in a written form.

Often a partnership failure is inevitable sooner or later for those who have not understood the importance of clear communication. Many missionaries with excellent leadership qualities sometimes fail to keep a long-term partnership due to their charismatic and dominating personality. They may also feel that they have resources and solutions for the evangelization of the nation. It is then necessary for them to bend their strong ambition and plan to be able to nurture and empower local leadership.

It is not easy to interpret people's minds and the intended meaning of their words. If the missionary uses unfamiliar gestures and facial and verbal expressions, it may cause the local leaders to feel uneasy. This uncomfortable atmosphere can even affect decision-making. Then, how do we minimize potential misunderstanding? The first step is for the missionaries to become acquainted with the host culture: the way of life, thinking pattern and language. Even if they have learned the host culture well, they will still experience conflict and friction as this is a part of human interaction. Cultivating good cross-cultural communication skills is a must for any missionary. Eugene Nida advocates four fundamental principles of approach to any society.

Effective Communication Based on Personal Relationship

The initial approach should be made to those who can effectively pass on communication within their family groupings. Time must be allowed for the internal diffusion of new ideas. The challenge for any change of belief or action must be addressed to the persons or groups socially capable of making such decisions.[18]

Ultimately, the key to a desirable ministerial partnership is the development of biblical character. Weak human personality tends to precede the Christ-like character. This is an area that all the Kingdom workers should be concerned about. There must be mutual ground where both parties can agree or give in to each other when necessary. For understanding is the key to an effective working relationship, in every area of ministry including church planting. Maintaining a good partnership is a great blessing for those who are working together to build God's Kingdom.

Trust

Trusting people is not a simple job. If we find it difficult to trust our own people, how much more difficult must it be for people from another culture. However, missionaries have to trust their ministry partners. If they fail, they cannot expect any success in mission. For some missionaries this is a very difficult area to

---

[18] Eugene Nida, *Customs and Cultures: Anthropology for Christian Mission* (Pasadena, CA: William Carey, 1954), 236.

develop but they have to cultivate their trust toward national partners, although certain negative experiences may be inevitable.

Our church planting work over fifteen years has only been possible because we placed total trust in the local church leaders. The mutual trust applies to every part: church planting, building fund, God's direction, and the whole process of the building project. In the past, a few local co-workers have failed us. Money that they received for church building was spent without evidence and no receipts were left. All the properties where church buildings stand must be titled under the General Council of the Philippines Assemblies of God. In spite of several unpleasant but isolated cases, our commitment of total trust has not been changed and we continue to trust our partners. Trusting each other in all respects forms a strong foundation for partnership.

Shared Responsibility

The partnership reflects an equal responsibility for every aspect of the work. Paul Hiebert notes that 'equality means equal opportunity'.[19] It is not that the party with more resources exercises more power than the other, but rather both should have an equal amount of responsibility. Therefore, it is essential for the local church leaders to establish firm leadership over and respect from their own people in order to mobilize their resources for God's work. In spite of the meager resources that the national counterpart can offer, missionaries need to help their national partners to take initiative in ministry, as missionaries serve as their assistants. However, more often than not, the opposite is the case.

In light of this, the missionary's role is significant in terms of encouraging their local partners to be responsible. The missionaries have historically practiced paternalism toward their national partners, and this attitude has produced negative consequences for the nationals who develop low self-esteem and inferiority complexes, and then rely too much on their partners. In order to make the nationals competent and accountable people, the missionary should consciously make an effort to give them an opportunity to take the initiative and make decisions without the missionary's presence. As a rule the design of the new church building, size and location is entirely decided by the congregation and its leadership. When the trust level is high and a job assignment is done in a sense of togetherness, church planting and any other mission work will go in a harmonious way.

Sharing

Developing a concept of sharing is important. When the church planting is under way, the natural expectation toward the missionary from the local church is unrealistic. They expect maximum assistance with minimal involvement from them. Also the missionary or a particular donor back home wants a church that is

---

[19] Paul G. Hiebert, *Anthropological Insights for Missionaries* (Grand Rapids: Baker, 1991), 127.

nice and big, regardless of the need and ability of the congregation. Also when the donor is generous and the local resources are meager, the missionary may feel responsible for covering the entire construction cost. In some rare exceptional cases it may be possible but obviously never advisable. That does not help them cultivate a sense of ownership and independence, let alone the possibility of reproduction.

How is sharing done? We never promise the whole amount of money for the church building although they desperately present the needed amount. We always encourage them to play their role in fully assuming the responsibility of sharing. In fact, as a rule, the church lot is always the responsibility of the congregation and so are most 'local' materials (such as sand, gravel and lumber) and expenses (labour, food and others). In a typical case, about one half of the total cost is shared by the nationals. There are several mid-way check points to ascertain that the pledged counterpart of the congregation is being received, before the outside assistance is released.

Multiplication

Our experience of being involved in church planting over the last fifteen years provides a method for effective church planting. This method has been working very efficiently.

Reinforced Emphasis on Reproduction

We emphasize, right from the inception of church planting, that reproduction is the ultimate goal of the new church. For reasons stated above, the time of the church dedication becomes a proper opportunity to remind the church of this emphasis. On this special and joyous occasion, the service rightly consists of lively praises, thanksgiving and a long chain of testimonies. However, in the midst of this celebration, we make a regular habit of challenging the church to open daughter churches in neighbouring communities. In fact, our covenant with the congregation is that only through the reproducing work, will our partnership continue. This is our commitment to assist or work with them in developing new churches. Such a covenant frequently serves to motivate them to start a new house church in a nearby village where there is no established Bible-believing church. In fact, some churches, expecting our strong emphasis on reproduction, have already started new works before their church building is dedicated.

Often such a new pioneering work meets under a big mango tree whose shade provides protection from the scorching sunshine. To our amazement, one by one, villagers begin to come to the meeting place to join the joyful gospel choruses. The quickest response normally comes from children. As they are not yet religiously oriented in their traditional animism, they are significantly receptive and open to the presentation of the gospel. Often a vacation Bible school in a totally strange place becomes an extremely effective means to draw children in. Soon their parents, who watched them from the distance, join this new Christian gathering. Labilab, an Ibaloi tribal village in Benguet Province, is a typical case. A nearby Ibaloi church sent a team to Labilab to offer a vacation Bible school. By the conclusion of the vacation Bible school, a new church was born. Now the church has its own building and about sixty active members are serving the Lord.

Multi-Generational Church Movement

Groups of newly established churches, after the completion of their buildings, have produced their 'daughter churches' throughout the region. This strategy empowers each local congregation to be actively missionary. In other words, the daughter churches are fast becoming mother churches, and this pattern continues to their daughter churches as well. This opens a potentially revolutionary possibility for reaching the unreached.[20] As this pattern continues, soon the third, fourth, and fifth generation churches are born. In fact, this appears to be one of the best ways to maintain the youthfulness and dynamism of the 'mother' churches, and to fulfill God's Great Commission.

Our frequent visits to pioneering churches throughout the mountains prove to be extremely fulfilling. Through consistent teamwork with the national workers and the commitment of local churches for 'multi-generational churches', in at least two areas, fifth generation churches have been established and the trend continues. Often all the churches in the system, that is, from the first to the fifth generation churches, join their efforts to pioneer a new work, that is, the sixth generation church. Through this joint effort, even the most unlikely places with a strong resistance toward the gospel find a Christian witness live and strong. The more generations we see, the stronger the gospel presence will become.

Networking

So far, our church planting strategies have resulted in 'local' networking among the churches in the area, and also mother and daughter churches. Pioneering work is assisted in various ways by the local network. Concepcion Tanzo is a lady evangelist and pioneering worker among the Ibaloi tribal group. Her church planting ministry is aided by a nearby sectional fellowship of the same denomination as well as a missionary who has a ministry not far from Concepcion's new congregation. Formal and informal meetings among the churches in the area greatly strengthen ministries. Recently a pioneering lady pastor had a wedding in a remote mountain village. More than half of the 3,000 guests were pastors and members of the area churches. The wedding feast quickly turned into an evangelistic meeting by the bride's design.

Also the networking takes place with an international scope. As many new churches have been partnered with various donors—individuals and churches in various Asian countries—often this relationship develops into a continuing working relationship. A Korean church in the States has partnered with eight

---

[20] For an elaborate study of this proposition, see Wonsuk Ma, 'Full Cycle Mission: A Possibility of Pentecostal Missiology', *AJPS* 8:1 (2005): 5-27.

churches, and now the church continues to work with the mother church in pioneering other daughter churches in the Philippines.

Conclusion

Church planting is an efficient way to spread the gospel and bring souls to Christ. My experience, together with that of my husband, clearly convinces us that this may be *the* best way to reach the unreached. The truth we have learned is that the plan of the Lord for reaching the unreached is through the church, his own body. As a visible representation of this universal church, local churches, as living organisms, are to reproduce themselves. The record of the early church is the established pattern for mission. A recent study found that reproducing churches grow more than those that do not. In fact, a self-content church is less than what the church is really supposed to be.

This biblical principle is not only found in the Scriptures, but also fully tried and tested by missionaries. In this process, the missionary's role is critical not only in providing assistance to the work, but also in doing it correctly. The bottom line is that the pioneering work never belongs to the missionary, but totally to the local congregation and leadership. The missionary's role is strictly secondary and yet crucial. This is where the missionary's qualification particularly in ministry principles and cultural understanding plays an important role. After all, almost everything in the non-western world is accomplished through a positive relationship, and church planting in Asia is not an exception.

Also, it is argued, that the goal of mission is about more than establishing a self-sustaining church. Until the church becomes a missionary church, eagerly reproducing itself here and elsewhere, the mission is not yet accomplished, even if the church, the very means for mission, is standing. Here is another crucial role of the missionary: to help the church to become a missionary church. There is no better qualified person to teach the church to become missionary oriented than the missionary him - or herself! This missionary goal, that is, reproduction, should be taught from the very beginning of the church's life. In fact, in many cases, by the time we dedicate churches, already their daughter churches are actively progressing.

Such church planting ministry, with multi-partisan involvement, better reflects the biblical principle. This has also proved to be effective and less 'risky' from the missionary's perspective. Only healthy churches can reproduce themselves, and this seems to be the primary task of all church workers, both national and missionary, to strengthen the churches and grow them to be reproductive. Pentecostals have demonstrated well that they have learned a unique strength through their church planting.

Chapter 9

Growing Churches in Manila: An Analysis

Introduction

The Philippines received the gospel around 1565 from Roman Catholics who came as the first Christian group. The Spanish Catholic priests arrived along with the Spanish invasion of the nation. The impact of this early Christian group was so great that the nation soon became the only Christian country, in this case Catholic, in Asia.[1]

Around 1945 some Filipino immigrants in the United States received Pentecostal experiences in an Assemblies of God Bible school in California and nearby churches. Some of them later came back to their country with a burning desire to share the gospel with their own people. First, these Christians spread the gospel among their own families and relatives through home Bible studies and soon the Pentecostal mission spread nationwide through missionaries and local ministers. Some years later, mission work began even among tribal groups in the northern Philippines.[2] Pentecostalism's unique message went through the hearts of animists and as a result, churches were established. They also marvellously established works in cities, such as Cebu, Baguio, and Manila. Some of the churches grew rapidly and became mega-churches within a short period of time.

In this chapter, I will attempt to study several Charismatic/Pentecostal mega-churches in Manila: Asian Christian Charismatic Fellowship, The Bread of Life Fellowship, and Cathedral of Praise. My selection of these churches did not have to do with their size, but rather with the common characteristics and general traits which these churches share with the mega-churches. My focus is to elucidate and analyze important factors which have contributed to the rapid growth of these churches. This will be followed by a discussion of the role and task of the church in society in the coming era.

---

[1] Rodney L. Henry, *Filipino Spirit World* (Manila, Philippines: OMF Literature, 1986), 10.

[2] T.C. Esperanza, 'The Assemblies of God in the Philippines' (M.A. thesis, Fuller Theological Seminary, 1965), 17-22.

Growing Churches

Asian Christian Charismatic Fellowship

BEGINNING

The church was founded in 1981 by Paul Klahr, an Assemblies of God missionary, in the center of Metro Manila. Paul Klahr pastored for seven years and then handed leadership over to a local leader, Nilo Jaren Lapasaran. At present, pastor Nicky Boy C. Valdez is the leader of the church. The church grew so rapidly that only a few years later the number in attendance was 700. By the year 1995, the fellowship had established twenty satellite churches in various parts of the country: Luzon as far as Pangasinan, Nueva Vizcaya in the north and Naga City, Bicol region in the south, as well as Cebu City in the Visayas region. The recent membership of the church has reached 5,000. All the pastors of these twenty churches meet regularly on a monthly basis at the Central Office. Later the church name changed to International Charismatic Service.

The church has a dream of reaching people not only nationwide, but worldwide and establishing a global outreach. In fact, the church sent leaders to different countries such as Spain, Japan, Canada, and the United States to establish more local churches.[3] The church has turned its perspective from narrow to broad.

IMPACT OF THE CHURCH LOCATION

The church was moved to the Ali Mall, with a larger space. There are two strategic reasons for moving to a shopping mall. First, this busy place easily attracts people to come to the service. Secondly, the place offers avenues to reach out to more unreached, the poor and street children. The church actively unfolds its wild dream of ministry in this attractive place provided by God. The church holds five services on Sundays, and each service has its own ministry team which includes members engaged in intercessory prayer, ushering for offering collection, greeting new comers, and other needed services.

GROWTH FACTORS

My next question was, 'What are the primary elements contributing to church growth?' The pastor enumerated the following factors as key to the church growth: the first is extensive Bible studies at home, offices and communities. The latter is called 'Barangay Bible Study'. Primarily, lay people are utilized for this teaching ministry, providing Bible studies not only for adults, but also for children. A Bible study combines prayer time and discipleship training. The church also provides children's crusades for spiritual growth and maturity.

---

[3] Interview with Pastor Jaren Lapasaran.

Second, the Sunday services include a unique feature called 'the background service' through which the members spend ten to fifteen minutes reviewing the message of the sermon. The members learn more specifically of the content of the message by studying the original meanings of various terms. There is an interaction going on between study group members and the leader. Questions can be raised at any time.

Third, the church has a great emphasis on personal evangelism. Every member receives an orientation or training for person-to-person evangelization. This method results in bringing many non-believers to the church. The church's feeding program for street children and ministry in orphanages have a clear goal of personal evangelism.

Fourth, the church allows the pastoral staff to exercise his or her leadership, and to maximize one's talent(s). The leaders are encouraged to attend seminars offered in Bible colleges and seminaries. Well-trained pastors are released to take charge of outreach ministries that are soon to become independent. This allows an outreach to become a prominent and dynamic church in its own distinctiveness.

Fifth, there is an adequate staff comprised of twenty-two people in total, with Pastor Ricardo Oasin as the Spiritual Overseer and the senior pastor Nicky Boy Valdez. This staff is assisted by nearly 130 lay leaders who are well trained for leadership to participate in church ministry. The church provides a training program for lay people through various modes, including Sunday Bible school, seminar conferences, couples and family ministry, and discipleship classes for young, middle and older adult groups.

Sixth, the senior pastor greatly emphasizes the teaching of God's word. The pastor believes that the pastoral staff should be prepared by the Word of God before sharing with people. With such an emphasis, all the pastors spend time together to study the message for the coming Sunday. Preparing the message with prayer makes an impact on the preaching.

Last, the church accentuates the dynamics and ministry of the Holy Spirit. The pastors teach the work of the Holy Spirit as God's power which can enable them to become victorious. Without hesitation, the pastoral staff prays for healing and for God's miracles. The church constantly reminds the members through teaching and preaching of the importance of the Holy Spirit in their life.

PARTICULAR ATTENTION

The church gives special attention to cell groups in a unique way: groups are formed in every department according to different age levels. A group is further divided into two groups – ministry and interest. In the first group are people who are willing to be involved in church ministry, while the second group consists of people who are interested in social interaction, seminars and hobbies. Unlike other churches, cell group meetings are not held during a week day but on Sundays after the main service. This arrangement is inevitable as the members' residences are scattered all over Metro Manila. It is just inconvenient, if not somewhat impossible, to gather during the week days. This system, however, fits in the church and is well accepted by the members.

The church leaders emphasize prayer. They provide prayer cell closets (rooms) in the church, leaving them open twenty-four hours a day for those who need to pray. Although the church does not own a prayer mountain, the pastor has a great concern for the prayer life of the members. The church has daily prayer meetings in the early morning and in the evening. They believe in the power and importance of prayer.

The church gives its attention to establishing outreaches oversees. As mentioned earlier, the church is attempting to globalize its missions work. The church is especially concerned about ministry among Filipino workers and business people overseas. The pastor states that God is opening more doors for the church to send pastoral staff members abroad.

The fundamental element for the church growth is the church's great concern for caring ministry among the members. There has been constant pastoral attention and ministry to each individual member with the Word of God and the power of the Holy Spirit. Through this ministry, the members are blessed, broken hearts are ministered to, the sick are healed, lives are transformed, and needs are met. They live Spirit-filled lives.

The church also does not neglect to provide recreation for young people. A basketball court is provided for those who are interested in athletic activities, which naturally attracts unbelieving young people to the church. The church constantly reminds itself that a church grows not by programs, but by giving proper care and adequate attention to its members' bodies, minds and spirits.

The Bread of Life Fellowship

Beginning

The church was started by Butch Conde. He served in a Full Gospel church as a Sunday school teacher. He is known as a person who sought the word of God earnestly. This led him to a seminary to learn theology, but soon he began to feel dry spiritually. After studying for some time he discontinued his schooling.

Conde, while serving in the church, had a strong feeling that God wanted him to leave the church and to start a new work. He simply resigned without telling anyone, in order to follow the inner voice of God. His first worship service took place in November, 1982 at the auditorium of Mary Knoll College, with quite a large number of 120 people in attendance. Seven years later the church moved to the Circle Christian Centre (a former cinema theatre) on Timog Avenue, Quezon City with the attendance reaching nearly 4,000 on Sunday. Presently, the Sunday attendance has reached about 12,000 members. The church had planted over sixty outreach fellowships in other parts of the country by 2000. One of the two fellowships in Cebu City reached over 1,000 regular members within two years.[4]

---

[4] Interview with Lanny Nicolas.

The mother church in Manila has twenty-four full-time workers, seven of whom are ordained pastors. In addition, there are sixty-five lay leaders actively involved in the church ministry. These leaders are taking care of small groups called 'cells'. Besides these, a sizable number of other members are available for ministry in various outreach fellowships. This indicates that the leadership puts a heavy emphasis on the role of laity and their training for ministry.

Recently the church built its own five-story church building. The building is designed in high standard, with modern facilities to accommodate diverse groups of people and to provide different functions. The church building even has a coffee shop, a book store, a small restaurant and other rooms where non-believers and believers can enjoy their time and fellowship. This can further provide a chance for the believers to engage in conversation with the non-believers in a natural way and to lead them to Christ. The church also provides music programs and concerts at different times of the year as a way of evangelizing people to the Lord. Of course, a message is shared between times in the concert. The church seems to be aware of the fact that it is in the world (not necessarily of the world) where the gospel should be shared by all means.

TRAINING PROGRAM FOR NEW COMERS

The church focuses on leading newcomers to cell group meetings. A church principle is to get new converts into the cell system first, and help them grow in the Word of God. Then the church leaders encourage them to attend the 'central congregational gatherings'. Further encouragement is given to them to attend a 'Life in the Kingdom Seminar'. The seminar provides training and teaching on how a new comer can become a true Christian and grow into Christian maturity. Life with the power of the Holy Spirit is the primary focus of the next stage of training, called 'Discovery Class'. This organized system enables about 800 members to get baptized within a year.[5]

GROWTH FACTORS

Associate pastor Lanny Nicolas attributed the fast growth of the church to four major factors. First, the church places a great emphasis on the teaching of the Word. The church believes that to study the Word of God is the most essential factor for members to grow in spirit. Bible Studies thus become an avenue to learn more of God's Word. Fellowships among men, women, young, and older people also provide an opportunity to study the Word.

Second, the church also places a heavy emphasis on prayer. Each individual is encouraged to regularly spend time in prayer. There are different prayer meetings for various age levels. With the emphasis on prayer, the church opened a prayer mountain in a suburb of Manila. This facility is probably the first full-fledged prayer mountain open to any Christian in the Philippines. Of course, the members take full advantage of this program.

---

[5] Interview with Lanny Nicolas.

Third, the church encourages the members to experience the power of God in their daily lives. Believing the Word of God, the members exercise their faith in time of need. They frequently experience divine healing and divine intervention in difficult circumstances. They also trust God to intervene in their emotional and spiritual problems. The church leaders are concerned about meeting various needs of the members with prayer. This ministry plays an important role in bringing people to the church.

Fourth, the church maintains competent leadership. A pastor leads his or her congregation with strong spiritual sensitivity. With the guidance of the Holy Spirit, Conde has effectively exercised his leadership in establishing new outreaches in many cities. His dynamic vision is well shared with junior leaders, who are normally in charge of other smaller fellowships. This is a mark of Conde's effective leadership. He pays much attention to deploying a staff member in various parts of the church ministry according to his or her talents and capability. The church often recruits some lay people into the pastoral staff after they have received training.

PRAYER MOUNTAIN

Pastor Conde places great emphasis on a Christian's prayer life. Through studying the Word, he felt that study of the Word should be paired with prayer. With such a strong conviction, he prayed to God for a property to build a prayer mountain. In 1984, Pastor Conde, together with a few deacons, visited Prayer Mountains in Korea. The sole purpose of the trip was to learn about Korean prayer mountains, and to observe their ministry and operation. In 1986, one of his members donated a property of two hectares in Antipolo, a suburb of Manila. In 1988, construction began for Touch of Glory Prayer Mountain. Through a great endeavor, in the following year the sanctuary was completed and the members could hold services.

Once a week the church members come and pray in the prayer mountain, and this provides a more intimate spiritual fellowship among members. A couple of times Pastor Conde, who is a friend of my husband, invited him to speak in monthly prayer rallies held at the prayer mountain. There were nearly 1,000 people gathered and they spend hours and hours in prayer. Many have experienced for the first time various ways to pray: corporate prayer, individual prayer in the mountain or in a prayer cell, and fasting. I discovered the dynamics of a prayer life being developed among members, as well as Christians from other churches. The building was sizable – it can easily accommodate nearly 2,000 people. The facility also included prayer cells and hostel-type accommodations. There are daily evening and dawn – watch services.

PARTICULAR ATTENTION

The church also set up the so-called 'values' class.[6] Once a week pastoral staff members conduct a Bible study in the police department where all Metro Manila police gather. Some other pastors are also leading Bible studies in colleges, universities and business companies. The church provides a program called 'Refuge Foundation' for street children. The church provides food and clothing, and even sends them to school until they are ready to work in society. This program is maintained through donations and funds from various church members. These particular ministries draw people to the church.

The church endeavours to plant new outreaches. As mentioned above, the church planted sixty fellowships in different parts of the country. The church utilizes qualified volunteer workers for pioneering works and members willingly respond to the call of the ministry in new pioneering works. The church requires all the workers to attend three meetings a week for coordination, feedback, and spiritual feeding.[7] Through participation, a leader will know what is going on among the hundreds of cell group meetings every week.

A unique system is that the church does not pay a regular salary to the pastoral staff. They all live by faith. Their simple faith is that God will provide and supply their needs as they work full time for Him. This is apparently an unusual way of serving the church and God.

The simple faith of Pastor Conde has produced much fruit in his ministry. There certainly is a divine support behind his ministry to expand God's kingdom. As the name of the church indicates, many souls who are hungry for the Word of God are fed from the ministries of Bread of Life Fellowship. As they continually work, the church's ministry and its expansion will flourish.

Cathedral of Praise

BEGINNING

In 1951 a few Assemblies of God missionaries, Rosendo Alcantara, Arilo Maypa, and Rudy Esperanza, came from the United States and pioneered this fellowship. Actually the great revival meeting held in Sunken Garden during the months of January and February encouraged them to start the fellowship. The speaker at the revival meeting was C. A. Erickson from the United States. The initial name of the fellowship was Bethel Temple.[8] Eventually, the leadership was taken over by a local pastor named Lester Sumrall and later by David Sumrall, nephew of Lester Sumrall. The church began to grow significantly under his effective leadership. Within the period of 1980 to 1987, the

---

[6] It is a teaching ministry offered by the church to different level of schools and communities.
[7] Oscar C. Baldemor, 'The Spread of Fire: A Study of Ten Growing Churches in Metro-Manila' (Th.M. Thesis, Fuller Theological Seminary, 1990), 72.
[8] Informed by Silvestre Cariño, Jan, 1997.

membership increased from 1,000 to 13,750. The church's goal was to reach 20,000 membership by the coming year (2000) and 27,000 by the following year.[9]

The church is operated by forty-five pastoral staff ministers and thirty-five lay workers. There are over 1,000 lay people, under the supervision of staff pastors, who serve in cell groups, evangelism teams, outreach teams, and other church activities. A majority of the pastors are members of the church who received their ministerial training in the Cathedral of Praise Bible School.

GROWTH FACTORS

In searching for core factors that result in the Cathedral of Praise being one of the mega-churches in this country, several stand out. First, the church provides an adequate discipleship program. The pastoral staff visits new converts at least three times a week. The pastors are readily available for counseling the new converts, who are well-guided from the first step of church life to the next. The teaching includes sessions for water baptism, discipleship and so on. However, not all the new converts are added to the church. They can integrate only 10% of them into the body. This may indicate that the pastoral staff is overwhelmed by the sheer number of the new comers.

The church has its own unique way of training new believers. They set three different levels of training. The first level is called 'The New Life Course;' the second 'Pressing Toward Maturity;' and the third 'Leadership Training'. After completing all three levels of training, they become cell group members.[10]

The church is comprised of three levels of membership. The first is called 'corporate membership'. They are actively involved in church functions as key leaders, such as cell group leaders, and they support church ministry with their finances. The second is called 'living stones membership'. These members are also strongly committed to the body and to the ministry of the church. They are faithful attendants of the worship services. The third group is called 'attenders'. These people show only shallow level of commitment to the church, although they are regular members.[11]

Second, the pastoral staff is highly committed. They eagerly visit new converts. They try to improve their ministerial skills by reading books and religious magazines. The pastoral staff, as full time workers, spends about 80 hours a week on the job. That is apparently double what is normally expected from a full time worker.

Third, the senior pastor is greatly concerned with preparing good and relevant messages for every Sunday service. He prefers sharing the message solidly from

---

[9] Oscar C. Baldemor, 'The Spread of Fire', 81.

[10] Oscar C. Baldemor, 'The Spread of Fire', 81.

[11] Oscar C. Baldemor, 'The Spread of Fire', 82.

the Bible, rather than integrating it with illustrations. The church offers four services on Sundays for the members' convenience.

Fourth, the teaching ministry is one important factor for the church's growth. Bible studies are held in close to 800 cell groups spread around the city. The church's intensive Bible studies aim at growing to 1,000 cell groups in the near future. Through the diligent Bible study programs, the members gain knowledge of God's Word and apply it in their lives.

Fifth, the church encourages the members who have received the three levels of training to be involved in church activities. They observe carefully to determine which ministry is suitable for participation according to their interests and gifts. This is one of the important reasons for the orderly and effective operation of the church.

Sixth, the church, having a Pentecostal background, emphasizes its healing ministry. The leadership allows the pastoral staff and lay leaders to readily pray for the sick. Particularly at the end of revival meetings the sick are invited to the altar to receive prayer. A common testimony is that while people are worshipping God in song and praise, pain often disappears. They feel a touch from the Holy Spirit. The senior pastor shares his testimony that his wife was completely healed of tuberculosis in both lungs during a worship service. A member by the name of Chua recounted his wife's healing experience. She had been suffering from a toxic goiter for many years. Doctors gave up on her, expecting her to die of this disease soon. However, she experienced the healing touch of God during a crusade. These living testimonies keep the church alive.

Seventh, the church continues to be active in expanding the Kingdom of God through reaching out to the unreached through dynamic crusades and a feeding program. The healing ministry during crusades seems to be a significant factor for the rapid church growth. The church sets specific growth goals, and strives to fulfil its missionary call.

PARTICULAR ATTENTION

The church operates its own Bible school which has a record enrollment in the country of 600 students. This training equips the young and old to go out for various ministries. The church is involved in a daily television program. Through this ministry many new converts visit the church. The church also established satellite churches in various parts of the country. This is a common strategy which big churches have employed to reach out to more people. A successful case is that of its outreach in Zamboanga City which has a 2,000 membership. Having grown bigger, the church decided to be independent rather than belonging to a denomination; however, the worship style of the Cathedral of Praise reflects its close fellowship ties with the denomination which they were formerly associated with.

The church is greatly concerned about evangelism and church planting. Out of such concern, the church holds evangelistic crusades three times a week. Cell group leaders conduct two crusades in their neighbourhoods. The third crusade is more regional, typically conducted in a plaza. It is sponsored by many cell groups in a given geographical area. The church sets up a goal for evangelism through the crusades. The dynamic activity and eagerness of the leaders are a critical element for the church's growth. The church also focuses on a ministry to the poor. Funds are set aside to help needy people outside the church as well as church members in need. The poor thus feel the love of Christ through the church.

Analysis

What Are Common Factors for Church Growth?

There are some important elements which have contributed to the growth of all the mega- churches under investigation. First, they all maintain well-organized cell groups. The cell group leaders are well trained for, and committed to, the ministry. The cell group meetings appear to function as the best opportunity for several important pastoral activities. They apparently become an avenue for the members to gain knowledge of the Scriptures through Bible study. These meetings also provide an opportunity to share needs. People are spiritually nurtured by corporate prayers. The cell leaders' great care and concern are directed particularly to new members. Through their acquaintance in the cell group meetings, they are drawn closer to the church activities. As the churches have larger numbers of membership, this system plays a vital role in bringing them into oneness and unity as the body of Christ.

The cell group system has been popularized by the Korean church. It has been probably the most effective growth strategy for churches in Korea. Yoido Full Gospel Church of Yonggi Cho is the best-known case. The churches have close to 700,000 members, and Cho repeatedly attributes the phenomenal growth to the cell group system and its effective lay leadership. This system also contributes to unity among the members. According to my knowledge, a cell group leader is a prayerful person with full understanding of the Scriptures. The leader also makes himself/herself available for the cell group members. In practice, the cell group leaders share the pastoral role with the senior pastor.

Second, the churches provide good training programs for lay leaders. They also fully utilize lay people once trained. Dedicated and committed lay people can provide an excellent service to the church ministries. Effective utilization includes allocating them for various church ministries according to talents and leadership styles. Since they are all voluntary workers, using them even helps the churches financially. It is also noteworthy that the training programs are extensive, including several levels of training.

Third, these churches all have Pentecostal backgrounds. Hence, they all acknowledge signs and wonders and the ministry of the Holy Spirit. The leadership and the pastoral staff are sensitive to the spiritual needs of the people. There are two vital effects when a church allows the Holy Spirit to freely minister in the church and to individuals. One is that the church experiences a rapid growth through God's interventions in individual lives. One classic example is that in Cathedral of Praise, once several healings were known through testimonies, the revival meetings became more alive, and more unbelievers came to the services. This results in an increase in membership of the church. The other one is personal maturity. The members are not only learning about God with head knowledge, but also learn about Him through tangible and personal experiences. Having a concrete experience with God certainly enhances Christian maturity. I believe that true Christian spirituality is to have the presence of God and to walk with Him in everyday life.

The churches emphasize the importance of prayer. Pastor Conde of Bread of Life, for example, established a prayer mountain to aid the members' prayer life. Many times, he and his staff visited different prayer mountains in Korea to learn from their prayer life and to adapt it into the Philippine setting. They believe that prayer is the source of spiritual power and strength to carry on effective ministries. Their belief is that prayer will ultimately lead the members to spiritual growth and maturity. All the churches in the present study, whether with or without a prayer mountain, strongly emphasize prayer.

Fifth, the sincere and deep commitment of the pastoral staff is noticeable. In the case of Bread of Life, the pastoral staff spends an average of 80 hours per week for ministry. The eighty hours would include the time for preparation of the Word, working at the assigned job, leading cell group meetings and visiting individuals who need counselling and care. It clearly indicates their serious commitment and service to the Lord and their given ministry. This commitment is extraordinary considering that one of the churches does not even pay any salary to its pastoral staff. When my husband and I met Pastor Conde in 1990, he told us that he and his family basically lived by faith, trusting in God's faithfulness. He shared his faith in expressions such as: 'The Lord always meets our needs through the hands of believers', or 'He manifests His faithfulness in my daily life'. Their total commitment strongly commends the same sincere commitment from the members.

Last, the senior pastors and pastoral staff spend much time preparing to preach the Word with study and prayer. They seriously commit themselves to study of the Word to feed the member's souls with spiritually rich food. The members love to learn the Scripture. It is certainly expected that after being nurtured with the Word of God, they will be in a teaching position in cell group meetings and Sunday school programs.

How Do They Multiply?

The churches organize dynamic activities, which I would count as important. Praying, studying the Word of God, training lay people, power ministry and tremendous dedication of the pastoral staffs are undeniable elements for church growth. One activity which I would consider an extremely important ministry in terms of expanding God's Kingdom is planting daughter churches.

After establishing their own churches, they all commonly exert their efforts to plant outreaches in other cities. The Bread of Life Fellowship, for example, has established sixty outreaches all over the country. Word for the World, another Pentecostal group, has established more than one hundred fellowships. This indicates that their attention is given not only to their own church's growth and activities, but to reaching out to unreached people nationwide. Asian Christian Charismatic Fellowship not only plants outreaches within the nation, but also abroad by sending out qualified leaders. Hence, their mission work extends globally. These outreaches, after setting up their own body of believers, again attempt to reach out still further to other cities. This is a biblical pattern of church growth. The disciples of Jesus themselves became examples by making disciples through intensive evangelism and training (Luke 10).

The mega churches have exerted a great effort to establish outreaches. They target not only one city but the entire nation. This unique phenomenon in the current magnitude is found only in the Philippines. There are many large Pentecostal/Charismatic churches in Korea, Singapore, Malaysia and other countries that are planting daughter churches, but not of a scope similar to the Philippine mega-churches. For instance, the churches in Korea have a rather narrow spectrum in their ministry area. Often it is limited to within the same city rather than going beyond. There must be some apparent reasons for this narrowness. In my analysis, the primary reason is the difficulty of recruiting leaders who willingly commit themselves and their families to engaging in a new pioneering work in other cities. This obviously requires much sacrifice.

It is remarkable that one church planted one hundred outreaches in diverse cities, utilizing its own church workers. This is one marvellous strategy for bringing people into the Kingdom. This valuable model should be followed by other churches in this country.

External Factors for the Growth

People in society face many social issues arising every day. And a church as a social entity is directly or indirectly affected by current social settings. All the churches surveyed above began their ministries toward the end, or right after, the fall of the Marcos dictatorship. Corruption in, and mismanagement of, the government slowly made the elite middle-class people seek a new avenue to express their disappointment and search for a new meaning in life. In this sense, these churches have ministered to the culturally dislocated masses.[12] Then the churches experienced the drastic turns of the modern national history: the fall of the Marcos dictatorship; the people's revolution; Aquino's fragile government; numerous coup attempts; natural disasters including the killer earthquakes and volcanic eruption, coupled with annual visitations of more than twenty typhoons; economic struggles; communist guerrilla wars; the departure of personnel from

---

[12] Harvey Cox, *Fire from Heaven: The Rise of Pentecostal Spirituality and the Reshaping of Religion in the Twenty-First Century* (Reading, MA: Addison-Wesley, 1995), 104-105.

the two large American military installations and its economic effects; a Muslim independence movement and armed struggle; and finally the establishment of the Ramos government, with many improvements.

Recently the Philippine government has greatly endeavoured to purge corruption smeared in government sectors and to construct a new policy to improve the country. The government also attempts to reshape the nation through bringing social justice. A new tax reform is a kind of the greatest reform, called 'mother of all reforms'[13] which intends to force the high-income taxpayers to pay their taxes, minimizing avoidance by present loopholes. The government officials are concerned about the well-being of the people through economic, social and moral revival.

The current government also has resolved several deeply-rooted political conflicts. One of them is the Muslim independence issue. The government initiated a series of dialogues with the Muslim sectors in Mindanao. The Muslims had engaged in an armed resistance to the government, and this constantly threatened the normalcy of life for civilians. According to one Korean missionary who works in Mindanao, often times he has witnessed the killing of innocent civilians by Muslim rebels. The reaction of the Muslims--as well as the majority of Christian civilians--to the government has been one of great resentment. This has been one of the core issues which the former governments dealt with only militarily. The current president, Ramos, eventually set up an anti-terrorism bill which, in many people's minds, may be developed into martial law. This has brought turmoil into the society. Former president Marcos' long dictatorship wounded the hearts of the people and left great devastation in politics and the economy. Finally, a peace pact was signed by a Muslim leader and the president, granting autonomy to several Muslim-majority provinces. The government also resolved the army rebel problem as well as the New People's Army issue.

Poverty became a serious issue. But the national economy, for the first time in many decades, began to show signs of recovery. In fact the Philippines recently joined the Asian economic tigers.[14] Yet the gap between the haves and the have nots is widening. Children's involvement in prostitution has become so serious that even the government cannot deal with the problem anymore. In spite of the president's campaign, corruption has reached the maximum.

The role of the gospel has become significant because of such radical social changes. The people need consolation and a secure place where they can lay their hearts. The unstable social situations have caused the people to become more open to the gospel. In any society, when the people face political and social crisis, they want to hear a voice of peace and comfort. When they experience injustice, they seek justice which brings fairness and equal rights into the situation.

---

[13] 'The War on Tax Dodgers', *Asiaweek*, Mar. 22, 1996, 33.
[14] 'From the Ashes', *Newsweek*, Nov. 25, 1996, 13.

The unique mission strategies these churches have employed meet the expectations of the people. Moreover, many of them have found ways to actively propagate the good news they have experienced. Their own involvement in the ministry makes them instruments to spread the message of hope, peace, and love. Their deep involvement in social ministries, such as helping needy people, educating young people, and conducting Bible studies in various social organisations and schools keep the churches in constant contact with the society.

Above all, one has to recognize the ministry of the Holy Spirit who constantly works behind human endeavours. Their prayers bring the power of the Holy Spirit into everyday human life. Both the ministry of the Holy Spirit and the hard work of His human agents brought the rapid church growth.

When China opened to the gospel, many missionaries rushed to the land to plant the seed of the Word. In the eighteenth century, Hudson Taylor went to that land with his 'faith mission'. His priority lay in evangelizing people with the pure gospel, not with any other means. This implies total trust in the gospel and its power. The Pentecostal revival swept into Korea right after World War II, when the people were suffering under poverty and depression. The gospel commended a tremendous appeal to the hearts of people, and great fruit was harvested. Since then, the Pentecostal churches have kept on growing rapidly, resulting in many mega-churches.

Personally, I hope that the mega churches maintain their vitality and distinctiveness as Pentecostal/Charismatic congregations. Their message should enable the people to transform their lives and their society. This can be accomplished only to the extent that the churches constantly rely upon the work of the Holy Spirit. They also need to be diligent, as they have been, in learning the Word and committing themselves to prayer. Transformation will begin first in the lives of the members, and their exemplary lives will be a challenge to their community, and will eventually result in social transformation.

Conclusion

This study has discussed the growth of several mega-churches in socio-economic and political change over the last ten years. These churches played a significant role in expanding His Kingdom through dynamic ministries inside and outside the church. As Pentecostal/Charismatic churches, their unique characteristics are reflected in their ministries. Significant elements contributing to the rapid church growth are prayer, ministry in the Word of God, unity, aggressive utilization of lay people in ministry, strong and respected leadership, well-organized church structures, and various church activities that are sensitive to the Holy Spirit's guidance and human needs.

However, these groups of churches have also experienced problems that are commonly found in any church. Recently Bread of Life Fellowship had a conflict between the central leadership and regional leaders, and this eventually resulted in a split among more than a dozen churches and their leaders. They formed an organized fellowship. Regrettably, this difficulty is not confined to the Bread of Life Fellowship alone. Upon hearing of this recent development, I began to wonder if splits are another way of the over-all growth of the large Christian church. Again, this is observed elsewhere. For instance, the phenomenal growth of Korean churches took place through countless splits. Today there are more than one hundred Presbyterian denominations and the number is still growing. Of course this is not a desirable thing at all.

In order for the mega-churches to continue to grow, I believe they should keep their distinctive messages. The church leaders and their pastoral staffs should keep spending their time in the study of the Word of God. Many lay leaders and pastors are, in fact, products of Bible studies. Well-prepared and Spirit-led messages will not only meet the needs of the members, but also help them grow in the knowledge of the Word. When they are nurtured by the Word, they will, in turn, become engaged in ministries as voluntary workers.

The churches should frequently remind themselves of their tasks and roles in their society. I believe that one of their roles is to transform each individual believer's life. As their lives shine with the living Word, this will influence people whose lives are constantly affected by the secular and materialistic society. Thus, Christians should live as salt and light through their transformed lives. I believe that the gospel, shared among non-believers, should be intertwined with the gospel bearer's holy and committed life. The churches ought to play their role in sharing the gospel with their unique ministry in the midst of turmoil and rapid social, economic and political change in the coming era.

Chapter 10

Proclamation and Manifestation

Introduction

There has long been an intense connection between proclamation and manifestation in the Pentecostal form of worship. Gathering together in the name of Christ is perhaps one of their favourite spiritual activities. Pentecostal worship helps believers experience the divine presence through hearing the word of God, praising, praying and other worship involvement. When one hundred and twenty disciples assembled together in one place, the Holy Spirit descended upon them and 'all of them were filled with the Holy Spirit and began to speak in other tongues as the Spirit enabled them' (Acts 2:4). The 'Gentile Pentecost' took place at Cornelius' home (Acts 10) in an amazing way when Peter spoke the word of God. The Holy Spirit was poured out upon them and they spoke in tongues.

In the same manner, Pentecostal mission is not complete if there has been neither active worship nor the exercise of spiritual gifts. This chapter explores the relationship between the proclamation of the gospel and the manifestation of the Holy Spirit in Pentecostal worship, and its implications for Pentecostal mission. Thus, this study consists of two aspects: proclamation and manifestation in worship and in mission. Throughout this discussion, my own experience of Asian churches and mission is reflected.

Proclamation

Expressions such as 'Pentecostal preaching' or 'Holy Ghost preaching' have been used in Pentecostal circles to characterize its distinct features in proclamation. [1] There are several elements in the preaching of the word, especially in its message and style of delivery. [2] As G. Duffield argues, all preaching begins with the preacher. A Pentecostal preacher is more than someone with a loud voice, lots of energy, frequent movement around the

---

[1] Guy P. Duffield, *Pentecostal Preaching: The L.I.F.E. Bible College Alumni Association Lectureship on Preaching for 1956* (New York: Vantage, 1957), 23.
[2] H. Vinson Synan, 'Preaching, A Pentecostal Perspective', *DPCM*, eds. Stanley M. Burgess and Gary B. McGee (Grand Rapids, MI: Zondervan, 1988), 722.

platform, and generous gestures, or even someone preaching without written notes.[3] A true characterization of a Pentecostal preacher, instead, begins with his or her own distinct Pentecostal experience, which is commonly known as the baptism in the Spirit. In fact, only a Pentecostal preaches a Pentecostal sermon with corresponding conviction and dynamism.[4] In this section, three elements will be discussed: the Pentecostal use of scripture in preaching; the content of Pentecostal sermons; and aspects of Pentecostal proclamation.

Use of the Scripture

In many ways, Pentecostals inherited the conservative approach to the scripture. Often higher criticism is an offence to the Pentecostal church. Scriptural records are accepted as fact unquestionably. In this sense, the Pentecostals have practiced a pre-critical literal reading similar to the Fundamentalists.[5] However, Pentecostals have more than an undivided loyalty to the authority of the word: they have an unshakable confidence in God's power to repeat ancient miracles in the lives of present-day believers. Charles Parham's early sermon epitomizes this:

> Many teachers will at once admit that all the prophecies concerning Christ's first coming were literally fulfilled, but they spiritualize the prophesies of His second coming. So with teachers, concerning the promises of justification and sanctification, declaiming that they are possible of perfect realization today, and why not the promises of healing?[6]

Thus, the word of God and its authority become a pivotal emphasis in Pentecostal preaching in church and in the mission setting.[7]

---

[3] Duffield, *Pentecostal Preaching*, 24.

[4] Duffield, *Pentecostal Preaching*, 26. The impact of spiritual experiences of Pentecostal leaders in a tribal setting is compared with leaders in the ancient Israelite society in Wonsuk Ma, 'The Spirit of God upon Leaders of the Ancient Israelite Society and Igorot Tribal Churches', in Wonsuk Ma and Robert P. Menzies (eds.), *Pentecostalism in Context: Essays in Honor of William W. Menzies* (JPTSS 11; Sheffield: Sheffield Academic Press, 1997), 291-316.

[5] William W. Menzies, 'Non-Wesleyan Origins of Pentecostal Movement', in Vinson Synan (ed.), *Aspects of Pentecostal-Charismatic Origins* (Plainfield, NJ: Logos, 1975), 85, detects the Pentecostals' 'strong sense of kinship with fundamentalism'.

[6] Charles F. Parham, *The Sermons of Charles F. Parham* (New York/London: Garland, 1985), 42.

[7] For instance, Duffield, *Pentecostal Preaching*, 38-58; Ray H. Hughes, 'The Uniqueness of Pentecostal Preaching', in L. Grant McClung, Jr. (ed.), *Azusa Street and Beyond: Pentecostal Missions and Church Growth in the Twentieth Century* (South Plainfield, NJ: Bridge, 1986), 91-100. Sung-Hoon Myung, 'Spiritual Dimensions of Church Growth as Applied in the Yoido Full Gospel Church' (Ph.D. dissertation, Fuller Theological Seminary, 1990), 206, characterizes Yonggi Cho's preaching as first of all 'Bible-based preaching'.

Another example of the Pentecostal use of the scriptures is observed in their understanding of interpretations of tongues and prophecy. Classical Pentecostals argue that their experience of tongues and prophecy must always 'line up with' scripture and not contradict anything already directly revealed in the Bible. It is not, therefore, a 'new revelation' in the sense of adding to biblical truth, but rather a special method of emphasizing a biblical truth, or of providing guidance (scriptural application) to real-life situations.

This timeless and universal application of God's word to contemporary settings has a direct implication for Pentecostal faith: the miracle-working God of ancient believers is the same God of today's believers and he is involved in mission work. In Pentecostal preaching, therefore, God's intervention is freely proclaimed and expected, based on this non-dispensational approach to the scripture.[8]

Also unique in Pentecostal preaching is the frequent use of narrative material. This is not just for theological reasons although the narratives in Luke-Acts are used to substantiate the Pentecostal doctrine of the baptism in the Spirit. On a more existential level, figures in biblical narratives are often identified with one's own personal Christian life. This 'narrative' theology becomes a favourite part of Pentecostal spirituality including the expression of their Pentecostal faith in the form of testimonies.

Sermons

When it comes to actual sermons, on the one hand, Pentecostal preachers have proclaimed standard Christian truth, which the historic church has upheld. On the other hand, there are features distinct and common to Pentecostal preaching. One should bear in mind that what was preached at the outbreak of the Pentecostal movement at the turn of the century will significantly differ from what is proclaimed in today's Pentecostal churches and mission field. In a similar way, today's Pentecostal sermons can vary from one socio-cultural environment to another. Several common topics are unique to today's Pentecostal preaching.

'CAN DO'

This contemporary Pentecostal approach has its roots in at least three elements. The first is the Pentecostal belief in God's intervention in human life. As discussed earlier, this has to do with the Pentecostal approach to the scripture. The second is a historical development during the rise of the charismatic movement in the 60s and 70s. Unlike the Classical Pentecostals, the second evolution of the Pentecostal movement brilliantly married the Pentecostal experience of a miracle working God, and prosperity in local and overseas

---

[8] John Goldingay, *Approaches to Old Testament Interpretation*, updated edition (Downer Grove, IL: Inter-Varsity, 1990), 66-96, terms this method as reading the scripture 'as the story of salvation'.

mission contexts.[9] The third is an upward mobility trend in the West as well as in some developing nations in the world (e.g. South America and Asia) which have traditionally suffered from chronic poverty. The majority of non-Western Pentecostal churches as well as many contemporary Western Pentecostal churches have been impacted by the evolution of the movement. The impact was not only experienced in the churches but also in mission work (powerful messages by missionaries stirred the hearts of people and power manifestations occurred with proclamation). For Sung-Hoon Myung, positive thinking preaching is a feature of Yonggi Cho's sermons.[10] One needs to remember that most non-Western Pentecostal churches began or grew during the 1970s and the following decades.

This phenomenon is not psychological escapism. In fact, Hughes describes it as a faith producing sermon.[11] It is 'faith of an unusual nature, immediate faith, miracle faith' produced as the word is proclaimed. In Pentecostal worship, one's faith is often challenged to believe in something humanly impossible.[12]

Cho's 'positive thinking' sermons made a striking contrast to traditional Korean Christianity which was predominantly influenced by the Presbyterian traditions. Until the 1960s, Korean Christians had been hearing of God's presence in the midst of human suffering. Considering the church's short history during the Japanese persecution in its first half-century, and Communist oppression during the Korean War in the 1950s, God was viewed as a sustaining force in human suffering. Cho describes traditional preachers as setting 'their pulpit in Mount Sinai to judge and condemn the souls'.[13] In contrast, he labels his sermons as a message of hope. When Cho began to preach his characteristic 'can do' sermons, he was severely criticized as propagating humanism, or even Shamanism.[14] In spite of these charges, Cho will be remembered as the one who reshaped the image of God among Korean Christians. His idea of God's blessing is holistic, encompassing spiritual well being, wealth and health based on 3 John 2. Cho obviously observed the social context in order to present an appropriate and relevant gospel to touch the hearts of the people. This contextualized message, in fact, played a role in lifting up souls in the society. Such 'can-do' messages, preached with power, affected churches and the mission field.

---

[9] Cheryl Bridges Johns, *Pentecostal Formation: A Pedagogy Among the Oppressed* (JPTSS 2; Sheffield: Sheffield Academic Press, 1993), 79.
[10] Myung, 'Spiritual Dimensions of Church Growth', 206.
[11] Hughes, 'The Uniqueness of Pentecostal Preaching', 93.
[12] Hughes, 'The Uniqueness of Pentecostal Preaching', 93.
[13] Paul Yonggi Cho, 'The Secret Behind the World's Biggest Church', in L. Grant McClung (ed.), *Azusa Street and Beyond: Pentecostal Missions and Church Growth in the Twentieth Century* (South Plainfield, NJ: Bridge Publishing, 1986), 102.
[14] Cox, *Fire from Heaven*, 224-26, argues for a strong link between Cho's sermons and traditional Shamanism in Korea.

'EXPERIENCE GOD NOW'

In a Pentecostal's life, experience is a human dimension that is frequently emphasized. Through singing, testimonies and prayer, people are expected to 'commune with God', that is, to experience God's presence. Preaching is a continuation of this expectation.

Experiencing God can refer to anything from an emotionally charged state, to the baptism in the Spirit, to physical healing. The transcendental God is viewed as the one who is imminent to his own people. In McGavran's words:

> Pentecostals...believe that God stands at our very elbows, knocking at the door of our hearts, speaking in our intuition and dreams. Pentecostals believe that God our Heavenly Father is instantly available, and powerful.... This common Christian doctrine is believed by all denominations but Pentecostals appear to believe it more than most others. [15]

God is experienced in Pentecostal worship in rather tangible ways. Consequently, many Pentecostal sermons deal with life-related issues such as illness, poverty, family problems, business, relationships, etc. [16] It is worth remembering that Pentecostal believers traditionally come from the lower end of the strata of a given society where missionaries work. They are often motivated to seek God's help more than the so-called mainline denominational believers whose socio-economic status is relatively higher.

This present-day orientation may be a contrast to the early Pentecostal mission movement, which understood itself as an eschatological reality. [17] Again, this could be a reflection of the second-generation evolution of the movement in the form of the Charismatic movement. This orientation towards life related issues is not only stressed in sermons, but also in the altar service after the proclamation. As an essential part of preaching, the altar service provides an opportunity for the audience to respond to the message. The most frequent invitation to the altar area is for salvation, healing, commitment/dedication, the baptism of the Spirit, praying over life's problems, blessing, business, children, marriage life, etc.

---

[15] Donald A. McGavran, 'What Makes Pentecostal Churches Grow?' in *Azusa Street and Beyond*, 122.

[16] Another characterization of Cho's sermons is 'life-related' preaching, Myung, 'Spiritual Dimensions of Church Growth', 206.

[17] The collection of Parham's sermons in the Garland Series, *The Sermons of Charles F. Parham*, includes twenty sermons, and about one-half of them deal with eschatological subjects such as 'Future of Nations', 'United States in Prophecy', 'The Bride', 'The Millennial Age', 'The Judgment Age', etc.

THE BAPTISM IN THE SPIRIT

The doctrine of baptism in the Spirit best characterizes Pentecostals. This is a 'life-transforming event' subsequent to conversion.[18] In many ways, this pivotal belief is frequently reflected in Pentecostal preaching. Since this makes one truly Pentecostal, many sermons end with an urgent admonition to seek this experience. Hence, even if Pentecostal theology books may say differently, a prevailing assumption among the congregation is that from the baptism in the Spirit, many other spiritual experiences flow.[19] As one is 'empowered' through this experience, true Christian service takes place. For instance, when there is the baptism in the Spirit, people will begin to speak in tongues. Although this functions as the initial evidence of the Spirit baptism, this gift will remain and can be expressed in various ways such as a prayer language.

In many ways, this experience is a defining moment in a Pentecostal's life. From my own experience I can testify to having suddenly heightened spiritual senses and awareness. I began to experience 'listening' to God in various ways including a strong impression in my mind, dreams, and clear convictions coming through the scripture. Many experience spiritual gifts listed in the scripture.

It is also true that around this experience, many people encounter physical healing, emotional liberation from various bondages, answers to prayers, various kinds of miracles, a call to ministry especially for evangelism, and others. From an experiential viewpoint, the baptism in the Spirit is a doorway event. Even if a sermon has little to do with this particular topic, it is not unusual for the preacher to conclude his or her sermon by inviting people to pray for the baptism in the Spirit. This invitation also includes 'old timers' wanting to experience the refilling of the Spirit.

'SOUL-WINNING'

Pentecostal preaching is the missionary nature of the Pentecostal movement. Pentecostals have believed, from the very beginning that experiences of God's reality in the form of spirit-baptism are the very essence of Pentecostalism; and this experience is viewed as God's empowerment for witnessing (Acts 1:8). In other words, mission is the very reason for Pentecostal existence. This is one reason why preaching on the baptism in the Spirit is critical in Pentecostal churches. Dynamic and meaningful witnessing becomes possible only after one is empowered by the Spirit, with speaking in tongues as the initial evidence. In

---

[18] Grant Wacker, 'Wild Theories and Mad Excitement', in Harold B. Smith (ed.), *Pentecostals from the Inside Out* (Wheaton: Victor, 1990), 21.

[19] This popular Pentecostal notion on the relationship between the baptism in the Spirit and the operation of spiritual gifts was recently challenged by Robert P. Menzies, 'Spirit-baptism and Spiritual Gifts', in *Pentecostalism in Context*, 48-59. He concluded that the 'spirit baptism is the "gateway" to a special cluster of gifts' which he refers to as more supernatural prophetic speech gifts (58-59).

the beginning, tongues attained a special significance as God's ultimate equipment for missionaries.[20]

In some non-Western Pentecostal churches, the original missionary zeal was not shared in its exact nature. For example, Yoido Full Gospel Church has had relatively few cross-cultural missionaries. Most of its overseas work has been in ministering among overseas Korean Christians. Nonetheless, an emphasis on soul winning has been consistent in preaching.[21] Cho's sermons have greatly challenged and motivated Christians to aggressively witness Christ to their neighbours. Naturally, this emphasis produces church growth. For this, Wagner argues that Pentecostals believe not only in miracle power, but also in soul-winning power.[22]

Preaching

In the process of sermon delivery, Pentecostals also share several distinct features. These are not often found outside Pentecostal churches today.

Probably the most noticeable is the active participation of the audience during preaching. The audience of a Pentecostal church freely expresses their agreement by voicing an 'amen' or 'Hallelujah'. This makes Pentecostal preaching a dialogue in a real sense. This element of making preaching extremely alive and responsive is regarded as having been influenced by black spirituality. Generous gestures and the lively tone of the preacher enhance this effect.[23] Pentecostal preaching in both its content and form creates a sense of expectancy. God's immanent presence is often felt strongly in Pentecostal worship. Even a call for Christian service and ministry is made with urgency. Another general characteristic of Pentecostal worship is its mood of celebration. With God's work in lives freely expressed through singing, testimonies and prayer, preaching often picks up this element and enhances the mood.

In Pentecostal preaching, one often notices the frequent use of illustrations. They come from the scripture and contemporary lives. Sometimes, the entire sermon takes a narrative form. This is especially true in many mission fields where a narrative is a highly esteemed and familiar form of communication.

Spontaneity is an essential element of Pentecostal worship, and preaching is no exception. It is not uncommon to hear a Pentecostal preacher share his or her struggle as the Lord gives 'another sermon just this morning'. Many Pentecostal

---

[20] 'New tongues missionaries' was probably the earliest term, which signifies the link between tongues and missionary work, *Apostolic Faith*, Nov. 1906, 2.

[21] Myung, 'Spiritual Dimensions of Church Growth', 206, terms this as 'mission-oriented preaching'.

[22] C. Peter Wagner, 'Characteristics of Pentecostal Church Growth', in *Azusa Street and Beyond*, 129.

[23] A comment during the dialogue by a Pentecostal delegate represents this, 'If Reformers have a problem with noise, we Pentecostals have a problem with silence' (Cecil M. Robeck, Jr. on May 13, 1997 in Chicago).

preachers may stand on the platform with a short sermon note, while others may not have anything but a Bible.

It is also frequently noted that the preacher can diverge from his or her original sermon outline. In the middle of preaching, the service can easily break into a time of prayer. Pentecostal preachers are sensitive to the need to be 'led by the Spirit' throughout the worship. Often 'anointed' preaching is understood to mean a sermon prepared under the direction of the Holy Spirit, and delivered with strong conviction, and power.[24]

Manifestation

In Pentecostal worship, the high expectancy of God's intervention, or his immanent presence, often results in the manifestation of various spiritual gifts which are bestowed to edify the body (for instance, 1 Cor. 12 and 14). There are two specific aspects of the gifts that affect the lives of believers.

First, the presence of the spiritual gifts themselves is a strong sign of God's presence and work among his people. The operation of the gifts brings a fresh recognition of a God who still works among his people in the present day. Thus, charismatic spiritual gifts often bring a living immediacy and freshness to a congregation and to the lives of their individual members. The operation of charismata, such as healing, casting out of demons and miracle working quickly brings one's attention to God. In this general way, God non-verbally communicates his existence and nature to his people.

Second, God, as the divine being, reveals and shows his will to his children through the manifestation of the gifts. God adapts to a specific individual and church and mission setting in which he reveals his specific will. The manifestation of the word 'gifts', for example in the form of words of knowledge, words of wisdom, prophecy, speaking in tongues and interpretation, fulfils this function of the gifts.

Although, it is an individual who experiences the manifestation of a gift, the entire congregation is 'edified', thus, underscoring the corporate nature of spiritual gifts. The manifestation of the gifts takes place, when God's people seek and desire them earnestly, and are thus a sign that the Holy Spirit comes upon a congregation in a personal and tangible way.

Healing

Throughout the Bible, healing is frequently used to manifest the presence, compassion and power of God (for instance, 2 Ki. 20:3; Mk. 1:29-34, 40-42; 2:1-12). This is a sign that the transcendental God is imminent in a specific human need, such as, sickness, weakness, or even death. Healing, therefore, is the manifestation of the supreme God who claims to be the Creator of all living things.

---

[24] Synan, 'Preaching', 722.

Paul notes that healing is one of many gifts (1 Cor. 14:9), which is intended to strengthen God's people. Healing is probably the most common manifestation of God's power among Pentecostal and Charismatic churches worldwide. The impact of healing manifestations in the mission fields of the Asian countries of Korea, Nepal, the Philippines, Singapore and Malaysia is particularly significant. This is because of their strong animistic orientations. Moreover, widespread poverty in many Asian nations causes supernatural healing to be favoured. In fact, traditional healing is practiced through various spiritual means outside of Christianity. Therefore, Pentecostal mission workers freely exercise the spiritual gift of healing in worship services and informal fellowships. When a member needs the healing touch of God, he or she normally asks the congregation to pray for them before, or after, a service. I understand that many Pentecostal church pastors and missionaries pray for healing as a regular part of the service and this prayer takes place following the proclamation of the word. This not only reinforces the reality of God as just preached, but also affirms that the powerful God is also a God who cares for the needs of his children. People are encouraged to have total trust in the Lord and the prayer session provides the opportunity to practice what has been proclaimed. Many members grow in their faith through a personal healing experience or that of someone close to them. Consequently, the sick are encouraged to go to a solitary place to encounter the power of the Holy Spirit.

Many healings take place in the mission field. I remember an elder in one of the local churches in the Philippines where my husband and I were working as missionaries. He suffered from cancer, and medically had no hope of being cured. Knowing this, he put his hope totally in God. In this desperate situation, the role of his pastor was crucial. The pastor not only stood by to support him but also encouraged him to believe in God's healing power. At the same time, the whole congregation was requested to join in prayer. During the pastor's frequent house visits, he proclaimed God's love and power, and always prayed for healing with the laying on of hands. This elder was healed and his healing became a great testimony to the congregation as well as to unbelievers who had been concerned about him.

In the Philippines, there are a good number of large Pentecostal-Charismatic churches. Since we have been working in this country for more than two decades, I have been able to do research regarding their growth factors. Such fellowships like the Bread of Life, Cathedral of Praise, Asian Christian Charismatic Fellowship and other churches have regularly exercised the gift of healing in church services as well as in home meetings.[25] The leadership of these churches strongly encourages their pastoral staff and lay leaders to actively pray for the sick.

---

[25] There are nearly twenty mega-churches in Manila, Philippines with over 2,000 members.

Revival meetings are an annual event for many churches, especially in Korea. Regardless of denominational affiliations, during this special period, churches suddenly become very much like Pentecostal congregations. Often at the end of a revival meeting, the worship leader will invite the sick to the altar to receive prayers. At other times, the leader or the preacher will simply lay hands upon those who are seeking God's special touch. A common testimony is that while people are worshipping God, they feel a touch from the Holy Spirit and their pain and illness often disappear. The senior pastor of Cathedral of Praise once shared that his wife had been completely healed of tuberculosis in both lungs during a worship service. Mr. Chua, a member of Cathedral of Praise recounted that his wife, who had been suffering from a toxic goitre for many years and was expected by her doctors to die very soon, experienced the healing touch of God during a crusade. These living testimonies keep the church alive and expectant.

In 1961, Nepal had no churches and only about twenty-five Christians. A current report states that there are over 2,000 local churches today. Although this country is a Hindu kingdom, it is experiencing a spiritual harvest. People in the Himalayas are coming to Christ with an openness to the supernatural demonstration of God's power, especially through healing. Tamang's testimony is a good example. When his mother was ill, his father and the village priest prayed to their gods for her healing and sacrificed several goats and chickens, but she did not recover. The priest went to a nearby village to buy more animals to sacrifice, but the mother soon died. In his grief, Tamang went to a Buddhist lama and pleaded with him to restore his mother's life. The lama visited the house and chanted prayers for several hours, but with no result. Finally, Tamang decided to call a group of Christians from a nearby village, hearing that they had the power to heal the sick. The Christians came to Tamang's home and prayed for his mother, while the entire village watched. To Tamang's amazement and joy, his mother came back to life. And as a result, he and his family, along with twenty other households, totalling more than 160 people, accepted the Lord. Today Tamang leads twenty new fellowships in the Himalayas and is closely associated with Asian Outreach.[26]

Praying for healing is not confined to rural or tribal areas. Pentecostal churches in Singapore and Malaysia also actively engage in prayer for healing. As people seek the manifestation of supernatural healing, they experience it. This experience enhances their faith in Christ and enriches their Christian spiritual life.

Also, Pentecostals understand that often demons cause physical and mental disorders and sicknesses. For this reason, exorcism is a regular part of Pentecostal preaching as well as prayer after proclamation. It is Third Wavers who have further accentuated this element of 'spiritual warfare'.[27]

---

[26] 'A Miracle for Tamang', *Asian Report* 222 (March, 1997), 8-9.

[27] For example, Charles H. Kraft, Mark H. White, Ed Murphy, et al. (eds.), *Behind the Enemy Lines: An Advanced Guide to Spiritual Warfare* (Ann Arbor, MI: Vine, 1994).

Speaking in Tongues

For Pentecostals, speaking in tongues has a critical significance; hence the common reference to them as tongue-speakers.[28] According to the Pentecostals, accounts in Acts and 1 Corinthians reveal more than one function for speaking in tongues. In Acts, glossolalia is viewed as the evidence of the baptism in the Holy Spirit. In 1 Corinthians speaking in tongues is seen as the gift (charisma) of tongues or the prayer language. Corinthian glossolalia occurred in a settled congregation and required the accompanying gift of interpretation to extend its usefulness beyond the speaker.[29]

Either way, speaking in tongues is common in Pentecostal worship. When the Holy Spirit comes upon a gathering of believers and the people are filled with the Holy Spirit, speaking in tongues normally takes place. Pentecostals hold to three distinct tongue phenomena.

First, when one receives the baptism in the Spirit (a popular Pentecostals term), it is regarded as an empowerment for service separate from regeneration (Acts 1:8) and speaking in tongues is considered as the initial physical evidence. Because of the frequent link between the 'empowering' nature of the baptism in the Spirit and speaking in tongues as the initial evidence, early Pentecostals once believed that tongues was a missionary gift of knowing a foreign language.[30] The baptism in the Spirit is normally considered a prerequisite for ministry within a Pentecostal setting. During the altar service, praying for the baptism in the Spirit with the sign of tongues is very common in a Pentecostal church.

Second, often during a time of reflection after a sermon, someone may speak in tongues publicly. This is believed to be the manifestation of the gift of tongues (1 Cor. 14:7). This is not a sign of the baptism in the Spirit, although this gift is often found among those who have experienced the baptism in the Spirit. When the congregation is contemplating the message of the sermon just preached, they are expecting God to give an 'utterance'. According to Paul, this gift, just like other spiritual gifts, is given to edify the body of Christ. Hence, congregations are strongly encouraged to pray for the interpretation of the message delivered in tongues. Often, the person who spoke in tongues or even the interpreter, if different from the original tongue-speaker, is not aware of what he or she has said. This spontaneous and often ecstatic message often reaffirms the word just proclaimed.

Third, tongues are also used as a private prayer language. Gordon Fee argues that the 'groaning' of the Spirit in Rom. 8:26-27 refers to speaking in tongues in

---

[28] This popular notion is reflected in Gordon L. Anderson, 'Pentecostals Believe in More Than Tongues', in *Pentecostals from the Inside Out*, 53-64.

[29] Russell P. Spittler, 'Glossolalia', *NIDPCM*, 338-39.

[30] Charles Parham's initial belief in tongues as xenoglossa is discussed by James R. Goff, Jr., 'Initial Tongues in the Theology of Charles Fox Parham', in Gary B. McGee (ed.), *Initial Evidence: Historical and Biblical Perspectives on the Pentecostal Doctrine of Spirit Baptism* (Peabody, MA: Hendrickson, 1991), 57-71, especially 64.

private prayer.[31] Paul clearly alludes to this use of tongues in 1 Cor. 14:14. That is, one prays in mind as well as in spirit. It is possible that the Corinthian Christians believed that this was the language of angels (1 Cor. 13:1). During Pentecostal worship, there are long periods of prayer for various reasons; and during this time it is not unusual to hear the pastor urge people to pray in their 'heavenly language'. There is often a strong release of one's emotional or spiritual burden through praying in tongues. Logically, those who have experienced the baptism in the Spirit with speaking in tongues will also experience this type of intimate prayer. Whether all three tongues phenomena are one gift with three different uses or they are two or three different gifts altogether is a matter of debate.

Often, these three phenomena appear together in a public worship setting. Just recently, my husband and I made a trip to Bakun, a municipality in Northern Luzon in the Philippines.[32] We held a Sunday service in a small tribal village. Sufficient time was given for various testimonies from members and then a typical Pentecostal sermon was preached with charged emotion and great expectancy of God's presence and work. Then, as is also typical of Pentecostal worship, the speaker urged the congregation to receive the baptism in the Spirit. He invited those who wanted the baptism in the Spirit to come forward and some young people came to the altar. While the whole congregation prayed for them, the preacher and other leaders laid their hands upon the young people and prayed for the baptism in the Holy Spirit. Soon they began to break out in tongues. One was weeping while another was lying flat on the floor. In the midst of prayer, one of them suddenly raised her voice and began to give out an 'utterance'. Everyone was aware that the Spirit was giving a message to the body and the congregation began to pray for an interpretation of the message. A few minutes later another lady who was standing beside them began to interpret the message. She was extremely hesitant at first. She tried to speak out but the words did not come out smoothly in the form of a sentence. However, after a short while, the interpretation was made with highly charged emotion. The message was something like: 'I love you. I will never forsake you. If you want to be baptized by the Holy Spirit, come forward. I will baptize you. Serve me continually...'. Since I was standing right behind her, I could closely observe her and listened to her interpretation. Then suddenly more hearts were opened and more people came forward for prayer. It was a tremendous spiritual encouragement to the congregation and this utterance reinforced the proclaimed message in a powerful way. There was a great movement of the Holy Spirit among the members of that church and when the Holy Spirit touched them, they spoke in tongues, were slain in the spirit and they wept. The service continued for three hours.

---

[31] Gordon D. Fee, 'Toward a Pauline Theology of Glossolalia', in *Pentecostalism in Context*, 24-37.
[32] The Assemblies of God has concentrated most of its mountain ministry in this area and has established many churches.

Prophecy

Along with traditional Christianity, Pentecostals share a basic theological belief concerning the primacy of the written word as God's revelation. However, they also believe in God's direct communication through various other modes. As mentioned above, an utterance can be given in tongues with corresponding interpretation. The gift of prophecy functions in a similar way, although it can come through other means such as visions, audible messages and dreams as observed in the scripture. In Pentecostal worship, prophecy is often a declaration spontaneously given to the congregation in a public setting. Paul equates the value of messages in tongues accompanying an interpretation, with that of prophecy for the building up of the body of Christ (1 Cor. 14:14-20).

The Bible provides an ample amount of evidence that prophecy is a manifestation of the Holy Spirit. The Book of Acts records that people saw visions, and prophesied after the day of Pentecost. Having been baptized in the Holy Spirit, people spoke in tongues and prophesied (Acts 8). Peter, by the Spirit, foretold the deaths of Ananias and Sapphira (Acts 5:1-10) and also saw a vision (Acts 10:9-16), which directly dealt with Peter's bias against the Gentiles and further substantiated revealed truth (v. 15).

As manifested in the book of Acts, Pentecostals and Charismatics experience the unfolding of God's will through dreams, visions, or personal messages, though God's written revelation functions as basic truth. However, in a real life setting, there are many situations that require decisions which have nothing to do with ethical or Christian principles. In these instances, 'direct revelation' is sought, and the word gifts, such as prophecy, find their place.

Paul notes that prophecy is given for 'strengthening, encouragement and comfort' (1 Cor. 14:4). Often this reinforces the message just proclaimed, as a prophecy often appears during the post-proclamation prayer time. The message of God tends to alert the people to be faithful in order to strengthen their spiritual life. Also visions are seen during both private and public prayer times. In the case of a vision, an interpretation is required. However, for a prophecy, no interpretation is required. Instead, Paul urges the rest of the congregation to 'weigh carefully what is said' (1 Cor. 14:29).

Blessing

The Pentecostal understanding of blessing is not much different from that of traditional Christianity except in two distinct ways. First, Pentecostals believe that God, in fact, blesses them here and now; and second, God blesses not only the spiritual, but also the physical, material and relational dimensions of human life. In this sense, the Pentecostal understanding of God's blessing is close to the Old Testament concept of shalom. They believe that God intervenes tangibly when they ask, and specific blessings are expected. An expectant and experiential dimension in their relationship with God characterizes the Pentecostal belief.

The message of blessing is often proclaimed in the pulpit. It is based on God's character: his faithfulness (Lam. 3:22), mercies, dependability (Deut. 32:4; Ps. 89:8; 1 Thess. 5:23-24), goodness (Ps. 100:5) and love. God also lavishly displays his love by providing rest and protection for his people (Deut. 33:12).

The message about God's character encourages his people to anticipate God's blessings. Pentecostals believe that blessings are given when they trust God and earnestly seek them out. Because of this, people implore God to meet their needs and are sacrificially devout in prayer, setting aside certain days for this very thing.

A story is told about a woman who had been longing for a baby and decided to devote herself to dawn prayer for three months. She woke up early every morning and prayed. On the last day of her three months of prayer, she went to a doctor for a check-up. She was pregnant. Some may say this was a shamanistic way of believing in God. On the surface, yes, it looked like she expected what she wanted; but on a deeper level, there was a fundamental difference. This woman truly believed in God, not on the basis of her devotion, but based upon who God is. The God who 'can do' in his goodness and faithfulness was part of her belief. This is only one example. There are hundreds of thousands of testimonies of God's blessing. Magazines like Charisma and Pentecostal Evangel regularly publish stories of miraculous healing. *Shin-ang-gye* [World of Faith], which has been published by Yoido Full Gospel Church, is the best-selling monthly magazine in Korea, and is full of testimonies of God's blessing in the form of healing, God's answers to prayer and miracles.

Secondly, many Christians believe in giving, and believe that it is a way of receiving his blessing. Often they give to God beyond their ability, trusting that God will be able to help them make up the difference. This behaviour certainly has the potential to promote a theological attitude which views God as a deity open for human control and even manipulation. One Korean church pledged to erect thirteen church buildings in the northern Philippines. It was a collaborative work of thirteen individual deacons and elders. Even one church would have been difficult enough to build, but their faith and dedication enabled them to fulfil their pledge. In Pentecostal preaching, dedication and God's blessing are among the favourite topics.

The expectation of God's blessing has as its basis God's own character, which is exhibited in his relationship with his people. God promises his blessing to his people based on the divine integrity. His blessing is intended for his people's experience in daily life. This experience is meant not only to be transcendent but also to be imminent, tangible and empirical as well. For this reason, Pentecostals do not hesitate to seek such blessings from God. Experiences enhance their relationship with God as they are drawn closer to him, and this leads them into deeper faith.

Conclusion

Pentecostal worship, like Pentecostal theology, incorporates most of the elements of historic Christianity. At the same time, differences characterize Pentecostal preaching in the church and in mission work. The distinctive aspect of the Pentecostal faith is the combination of God's supreme reality and its intimate relevancy. The platform where this combination is experienced is our everyday life! Pentecostals have a constant immanent encounter with the ultimate transcendental being. The catalyst of this uneasy combination is a unique Pentecostal experience called the baptism in the Spirit.

Pentecostal preaching in the mission field is one of several effective avenues where this unique Pentecostal combination is taught, proclaimed, reinforced and elaborated. Although in the popular preaching of some televangelists, health and wealth receive disproportionate attention, all the blessings are perceived as a means, or part of the empowerment to be an effective witness for Christ. This makes Pentecostal worship and life dynamic and alive. Preaching communicates this element not only in its content but also in its form of delivery.

As Pentecostals expect the manifestation of God's reality in everyday life, preaching becomes a vehicle of affirmation. There are various gifts through which one experiences God's presence and power in public Pentecostal worship. Pentecostals believe that these gifts, which were common in the early church, are also intended for today. As indicated in the Book of Acts, these gifts brought renewal and strength to a believer's faith and revival for the church. The same result is observed in the Pentecostal mission field when God's power and love are manifested in worship. God's overwhelming presence becomes real. God is never miniaturized but remains a powerful and ultimate transcendental force. God becomes immanent and tangible in human experiences through the intimate worship and fellowship in the believer's life.

Chapter 11

Mission with Empowerment in a Tribal Setting

Introduction

Mountain tribes in the northern Philippines are collectively called Igorots[1] During the four-centuries of Spanish rule, the Igorots were exempt from 'Christianization' by the Spanish Catholic missionaries, due to the effective military resistance of the Igorots against the Spaniards, and they have maintained their animistic religion and culture to this day. The Kankana-eys are one of fourteen Igorot tribes, and have their own dialect, religious practices and lifestyle. Although the Kankana-eys share many cultural practices with other Igorot tribes, each tribe has substantially unique practices.

In the early stages of the Assemblies of God mission movement in the U.S.A., the participation of female leaders was well established around 1914. In fact, it is considered to be one of the most important factors in bringing about the revival and advancing mission work further.[2] Both single and married women were called, and responded to various ministries such as church planting, evangelization, nursing and teaching, in the far-flung corners of the world. They were anointed by God for specific tasks, and that was more important than human authorization.

The Assemblies of God started its ministry among the Kankana-ey tribal people in 1947, initiated by a single woman missionary from America, together with a few national leaders. Elva Vanderbout was commissioned by the Foreign Missions Department in Springfield, Missouri in 1946.[3] Until she launched her work in the mountains, neither missionaries nor national workers of the Assemblies of God had attempted mountain ministry.

---

[1] According to Albert E. Jenks, *The Bontoc-Igorot* (Manila, Philippines: Bureau of Printing, 1905), 27, Igorot in English is 'mountaineer' (i.e., 'one who dwells in the mountains'). W. Scott, *On the Cordillera* (Manila, Philippines: MCS Enterprises, Inc., 1969), 155, further elaborates that the archaic term *golot* ('mountain chain') and the prefix *'I'* ('dweller in' or 'people from'), suggests that *Igorot* carries the meaning 'mountaineer'.
[2] Gary B. McGee, *This Gospel Shall Be Preached* (Springfield, MO: Gospel Publishing House, 1986), 46.
[3] Elva Vanderbout's Application for Appointment to Department of Foreign Missions, Springfield, MO (1946).

Vanderbout approached the tribal people with a unique Christian message: God's power. Through the message of divine power and its manifestation, churches were established and the mountain ministry of the Assemblies of God was successfully carried out. The goal of this study is to describe her mission work in various contexts and to analyze and evaluate her ministry.

The Life and Ministry of Vanderbout

The Call of God to Elva Vanderbout

In 1944, a missions' convention was held at Bethel Temple in Los Angeles, where Vanderbout regularly attended. One of the speakers was Howard Osgood, a missionary to China.[4] The second morning of the convention, Vanderbout took a seat at the very front of the church auditorium. When the song service started, she felt a great sense of the presence of the Holy Spirit in her heart. Mission songs seemed to speak to her more personally and directly than she had ever experienced. When the speaker shared a message about millions of people who were idol worshipers, walking in the darkness of paganism, the message pointedly reached her. At the end of the preaching, the speaker invited members to give their lives for the lost. Her heart was broken as she sensed the presence of God, and Vanderbout was one of the first to respond. She almost ran to the altar, put her hands up in a gesture of total surrender and prayed, 'I give myself to you! I will do what you ask me to do! I will go where you ask me to go! Oh God'. Then she heard the voice of God, 'Whom shall I send, and who will go for me?' From the depths of her heart, she answered, 'Here am I. Send me'.[5]

In the meantime, Vanderbout's husband was terribly ill, due to a cerebral haemorrhage. The disease paralyzed the left half of his body, rendering him bed-ridden and in need of full-time attention. When her husband died, Vanderbout's heart was indeed broken.[6] A few months after the funeral, Vanderbout turned her thoughts to where she should go. One day the pastor's wife asked her if she had decided which country she wanted to go to for her mission work. Mrs. Turnbull, the pastor's wife, mentioned the Philippines, and upon hearing the name of the country, she realized that she loved thinking of going to the Philippines.

Sometime later, an opportunity came for Vanderbout to make contact with a missionary couple in the Philippines, and she obtained the necessary information about the country from them. She was then all the more excited about going to the Philippines as a missionary.[7] She was officially ordained to be a missionary

---

[4] Inez Sturgeon, *Give Me This Mountain* (Oakland, CA: Hunter Advertising, 1960), 28. *GMTM* henceforth.

[5] *GMTM*, 30.

[6] *GMTM*, 36-47.

[7] *GMTM*, 54.

in the year 1946, by the Foreign Missions Department in Springfield, MO, U.S.A.[8]

On December 15, 1946, Vanderbout left her own land to take up residence in the Philippines. She travelled by ship, which went to the Philippines via different countries. The ship was jammed with adults and children, so much that she could hardly find a space to lean her body, and Vanderbout felt unutterable weariness with the situation. She managed to find a tiny space on the third deck, which was the worst place.[9] However, she attempted to get through the long days and nights with prayer. After twenty-three days of a long and tedious journey, the islands of the Philippines began to loom near. Vanderbout sparkled with joy at being able to reach the destination that she was longing for.

On January 7, 1947, Vanderbout finally trod the soil of the Philippine Islands to begin her mission work. After a twelve day stay in Manila, she left for Baguio City where she would eventually begin her ministry among Igorot people.[10] The road was extremely rough. Most of the bridges had been bombed during the war and had not yet been rebuilt, so the bus had to ford streams and gullies. At that time the population in Baguio City was about 30,000. Much of the city had been demolished during the war.[11] However, Vanderbout was warmly welcomed by members of the Assemblies of God church.

Vanderbout's clear call from God eventually directed her to the Philippines. It was apparent that God's hand was upon the specific path of her decision, as God's divine intervention in her life was vivid and vital. Her desire and burden to reach out to the mountain people was thus slowly coming to realization.

Vanderbout's Initial Ministry

In 1947, Vanderbout began her ministry in Tuding,[12] Itogo, Benguet Province. The place was well known locally as a notorious nest of criminal elements and the most wicked and sinful town in the mountain province after World War II. Robberies, assaults, knifings, and police raids were part of everyday life there. About 2,000 people lived in Tuding and 21,000 inhabitants in its surrounding areas.[13]

One night, Vanderbout visited Tuding to observe what sort of place it was, and when she returned home that night, she could not erase from her mind the picture of the Tuding Barrio, and she became deeply burdened for the people. Filipino leaders advised her not to begin her ministry in such an evil place; it might endanger her own life. But Vanderbout persisted and started her ministry in Tuding. In spite of the perils she would encounter, she was assured that God

---

[8] Vanderbout, Application (1946).

[9] *GMTM*, 69-75.

[10] *GMTM*, 76-80.

[11] Elva Vanderbout, 'A Westward Move', *Our Missionary*, August 1962, 1.

[12] Tuding is located in Itogon, Benguet Province in Northern Luzon , Philippines.

[13] *GMTM*, 1.

had called her to these people.[14] Vanderbout thus sincerely responded to the call of God and her commitment paralleled the call.

For a few months, Vanderbout wrestled with how to begin her ministry among these people. Of course, she spoke in churches in Baguio, the summer capital of the Philippines. She also started Bible study classes and conducted prayer meetings. But she wanted a stable ministry in Tuding to win souls who were in darkness.

With much prayer, and understanding that a woman would find it difficult to approach pagan people with a new religion, Vanderbout thought of the children in a public elementary school in Tuding. She visited Tuding Elementary School to meet the principal and to introduce her idea. To her amazement, the principal granted her permission to open a Bible class.[15] It was marvellous for a single woman to get permission to do ministry in any local public school in the male-dominant mountain world. This was another apparent work of the Holy Spirit. This public school ministry later became a stepping stone for spreading the gospel among the mountain people.

July 26, 1947 was her first day at the Tuding school. Vanderbout presented the gospel through the interpretation of a national Christian worker. She supplemented her words with interesting visual materials which fascinated the children; they had never seen such objects. The visual aids drew their rapt attention to the message of the gospel.[16]

As Vanderbout continued her ministry among the children, especially the fifth and sixth grades were most interested in the gospel. The children comprehended the message quite well and responded with a warm heart.[17] As Vanderbout continued her ministry among these school children, some girls and boys wanted her to visit their parents. She prayed earnestly about her visitation to their homes. The Holy Spirit spoke to her that this was the very door that God had opened for her through which to reach these people. She made up her mind to accept the invitations to visit the homes. She and the national workers who assisted her in interpretation hiked twelve miles to visit the children's homes. The parents, indeed, positively responded to the gospel message; and this was the first time for them to hear the Word of God.[18]

One particular experience with the sick father of one of her 'students' became the turning point in her ministry. When she visited the girl's home, she found the father was paralyzed on the entire left half of his body and had been on the floor for six months. Their living conditions were so poor that there was not even a blanket or pillow for the patient. This scene broke Vanderbout's heart, especially

---

[14] Leonardo Caput, A Personal Letter to the Author (Mankayan, Benguet, Philippines, March 15, 1993).

[15] Caput, Letter (1993).

[16] *GMTM*, 87.

[17] *GMTM*, 87.

[18] Caput, Letter (1993).

in retrospect of her husband's death. A burden to share the gospel welled up in Vanderbout's heart, and she regularly and faithfully began to visit and share the living Word of God with the paralyzed man. Through her ministry, the whole family found the Lord as their Saviour.[19] After many such conversions, many of these parents became the pillars of what was later to comprise the Tuding church.[20]

Even though she was a female, single missionary, Vanderbout was well accepted by native Kankana-ey people because of her passion and love for them. One advantage for Vanderbout, in spite of being a female, was that she was a white woman, and the mountain people tended to respect white people. Above all, the Holy Spirit intervened in her ministry to bring effectiveness.

Pentecost in Tuding

Vanderbout did not confine herself just to children's ministry. She wanted to expand her work in Tuding, Itogon. She and her ministry team thus started evangelism in Tuding. She soon found that each time they preached the gospel, more and more people were coming to hear the message of God. Vanderbout eventually decided to hold open-air services to accommodate the crowds. As she frequently met these people, she noticed that many were afflicted by diseases. She also learned that during the war, most of the mountain people lost all of their possessions, and this left them poverty stricken and devastated. Poor living conditions caused them to lose bodily resistance to disease.[21]

Before Vanderbout's ministry, there were some Christians in town, and Paran Bukayan and a few of his relatives were some of them. Bukayan opened his house for Sunday morning and evening services.[22] When Bukayan heard about the ministry and compassion of Vanderbout among the mountain people, he invited her to speak in his worship service. By this time, she had become well known among the village people of Tuding. News of Vanderbout's preaching in this service spread among them through Bukayan's relatives. Pagan people came to the service with interest in what a white woman had to say.[23] The message had a powerful impact on the people gathered there, and many turned to Christ. The power of the Holy Spirit was manifested among them. The good news of Christ began to change people's hearts, and the congregation of the house church grew larger.

In 1948, Vanderbout and several national ministers held revival meetings in Tuding week after week, besides having regular services on Sunday nights. The Holy Spirit moved among the gathered people and many non-believers were

---

[19] *GMTM*, 88, 89, 92.

[20] Caput, Letter (1993).

[21] *GMTM*, 93.

[22] Juan B. Soriano, 'Pentecost in the Philippines', *Pentecostal Evangel* (August 7, 1948), 2-4.

[23] Caput, Letter (1993).

saved, and at one time more than 150 were baptized in water. Old, young adults, and children shared wonderful testimonies of the power of God which saved their lives from darkness and the bondage of sin. They rejoiced over salvation and became new creatures.[24] In every Sunday evening service, many were baptized with the Holy Ghost and fire, according to Acts 2:4. It was like old-time Pentecost.

What attracted the animists to her ministry? It was apparently God's power revealed so vividly through the message and prayer. The power they experienced was something different from the power of ancestor spirits mediated by a pagan priest. Many received visions from the Lord and many were called to God's service.

Construction of the Tuding Church

As more people came to God every week, Vanderbout felt the need for a church building where all the people might comfortably worship God. She began to pray with strong faith to be able to build a church in Tuding. But it was not an easy job to do, because the first materials purchased cost $2,000. For several months, Vanderbout wrote to her former pastor, Rev. Turnbull, regarding this project and her needs. To her surprise, Pastor Turnbull sent a check for $2,000. Later the Foreign Missions Department sent a sizeable amount toward the church building. Vanderbout set about purchasing property on which to build a new church building right away.[25] At last the building was sufficiently finished for dedication, even though the ceiling and the interior were not complete. The dedication service was held December 9, 1949. Vanderbout invited Rev. Howard Osgood, the former missionary to China, who was the speaker at the missionary convention in Bethel Temple Church where Vanderbout had received her call. A mass of people flooded into the service.[26]

Juan Soriano, a mountain ministry team member, was chosen to pastor this church.[27] Why was Soriano selected as the pastor for Tuding Church? Was Vanderbout not qualified herself to be the pastor? First of all, Soriano was enthusiastic and dedicated to evangelism ministry. He was thus well suited to pastor this newly established church. In the Kankana-ey culture, men are dominant in every part of social activity. That probably influenced the selection of this leader over Vanderbout, although she had endeavoured to build the church building. A native pastor was also preferred over the foreigner, in order to effectively lead the congregation. Later, the Tuding church became a ministry centre conducting seminars, short-term training of church leaders, revival meetings, and various other gatherings.

---

[24] Soriano, 'Pentecost in the Philippines', 2-4.

[25] *GMTM*, 111.

[26] Elva Vanderbout, A Personal Letter to the Foreign Missions Department (Aug. 1961).

[27] Elva Vanderbout, 'Talubin Christians Re-Enact Conversion', *Missionary Challenge*, Mar. 1958, 1.

Evangelism and Power Encounter in Tuding

Vanderbout conducted weekly open-air services in Tuding during the year 1954. Frequently, she proclaimed the healing power of God during the service, based on Mark 16:15-18: 'They shall lay hands on the sick and they shall recover'. She also saw the needs of the people, and with simple faith in the Word of God, called on her ministry team to pray for the sick.[28]

A fourteen-year old boy had ulcers on his leg. When this boy was seven years old, he had fallen down and his leg was broken right at the knee. The next five years of his life were very difficult, because as the leg healed the bones grew together bent. His leg was stiff and he could not straighten it. He could not touch the ground, which meant he could not walk, only hopping along with the help of a stick or by just crawling along on the ground, and he had certainly lived a miserable life.[29] He had been somewhat treated by witch doctors, but he could not be cured.

The boy's mother became a Christian and the parents gave up their pagan worship, determined to follow Christ. Vanderbout and her ministry team came to the boy's home to visit. She laid her hands upon him and prayed, believing in Christ to heal. This boy threw away his stick, believing in the healing power of God.[30] From that time on he did not use his stick any more, and little by little his leg straightened out, and the ulcers disappeared by God's power. Many souls were saved through healing experiences as God's power was manifested in the ministry of Vanderbout and her team members.

There was a little girl who had not been able to walk for a couple of years, and she began to walk by a miracle of God. Her parents turned to Christ through their daughter's healing, and they attended the services regularly.[31] Such testimonies of healing caused the revival to grow and added to the number of believers. The crowd attending her services normally comprised the whole barrio population. The revival in Tuding was to shake the whole of Benguet Province, and this news was spread far and wide to sow the seed for the work to be done throughout the mountains.

Salvation-Healing Ministry in Baguio City

Baguio City, located 6,000 feet above sea level, is only about a fifteen minute drive from Tuding, and is an access point to different provinces. In fact, within a thirty minute drive from Baguio City, people can reach places where tribal people still maintain their traditional lifestyle. In 1955, Vanderbout drew up a plan to conduct a revival meeting for salvation and healing in Baguio City. She first went to the mayor to obtain a permit for Burnham Park, the most eminent

---

[28] *GMTM*, 95.

[29] Elva Vanderbout, 'Report on Trip to the Alsados', *Missionary Challenge*, Apr. 1954, 3.

[30] Elva Vanderbout, 'A Work of Mercy in the Philippines', *Foreign Field Report*, July 1954, 3.

[31] Elva Vanderbout, A Personal Newsletter (May 1957).

and largest spot in the city. The mayor's response was somewhat negative due to a time conflict. A carnival had been planned to use the same place. Vanderbout again asked the mayor to reconsider her request and when the mayor checked with his clerk to confirm the dates, the clerk told him that the carnival had been rescheduled for a later date. Vanderbout thus received permission from the mayor to use that place. She almost shrieked for joy because it was the first time that this place had ever been used for a religious gathering.[32] Vanderbout finally set the date, March 1, 1955, for the revival meeting. The speaker was Mrs. Ralph Byrd from America, and about 1,500 came to the morning meetings. Through those services, hundreds of people accepted Christ as their personal Saviour.

God also performed miracles of healing in different services. One girl eighteen years of age, who had suffered as a deaf-mute for twelve years, was instantly healed. During each morning and night service, the sick lined up to be prayed over for healing.[33] God healed deaf mutes by the scores; the blind received their sight and paralytics were healed. People suffering from tuberculosis and many other sicknesses were healed. One famous woman in the city was healed of a very large goiter. It partly diminished when she was prayed for on Saturday night, and when she returned to the Sunday morning service, it had completely disappeared. A man of twenty-eight years of age, who had been a deaf-mute all his life, was cured instantly one morning.[34] The eight-day salvation and healing revival was marvellous and countless people came to the Lord and myriads of sick people were healed. During the meetings, there was a mighty outpouring of the Holy Spirit and nearly forty were baptized in the Holy Spirit. There were several outstanding conversions of distinguished government officials, including the deputy-governor of the sub-province, his wife and daughter. The mayor of a nearby town was saved and healed from sickness. He gave a resounding testimony. These phenomena were recognized as the work of the Holy Spirit.

Salvation-Healing Ministry in Mountain Provinces

Vanderbout wanted to hold consecutive salvation and healing meetings in Mountain Provinces. Since the missionary already had empirical experience with the power of healing in previous meetings, she expected to repeat the effect in Mountain Provinces, not fully understanding the true empowerment of the Holy Spirit.[35] She loaded her car with camping equipment, a public address system, and an electric light system. The missionary and national workers drove nearly

---

[32] Elva Vanderbout, 'Salvation-Healing Revival in Baguio City, Philippines', *Pentecostal Evangel*, June 1955, 2.

[33] Vanderbout, 'Salvation-Healing Revival in Baguio City', 4.

[34] Vanderbout, 'Salvation-Healing Revival in Baguio City', 4.

[35] Vanderbout, 'Talubin Christians Re-Enact Conversion', 2.

all day over rugged, mountain roads into head-hunter's territory. Almost the whole community came out to the meetings.[36]

In the place where they held a service, hearts were stirred by God's power, and the Holy Spirit moved among the people and many miracles of healing took place. Many of the new converts took a clear stand for Christ, even in the face of persecution and the raving of the heathen priests and witch doctors.

In another large mountain town, with many surrounding villages, God gave Vanderbout and local workers a marvellous six days of meetings. Hundreds came from all different directions and filled the town market place to hear the gospel. For most of them, it was the first time in their lives to hear the gospel message. Vanderbout recognized this was exactly what Christ came into the world to do: to minister with power, to save the lost and to heal the sick.[37]

Miracles continually took place. An old man was carried by his friends from another village to attend the meeting. He was all bent over, and could walk only on his hands and feet like an animal. The man instantly stood up and walked. He gave his life to Christ, and began to preach to the people with excitement. He did not go back to his home, but stayed at the meeting place, telling everybody what God had done for him. He almost joined the evangelistic team to share his testimony.[38]

Many sick people experienced the healing power of God. An old man who had been deaf in both ears since he was a young man was instantly healed in the service. There was an old woman who had been blind in both eyes since 1942. She was also healed, with complete recovery of sight in both eyes. One paralyzed woman spent most of one Sunday morning crawling to attend the service. God instantly healed her, and she stood and walked across the ground to the platform to testify of God's healing power. An old, blind woman attended one meeting, at her granddaughter's encouragement. God instantly opened both of her eyes, and she pointed out the lights and different objects. People in the meetings were amazed by such incidents and glorified the name of Jesus Christ.[39] As a result of these meetings, believers in a community, numbering 12,000 people, wanted to build a church. In another village, known for their head-hunting practices, men had already started to build their church. Vanderbout opened a short-term Bible school, as well as special classes for the new converts.

Establishing an Orphanage

In the course of her ministry, Vanderbout noted that there were many babies suffering from sicknesses and malnutrition. Opening an orphanage was not part of her original plan, but she did it out of necessity. As Vanderbout became

---

[36] Elva Vanderbout, 'Here and There', *Midland Courier*, Jan. 26, 1958, 3.

[37] Elva Vanderbout, 'Salvation-Healing Meetings in Mountain Province', *Missionary Challenge*, Feb. 1958, 2.

[38] Vanderbout, 'Salvation-Healing Meetings in Mountain Province', 3.

[39] Vanderbout, 'Salvation-Healing Meetings in Mountain Province', 3.

known as the white missionary who had a loving and caring heart for the mountain people, believers and even non-believers sought her help for their needs, including problems with their children's sicknesses.[40] There was a baby who was badly crippled and needed an operation almost immediately, without it he would die. The mother of this baby desperately searched for a way to save her baby's life. The only person in whom the mother put her trust was the missionary, and she pleaded with Vanderbout for help. The next morning Vanderbout took the baby to Baguio City to her doctor. After carefully examining the baby, the doctor said that the baby's foot would be all right after five weeks of treatment. As the doctor had estimated, the baby's foot indeed recovered, exactly after five weeks of treatment. Even though he had a slight limp, it was hardly noticed.[41] Vanderbout's sacrificial love for a little soul touched the hearts of many people, who then turned to the Lord as news spread through the villages that such supernatural works of the Lord frequently took place.

Vanderbout met more sick children, and orphans and children who did not have places to live who were also brought to her. A number of children, who would certainly have died were kept alive, because the missionary took them in and nursed them back to health.

Vanderbout began to feel the pressing need of erecting a building to accommodate the children continually coming to her, and she began to pray. Her prayers were answered through the Rotary Club of Baguio City. They gave a generous offering for the building of an orphanage, and in 1953, the new building was quickly finished to allow children to live in it. The orphanage was named Bethesda Children's Home.[42] Undoubtedly, more children were added after the opening of the orphanage.

The orphanage also brought many more works as well as exotic experiences to Vanderbout. An unwanted young girl had been put in a cage by her father and stepmother, in the village of Bua. She had been in there for many days; in fact, no one could tell how long. Her body was deformed and her hair covered her face like a jungle creature. The child also had an oversized chest, a clubfoot, a paralyzed right hand, and very big eyes. The child was brought to Vanderbout. The missionary's compassion and love saved the life of this little child.

Another of Vanderbout's testimonies was about twin boys who were abandoned by their parents. People in the mountains believed that twins were bad luck, so these boys were left on the floor of a hut with only a thin blanket. Two of Vanderbout's workers found the twin boys and carried them out. When they reached Tuding, the children were already blue and near death. However,

---

[40] *GMTM*, 121-22.
[41] *GMTM*, 121-22.
[42] *GMTM*, 130-31.

their lives were saved. Vanderbout then had twenty-two children in her orphanage.[43]

Another unusual story was how a twelve-year old boy from the city jail in Baguio became a family member at the Bethesda Children's Home. This boy was repeatedly in and out of the city jail; and one time he spent five years in Muntinlupa National Prison, a maximum-security facility near Manila. While this boy was there, he indeed was touched by someone who shared the transforming message of Jesus, and he gave his life to the Lord. When he came back to Bethesda Children's Home, he was a new person and he even sought to go to Luzon Bible Institute out of his own desire. This boy grew to become a wonderful minister for God's Kingdom.[44]

The first child to enter Bethesda Children's Home was Gervacio Tavera, Jr., who later became an ordained minister. He also served as one of the most capable interpreters in the Philippines. Many of the children from the orphanage became marvellous Christians and Christian workers.[45]

For Vanderbout, opening Bethesda Children's Home was not just to establish an institution for social work as other people did; nor was it merely a place for homeless, sick and poor children to live together. Vanderbout's intention for the Home was to help children grow in the living Word of God, so that they would become messengers of Christ.

Development of Children's Ministry

Vanderbout continued to develop her ministry to children. She envisioned children as future workers for the mountain ministry, and she organized various activities with this in mind. One of them was a kid's camp in 1961. Since the concept of a kid's camp was unfamiliar to local churches in the country, her kid's camp became the very first one in the Philippines. About seventy children came, and thirty-five of them received Christ as their personal Saviour. About ten were baptized in the Holy Spirit. During the camp, unusual experiences for the children included seeing visions of the Lord, feeling the sweet presence of God during the time of prayer, and so on. God mightily poured out His Spirit upon these precious boys and girls, and kid's camp served as an evangelistic avenue.[46]

She also organized the first Missionettes Club at the Tuding church, another first in the Philippines. Its purpose was to train all children and teenagers to be missionaries in the future. Children were intensively trained to memorize Bible verses to prepare themselves to be soldiers of Christ. In the opening ceremony, an impressive candlelight and pledge-signing service was conducted for twenty-two Missionettes and thirteen Junior Missionettes. District officers of the Philippine Assemblies of God and a number of sectional presbyters attended the

---

[43] Vanderbout, 'A Work of Mercy in the Philippines', 3.
[44] Vanderbout, Letter (Aug. 1961).
[45] Vanderbout, 'Report on Trip to the Alsados', 1.
[46] Vanderbout, Letter (Aug. 1961).

service.[47] Each girl proudly wore her Missionette uniform, consisting of a navy blue skirt, white blouse, and light blue vest. The Missionette emblem was embroidered on the left side of the vest.

Occasionally Vanderbout had special prayer meetings during which children and teenagers were spiritually saturated or bathed in prayer. A number of children were baptized with the Holy Spirit. Later, many of these children became beautiful Christian ministers.

Training Young People

In 1962, as Vanderbout continued with the mountain ministry, she came to feel the need for more help in reaching out to more people with the gospel. She also felt a need for training young native Christians to reach their own people. As a result of her work among the young people, four from the mountain provinces graduated from a Bible School and became pioneer workers. Others graduated and became evangelists in remote and deep areas of the mountains where no Assemblies of God workers had ever penetrated. These young people were enthusiastic to hike through dense forests to preach the gospel, in spite of difficulties and danger.[48]

When Vanderbout started the mountain work, there were only two national ministers for the mountain ministry. But ten years later, twenty-two full-time national workers were involved in the mountain ministry, and fifteen young people were ready to go to Bible school to prepare themselves for future ministry. The mountain ministry continued through the young ministers with vitality and abundant fruits.

Analysis of Vanderbout's Ministry

In the preceding discussion, I have presented narrative accounts of Vanderbout's ministry among the mountain tribes of the northern Philippines. Next, it will be appropriate to analyze her ministry and highlight a few of the approaches and elements she used, which made her ministry successful and in turn made it possible for her to spread the gospel among the Kankana-ey tribe. These may also exemplify the uniqueness of Pentecostal approaches to mission.

Empowered Ministry

As a Pentecostal, she approached the animistic people with the message and demonstration of God's power. As delineated above, God's power was revealed in various forms such as healing, casting out demons, and others. This approach was indeed efficacious to bring animists to Christ, because there are similarities in the world views of Pentecostals and animistic people. For instance, the

---

[47] Charlotte Schumitsch, 'Missionettes in the Philippines', *Pentecostal Evangel*, March 25, 1962, 1.

[48] Vanderbout, Newsletter (May 1957).

animists believe that their gods and the spirits of the deceased obtain power to heal the sick, bless their lives and/or bring curses. Thus, when any one is sick, people implore the spirit to cure the sick through the help of a mediator (priest). The people perceive that common people are not able to communicate with the gods or spirits, but only the priest can.

Therefore, when the power of God was demonstrated among them, they immediately recognized that the power of the Christian God was greater than that of their gods. This provided a turning point in their religious understanding. Soon their allegiance shifted from their traditional deities to Christ. This change of allegiance also resulted in an economic benefit. Often, they offered many sacrifices until the sick got healed. Due to the high cost of sacrificial animals, such as native pigs, they had to borrow money from their relatives or friends in order to prepare a sacrifice. Receiving healing from God without offering material sacrifices was something new to them. From my own later observations, I believe the spiritual power encounter was the key to winning souls to Christ.

Recognition of a Woman in Leadership

In a tribal culture, it is difficult to accept a woman as a leader of the village or community, as man's authority has been prevalent. When there are special occasions such as a funeral, a wedding ceremony or a ritual practice, males are expected to lead. Throughout my experience in close association with them, males dominate in every leadership position.

In such a cultural setting, it was radical that a woman missionary would become an accepted and effective leading figure. Circumstances were not favourable for her, as Vanderbout had settled in a notorious place (Tuding) where even national ministers were reluctant to live among and associate with the people there. However, her determination to live in such a place perhaps showed the native leaders her potential capability to work for their people. Probably this attitude and determination drew the attention of native pastors and it led them to assist her in ministry. Secondly, the presence of spiritual gifts also attracted many to follow her. As described above, what happened in Vanderbout's ministry reflected the Pentecostal ministry in the West and, furthermore, the early church as depicted in the Book of Acts. When the apostles were empowered, they performed diverse miracles. Those who witnessed such extraordinary works of the Lord naturally accepted the apostles' preaching. Some even followed the apostles and they, themselves, became instruments of God's mission. The apostles naturally became leading figures, and in this sense, the presence of the spiritual gifts enhanced their leadership, although the gifts might not have served to bring them into leadership positions. Thirdly, I assume that Vanderbout's zeal and great ambition to spread the gospel among the mountain villages moved the hearts of national pastors to support and follow her. She was bold enough to invade pagan territories where the people had never known Christ. It was tremendously difficult for a foreign religion or gospel to break into the air-tight traditions. Her adamant will to fulfil the divine task made her a self-made leader.

Assistance of National Ministry Team

Throughout her ministry, the assistance she received from a national ministry team was vital. There were sincere and committed pastors to assist her work. Certainly, she was not able to perfectly speak the native dialect, and this meant that she needed someone who could interpret her preaching, counselling and serious conversations with church members. Furthermore, she was not familiar with geography and trails in the mountain. This presumes that someone had to accompany her wherever she went. The role of the ministry team might not have been significant, but it was essential. A few national pastors who were trained under her spiritual leadership experienced the empowerment of the Holy Spirit and later were able to exercise spiritual gifts in their own ministries.

Leadership Training

Vanderbout, in the midst of busy activities, did not neglect to train local leaders. She sent prominent and ambitious young Christians to the Bible school for future ministry in the mountains. As indicated above, she saw the need of having national ministers join her ministry. She alone could not hike to many communities in the mountain region; besides, she was an outsider who lived in the Philippines always with the possibility of having to leave the country when it would become necessary. It is also plausible to assume that the national pastors were far more effective in their ministry among their own people with their vernacular language. Needless to say, the training of national leadership was a marvellous investment for the tribal ministry. We have to wonder what would have happened if there had not been trained leaders? Would there have been successful church planting and evangelism by Vanderbout alone?

Why are Power Manifestations not as Intensive Now as Before?

This question has been in my mind for a long time. Although Pentecostals have experienced a paradigm-shift in their belief that our practices are no longer effective in certain contexts, thus, we need new additions; we have to remember that power ministry has been one of the essential distinctives of Pentecostals. It is not a problem to add more practices into it, such as social action or social transformation, but it is important to keep our proud gift. If we lose it in order to have other additions, this is not the right way to honour our gift.

The Book of Acts clearly shows how the apostles spread the Word of God. The two vital elements in their ministry were power encounter and teaching the Word. Not only did these two significant factors appear in Acts, but Jesus also used them in his ministry. I notice that when the gospel was first launched among the Kankana-eys, they experienced tremendous power in almost all the revival meetings and even regular services. However, as the years have gone by, the power does not manifest the way it once did, although in their hearts the people still want it. Is the motivation of their prayers not right? Do they no longer eagerly pray? I will examine possible answers to these questions, based on my own observations and evaluations, as follows:

Many years later, established churches in the mountains pioneered house churches, and they started with Bible study. This method was easy and handy to gather people into a group. It was also effective in terms of drawing non-believers, especially young people. They would not only study the Word of God, but they would also have a time of fellowship. Perhaps this was a place where the opposite sex became interested in each other. And, this should be a good way to begin a pioneering church. However, they lacked power ministry such as it was during the ministry of Elva Vanderbout: praying intensely for healing of the sick and earnestly exercising spiritual gifts. As mentioned above, the effective mission that the apostles fulfilled was through both teaching the Word and power manifestation. It is not that one is needed more than the other, but both must be incorporated in Pentecostal mission. If the gospel is for all Christian groups, both should be applied in mission work as well.

In later years the tribal people were able to have the benefit of medications more than ever before through various ways. During the earliest period of the Pentecostal ministry, there was no way to receive such a benefit. Perhaps it became available through missionaries (mission medical teams) or transportation, which could now take people to a nearby small city where they were possibly able to get what medications they needed. I am not negative towards taking medication. I believe it is what God gave us to use for healing. But having the benefit of modernization should not be interpreted as being all right to lose the other benefit of healing. I personally have a strong desire for Pentecostals to experience divine healing, whether we have medicine available or not; and, at the same time, using medicine is advisable because God uses it also. But, our belief for healing should continue to be practiced in times of need.

Materialism with technology also crept into almost every place in one way or another. City people became more materialistic due to more exposure to material worldly goods, than perhaps others who were in more remote areas. But, this also happened in the lives of the tribal people. Some villages have electricity which enables them to have a TV set, VCR player to watch movies at home, and other modern conveniences. They sense that being rich is good, because they can enjoy their lives. And some young people do not mind leaving their families to go abroad to make money through various job involvements; even wives leave family behind in order to be a domestic helper and they will send money back home out of their salary.

Having a comfortable lifestyle is very important to all humans, because we are physical beings. However, tasting physical comforts may cause us to tend to want to be more into that and to neglect our spiritual life. I observe that some Pentecostal church services on Sunday seem to be more Anglican in their worship style: very calm, too orderly, and they have no time of prayer for healing. I do not mean that it is influenced by the people's lifestyle; however, it reminds me of a city church service that is punctual and goes according to time, rather than events. My earnest desire is to bring back our typical Pentecostal worship style: more alive and dynamic and in particular, praying for healing and meeting needs, so that the people may experience God's power in a tangible way.

Concluding Remarks

Many villages were entirely transformed because of Vanderbout's dedicated work. She fearlessly entered pagan villages and head-hunters'[49] communities. She preached the message of Christ straightforwardly; and she trusted that God would protect her from harm.[50] Her ministry among the Kankana-ey tribe and other tribes impacted many communities and individuals. Memories and records of her life and ministry were not properly collected, and her powerful ministry deserves much serious study.

The desire of her heart to live and minister in the mountains was fulfilled, and with it came the satisfaction of knowing that her work was not in vain. Surely she will receive her crown in heaven, and her work will not go unnoticed by the Lord.

From the beginning of Vanderbout's ministry in 1947 to 1959, eight churches were constructed under her direction. There were over one hundred preaching points throughout various mountain areas, and she reached more than one hundred villages with the gospel. In 1955, she started to work in villages of the head-hunting mountain people. This is considered as the singular accomplishment of her thirteen years of ministry in the mountains.[51] In addition to the ministry of evangelism and church planting, Vanderbout did not neglect training devoted young people. As a result of her labour, approximately one hundred young people from the mountains went to Bible schools, and a majority of them became ministers to reach their own people. Out of necessity, Vanderbout opened an orphanage to care for poor, neglected and abandoned children. She took care of fifteen of the original children of the orphanage.[52]

However, after thirteen years of mountain ministry as an Assemblies of God missionary, she left the denomination to begin a new ministry, but still in the same mountain region. She married the national pastor, Juan Soriano, who had accompanied her to assist her in ministry. After leaving the Assemblies of God, she and her husband continued to work in evangelism, church planting and training mountain leaders in a new setting, without associating with any denomination.

---

[49] Head-hunting was prevalent among the mountain tribal people during those days. In particular, the Bontok tribe practiced it exceedingly. Headhunting had two purposes: one was to take revenge, and the other was to show a man's bravery to the one he loved.

[50] Vanderbout, 'A Westward Move', 3.

[51] Vanderbout, A Personal Letter to the Foreign Missions Department (Aug. 1959).

[52] Vanderbout, Letter (Aug. 1959).

Vanderbout's marriage was not acceptable to the Department of Foreign Missions of the Assemblies of God, U.S.A. The policy was the same for all female missionaries. As a consequence, in 1966 Vanderbout resigned her missionary position, both from the Department of Foreign Missions and the Philippine General Council of the Assemblies of God.[53]

It is impossible to present a complete picture of Vanderbout's life in this one short study. But it is evident that from the day of her arrival in the Philippines, the Lord directed her life, and she ceaselessly laboured to fulfil His will. I assume that there was much more accomplished by Vanderbout, prior to her leaving the Assemblies of God, than what is known through written records which have survived today. The ministry that Vanderbout established among the mountain people is continuing on through the dedicated young people who were trained by her.

---

[53] Elva Vanderbout, A Personal Letter to the Foreign Missions Department (Feb. 17, 1966).

Chapter 12

Power Encounter

Introduction

Demonology, long neglected by traditional theologians, has suddenly become a hotly discussed issue in theological discussions, especially since the rise of the Third Wave in the 1980s. The subject has inherent elements of controversy, and that is the primary reason why the recent discussions make many churches uneasy. This uneasiness is especially obvious among western Christians as well as mission-initiated churches in the non-western world. This has much to do with the western worldview which collapses the world of angels, demons and miracles into the two-tier worldview, the supernatural and the natural worlds. Theology, as a product of their worldview, naturally ignores or 'demythologizes' this part. The Asian church, like other 'Southern' Christianity, received this 'sanitized' version of Christianity, and has struggled to live between its traditional worldview, which incidentally is holistic and much closer to the biblical worldview, and the transmitted 'Christian' theology, for some time. This distancing is further reinforced by unconscious attempts to sever emotional ties with the old 'superstitious' and 'demonic' religious traditions. As a result, any discussion of angels and demons, or demonization, healing, and miracles, for the most part, has been deliberately avoided in our theological reflection.

The growth and maturity of the Southern church and its theological thinkers has constantly challenged the validity of such western theology in the southern context. This reassessment of the 'received' theology is in fact one side of the same coin; the other is their earnest desire to construct theologies that are relevant to the local context. The theological minds in the south did not overlook the fact that locally 'initiated' versions of Christianity, be it African Initiated Churches, Chinese house church Christians, or even doctrinally questionable groups in Japan, always includes the activities of spiritual beings in their theological framework. This may prove that the 'primitive' form of Christianity, including the early church, inevitably embraces the worldview that is closer to the non-western ones.

One outcome of this tension is the creation of what is called 'split-level' Christianity, where the theological system provides no room for the supernatural world in their Christian beliefs and practices. Their allegiance is divided: for 'higher religious' concerns such as sins, salvation and others, the church provides answers; for 'lower religious' concerns such as dreams, healing, and others, the old and indigenous religion provides answers. This shows that we have lived with a one-sided or handicapped version of Christianity for quite some time. This dilemma also presents a new possibility for Southern theological minds to revisit the biblical evidence through a new set of lenses of worldview, and this will shed new light on the study of demonology.

This present study is an overview in nature to explore the locus of Pentecostalism in the wider context of demonological discussion. The study traces three major groups within the Pentecostal movement and their contribution to the present discussion: classical Pentecostalism and the Third Wave. The concluding section summarizes Pentecostal contributions to theology, missiology and practical ministry. Also, challenging areas where further attention is required are discussed in each area, to avoid foreseeable risk and to offer a positive contribution to the future of Christian theology and ministry. As an Asian Pentecostal, I certainly explore this topic from an Asian perspective.

It is helpful to remember that Pentecostalism, although when popularly traced has its origin in North America, has sufficient Southern characteristics. Walter Hollenweger coined the idea of the 'black oral root' to express this Southernness as its worldview, theological expression and spirituality.[1]

Pentecostals and Demons

Classical Pentecostals

The rise of Pentecostalism, also often called Apostolic Christianity in the early twentieth century, has usually been traced back to North America, either to Charles Parham of Topeka, Kansas in 1901 or more popularly to William J. Seymour of Azusa Street Mission in Los Angeles in 1906-1909. The recent celebration of the Azusa Centennial in 2006 demonstrates that the scholarly opinion has been tilted more towards the latter. However, recent 'discoveries' of several similar movements in different parts of the world around the turn of the century have added weight to the argument that Pentecostalism did not have one source, but several.[2] Most likely this discussion will continue in the future.

Often identified as denominational Pentecostals (later called 'classical Pentecostals'), in the first half of the twentieth century particularly in the West, Pentecostals were relatively easy to identify. Early Pentecostals trace their theological and spiritual roots to the holiness movement of North America in the

---

[1] Walter J. Hollenweger, *Pentecostalism: Origins and Developments Worldwide* (Peabody, MA: Hendrickson, 1997), 18, considers this the most important characteristic of Pentecostalism.

[2] E.g., Hwa Yung, 'Endued with Power: The Pentecostal-Charismatic Renewal and the Asian Church in the Twenty-first Century, *AJPS* 6:1 (2003), 63-82.

nineteenth century. In fact, expressions such as 'baptism in the Holy Spirit', which have become characteristically Pentecostal, were already used among holiness believers throughout camp meetings.

HEALING MOVEMENT

One important continuity between the Pentecostal and the holiness movements was the belief and practice of divine healing. Healing ministry was so popular that healing homes were established throughout the United States. Following on after its holiness predecessor, Pentecostals established a theological position that healing is based on atonement. For example, the Declaration of Faith of Church of God (Cleveland, TN) has, 'Divine healing is provided for all in the atonement'.[3] The Assemblies of God, USA has a more elaborate statement, but the belief is identical: 'WE BELIEVE...Divine Healing of the Sick is a Privilege for Christians Today and is provided for in Christ's atonement (His sacrificial death on the cross for our sins)'.[4] Its full elaboration of this doctrine is found in a position paper entitled, 'Divine Healing: an Integral Part of the Gospel'.[5] This official document approved by its General Presbytery further identifies its scriptural base as Isaiah 53:4, 5; Matthew 8:16, 17; and James 5:14-16. Classical Pentecostals throughout the world subscribe to similar doctrinal positions.

An excellent example is found in David Yonggi Cho's ministry on January 14, 2007. In his second Sunday service, as usual for several decades of his ministry, he administered a healing ministry.[6] The title of his sermon was 'Through God's Grace', and his message was based on the parable of the prodigal son. He stressed the overwhelming grace of the Father in receiving his wayward son. Regardless of his sermon title, healing ministry is a regular part of his worship. The summary of this healing session may be close to what follows, although some words are borrowed from his January 21, 2007 service:

> If you come with disease and life's problem, please stand. If you are sick, please lay your hand upon the suffering part of your body. If you come with a life's problem, lay your hand on your heart. Let us pray, 'God, our father, we come to you with our weakness and disease. Through the work of your son on the cross, please heal every disease. Please heal them now, heal them now, heal them now. All kinds of disease and suffering, I command you in the name of Jesus Nazareth to loose your grip right now. Leave now, leave now, leave now. Enemy and demon, I command you to

---

[3] 'Church of God Declaration of Faith' (http://www.churchofgod.cc/about/ declaration_of_faith.cfm, 2005), accessed on Jan. 19, 2006.
[4] '16 Fundamental Truths of the Assemblies of God' (http://ag.org/top/Beliefs/ Statement_of_Fundamental_Truths/sft_short.cfm, 2006), accessed on Jan. 19, 2007.
[5] 'Divine Healing: an Integral Part of the Gospel' (http://ag.org/top/Beliefs/ Position_Papers/pp_4184_healing.cfm, 2006), accessed on Jan. 19, 2007.
[6] The entire worship can be viewed (in Korean, but sometimes with English text) at http://www.fgtv.com/fgtv/player/PF_vod_player_email_new.asp?CODE=0&SECT=1a_ 1&TSECT=m1&DATA=1a070121l&VTITLE=&VBODY=, accessed on Jan. 27, 2007.

leave, leave, leave. Lord, through your work on the cross through the stripes, bring healing to us, we plead. Do your miracle now. As you promised in 3 John 2, prosper every spirit, blessing everything they do and make everyone strong. In Jesus' name we pray. Amen'. God is healing now. He is performing miracles now.

The healing ministry did not end there. Before the conclusion of the worship with his benediction, he pronounced various healings which took place in that service. He does not specify how he obtained this information, but in other services, he said, 'God spoke to me...' or 'I see...'. This implies the exercise of a spiritual gift, either a word of knowledge, or a simple revelation by God to him. His declaration was as follows:

God says that a deal was healed. A brain tumour was healed. Someone with a neck problem has been healed. An intestinal cancer was healed. A muscle pain is healed. Someone with back pain has been healed. An acute skin disease has been cleaned. God want to heal you. Trust him.

This is only a small window into Pentecostal healing practices. However, this provides a useful scene to bring our discussion forward.

Before we move on, it is important to clarify that healing is not the most distinct feature of classical Pentecostalism. Its main theological emphasis is on the empowering aspect of what is called 'baptism in the Holy Spirit'. As almost all the classical Pentecostal groups subscribe to speaking in tongues as the initial and physical evidence of Spirit baptism, the movement has been more popularly known for this feature, which is rather unfortunate.

THEOLOGICAL BELIEFS

The Pentecostal practice of divine healing, considered from their theological orientation, is well illustrated in the example above, and can be characterized in several ways. However, our discussion is specifically focused on Pentecostal demonology and its pastoral response.

First of all, Pentecostal faith has brought a new Christian worldview and has made a significant impact on world Christianity. As discussed in various places, the birth of the Pentecostal movement was also the rise of a Christian holistic worldview, which takes the supernatural world seriously. Only with such a worldview milieu, is expectation for healing and miracles possible. Therefore, the presence or absence of such has much to do with the worldview within which Christian theology and ministry operates. That classical Pentecostalism traces its origin to the West is significant in that the worldview of the New Testament church was holistic, and this makes the movement a restorational kind.

Secondly, expressed through Pentecostal healing practices, at least some cases of disease are attributed to the work of evil spirits or demons. Determining the cause of a disease is difficult. However, using the New Testament evidence, Pentecostals tend to significantly overemphasize the role of demons in causing disease and disturbances to God's work. Albeit the lack of theological sophistication, Pentecostals have acknowledged the presence and potent of demons and evil spirits. In Pentecostal minds, they are active in human lives, causing diseases, misfortunes and distractions against God's work. Particularly, mental illness is easily attributed to a demonic activity, and power encounter, in its true sense, occurs in Pentecostal life. Some Pentecostal-Charismatics suggest that the spirit which causes a disease actually has the same disease, that is, the spirit causing blindness is blind itself. As seen in Cho's prayer, Pentecostals often personify diseases and unfavourable circumstances such as poverty. They are called and commanded out in the name of Jesus, just as demons are treated.

Third, in confronting demons, Pentecostal theology shows a strong Christo-centric orientation, especially the image of *Christus Victor*. Except in the mention of the gift of healing, there is a surprisingly limited role of the Holy Spirit in this belief. In Pentecostal beliefs and practices, healing is anchored in the atoning work of Christ on the cross. The Assemblies of God (USA) position paper established a doctrine of 'healing in atonement', arguing for the possibility of healing for every case. However, popular belief among people in the pew is clear in acknowledging the problem of such a tight doctrine, and they have learned to live with the tension. Although not always articulated, the present life in an eschatology tension appears to have provided a satisfactory explanation.[7] Christo-centrism is also expressed in the most popular phrase which Pentecostals use in their prayers, 'In the name of Jesus...'. They take the teachings of Jesus seriously, e.g., 'they will place their hands on sick people, and they will get well' (Mark 16:18).

Fourth, consequently Pentecostals maintain the attitude of an upper hand, with their prayers full of commands and rebukes. Pentecostals seldom 'discuss' with the evil spirit during an exorcism event. It is based on at least two assumptions: 1) demons are liars, and 2) Christians already have authority as God's children to rebuke and command them. Having said that, it is important that in practice the exorcist is required to have spiritual insight (e.g., the gift of discernment), or spiritual power through prayer and fasting. Taking Matthew 9:29 (taking one textual tradition!) seriously, Pentecostals have taken prayer and fasting as the primary way to confront the devil.[8] Combining a few rites, such as

---

[7] Only recently have studies among Pentecostals begun to appear on 'non-healing'. E.g., Erlinda Reyes, 'A Theological Framework for Non-healing in the Pentecostal Perspective' (ThM thesis, Asia Pacific Theological Seminary, 2007); also on the issue of suffering, see Veli-Matti Karkkainen, 'Theology of the Cross: A Stumbling Block to Pentecostal/Charismatic Spirituality?' (150-63) and William W. Menzies, 'Reflection on Suffering: A Pentecostal Perspective' (141-49), in *The Spirit and Spirituality: Essays in Honour of Russell P. Spittler*, eds. Wonsuk Ma and Robert P. Menzies (London: T & T Clark, 2004).

[8] For example, see ch. 16 for a Korean example. Similarly, Harold R. Cole, 'A Model of Contextualized Deliverance Ministry: A Case Study: The Cordillera Rehabilitation Centre', *JAM* 5:2 (2003), 259-273.

anointing with oil and laying on of hands, sometimes spiritual confrontation is a long battle, even if surety of victory is not questioned.

Fifth, how Pentecostals have formulated their demonology is revealed only implicitly in various anecdotes of healing and exorcism. Although much attention is given to demonic activities in individuals, the concept of territorial spirits is imbedded in their holistic worldview. Never developed to its sophistication, certain places are known for the presence of demonic influence. Also implicitly recognized are different degrees of demonic control over individuals or places. Therefore, 'demon possession', in Pentecostal minds, represents only the worse case of demonic control.

Third Wave

The rise of the Third Wave, or the 3.0 version of Pentecostalism after the classical Pentecostal and Charismatic movements or Neo-Pentecostalism, traces its genesis in the first part of the 1980s. John Wimber was a catalyst in transforming the worldviews of C. Peter Wagner and Charles Kraft of Fuller Theological Seminary through the controversial course, 'Signs and Wonders'. However, both Kraft and Wagner had struggled with what is called 'powerless' Christianity in their own missionary settings, and they were in a deep quest for an answer.

However, the significant contribution of the Third Wave in the discussion of demonology, especially among the Evangelical circles, cannot be underestimated.[9] Although diversity of Third Wave thinking is expanding rather than decreasing, from the very beginning, the main focus of this branch of Pentecostalism has been power encounter. It is generally agreed that power encounter is broadly divided into two categories: lower (or personal or ground) level power counter and higher (or strategic or cosmic) level power encounter.[10] Some related concepts to the former are inner healing, deliverance and inter-generational curses, while the latter is expressed through ideas such as territorial spirits, spiritual mapping and prayer walks. This has a strong missiological implication. Between Kraft and Wagner, the former seems to have produced more reflections on the lower level power encounter, while the latter on the strategic level power encounter, especially with his House of Prayer for the Nations in Colorado Springs, Colorado.

Unlike classical Pentecostals, its predecessors, the leaders of the Third Wave are articulate popular teachers and writers, and authors such as C. Peter Wagner,

---

[9] The authors, more practitioners than traditional theologians, have developed demonological discussions as they construct theories and practices of 'power encounters' with evil spirits.

[10] Varying categories have been used among Third Wave thinkers. E.g., Charles H. Kraft, 'Contemporary Trends in the Treatment of Spiritual Conflict', in *Deliver Us from Evil: An Uneasy Frontier in Christian Mission*, eds. A. Scott Moreau, et al. (Monrovia: MARC, 2002), 177-202.

Charles Kraft, Neil Anderson, and others have produced countless books on theories and practices of power encounter, and new, the restoration of the apostolic and prophetic offices, and others. Now loosely networked among what is called 'post-denominational churches' in North America and elsewhere, books and conferences have proven to be the most effective tools in propagating Third Wave beliefs.[11]

Considering the diversity at hand, my reflection is around Kraft. I found him to be a respectable scholar with a deep pastoral and missional commitment. Also I have a better acquaintance with his way of power encounter, through his teaching (with his ministry session before the class) and his helpful publications.

SPIRITUAL WARFARE

Earlier, I analyzed Kraft's theory and practice of deliverance from a classical Pentecostal perspective. In that study, I described a ministry session he conducted years ago, and readers are encouraged to review the material.[12] I found one of his earlier books entitled *Christianity with Power* extremely helpful and useful.[13] As the title suggests, he has an extensive discussion of western worldview which provided a conceptual framework for Christian theology and practices. This 'defective' worldview which simply does not have a proper category for 'supernaturals' has inevitably affected Christian ministry for centuries, without proper handling of demons. As a cultural anthropologist, Kraft takes the reader onto a path to the new discovery of Christian life with power and authority. Well woven with his own testimonies, the book shows how one can overcome the typical evangelical limitations in reaching the scripture as presented, especially in our holistic worldview.

Equally helpful and sound is his later chapters on conducting a power ministry. His principles are biblically based and theologically sound. Although his discussion leaves several topics for further exploration and discussion, his theoretical presentation and practical steps presented in this particular book are highly recommended for Christian workers. The 'sensitive' topics include the possibility of Christians being demonized, inter-generational curses and also demonic influence attached to objects.

This book represents the author's long journey which 'only just begun'.[14] His subsequent writings acquire sophistication in theory and practice. My earlier analysis represents a more developed stage, which now includes controversial

---

[11] Kraft, 'Contemporary Trends', 177-202 provides a valuable summary of the development of Third Wave thoughts, while 182-87 present details of publications and conferences.

[12] Wonsuk Ma, 'A "First Waver" Looks at the "Third Wave": A Pentecostal Reflection on Charles Kraft's Power Encounter Terminology', *Pneuma* 19:2 (1997), 189-206.

[13] Charles H. Kraft, *Christianity With Power: Your Worldview and Your Experience of the Supernatural* (Ann Arbor, MI: Servant, 1988; reprint by Manila, Philippines: OMF Literature, 1990).

[14] Kraft, *Christianity With Power*, 177.

concepts such as the 'inner child', increasing the pain level to force demons to reveal information or to induce their obedience, cutting their arms and legs, commanding the demons to jump into a box, and others.[15]

Now, with strategic or cosmic level spiritual warfare, several names are readily identified: C. Peter Wagner,[16] Cindy Jacobs, John Dawson and others. Kraft proposes three categories of spirits involved: 1) 'territorial spirits' that are assigned to various levels of territories including nations, cities, and regions; 2) 'religion/institutional spirits' that are 'assigned to religions and organisations', and 3) 'vice spirits' that have to do with vices.[17] Using Argentina as the most popular case, Kraft summarizes a common strategy:

> ...Cosmic-level warfare approaches the breaking of the power of cosmic-level rats through dealing with cosmic-level garbage. This garbage includes sin on the part of human populations (both present and in the past); the breaking of satanic power gained through past dedications and/or sinful use of a place; disunity and competition among spiritual leaders; and neglect of godly use of a place or territory.[18]

This cosmic level spiritual warfare employs approaches such as repentance, spiritual mapping and intercessory prayer walk. The most obvious confrontation, however, occurs when the 'strong man' is identified and 'bound'. To break satanic power, originally gained through religious dedication or sinful use of a territory, warfare prayer is the key and the ultimate goal is evangelism.

ANALYSIS

There are several features which became evident during the last two decades of development.

The first is its pragmatic approach. Motivated by pastoral and missionary concerns, Third Wave demonology has been shaped through the combination of biblical evidence and a good dose of experience-based theories. In fairness, this is not the fault of Third Wavers at all. The scripture does not provide sufficient data to construct a totally biblical demonology. The problem is that most of the biblical 'holes' are now sometimes filled by less than biblical concepts. For example, the problematic idea of an 'inner child' has no biblical support whatsoever, although it is argued that the world of psychology has long used a

---

[15] Charles H. Kraft, 'Dealing with Demonization', in Charles H. Kraft, Tom White, Ed Murphy et al, *Behind the Enemy Lines: An Advanced Guide to Spiritual Warfare* (Ann Arbor, MI: Vine Books, 1994), 79-120 (114). See also Ma, 'A 'First Waver' Looks', 191-92.

[16] E.g., C. Peter Wagner, 'Twenty-one Questions', in *Behind the Enemy Lines*, 123-47, presents his answers to critical questions raised to the 'four-year old' discipline of strategic power encounter.

[17] Kraft, 'Contemporary Trends', 189.

[18] Kraft, 'Contemporary Trends', 193.

similar concept. It is important to remember that not everything that allegedly works among Christians is biblical, such as the imaginary cage and punishment schemes.

Now, this brings a serious theological challenge: what is the limit of theological inquiry, especially when the scripture does not provide necessary evidence? This problem has been with us throughout Christian history, just as Judaism invented many new interpretations of the law during the exilic and post-exilic era. It is quite clear that the church is to live with certain theological ambiguity, and yet pastoral concerns often push the limit. Personally, I have benefited significantly from Third Wave emphases on, among others, the believer's inherent authority to confront evil power and the believer's responsibility to remove sin (garbage) rather than the devil (rat).

The second is the role of experience in theological construction. It is a little different from the case of classical Pentecostals who were criticized for building their Pneumatology based on experience. Often serious charges are made that much of experiential data comes from demons themselves who are by nature liars. Third Wavers would argue that they were forced to provide valuable information. Another example is the general consensus among Third Wave thinkers that believers can be 'demonized'. Although the new term proposes a broader spectrum of demonic influence than demon-possession, there is theological homework to be done. There is no doubt that experience can be a valuable resource for theologization; yet it should come under the judgment of the Scriptures.

The third is the 'sensational' tendency of some concepts. For example, the theology of inter-generational curses has raised an unusual interest among Korean Christians and often sessions are held to 'cancel' such curses through inner healing. By insensitive leading, sometimes family conflicts arise with serious pastoral and ethical questions.

The fundamental question, however, is whether the amount of attention given to evil spirits is theologically healthy. This is a matter of theological balance. In a theological framework where the devil somehow takes the centre of Christian attention (as we saw in several places), a distorted theology is formed where 'God's whole redemptive activity is narrowed to destroying the devil'.[19] In a way, classical Pentecostals also share this unhealthy view as they tend to view the Spirit's empowerment (e.g., Acts 1:8) in terms of spiritual confrontations. Now again to be fair to Third Wave leaders, it is certain that such disproportionate attention to demons is never by their design. Kraft once said that he did not look for demons, but he cast them out when they were found.

The fourth is the controversy around territorial spirits. This is a hermeneutical issue as to whether one can build a theological pattern based on limited scriptural

---

[19] Carolyn Denise Baker and Frank D. Macchia, 'Created Spirit Beings', in *Systematic Theology: A Pentecostal Perspective*, ed. Stanley M. Horton (Springfield, MO: Logion Press, 1994), 179-213 (207).

evidence. As commonly known, the concept of territorial spirits is based on Daniel 10:13, where the messenger of God was 'detained' by the 'prince of the kingdom of Persia' for twenty-one days before Michael the archangel came, so he could bring God's message to Daniel. Here the 'prince' is interpreted as the evil spirit assigned to Persia, and it tried to hinder the work of God. Third Wave thinkers tend to believe that this is a pattern to be applied to every region and political system. In the absence of sufficient biblical support, such a notion appears to be overly simplistic and speculative.[20]

Promises and Challenges

Obviously the development of demonology in the twentieth century through the emergence of various streams of Pentecostalism has brought both contributions and challenges.

Theological

The first area is theology. This short survey has illustrated how Pentecostal Christianity has contributed to this problematic and yet important part of Christian theology, which has long been ignored. The demonstration of God's power through the Spirit of God over the evil ones has been the typical sign of the presence of God's kingdom (Matt. 12:28). The general absence of such an important feature of the kingdom of God may be attributed to the ignorance of demonology all together. Thus, the rise of Pentecostalism has renewed the church's awareness of this aspect of theology and pastoral ministry.

Yet, its theological challenge remains unchanged. The inherent difficulty, which any theologian would face in the study of demonology, comes from various directions and some of them have already been introduced. Also, with its explosive nature, demonology must be 'handled with care', within the full context of theology, particularly taking into consideration eschatology, Christology, and ecclesiology. Demonology poses a serious theological dilemma between the ultimate victory of Christ over Satan through his death and resurrection and the reality and potent of the principalities and powers in this age. The New Testament does not deny this tension. Even a slight tilt towards the power of the atonement will result in the 'kingdom now' notion with its triumphalistic attitude. This, while rightly maintaining Christ as the centre of theology, may result in the inadvertent ignorance of pastoral reality which people in the pews experience daily. Typical western evangelicals represent such a position. On the other hand, any tilt towards the reality and potent of evil forces will move the centre of theology away from the atoning work of Christ thus reducing the Christian life into a struggle with evil spirits. Pastoral sensitivity and commitment cannot justify such a shift in theological attention. The very eschatological nature of our present life should provide the needed balance.

---

[20] Baker and Macchia, 'Created Spirit Beings', 200.

In general, a well thought out attention to demonology is essential. Barth may mean this when he advised to 'give only a quick, sharp glance to the area of demonology'.[21] He warned against granting any more attention to demons than deserved. Early Pentecostals were known for blaming demons for things they never did, and I am afraid that Third Wavers have not improved the situation.

Missiological

Classical Pentecostals were not intentional in linking their healing and exorcism with evangelism and world mission. Considering the unmistakable pattern of Jesus' proclamation of the presence of God's kingdom through healing and exorcism, Pentecostals generally failed to articulate their missiological implication. However, their missionary work regularly included 'signs and wonders'. It is to the Third Wave's credit that spiritual warfare, particularly strategic level one, was specifically motivated by and applied to evangelism and mission.

Their influence along with other Pentecostal leaders was rightly exercised in the process of the Lausanne movement, so that the 1989 Manila Manifesto now includes more sharply articulated spiritual warfare language. Particularly noted are two paragraphs under Section 5, God the Evangelist:

All evangelism involves spiritual warfare with the principalities and powers of evil, in which only spiritual weapons can prevail, especially the Word and the Spirit, with prayer. We therefore call on all Christian people to be diligent in their prayers both for the renewal of the church and for the evangelization of the world.

Although the miracles of Jesus were special, being signs of his Messiahship and anticipations of his perfect kingdom when all nature will be subject to him, we have no liberty to place limits on the power of the living Creator today. We reject both the scepticism which denies miracles and the presumption which demands them, both the timidity which shrinks from the fullness of the Spirit and the triumphalism which shrinks from the weakness in which Christ's power is made perfect.[22]

As part of this Lausanne process, a study group was formed and its several conferences resulted in a very useful book.[23] Particularly valuable is the 'Deliver Us from Evil Consultation Statement',[24] which presents the current state of affairs. This is a 'balanced' document because it reflects views of varying persuasions, including western and non-western as well as advocates (such as Third Wavers) and more 'reserved' ones. It also takes the subject matter

---

[21] Karl Barth, *Church Dogmatics*, III/III, 519.
[22] The Lausanne Committee for World Evangelization, 'The Manila Manifesto' (http://www.lausanne.org/Brix?pageID=12894), accessed on Dec. 30, 2006.
[23] A. Scott Moreau, et. al., eds. *Deliver Us from Evil: An Uneasy Frontier in Christian Mission* (Monrovia, CA: MARC, 2002).
[24] Moreau, *Deliver Us from Evil*, xvii-xxviii.

positively, while issuing due cautions against any excess. Equally useful is the lead chapter by an Asian theologian.[25]

A serious challenge rises in a non-western context where some of the newly developed Third Wave ideas are presented. It is one thing to preach them within the West where spiritual beings were totally ignored; but, it is an entirely different case when they are introduced to a cultural context which is already crowded with myriads of good and evil spirits. Kraft's contention that demons can be 'attached' to an object which can affect the occupants of a building sounds more like an animistic belief than a biblical one.[26] Years ago, a prominent South African Pentecostal church formally adopted a position to denounce the belief in inter-generational curses, although it was enthusiastically adopted by many African indigenous churches. So, with its many theological 'holes', demonology has slippery edges as it interacts with a local culture.

Pastoral

Demonology has deep pastoral implications. Pentecostalism has brought a significantly added dimension to Christian ministry. Now much responsibility is in the hands of local pastors to bring a balanced demonology to the actual life setting.

There are two things included in my personal appeal to my fellow Pentecostals. The first is to pay attention to the community dimension of power encounter. Traditionally, healing has been completely a personal matter. As ministry takes place in a local church, it is then essential to explore the community dimension of such experiences. Non-western churches may suggest ways to involve and also benefit the community of faith through healing ministry. In many small village settings in Asia, the healing experience of an individual is often jointly owned by the entire community; in fact, such is often the case for church planting.[27]

Another dilemma that any Pentecostal pastor faces is the problem of long-term suffering. As much as there is a tension between Christ's victory and the devil's reality today, any long-term suffering by a faithful believer cannot simply be explained by a theological declaration, such as healing in the atonement. If salvation has been achieved through the atoning work of Christ, and yet, the full realization of it still awaits the appearance of the Lord, so may

[25] Hwa Yung, 'A Systematic Theology that Recognises the Demonic', in *Deliver Us from Evil*, 3-27.
[26] Edward Rommen, ed., *Spiritual Power and Missions: Raising the Issues*, EMSS 3 (Pasadena, CA: William Carey Library, 1995) devoted the entire discussion to spiritual warfare. Robert J. Priest, Thomas Campbell, and Bradford A. Mullen, 'Missiological Syncretism: The New Animistic Paradigm', 9-87, lodge a strong criticism again the emerging theories and practices of power encounter. See Charles H. Kraft, "Christian Animism' or God-Given Authority?' 88-136 for his response.
[27] For example, J. Ma, *When the Spirit Meets the Spirit* reports numerous cases of healing which resulted in church planting in the Northern Philippines.

healing. Pentecostals are challenged to continue to preach the good news of divine healing, but also to minister to those who are living with suffering. How to minister to HIV/AIDS infected individuals is a case in point. Recently the Commission of World Mission and Evangelism of the World Council of Churches proposed two concepts, 'cure' and 'healing'. Healing ministry, then, may be much broader than just bringing a cure. Victory over infirmity and disability through the grace of God, even if the actual cure is never experienced, may be a more theologically desirable goal of healing ministry. Also to be revisited is the controversial argument of the demonization of believers.

Within the Pentecostal family, we can learn much from each other. Thus, as I did once, an open dialogue between different streams of Pentecostalism will benefit one another. With the explosive growth of indigenous Pentecostal groups, including Pentecostals who do not think they are, a gracious offering of established Pentecostal theologians would help them to articulate their beliefs. Chinese house church networks are in my mind. It is, however, critically important, in the course of such an exchange, that the helping hands do not insist on their theological discourses and categories. Rather, their job is to help the others to discover their God-given spiritual and theological gifts. With the widespread of Pentecostal-charismatic beliefs and practices among Asian churches, how can we Asians formulate demonology that is theologically balanced and yet contextually and pastorally sensitive?

Chapter 13

Women in Mission

Introduction

The day of Pentecost was customarily celebrated only by Jewish males. However, both men and women experienced the outpouring of the Holy Spirit on that day (Acts 2). Peter's preaching from Joel 2:28-29 is that 'sons and daughters' would prophesy, and this has since been the key encouragement for women in Christian ministry. This was particularly true for those with roots in the nineteenth century Holiness movement.[1]

Pentecostals strongly believe in the notion of the call of God; and both married and unmarried women have worked in various ministry settings primarily to fulfil their sense of calling. They work as church planters, preachers, counsellors, teachers and doctors in far-off corners of the world. Their God-given gifts and empowerment are used for particular purposes and tasks, and this sense of divine call is more significant than qualifications set by institutions and mission organisations.

In local ministry settings, women are also used effectively. Some women have had enormous influence on churches, schools, and prayer mountains (in Korea). Women work hard with their distinctive spiritual gifts and strong commitment. However, Asian women in general have often been deprived of their calling and their potential, because Asian culture has commonly failed to recognize the capability of women in leadership roles, both in society and the church. Although there have been some changes in women's' working roles due to global influence, recognition of women is still minimal.

In this chapter, I will discuss several critical women's issues arising in Asia, women's involvement in mission in the field, and ministry in a local setting.

Reflection on Personal Experience

While becoming a working team as a couple, I experienced a rather uncomfortable change. Korean culture expects a pastor's wife to be active at

---

[1] Barbara Cavaness, 'God Calling: Women in Assemblies of God Mission', *Pneuma: The Journal of the Society for Pentecostal Studies* 16:1 (1994), 49-62.

home, but not in ministry. However, once we were in the mission field, both husband and wife were expected to be active. I had to push myself hard so that I would not remain as an 'indoor mama', just doing household chores. Although I had to push myself, I could not grasp just how far I should go and how much I should do. If I went too far, people might criticize me; on the other hand, if I remained as a typical Asian woman, and kept quiet, I would never be anything more than a housewife. I made a decision to stretch myself as much as I could within a given opportunity. In particular, our ministry among the Kankana-ey tribe has helped me to see new horizons for a woman's role in God's Kingdom.

A historical study of the Assemblies of God mission among the tribal groups of people in the mountains in northern Luzon in the Philippines reports an interesting truth that the initial ministry among the Kankana-ey tribe was started by a single widow missionary from America, together with a few local leaders.[2] Until she began her mission in the mountains, no missionaries or local ministers of the denomination had attempted mountain ministry. Elva Vanderbout reached this tribal people with the distinctive Christian message of God's power. Through the gospel of divine power and its manifestation, churches were built and the work was effectively carried out. Her deep devotion to spread the gospel was remarkable and resulted in many souls being brought to Christ.

Through this study, I would like to strongly encourage Asian women to find their unique self-identity as Christian women. Many Asian women tend to keep themselves within the home or in other limited areas, and I also encourage Asian women to liberate themselves from this unjustifiably restricted perspective.

Women of the Bible in Ministry

Deborah is an outstanding woman leader in the Old Testament. Judges 4:1-15 notes a story of conquest through the leadership of Deborah. This narrative is about Israel in combat with Canaan. They are understood to be a sturdy nation with a strong military.[3] The Israelites were, for a long period of time, brutally exploited by the Canaanites. Unbearable persecution from the Canaanites finally caused the Israelites to implore the help of God (Judges 1-3). The brave Judge Deborah, the woman who led Israel during this time, determined to do something by battling with Canaan. Deborah commanded Barak, son of Abinoam, to get ten thousand men of Naphtali and Zebulun and direct them to Mount Tabor. A fascinating fact in this description is the human plot incorporated in God's strategy (v. 7). Deborah said, from what she heard from God, 'I will lure Sisera, the commander of Jabin's army, with his chariots and his troops to the Kishon River and give him into your hands'. Deborah revealed her tremendous faith, bravery and wittiness, all of which enabled Barak to succeed. She ascertained for

---

[2] Julie Ma, 'Elva Vanderbout: A Woman Pioneer of Pentecostal Mission among Igorots', *JAM* 3:1 (2001), 121-40. See also ch. 11.

[3] Arthur E. Cundall, *Judges and Ruth* (Downers Grove, IL: InterVarsity Press, 1968), 88.

herself, and Barak, the fact of God's victory upon her nation.[4] Deborah ordered Barak, 'Go! This is the day the Lord has given Sisera into your hands; has not the Lord gone ahead of you?'. As Deborah prophesied, God routed Sisera, the commander of Jabin's army of Canaan, and all his chariots and army. Sisera deserted his chariot and darted away on foot (vv. 14-15).

Deborah's leadership was recognized in the battle with Canaan. Her wisdom was used for the battle and to bring about the victory. Surely God was with his people and fought for them.

In the New Testament, other women, who did not necessarily occupy major positions, were magnificently used by God to complete his purpose. Women who followed the Lord during his ministry witnessed the final moments of his death.[5] Matthew 27:55 records the account of women who followed Jesus from Galilee to care for his needs: they are Mary Magdalene, Mary the mother of James and Joses, and the mother of Zebedee (v. 56). These women never left the tomb where the body of Jesus was placed. This shows their heart and love for the Lord, even against fear from cultural expectations and the guards. Matthew 28:5-7 notes, 'The angel said to the women, "Do not be afraid, for I know that you are looking for Jesus, who was crucified. He is not here; he has risen, as he said"'. Then, the angel commissioned the women to move promptly to Galilee and report to the disciples, (v.7) who were in fear that the Lord had not risen from the dead. With great joy, the women went on their way to Galilee and they encountered Jesus. He gave them the same identical order as the angel, to go to Galilee and tell his disciples that he would appear to them (v. 10).

These women became the messengers who brought the good news of the resurrection of Jesus to the disciples. Although the women never spent very much time with Christ, they proved that their faith in him was much stronger than the disciples and they were used amazingly in the final moments.

Women's Issues in Asia

I will highlight a few issues, out of many, in this section.

The Degeneration of Women

In some countries in Asia, women are dehumanized. Although women are offered more opportunities in society and are better treated in the new century, the old traditional attitude toward women still persists. Women are not properly considered and recognized for their role in society and churches. Many decades ago, women were victims of government, military and society oppression. One particular woman's organisation, Christian Conference of Asia Women's

---

[4] J. Ma, *When the Spirit Meets the Spirits*, 166.

[5] Julie Ma, 'A Missionary Challenge to Asian Pentecostals: Power Mission and Its Effect' (A Paper Presented in Asian Pentecostal Society Annual Meeting, Manila Philippines, 2000).

Concerns Consultation, held a conference in Ginowan Seminar House (also known as The Ecumenical Peach Centre), Okinawa, Japan, from June 19-25, 1992, under the watchwords, 'Called to be Peacemakers'. Participants came from Korea, Japan, Taiwan, Philippines, Hong Kong, Sri Lanka, Australia and Papua New Guinea.[6] From the many striking facts reported from this conference, I want to consider the 'issue of the dehumanization of women' in order to present an overview of women in the past.[7]

Seventy percent of the world's 13 million refugees are women. Such cruel confinement in refugee camps destroys their humanity. This kind of treatment led women to kill their babies in Okinawa in World War II; which led to the suicide of Korean 'comfort women' in Japan; which leads through poverty to the sale and theft of women and children in the Philippines, Taiwan, Thailand and other Asian countries; which leads to women being prostituted especially around military bases and for the entertainment of tourists, in many parts of the world; which leads to the perversion of children in military training; which leads to women taking up arms in Sri Lanka where they are encouraged to commit suicide if they are caught. This clearly shows that women were indeed the victims of war and were indeed heart-wounded.

How about in the current era? Are women any less the victim and are they treated better than before? My immediate response is a qualified 'Yes'. But, being better treated does not necessarily mean being treated equal with men. I am not talking from a feminist activist's viewpoint, but rather from the viewpoint of justice for all humanity.

In Vietnam, girls have less chance to benefit from an education than boys. There are primary differences in the opportunities for boys and girls who finish primary schooling to proceed on to government secondary schools. Places are normally rationed by examination, and frequently the girls have lower chances due to their poor performance on the exam. The primary reason for this is that the girls may be spending far more time than boys working for household resources.[8]

In 1955, Malaysia formulated the Employment Act which is beneficial to workers.[9] This is the core legislation that governs the function of all 'labour relations'. Some areas apply in an equal manner to men and women, such as contracts of service, salary, break time, amount of working time, holidays, annual leave, sick leave, and so on.[10] Certain aspects of this provision, however, are unfavourable to female workers. Against stipulations in the Act, female

---

[6] Jeanne Hayes, *Sowing the Grains of Peace: A Resource Handbook for Building Peace* (Okinawa, Japan: Northeast Asia Subregional Women's Consultation Ginowan Seminar, June 1992), 1.

[7] *Sowing the Grains of Peace*, 33.

[8] Margaret McDonald, *Women in Development: Viet Nam* (Manila: ADB, 1995), 43.

[9] Aminah Ahmad, *Women in Malaysia* (Manila: ADB, 1998), 12.

[10] Ahmad, *Women in Malaysia*, 12.

employees are paid lower wages compared to male workers, for doing an equal amount of labour. 'Women in the private sector are subject to wage discrimination as compared to their male counterparts'.[11] In the public sector, women are given the same pay for the same amount of labour. A policy has now been developed which ensures that Malaysian women are given growing opportunities to participate in the national growth of the country in areas of the economy and work market as well as better admission to education and health.[12]

In China, women encounter unfair treatment when seeking employment. A 1997 investigation, authorized by an official newspaper for students, discovered that female graduates from colleges and universities face greater rejection rates than male graduates in the labour market. Women accounted for 34% of the graduates in 1996. However, 27 out of 42 government organisations, at a 1996 employment conference in Beijing, refused to interview female candidates. According to the Beijing Graduate Employment Consulting Centre, 'Discrimination against women is a social difficulty, which can only be resolved when social and economic standards have risen'.[13]

Women have gradually moved into a better place and are treated better than back in the 1940s. However, there needs to be more improvements in women's positions, opportunities, and recognition in society and in churches.

Violence against Women and Girls[14]

'The Universal Declaration of Human Rights' provides liberty for every individual - male or female – which is fundamental to human life.[15] For women, these rights have been violated in the following ways: sexual assault, sexual harassment, and verbal mistreatment intended to disgrace them. The use of a woman's body to sell cars and other goods makes objects of women. Moreover, scenes of rape and other violations against women are needlessly shown in films, soap operas, and comic books.[16]

Men in Korea are offered military service when they reach around the age of 19 or 20. Certain male characteristics are reshaped during the military training. The influence of Confucianism in the minds of Korean men is another factor, particularly in the valuing of women.

Sowing the Grains of Peace well depicts the attitude of men in Korea. From an early age, men receive military training and in adulthood they join the army and continue to live in a militarized society. From there they acquire militaristic

---

[11] Ahmad, *Women in Malaysia*, 12.
[12] Ahmad, *Women in Malaysia*, 4.
[13] Aminah Ahmad, *Women in the People's Republic of China* (Manila: ADB, 1998), 35.
[14] Jeanne Frances I. Illo, *Women in the Philippines* (Manila: ADB, 1997), 16.
[15] Rina David and Penny Azarcon de la Cruz, 'Towards Our Own Image: An Alternative Philippines Report on Women and Media' (Pamphlet Series No. 1, Philippines Women's Research Collective, Quezon City, Philippines 1985), 16.
[16] David and de la Cruz, 'Towards Our Own Image', 16.

values and ways of thinking and this becomes tied to the Confucius value system, which emphasizes the dominance of man over woman. They regard women as objects, with a low position, as assistants or the subdued ones. Assault and battery of wives, discriminatory treatment, low wages at work, human trafficking (kidnapping women for prostitution) sexual torture and physical violence are committed by men who are deeply influenced by militarization.[17]

Some years ago, a policeman in Korea detained a girl student and abused her sexually. In another incident, a group of policemen raped a woman. In 1980, a fresh military occurrence appeared, which was called the '35 policy'.[18] The policy aims to restrain people's awareness through sex, sports and the screen. Information relating to the use of women in the 'enjoyment industry' in South Korea demonstrates that 5% to 7.5% of the female populace (1,200,000 – 1,500,000) is drawn in. This statistic also includes the women who followed the locations of the US Army in Korea.[19]

The Philippine government's survey noted that, on average, one in every ten women has been beaten; a much smaller percentage has been pushed to engage in sex with someone. Some of the victims searched for places of help, such as the 'Women's Crisis Centre', *Lihok Pilipina* in Cebu City and in Metro Manila, and hospitals like the Philippine General Hospital.[20] It should be noted that physical and sexual exploitation is not only a problem of human rights in a society, but is also part of the economic issue. Women who work at night report incidences of broken bones or badly bruised wounds. They often hide the signs of their pain from follow workers.[21]

Children are also victims of local violence. A survey shows that from 1991-1996, 8,355 cases of child maltreatment were reported to the 'Department of Social Welfare and Development'.[22] All the victims of child abuse were girls, ages between 11 to 17 years old. More than half of the girls had been sexually abused. Thus, the victims indicated or showed symptoms of sexually transmitted diseases (STDs).[23] Most incidents of child abuse occurred at home while the

---

[17] Hayes, *Sowing the Grains of Peace*, 13.

[18] Hayes, *Sowing the Grains of Peace*, 13.

[19] Hayes, *Sowing the Grains of Peace*, 13.

[20] Illo, *Women in the Philippines*, 17.

[21] Illo, *Women in the Philippines*, 16-17.

[22] Illo, *Women in the Philippines*, 17.

[23] University of the Philippines Centre for Women's Studies and the United Nations Children's Fund (UCWS/UNICEF), 'Breaking the Silence: The Realities of Family Violence in the Philippines and Recommendations for Change' (a report undertaken by the UCWS Foundation, Inc. for Women in Development Interagency Committee Fourth Country Programme for Children, with funding assistance from the United Nations Children's Fund, 1996).

victims were alone, while parents were away for work. The majority of the perpetrators were found to be male relatives.[24]

A common form of violence affecting women is sexual abuse. They become prey to sexual exploitation by men. I have speculated on this issue and considered how long it will continue, and if there are any possible ways to minimize sexual abuse.

Less Opportunity for Education

Philippine women are fortunate to have the benefit of education. At the national level, there are virtually no gender gaps in literacy and school attendance rates, although there are regional variations. For example, about 50% of children drop out before they reach the sixth grade. Among adults, female illiteracy dramatically exceeds male illiteracy. The illiteracy problem in Mindanao can be traced back to two factors, with divergent gender effects: the peace and order problem, which has affected the school attendance of boys, and cultural prescriptions that inhibit the education of girls.[25]

As I have briefly mentioned in the previous section, women in Vietnam have few educational opportunities. Poverty is one of the main reasons why women lose their chance of schooling. There is a considerable burden on needy families in sending their children to school. Furthermore, girls in poor families experience severe disadvantages. If parents are forced to take their children out of school due to financial difficulties, they will take the girls out first rather than boys.[26]

In China, according to a survey in 1998, female school enrolment at the primary, secondary and higher education levels, as a proportion of entire enrolments from 1982-1996, showed a general increase in female enrolment over this period. However, there is still a gap between male and female enrolment, with the gap broadening as the education level increases.[27]

In some Asian countries such as Japan, Korea, Singapore, Malaysia and Hong Kong, women may have a better chance of going on to higher education, than women in Muslim countries who unfortunately, have very little opportunity to experience higher education.

Selected Asian Women in Pentecostal Ministry

There are many Asian women who have sincerely responded to a call from God. Below, I have described several outstanding women whose impact was enormous on the Pentecostal church, and beyond.

---

[24] UCWS/UNICEF, 'Today's Girl-Children: Tomorrow's Women' (an Info Kit for the launching of the Week of the Girl-Child, 1997).
[25] Illo, *Women in the Philippines*, 58.
[26] Asian Development Bank, *Poverty in Viet Nam* (Manila, Philippines: ADB, 1995), 28.
[27] Ahmad, *Women in the People's Republic of China*, 30.

Jashil Choi

Although Choi is discussed in detail in the chapter, Korean Pentecostal Spirituality: A Case Study of Jashil Choi, it would be well to briefly address her ministry in this chapter too because she is one of the rare and outstanding women in Asia, in terms of her strong commitment to the work of the Kingdom of God. Her work particularly focuses on leading small children to Christ, out of a conviction that earlier conversion is better than later conversion, in terms of building a firm spiritual foundation in a life.

WITNESSING FOR CHILDREN

Since the early days of her Bible college, Choi was extensively involved in the evangelism of children. A motivation for this ministry came from Matthew 5:16, 'Let your light shine before men, that they may see your good deeds and praise your Father in heaven'. She did not mind spending time with them, until the children felt comfortable being in her presence. Then she slowly took out the Bible and began to share stories of the gospel. These children, who grew up in her church, later became missionaries, pastors, scholars and leaders in the church. It implies that Choi had a distinctive gift for approaching little children for evangelism. This natural ability helped her to draw many of them to Christ. This example teaches me personally that child evangelism is as important as adult evangelism, perhaps in a sense more important, because the earlier conversion takes place, the more it may help a child to grow in the knowledge of the Word of God.

Her ministry was normally characterized by intense and earnest prayer. She spent more time in prayer and fasting for effective evangelism than for ministry itself. It is well known that her prayer with fasting was a significant support for church growth. However, her eager desire to win souls, particularly targeting children, was also a prominent part of her work. Of course, Yonggi Cho's charismatic leadership with a pastoral gift was a prime factor for the rapid growth of his church. But, Yonggi Cho did not hesitate to attribute this unprecedented growth primarily to Choi's spiritual insights and gifts. At that time, the church became particularly known for its healing ministry.[28]

SIGNS AND WONDERS

Laying her hand upon the sick was part of her ministry besides preaching in service. Her compassionate heart draws her to those who suffer from disease to pray for them. Her customary fasting with prayer was a strong spiritual source for power manifestation for healing. It was noted that signs and wonders occurred during prayer time, particularly in Japan where the gospel had hardly penetrated. Cho's ambition for Japan was to let people hear the good news and bring as many as possible to the gospel through a variety of means. The more she felt urged, the more she fasted with prayer. This brought an amazing result in that

---

[28] Jashil Choi, *I Was a Hallelujah Woman* (in Korean; Seoul: Seoul Books, 1978), 355-56.

many Japanese Christians had an experience of healing through her prayer. This good news was spread among churches by the word of individuals and eventually led those who critically suffered from cancer or incurable disease to Osan-ri Prayer Mountain in Korea to pray intensely with fasting for the healing touch.

Seen-ok Ahn

Seen-ok Ahn (Kim before her marriage) was born in Pyoungyang, the capitol city of North Korea, on August 22, 1924. She started attending a church in her childhood, even though her parents were not Christians. Her first ministry experience was at an orphanage, where she met her husband who took care of the orphans. As the Korean War broke out in 1950, they fled North Korea and moved to the south.[29]

EDUCATIONAL MINISTRY

In 1953 Ahn and her husband began to teach war refugee students. This soon grew into a formal Christian school in Daejon City. Now the ministry comprises six different schools in the city with approximately 8,000 students and 400 teachers.[30] While working in this ministry, God opened a door for her to receive theological training in the United States. This experience helped to broaden her perspective on educating young people.[31] The school holds chapel services on a regular basis, which enables the students to hear the Word of God and to accept Christ into their hearts. Also, the schools incorporate a Bible subject in their curriculum, which is an indirect means of evangelism among the students. In fact, many students who have graduated from the school have committed their lives to full time ministry and mission work.

PRISON MINISTRY

Ahn did not just limit herself to being involved in the educational arena, but she expanded into other works. She was involved in evangelism among prisoners for more than twenty years. She preached the Gospel to a diverse range of criminals and subsequently won many souls to Christ. Her boldness for Christ led her to auspicious places like prisons where men were dominant and she presented the

---

[29] Yeol-soo Eim, 'Pentecostalism and Public School: the case study of Rev. Dr. Seen-ok Ahn' (A paper presented in the first Asian Pentecostal Society at Four Square Seminary, DaeJun, Korea, May 21, 1999), 2.

[30] Eim, 'Pentecostalism and Public School', 3, reports specific names of the school. The names of the school are Daesung Junior High School (boys only), Daesung Girls' Junior High School, Daesung High School, Daesung Commercial Girls' High School, Sungnam Junior High School, and Sungnam Junior School (boys and girls).

[31] Department of Planning, *The Statistics of the School in 1999* (Daejon, Korea: Daesung Christian School, 1999).

good news to them as well. Working together with the Holy Spirit, the results of her ministry were over-whelming.

Ahn also pioneered a church and it grew rapidly in numbers, to the point of being the largest church among the Foursquare churches in Korea. Her spiritual life was so remarkable that when she was sixty years old, she committed herself to forty days of fasting. People around her were very concerned about her health, but she went through it well.[32] Ahn continues to exercise her spirituality in prayer and fasting, even to date.

Trinidad Seleky

Trinidad Seleky (Esperanza before marriage) was born November 6, 1922 in Pangasinan, Philippines. She was one of a few prominent women among Pentecostal churches. Seleky graduated from Bethel Bible College in 1948, Northwest College in Kirkland, Washington in 1962, and completed her Master's Degree at Fuller Theological Seminary. In fact, she was the first Filipino graduate from this seminary. The most significant contribution she made was educating and training future Asian leaders at Asia Pacific Theological Seminary. In 1967, she joined the teaching staff and served for many years in its administration. Besides teaching courses in education at the seminary, she conducted seminars, and was involved in various ministries such as vacation Bible school, youth camps, children's crusades, Sunday school curriculum development, and training Christian education workers. She has travelled all over the Philippines teaching and sharing her burden for Christian education ministry.

From 1980-87 Seleky served the Philippine General Council of the Assemblies of God as Treasurer, as well as National Director of the Sunday School Department. She liaised between the Seminary and the rest of the evangelical works in the Philippines. She also provided leadership for Philippine Association of Christian Education which developed the Doctor of Education program. In May, 1987, Seleky received a Doctor of Divinity from Southern California Theological Seminary. Her dedication to teaching and God's ministry is remarkable.[33]

D. *Virgie Cruz*

Virgie Cruz was a Filipino, born on October 5, 1930 in Paete, Laguna, Philippines. Cruz ministered as an international evangelist and was founding pastor of a large church in Manila. She conducted many evangelistic crusades in mega cities within the country and oversees. The results were immense, in that hundreds gave their lives to Christ and further committed to his service. Her dynamic message together with the work of the Holy Spirit penetrated the hearts

---

[32] Seen-ok Ahn, *Fasting Prayer* (audio tapes, Jan. 15, 1988).
[33] Lou Gomez, the President's Secretary at Asia Pacific Theological Seminary, Baguio City, Philippines, October 5, 2001, provided the information.

of the people and made them repent. Cruz was used not only in evangelism, but also in pastoral work. Her vibrant leadership caused church members to become involved in active evangelism. While the church was growing, it also expanded its ministry into diverse realms: caring for the community, helping the poor, reaching young people, and so on. Cruz influenced and challenged numerous young people during her pastoral work to become engaged in the ministry of the Gospel.

Other Women

God has used countless Asian women. For instance, in Malaysia, Susan Tang has, for more than twenty years, been planting and pastoring churches in Sabah. Her dedication to God's Kingdom has resulted in not only many converts and churches, but also countless pastors and evangelists.

Another woman, Teo Kwee Keng, has pastored a thriving church in Batu Pahat, Malaysia for fourteen years, pioneering at least four other churches in the area during that time, and serving at a number of preaching points.[34]

Norma Lam from the same country has served as a woman missionary in the Philippines, teaching at an international seminary for twelve years. While she was teaching at the seminary, she also extended herself for local mission work, together with Filipino missionaries, Anita Swartz and Adeline Ladera, who have worked together in the Ministry Development Program of the seminary. The regular mission works consist of evangelism, medical services, preaching, and teaching in mountain village churches. Her ministry extends to the Philippines, Cambodia, Indonesia, China, Malaysia (her home country), Singapore, and many other Asian countries.

Numerous Asian women serve as cross-cultural missionaries: Nora Catipon, a Filipino single missionary went to Cambodia to teach in the Bible School; another woman, Erlinda Reyes has joined an international training ministry working with missionary staff from many other countries.

In the 1960s, Maria Gomez in East Timor was called to service at a particular Island where a prison stands and various criminals were confined. She and her husband spent many years planting the seeds of the Gospel through the means of building churches and training young people. One night when they had an evening service, the Holy Spirit fell upon the congregation and people confessed their sins and great healings took place. Now the whole Island is called an Assemblies of God Island. Gomez is the current General Superintendent in East Timor.[35]

---

[34] Cavaness, 'God Calling', 49-62.
[35] Bill Snider, speaking at the Missions Emphasis Week at Asia Pacific Theological Seminary, October 10, 2001.

In Singapore, from 1950-1960, Lula Baird, Lau To Chan, Sarah Johnson and Jean Wagner were instrumental in the establishing of Grace Assembly. It is now a thriving church of nearly 1,700 parishioners.[36]

There are several other devoted women in the mountains in northern Luzon. Pynie Pacasen is one good example. She is a Kankana-ey tribal woman, who crossed a tribal boundary line and has preached the Gospel to the Kalango-ya tribe for more than ten years. She has established five congregations among the Kalango-ya tribe. Her ministry has involved hiking mountain trails for more than ten hours every week, often in heavy rain or under treacherous heat, and the mountain trails were heavily infested by Communist guerrillas for many years. Through her ministry, many young mountain people have been trained as Christian workers.

A broader perspective of Asian Pentecostal women's involvement in ministry is well summarized by Cavaness:

> Women made up 26 percent of the list of the Assemblies of God ordained and licensed ministers in Indonesia, 36 percent of the list in Malaysia, and 34 percent of the list in Singapore (totalling over 250 women). The Assemblies of God in the Philippines has a lot of women pastors and workers, and women make up about one-half (100) of the number of foreign missionaries being sent out from Singapore AG churches. The more than 130 AG Bible schools and one seminary in Asia Pacific have large contingents of female students preparing for ministry.[37]

Asian women may have received their encouragement from women missionaries, such as is seen in the case of Elva Vanderbout. Also, Ruth Breusch was a missionary to India and made a great impact on local churches, while Naomi Dowdey in Singapore founded and pastored the largest Assemblies of God church.[38] Lillian Trasher a missionary to Egypt (1910), who broke her engagement to answer God's call, served Egyptian children for twenty-five years with no furlough. When she died in 1961, she was greatly honoured by the Egyptian government for her social service, taking care of 1,400 children and widows at the orphanage in Assiout, Egypt. In fifty years she ministered to more than 20,000 children and widows.

Challenges and Conclusion

God does not call people on the basis of gender, race, abilities, education, or economic status, but calls both men and women to fulfil his work. Pentecostals assert that God endows power to those of his people who act in faith and

---

[36] Fred Abeysekera, *The History of the Assemblies of God of Singapore* (Singapore: Abundant Press, 1992), 206-13.

[37] Cavaness, 'God Calling', 59.

[38] Cavaness, 'God Calling', 58.

obedience, nothing else. David Roebuck remarks about the early stage of Pentecostal women ministers:

In almost every case discussed, a female minister significantly influenced these women's understanding of their call to ministry. Without denigrating the role of the Holy Spirit or of the significant males in their lives, the presence of a powerful female role model was remarkable.[39]

If we acknowledge that the call and empowerment of God applies to males as well as females, a woman's role in various ministries such as teaching, preaching, leadership, mission, and administration should be recognized and even encouraged without limitation. However, in churches, almost all leadership positions are taken by men, who have powerful voices for decision-making. It is interesting that in most congregations, there are more female than male members. This gender imbalance in the leadership is also common in institutions and mission organisations. It is particularly true among Asian churches, because of their male dominant culture. Thus, Christian women in Asia have more challenges to overcome.

Women should be given an opportunity for higher education through which they can develop their academic skills. According to Ruth Peever, a TESOL professor at Asia Pacific Theological Seminary, and a former missionary in China for fifteen years, who delivered a lecture on the advantages of higher education among young people, in Korea in August, 2001, her experience in China was that her doctoral degree suddenly opened many doors, especially to places that were exclusive and had a high profile, for ministry. The president of a university in China honoured her for her high academic degree. Asian women should be encouraged to strive for higher education and academic challenges for better involvement in ministry.

Women ordination is not permitted in many denominations in Asia. A simple answer from a denominational leader in Korea was, 'You'd better get married'. I personally do not have a strong desire to be ordained; however, ordination may be able to open doors for ministry that would not be available without the ordained position.

Pentecostal denominations have stood out in this socio-ecclesial culture of Asia. Although not uniform, the majority of Pentecostal denominations of Asia have ordained women for ministry. For instance, the General Councils of the Assemblies of God in countries like the Philippines, Malaysia, and Singapore have an impressive proportion of women ministers. In Korea, the number is also rapidly rising. Their achievements are especially noticeable in mission. However, when we look at their leadership role, it is still a male-dominated world.

---

[39] David G. Roebuck, 'Go and Tell My Brother?: The Waning of Women's Voices in American Pentecostalism' (a paper presented at the Twentieth Annual Meeting of the society for Pentecostal Studies, Dallas, TX, November 8-10, 1990), 18.

If Christ liberated all humanity, including women, on the cross, Pentecostals should endeavour to liberate women in every area of ministry, not just in a few selected areas like Christian education. Historically, the Pentecostal movement liberated social outcasts, like the Native Americans, women, and laity. Since we know that God called and empowered both women and men, they have to have the same opportunities to fulfil their calling.[40] I also believe that women themselves have to make an effort to improve themselves. Thus, women must encourage themselves and one another. The bottom line is that everyone, man or woman, should have a chance to fulfil their God-given calling.

---

[40] For example, Cheryl Bridges Johns, 'Pentecostals and the Praxis of Liberation: A Proposal for Subversive Theological Education', *Transformation* 11:1 (January/March, 1994), 11, notes that 'the active presence of the Holy Spirit…calls for a radical balance in the ministry of males and females, blacks and whites, rich and poor'.

Chapter 14

Santuala: Contextualisation and Syncretism

In 1565, the Roman Catholic Church launched its missions among the Igorots. Several other Christian groups, such as the Anglicans, United Church of Christ of Philippines (UCCP), and the Baptists, followed shortly after the Catholic work began. Since 1947 the Assemblies of God has concentrated on evangelism and church planting. During the past ten years, my research and ministerial experience among the Igorots has revealed that syncretistic phenomena occurred among Christians, particularly among non-Pentecostal believers. Often people attend Sunday morning service and then join in a traditional religious practice in the afternoon. This syncretistic attitude can be traced by two factors: 1) Some church leaders did not teach a distinction between cultural and religious practices. Obviously, religious rites and rituals are conveniently packaged together. Thus, some Christians consider it permissible to participate in a ritual performance. 2) Generally, churches did not teach people to make a full-pledged commitment to Christ after conversion, nor did they emphasize that a new belief in Christ replaces old beliefs. As a result, many Christians maintain a dual allegiance, practically worshipping two different (groups of) deities.

According to Paul Hiebert, syncretism takes place when the gospel is uncritically contextualized in cultural forms. In order to avoid syncretism the congregation should critically evaluate their own customs and cultural elements in the light of new biblical principles.[1]

A religious group in the mountains called *Santuala* is a good example of syncretism. This religious group has spread widely in the mountain region. The *Santuala* group has employed the Pentecostal worship style and some of the Pentecostal religious practices, such as healing and blessing. Like many other *quasi*-Christian groups, the *Santuala* share basic beliefs with traditional Christianity, such as the existence of God, the work of the Holy Spirit, healing, blessing, and undertaking missions, particularly through healing the sick.

This chapter will first briefly discuss the history of *Santuala*, tracing its establishment, spread, essential goals, specific worship forms, and beliefs. Particular attention will be given to Pentecostal worship forms that they have borrowed and developed into their own model. Although the group does not claim to be Pentecostal, their beliefs and practices include many elements that

---

[1] Paul G. Hiebert, *Anthropological Insights for Missionaries* (Grand Rapid, MI: Baker, 1985),186-87.

are generally found in Pentecostal Christian worship. Their forms of religious practices will be analyzed, and their syncretistic phenomena will be investigated to discover its possible origins. Finally, suggestions will be made to assist Pentecostal churches in preventing, or at least minimizing a tendency toward syncretism among tribal people.

Since there are practically no written records, either by *Santuala*s or researchers, data gathering took place through interviews with *Santuala* believers and several Igorot Christians who once were *Santuala* members. All of the interviewees had had many years of involvement with *Santuala*. In fact, a few of them had been in key leadership positions for many years before they turned to Christ. They now serve Him sincerely today.

The Beginning

The *Santuala* group was founded around 1950 by an Ibaloi tribal woman named Maura Balagsa, a native of Kabayan in Benguet Province who was born around 1880. She became critically ill when she was seventy years old. No doctor was able to discover the cause of her sickness, thus, no medicine could help her. Her illness kept getting worse and she reached the point of death. Because of her long illness, her family members, relatives and neighbours stopped nursing her and decided to move her to a riverside spot near the village and leave her alone there so that she could die a natural death.[2] During the rainy season the river swells and flows over and they believed that she would then be swept away by the floodwaters. However, as this final plan was underway, a Christian pastor from a church visited her and prayed for her. During his prayer, she saw a vision of herself going around to different places and preaching about Jesus and healing many sick people. Soon after this experience she was miraculously healed. The news soon spread among the mountain villages and it became a great event. The impact was particularly felt in Bito, Bagon, where she was miraculously cured.[3] Numerous sick people came to her and received her prayer for healing and many became her followers. From the 1950s to the 1970s, this religious group had great success and hundreds came to join them. The *Santuala* movement did not confine itself to one province but spread to other provinces as well. Old people and the sick were especially fascinated by unique *Santuala* practices such as seeing visions and praying for healing. The founder, Maura Balagsa, died at the age of 120. There is no doubt that she had great longevity, although she continued to fight severe illness after her initial healing.[4]

---

[2] There are six mountain provinces in Northern Luzon. Benguet Province has access both to the south, all the way to the capital city, Manila, and to the north until Kalinga, Apayao and Abra provinces

[3] Bakun is one of thirteen municipalities in Benguet Province.

[4] Interview with Luciano Calixto, a member of Lamut Assembly of God Church, La Trinidad, Benguet Province. He was converted from Santuala. I also interviewed Teodoro

Characteristics of Santuala

Many unique characteristics of *Santuala* were cultivated through the years. As briefly mentioned above, the worship styles and forms are similar to those of Pentecostals. For instance, during their services, they sing with much emotion, dance and clap their hands, see visions, and gather around the sick and pray for them. These practices are interwoven with other less Christian practices. Their official gatherings are on Fridays and Sundays when the members do not engage in any work, with meals being prepared on the previous days. This strict observance signifies their commitment to holy life and worshipping God. However, when there are special occasions such as a funeral or wedding, they also gather on these particular days.

In their services, there is neither Bible study nor a time for preaching. However, they do spend a great deal of time singing. The group does not have formal leadership during the service, but an elder or elders will be in charge of major activities. Very few members have their own Bible. If they do have one, it is perhaps considered to be a symbolic item whose function is similar to that of a small *Santo Nino*, an image of the infant Christ, which most Catholic believers carry for divine protection.

Pentecostal Features in Santuala Worship

In a typical *Santuala* worship service, the members offer three songs, each one from a traditional hymnal. It is probable that choruses have not been available to them or it could be that they refrain from using them due to their conservative orientation. When I asked why they sing only three songs in every worship service, they were not able to give me an adequate answer. It is likely that they were influenced either by the notion of the Trinity or by the prescription of their traditional native practice to offer sacrificial animals only in odd numbers.[5] According to Teodoro Gaiwen, members sing and are accompanied by people dancing for joy and gratitude for healing and blessing.[6] The dance employs various actions, such as hopping, jumping, stepping, and swinging their hands in the motion of a butterfly while turning their bodies. Singing and dancing are always combined with hand clapping by the congregation. This expressive and enthusiastic mode of worship resembles Pentecostal worship. As commonly recognized, Pentecostals freely express their emotions in bodily movements.

Gaiwen, an elder of the same church, who is a former member of Santuala. All the interviews, unless stated otherwise, took place in January 1998 in Lamut, La Trinidad, Benguet, Philippines

[5] The Kankana-eys, one of nine major tribes in Northern Luzon, kill animal(s) for sacrifice by odd number, one, three, five, seven and the like.

[6] Teodoro Ganiwen is a sincere and faithful Christian. In fact, he is in the position of an elder in Lamut Church. His parents and some relatives are active *Santuala*s. He is the only one in the family who has converted to Christianity.

Pentecostals are particularly known for their 'affective action' in their worship.[7] They never conceal their emotions when they praise God.

One of their favourite songs in worship is *Balligi* meaning 'victory', which is also favoured by Pentecostals in the region. The chorus of the song reads:

Ballige, wen balligi,	Victory, and victory,
Alleluya ken Jesus,	Hallelujah I am free,
Intedna ti balligic,	Jesus gives me victory,
Gloria, gloria alleluya,	Glory, glory Hallelujah,
Madaydayaw Naganna,[8]	He is all in all to me.

It is also apparent that some of the *Santuala* worship forms are borrowed from their native ritual practices. Dancing is one of the critical elements in the native ritual of inviting and appeasing the spirits. In fact making the motion of a butterfly by swinging the body is quite similar to an Igorot dance in a native ritual.

The next important component of *Santuala* worship is prayer. The congregation actively participates by reciting amens. Each prayer must consist of six sentences, and after each sentence the congregation responds with a loud amen. Thus, a prayer is inflexibly set in six lines to receive six amens. This formula is a unique part of *Santuala* worship. Responding with amens reflects a Pentecostal worship characteristic. Pentecostals want to affirm their prayers with verbal expressions, such as 'amen' or 'Yes, Lord!' The *Santuala* have the same desire to assure themselves of God's answer to their prayers. They call it a 'six-amen prayer'. One example of prayer is:

Thank you Lord for this day amen,
For gathering us together amen,
Bless this service amen,
Forgive us amen,
Heal us amen,
Forgive our first, second, and third ancestors' sins.
Amen.

After offering a prayer, three people go around the congregation and shake everybody's hands and pat everyone on the chest a few times. Then, three people stand at the centre of the gathering and repeat the same thing among themselves, whilst shaking hands and tapping the chest of one another.[9] This signifies the

---

[7] Margaret Poloma, *The Assemblies of God at the Crossroads* (Knoxville: University of Tennessee Press, 1989), 5.
[8] The words are in the Ilocano dialect, which is the trade language among the mountain tribes in Northern Luzon.
[9] Interview with Belina Igualdo, the pastor of Lamut Church.

heart-felt love of each member. The love of Christ is expressed more by gestures and motions rather than verbal expressions.[10]

They then sing three songs again and also recite six amens in the second prayer time. An intercessory prayer follows, just as in Pentecostal worship. They never fail to include prayer time for healing, which is also another common feature readily shared by Pentecostal churches, particularly in the mountains. Perhaps the most remarkable part of their service is when the intercessor(s) and an elder invite the sick to come to the front. After identifying the illness of a person, the intercessor earnestly asks God to touch and heal the sickness. The intercessor lays both of his hands on the head of the sick person and there is full confidence among the sick that God will speak to the intercessor as to what they should do. The sick also believe that God will answer their prayer through the intercessor.

After the intense intercessory session, every member spends time seeking visions. The *Santuala* are particularly interested in visions. They believe that God reveals desirable ways to His children through visions. This form also mirrors the Pentecostals' practice. The Pentecostals in the mountains tend to see visions during prayer. A vision is also accompanied by an interpretation. Frequently, elders of the *Santuala* see visions. Yet, this experience is not confined to certain people. Any member can see visions but not all visions are valid. The elders examine and discern the visions.

Agapita Cuyapyap, who is a long-time member of *Santuala*, has actually seen a lot of visions. In an interview, according to her, a vision is like seeing a movie or a television program where pictures move consecutively.[11] She once had a vision of a *Santuala* member who committed adultery, but was never exposed by anyone. She quietly approached that person and shared what she had seen in her vision. The person was strongly convinced by the vision. Hearing internal or audible voices is another way of receiving a divine revelation. These experiences also edify and strengthen their spiritual life.

As mentioned above, a vision always requires an interpreter. An interpreter is normally an elder who possesses the gift of interpretation. No member is expected to interpret his or her own vision, only an interpreter does this. Often the interpreter becomes very specific when he hears the vision of a sick member. It is common for the sick person to be asked to repent of his or her sin, together with their forefather's sin. Often the deliberation goes something like this, 'It is because your forefathers did not conduct a proper ritual performance, that you now have a terrible headache'. The prescription will then be something like, 'You have to confess the sin of the ancestors in four generations. Then you will be healed'. Without exception, the sick do exactly what the interpreter requires.[12]

---

[10] Interview with Gaiwen, Teodoro.

[11] Agupita Guyapyap is an elderly woman and has been devoted to *Santuala*. She is one of their prominent seers.

[12] Interview with Jenny Salipnget, a convert from *Santuala*.

Another example of a vision is that, in a vision, someone cleans a winnow, fills it with rice and gives rice to each member apart from one particular individual. The interpreter explains that the member who did not receive rice will not receive a blessing from God.[13]

Toward the end of the service, the elders go to sick people and stroke their backs. Then, they spend time singing three songs and six amens. At this time, they sing fast songs and dance in a lively way while circling around the area. Then they sing more songs, six or even nine, depending on the level of their excitement. If a person is very sick, they repeat the whole thing again.

As part of the service they dine together. They consider eating time to be important. The food has been prepared beforehand. The schedule of the meeting is decided ahead of time. After eating, they sing songs and pray with six amens again. Finally, at the end of the service, four people (instead of three) go around and shake the hands of the members again three times.

The service does not include the sharing of testimonies or preaching. The service primarily consists of brisk activities, such as the four rounds of singing, praying with six amens, prayers for healing, and seeing visions. At any meeting, these components are always present.

Pentecostal Beliefs Reflected in Santuala

God

*Santuala*s believe in the existence of God. They call upon God in their prayers and approach Him in anticipation of His power to heal and bless. Although they may not possess a sound understanding of God as revealed in the Bible and presented in traditional theology, they are assured of His mighty power. This perception is derived from their own experiences and those of other members. Empirical experience enhances their belief in God and heightens their desire to experience Him. Such experientially oriented expectation shapes their perception of the image of God. Their understanding of God is not that He is transcendental but rather that He is imminent. His presence is not aloof but nearby them. Comprehending God in such a way is extremely similar to the view of Pentecostals. Pentecostals also want to feel the Divine Presence in their daily lives.

Healing

Healing occupies a very important place in the *Santuala* life, since their founder, Maura Balagsa, had a tremendous encounter with God through healing. Her followers naturally adopted the same pattern. As mentioned above, such miraculous events became the key element in drawing people into the

---

[13] Interview with Manido Taypoc, a former member of *Santuala,* who now attends Lamut Assemblies of God Church.

movement. Thus, they invariably include lengthy prayer times for the sick in all *Santuala* services. Even the time for visions often has an unmistakable link to healing, because they often pray for the sick after seeing a healing vision of someone. Due to their deep belief in, and expectation of God's healing touch many members are involved in a so-called 'healing ministry' in various mountain regions. Details of their mission work will be discussed below. Their heavy emphasis on healing shows a resemblance to Pentecostal practices.

Blessing

Believing in God's blessing is another important element of *Santuala* belief which is considered to be almost as significant as healing. Although they do not include a time of thanksgiving in their regular service, they hold it at a separate time during special occasions. The service of thanksgiving is a great moment to recall what God has done, and to look forward to more blessings in the coming days. In this service their joy overflows with expressive body language. It definitely signifies God's abundant and unlimited blessing upon their lives. The heavy emphasis on God's blessing is undoubtedly similar to that of Pentecostals.

The Holy Spirit

The *Santuala* tend to weave their spiritual practices with a belief in the power of the Holy Spirit. They believe that healing takes place when the Holy Spirit moves through the faith of believers. When they are involved in a healing mission through a visionary experience, they believe in the healing power of the Holy Spirit. They believe that the Spirit brings healing and works miracles in specific circumstances. They exercise their faith when they are in far-flung areas to pray for the sick. *Santuala*s, thus, believe in the ministry of the Holy Spirit through human agents.

Two Specific Services

Throughout the interviews, the interviewees highlighted two particular services: thanksgiving and funerals. For significant thankful occasions, members want to exhibit their gratitude to God through worship. The funeral service is another important service. Their practices indicate the combination of both Pentecostal and traditional religious practices.

Thanksgiving Service

For special occasions like weddings or harvest, a thanksgiving service is held and the people involved are required to bring offerings. They are grateful to God for the granting of His favour. At the same time, people anticipate divine blessing. According to their understanding, God's blessing comes only through worship services with offerings. This clearly reflects their old religious practices associated with animism.

As usual, prior to the commencement of the worship service, an elder sees a vision. As indicated earlier, seeing a vision is necessary before any religious activity begins and because of this they set aside a time for seeing visions, so that they will know God's divine will and then earn His favour. Upon seeing a vision, they set a date, time, and place to prepare for the worship. This implies that the service should not be held in the usual places, for example, a member's home. A garden belonging to either the person or the couple who offer this service, is preferred.[14]

In the case of a wedding service an elder is primarily in charge of conducting the whole affair, with the assistance of a few assigned members. First of all, prayer is offered and then they dance around the sacrificial animal. Their form of dance is a lot like a pagan ritual and non-believers would have difficulty discerning between Christian worship and the age-old native sacrifice ritual called *canao*.[15] Following the dance they kill a pig. Some aspects of their procedure for butchering the animal are certainly borrowed from pagan ritual practices.

Having killed the pig, the *Santuala* elder holds a cup of water and offers another prayer of thanksgiving and pours the water on the spot of blood. Then they singe the butchered pig and boil it in a big pot. They again offer another prayer, which is the last part of the service. After the service, the members feel free to move around and converse with one another. When the meat is cooked, it is served to the people.[16] The Thanksgiving service is, thus, important in two aspects: expressing their thanks to and expecting a blessing from God.

Funeral Service

Commonly, the *Santuala* hold a three-day funeral service; however, this can be stretched to nine days. The age of the deceased person affects the length of the funeral period. If the person was old, they would have more days than if they were young. The funeral service is almost identical with other services. They offer songs related to a funeral theme, and prayer for the salvation of the dead and comfort for the family. Although *Santuala*s do not give emphasis to earthly salvation, they firmly believe in life after death. Their belief system includes the notion of hell and heaven.

There is no prescribed number of animals one should butcher. If the family possesses many animals, they kill in quantity, but if they are poor they may not

---

[14] Interview with Teodoro Gaiwen.

[15] *Canao* is a pagan religious practice held for various thanksgiving occasions and healing purposes. It also serves to consolidate the Igorot community through the fellowship involved in the ritual performance. Usually when the *canao* is held, the host invites his or her village friends, neighbours and distant relatives. Therefore, through this occasion, they discover their individual identity as mountain people.

[16] Interview with Teodoro Gaiwen.

kill any. The procedure for killing the animal is similar to that of the Thanksgiving service.[17]

Nine days after burial of the dead person, the family is allowed to go to the field and work. But during the first nine-day period the members of the family just rest and stay at home. On the ninth day, they kill an animal and again invite neighbours to dine with them. Perhaps this is to express the family's gratitude to those who extended help during the funeral. Nine months after the funeral, they hold another service for the dead. This also requires the butchering of a pig or pigs. The elder offers a prayer for the dead and also for the family members for forgiveness of their sins. Praying for forgiveness is commonly included, regardless of whether the family is considered to be guilty or not. In the ninth year after the death, the family of the deceased gathers together for the remembrance of the dead. After this, no more ritual is required.

Ritual Practices of the Mountain People

Since I have frequently observed traditional religious practices, I would like to discuss *Santuala* ritual practices in the light of native religious practices. The procedure for their rituals is strictly prescribed. When the mountain people perform rituals, they first offer a prayer to the ancestral spirits, with only a priest having authority to pray. They then butcher sacrificial animal(s). While the animal is still alive, assigned butchers prick the heart of the animals with sharp bamboo sticks. Due to pain, the animal screams at the top of its voice. When the shriek comes down, and the animal has little strength left, people cut parts of the animal's body. Animals are butchered in odd numbers, one, three, five, seven and so on. The family that offers a sacrifice always consults with a village priest for the date, place, time, and the number of animals to butcher. The number of sacrificial animals increases by two from the previous ritual.

There are two main occasions for which people perform rituals: thanksgiving and healing. Thus, rituals are performed during the time of harvest and illness. One tribal group named Ifugao holds the Thanksgiving ritual more frequently than do other tribal groups. Of course, other tribes are not exceptional. Ifugaos are rice planters and have cultivated tremendous rice terraces, which even attract tourists. There are two major phases: the time of preparation, starting from August to March; and the time of harvest from April to July. In every phase, from seedling to harvest, they perform rituals for blessing.

The healing ritual is performed when a family member is sick. In an animistic environment, malevolent spirits are believed to cause the sickness. I hear quite often that they believe that sometimes a terrible dream makes a person ill. The sick person is taken to the priest for an examination of the dream and for the prescription of a ritual for the cure. Often the priest blames the illness on their

---

[17] Interview with Tino Altaki, who was a *Santuala* for a few decades and has now become the head leader of the regional group.

negligence in caring for their ancestors. According to their beliefs, offering a sacrifice is the best way to appease an offended spirit. Venerating deceased ancestors is one of the most important roles that they must fulfil and this can only be done through prescribed rituals.

Missionary Works

Missionary work often takes place because of a vision, the primary mode being that of receiving a divine revelation among *Santualas*. Since the founder was miraculously healed, healing has become a critical part of their religious life. Indeed, all members are required to be involved in the healing mission. However, prior to missionary work, the elder needs to see a vision and be directed accordingly. First of all, destiny is decided. For instance, if an elder sees a vision of a pipe that is connected to Baguio City,[18] he immediately interprets that a member should go to Baguio to look for the sick and pray for their healing. If the elder sees a particular mountain village in his vision, he commissions a few members to go there. Sometimes, it is not always easy to discover the sick, but they often find him or her by inquiring around. If any member refuses to accept a task given by their elder, a divine punishment is expected and it usually happens.

Strangely enough, when members pray for the sick, healing takes place. This phenomenon has apparently attracted many people to the group, and thus it has grown in numbers. Normally, a new *Santuala* group is established in a different community through a missionary pilgrimage. The healing experience is a profound testimony among the animists. In their belief system, spirits have the power to cure them. The people follow the deity who demonstrates the strongest power for healing. Thus, the missionary journey becomes the hallmark of the *Santuala* group. It is the only explicit missionary activity considered highly significant.

Concept of Forms and Meanings in General

The study shows that the *Santuala* group has combined both the Pentecostal and native ritual forms and their meanings. Since different forms are used in their worship, I felt it necessary to analyze them. But before doing that, I would like to first examine the diverse results from various forms and meanings employed in

---

[18] Baguio is located a mile high above sea level. This city was developed as the summer capital and resort area for American military personnel, since the American colonization of the Philippines in 1898. Certain developed areas like Camp John Hay were continually used and were under the control of the American military to serve the same purpose. It was handed over to the Philippine government when the American soldiers were completely evacuated from the Philippines in the early 1990s. Baguio is the only chartered city in the mountain region of Luzon. During the Easter and Christmas breaks, in particular, the city is flooded with hundreds of people.

Santuala worship. According to Charles Kraft, there are four types of results one can expect.[19]

Forms	Meanings	Result
Indigenous	Indigenous	No Change: Traditional Religion
Foreign	Indigenous	Syncretistic Church
Foreign	Foreign	Dominated Church (a kind of syncretism)
Indigenous	Christian	Biblical Christianity

The only ideal contextualization of the gospel is the combination of indigenous forms with Christian meanings. However, it is critical that indigenous forms are carefully selected and analyzed before putting them into an actual practice. Often churches are encouraged and challenged to use traditional musical instruments, art forms, dance and other forms in worship, but there is a strong hesitancy among Evangelical Christians to use these. This caution prevails among local pastors and missionaries today.

Tribal churches are no exception to this contextualization rule. Members of a local church may not understand how to bring the two forms together unless a church leader gives proper teaching. Syncretism occurs when the pastor probably lacks either knowledge of it, or cannot creatively utilize native forms to communicate the Christian message. Such negligence naturally leads to confusion or even unguarded syncretism.

For example, in one communion service a church used native rice wine, or *tapey,* in place of grape juice. For native mountain people, *tapey* is an important element for certain occasions such as cultural festivals, fellowship among clans, and performance of rituals. Culture varies and in some provinces it is used strictly for ritual performance, but in other provinces it is allowed for non-religious occasions. When this church used *tapey,* some members were not able to distinguish between participating in the Lord's table and attending a native ritual performance. This clearly indicates that without proper teaching, the utilization of a cultural form often associated with native religious practices can result in a rather confusing or even destructive effect on Christians.

Analysis of Forms and Meanings of the Santuala

As noted in the beginning of this study, the *Santuala* group came into being through a unique event. In contrast to an average Christian church, there are no trained or ordained pastors, proper programs, or teaching in the Santuala group. The group seems to be highly interested in spontaneous and visible external practices in spite of the other standard doctrines they subscribe to, such as the

---

[19] Charles Kraft, *Anthropology for Christian Witness* (Maryknoll, NY: Orbis books, 1996), 158.

existence of God and His almighty power. At the time the *Santuala* came into being, if there had been a spiritual leader who was able to carefully guide the spiritual life of members, the result would not have been what we see today. As a result of this lack of proper guidance, the *Santuala* group created its own model of contextualization by combining both indigenous and Pentecostal worship styles. This resulted in a rather unique syncretistic religion:

Forms	Meanings	Result
Non-Christian ritual form	Pentecostal worship meaning	Syncretism
Pentecostal worship form	Non-Christian ritual meaning	Syncretism

Above, I have already discussed the Pentecostal elements found in *Santuala* worship. In this section, it is necessary to make a detailed analysis. Some worship features common to both groups will be examined. First of all, singing songs from hymnals accompanied by dancing may be found in both *Santuala* and Pentecostal worship. However, the movement of the body in *Santuala* worship is exactly like the pagan ritual dance. Prayer is offered in ways commonly shared by Pentecostals, yet the *Santuala* have developed their own style by reiterating 'amen' after each sentence of prayers. Responding to a prayer with 'amen' is also a common feature in Pentecostal worship. This expression affirms the prayer and, thus, the congregation participates in the prayer itself.

Praying for the sick by the laying on of hands is exactly like the Pentecostals. It is done with earnest anticipation that God will perform an awesome miracle for the sick one. However, praying for the forgiveness of ancestors' sins is not found in Pentecostal worship, although recently, the Third Wave practices inner healing in a similar manner. I remember a Malaysian pastor sharing that a pastor taught his members to pray for the sins of their ancestors, so that their souls would be saved. This resembles the Roman Catholic teaching that the souls of ancestors are in purgatory and will be transferred to heaven through the prayers of their descendants for the forgiveness of the sins they committed while they were on the earth. In the pagan ritual performance, the priest offers prayers to the spirits, often confessing the sins they committed in the world.[20]

Seeing visions is a unique component in the *Santuala*'s worship. For them seeing a vision is the only way to discover the will of divinity. It is true that Pentecostals also expect to see a vision or hear the voice of the Spirit during their prayer time, but not as part of a worship service. This experience has many positive effects causing believers to be drawn closer to God. In Pentecostalism it never overrides the Word, which is the ultimate revelation of God. The interpretation of visions is extremely subjective and they cannot be self-generated.

Tapping one's chest is a way of showing affection and love among *Santuala* members. Although Pentecostals may not exactly share this particular motion,

---

[20] Interview with Tino Altaki, April 1998.

external bodily expression is well suited to both the Pentecostal style and a native cultural form. This could be an equivalent to hugging or touching each other's shoulders among Western Christians. Had this particular motion been brought to a specific culture by missionaries along with the gospel, it may well have been blended with the existing culture. In fact, tribal cultures provide much space to express their affection and warm feelings. They freely show friendship and kindness to the strangers and guests. Giving is one of their favourite signs of love. Although some tribes, such as the Bontoc and Isneg[21] cruelly practiced headhunting until around the turn of the century, the tribes basically possess pleasant characteristics. This might have been reflected in worship through tapping their chest.

Another important element in *Santuala* worship is eating food during the service. Many churches in the mountains have a fellowship meal after the service. Any available food is offered for the table. It is observed that after ritual practices, villagers who attend also eat together. Meat, rice and drinks are prepared for the guests. It is possible that such cultural religious practices have influenced their worship.

Hand-shaking in *Santuala* worship is an expression of showing gladness to one another. Through this bodily contact, the level of intimacy may be increased. Shaking hands is not unusual among the Pentecostals, although it is done either early in the service or afterwards. *Santuala* missionary work is done only through healing, with the possibility of the establishment of a new *Santuala* congregation. This seems to be their primary commission. The whole process, such as the place and time for this ministry, is revealed only through a vision. This practice is unique to the *Santuala*.

This analytical study reveals that the *Santuala* group practices syncretism by mixing the worship styles of different groups. This has resulted in their unique worship style. Three forms practiced in their worship are noted below. The two main sources for *Santuala* worship are Pentecostal and traditional practices, and they can be seen below:

Pentecostal Worship	
Forms	Meanings
Singing songs	Praising God
Dancing	Praising God
Praying to God for the sick	Healing
Seeing visions	Discovering divine will and direction
Saying amen in prayer	Confirming that He will answer prayers

Native Religious Practices

---

[21] The Bonctoc tribe inhabits Mountain Province, which is one of six provinces, and the Isneg tribe dwells in Apayao Province.

Forms	Meanings
Dancing in a form of ritual dance	Calling and appeasing spirits
Praying for forgiveness of ancestral sins	Concern for the ancestors
Butchering animals	Sacrifices

In the case of *Santuala*, the two source traditions were appropriated and then developed into the following syncretistic system:

Santuala Religious Practices	
Forms	Meanings
Tapping each member's chest	Showing love and affection
Eating together as part of the service	Sharing community life
Shaking hands in the service	Greetings
Travelling to different places to pray for the sick	Fulfilling God's work
Seeing vision in a lengthy time (animistic aspect)	Looking for immediate answers

Why Did Syncretism Take Place?

It is appropriate to deal with several primary problematic issues, which brought about syncretistic results.

Lack of Theological Teaching

Through a brief description of their history and worship, it becomes apparent that *Santuala* worship never includes a time for preaching or a time for Bible study. They do keep the Bible, but more as a symbolic object. The interviewees commented that *Santuala* members have devotions on a regular basis, but do not read the Bible. Consequently, the members have never had a chance to learn the Word of God. This means that they often have a very poor or incorrect understanding of God, the Holy Spirit, healing, visions, and other Christian beliefs. Instead these important concepts are learned through informal and casual settings. They concentrate on proper religious practices that meet their immediate needs, such as healing.

Lack of Stable Leadership

Structural leadership is missing in *Santuala*. The closest person to a leader figure is the elder, but their role is restricted to that of a mediatory function between the members and God, very much like a shaman. The elder simply directs the people through external signs. None of the interviewees have knowledge as to why there has been no official leader since its establishment. The *Santuala* lacks the leadership that will guide members into spiritual growth, and this deficiency is critical.

Diverted Focus

The motif of the members' belief is limited to only two effects: healing and blessing. The regular members of Santuala worship are more or less those who have experienced healing or blessing. As the founder herself had a great experience of miraculous healing, her followers tend to focus on acquiring the same experience. Thus, in a sense, healing is the central focus of their belief system. Their so-called missionary work is only an extension of this expectation. This shapes the nature of the group as a religious community with an expectation of God's instantaneous healing.

Another important emphasis is on blessing. Believing in God is directly linked to receiving divine blessing. However, the blessing is conditioned by the offering of material goods, and this is a deviation from Christian teaching. This indicates that they have inherited the old traditional belief where a sacrificial offering is imperative to expect blessing from their ancestors. They do not understand the concept that God's blessing is given freely because of the loving relationship between Him and His children.

What Should Pentecostals Learn from Santuala?

Based on the above discussions, I would like to make suggestions to Pentecostals as to how to approach animists. My motive is to avoid or minimize syncretistic outcomes when Pentecostal beliefs interact with culture and native religions.

Focusing Not Just on Miracles

When the Pentecostal message spread at the turn of the century, signs and wonders accompanied the preaching of the gospel. People came to the Lord in their scores through the experience of God's miraculous power, and instant healings became particularly prominent. The history of the Pentecostal ministry in North America and Asia reveals that healings took place in almost every place where the Pentecostal message was proclaimed. Divine healings occurred widely regardless of race, location, or types of illnesses. When the Assemblies of God ministers initially brought the gospel to the tribal people of northern Luzon around 1947, healings became a common miracle from God. The expectant atmosphere in healing revival meetings in various mountain regions reminds us of the Book of Acts. As a Pentecostal, I am thankful to the Lord for this unusual and important gift. It is also true that, without a doubt, healing is an attractive element that draws people to the love and power of Christ, so that they can have a personal experience with God. However, I believe that healing or any miracle should not be an end, but a means to the end. The ultimate purpose of healing should be that of leading people to spiritual growth, a dynamic Christian life and maturity in Christ, thus the miracle of healing functions as a 'sign' pointing to a true reality. If one constantly relies on empirical experiences, our spiritual life will not be healthy and balanced. Pentecostals need to clearly comprehend the role of the gospel rather than simply underscoring distinctiveness in its parameter.

Biblical Guidance with Proper Experience

In my judgment, due to their heavy inclination towards empirical experiences, *Santualas* tend to neglect the Word. It is noticeable that when a church focuses on learning truth, experientialism is downplayed. On the other hand, if too much credit is given to empiricism, learning is overlooked. When I served in an evangelical church in the States as one of the associate youth directors, I was able to observe the nature of the church. The members appeared to be eager to study the Bible. The church had Bible studies throughout the entire week, and different groups come to study the Word on different nights. However, when they encountered critical problems or physical illness, their minds did not quickly grasp the meaning of healing in the Bible. Rather, in most cases they looked for human resources to resolve their problem. An elaborate Bible study program does not always seem to provide relevant application. Because the leaders in the church did not have tangible experiences in this area, they had no confidence, or expectation, of divine healing from God. This reminds me of the importance of gaining the empirical experience in our Christian life. Pentecostals need to maintain a balance between the two, the Word and experience.

Emphasis on Pentecostal Beliefs and Practices

In this changing social context, it is crucial to remain true to the Pentecostal heritage by adhering to its beliefs and practices. It is often observed that second and third generation Pentecostals begin to lose their roots and heritage. In the end, we may see people who claim to be Pentecostal but do not maintain its distinctive beliefs and practices, thus, they may be called 'nominal Pentecostals'. According to one survey, sixty percent of self-proclaimed Pentecostals have never had any of the 'Pentecostal' experiences that our forefathers and mothers had.

Why is this happening? Why do the younger generation of Pentecostals seem to care little about the identity of Pentecostalism, its roots and its uniqueness? Has the first generation neglected to pass on its heritage? The expectation of the Lord's soon return may have caused the pioneers to be good evangelists and missionaries, but not writers and reflective thinkers. The lack of reflective literature by them supports this contention. Some Pentecostal churches in Korea favourably follow the worship style of the Reformed Church, while some Presbyterian pastors eagerly adopt the Pentecostal worship style and message. In certain respects it is good to be open to other traditions, but not to the degree that we lose our own distinctives and become 'Pentecostal Evangelicals'. Therefore, Pentecostals must maintain Pentecostalism's unique faith and practices. Teaching with this emphasis should take place not only in local churches, but, more importantly, in theological institutions and ministerial training programs.

Conclusion

The *Santuala* group is certainly an interesting phenomenon for Pentecostals to consider as it provides an example of Pentecostal syncretism. The founder, Maura Balagsa, and her experience set their theology and ethos with a primary focus on divine healing. Healing became a powerful entry point for many *Santuala* members. The influence of a single leader is noted here, and this is what we have observed in Pentecostal/Charismatic Christianity. Even though the *Santuala* acknowledge the work of the Holy Spirit and, thus, call on the Spirit in prayer for healing, it is sometimes doubtful if healing takes place through the Spirit because of their syncretistic practices. One needs to remember that Baguio, the largest city in the mountains, is a haven for famous faith healers who definitely display their syncretistic beliefs. And yet, the members' trust in divine power seems to be genuine and serious, as no member is expected to take medicine or go to a hospital. If a member gets sick, all members devote themselves to prayers for healing.[22] This strengthens not only their faith in God but also their solidarity among themselves. This community orientation is another feature commonly shared by Pentecostals. Noticeably, the group recognizes the importance of divine blessing although they tend to give it less emphasis than healing.

Individuals expect divine revelation through a vision, which enables them to discover God's divine will and direction. If an individual does not receive visions during prayer time, when he or she is supposed to, their faith and authority will be severely questioned. On the basis of what the elder sees through the vision and the explanation given during the interpretation, the group is able to move. It is unfortunate that among Pentecostals, theological learning sometimes replaces prayer time and expectation of God's revelation to affirm what is revealed in the scriptures, and to receive guidance for a specific individual or situation.

The *Santualas'* lively and participatory worship is epitomized by their dancing. It is acknowledged that the people simply adapt the ritual dancing style without evaluating whether it is suitable or not. Offering animal(s) for sacrifice in a Thanksgiving service is another interesting practice, as is praying for, or repenting of, ancestral sins. Several important native religious ideologies have entered into the *Santuala* beliefs, and there is no biblical support for these practices. On the other hand, some practices are similar to those of the Pentecostals. For example singing briskly, clapping hands, and dancing are elements which one can often find in Pentecostal worship.

This study shows that the Santuala group developed a belief and worship system, which is similar to that of the Pentecostals, but they have never claimed to be Pentecostals, although they do enthusiastically identify with Christianity. Although we do not know how much influence the founder received from the

---

[22] Interview with Tino Altaki.

Christian minister who prayed for her healing, his influence may have been great regardless of whether it was right or wrong. It is probable that the Sanutualas' heavy emphasis on empirical experience may have come from this minister. This reminds us of the important role Christian leadership plays in the development of a new convert's life.

The preceding discussion of the *Santuala* group provides many lessons for the Pentecostal church. As the Pentecostal message has been planted in many Asian hearts, where there is an animistic orientation, it is critical to reflect on several models of syncretism as well as the ideal contextualization. Indonesia and some parts of Africa may provide other models. [23] This study also reveals the importance of Pentecostal spirituality. [24] While we can expect spontaneous answers from God, it is indeed important to balance this expectation with a deep understanding of the Word.

---

[23] For Southern African cases, see Mathew Clark, 'The Challenges of Contextualization and Syncretism to Pentecostal Theology and Missions in Africa', a paper presented at the Theological Symposium, the 18th Pentecostal World Conference, Seoul, Korea on Sept. 21, 1998, 263-83.

[24] See the book by an Asian Pentecostal, Simon Chan, *Christian Spirituality* (Downers Grove, IL: InterVarsity, 1998).

Chapter 15

Local Church, Worship, and Theological Formation

Introduction

The growth of Pentecostal Christianity in the second half of the twentieth century, particularly in non-western continents, has been the object of a stream of studies from a variety of perspectives: theological, sociological, historical, psychological, contextual and missiological. The publication of *World Christian Encyclopedia* by David Barrett (1982 and 2001) and his annual updates in *International Bulletin of Missionary Research* have continually provided a trajectory of the global Christian movement, including Asian Pentecostal churches. Also in the last decade or so, studies on Asian Pentecostalism have progressed remarkably. The launching of the *Asian Journal of Pentecostal Studies* signaled serious academic reflection among Asian Pentecostals, and the publication of its supplement series is another important development in Asian Pentecostal studies. The formation of the Asian Pentecostal Society in 1998 was another important step towards networking among emerging Asian Pentecostal minds.

Pentecostal worship in Asia is an incredibly complex subject. It is in fact a contextualization process on a daily basis, as several important elements shape how one congregation worships in a given location and context.

The first element is the spiritual and theological tradition of Pentecostalism as it was introduced to them. Interestingly, although it is claimed that North America is the source of the tradition, it is not that simple. For example, in many parts of Asia, understandably North American, often Azusa Street Mission Pentecostal missionaries brought the new message. But, in some areas, European Pentecostal missionaries from England and Finland were active, while in Korea, the first group of national workers, who worked under the first North American Pentecostal missionary, was trained in Japan.

Second, the local spiritual milieu greatly alters the original form of spirituality. Whether it is Christian or not, Asia is rich in spiritual awareness and every Asian religion has a good dose of spiritual beliefs and practices. This explains why Chinese Christians practice different forms of spirituality, including worship, from let's say, an Indian counterpart. This has, in part, to do with the religio-cultural soil of a given location. For another example, a powerful revival took place in Korea in 1904-1907, prior to the arrival of the first Pentecostal missionary, and several forms of spiritual exercises had already been shaped. These include the daily early morning prayer meeting, unison prayer in loud voices, repentance as the mark of the Spirit's presence, and others.

The third is the changing social context of the congregation shaping their spiritual tradition, which in turn influences how they worship. Political, economic, and social situations easily condition one's prayer, selection of songs, and even the mood of worship. Affluent Singaporean Pentecostal worship is radically different from how people in a Chinese house church network worship and this can be explained by their social context, among others. What I try to illustrate here is the diversity in Pentecostal life and worship in Asia.

In spite of the formidable nature of this study, I will attempt to deduce a set of common features of Pentecostal worship in Asia in the following way. First, I am selecting an Asian Pentecostal church that may provide a reasonable model for Asian Pentecostal worship. Through a descriptive presentation, an example of Pentecostal worship in Asia is introduced. This church or its particular worship service we are going to observe is, by no means, a perfect example or representation of Asian Pentecostal churches, but nonetheless, it will serve as the starting point for our discussion. Then secondly, based on an observation of the sample Pentecostal worship, as well as many other Pentecostal churches that I have observed, several characteristics will be discussed. In this process, we will use Albrecht's illuminative study.[1] Also coming into play in this general characterization is the socio-religious context of Asian Pentecostals. Any unique features of Asian Pentecostal worship, particularly in comparison with non-Pentecostal churches, surrounding this sample church will be discussed. Interwoven with the characterization are the theological presuppositions and, often implicit, theological motivations that produce certain distinct features of Asian Pentecostal worship. Also in discussion is the contribution of worship experience to the formation of Asian Pentecostal theology. Thirdly, I will move to the correlations between worship and theology, with a concluding proposal for the healthy future of Asian Pentecostalism.

A Visit to the All Gospel Church

San Fernando (population: 115,605 in 2002 projection),[2] a port city by the South China Sea in the archipelago of the Philippines, is a major financial, political and commercial center of what is called Region I (estimated population for 2005 as

---

[1] Daniel E. Albrecht, 'An Anatomy of Worship: A Pentecostal Analysis', in Wonsuk Ma and Robert P. Menzies (eds.), *The Spirit and Spirituality: Essays in Honor of Russell P. Spittler* (London: T. & T. Clark, 2004), 70-82.

[2] City of San Fernando, 'Baseline Profile' (http://www.sanfernandocity.gov.ph/quick.html), accessed: June 23, 2006.

4,481,820 [3] an administrative region comprising several provinces predominantly speaking the Ilocano dialect. This region is also known for its strong presence of the Roman Catholic Church and Aglipayan (Philippine Independent Church), the national version of the Catholic Church.

Established in January, 1988 in a rented second floor of a deserted commercial building, the All Gospel Church has steadily grown under the leadership of Rev. Conrado Lumahan. He currently serves not only as Senior Pastor of this church and its 20 daughter churches in nearby towns and villages, but also as Superintendent of the Northern Luzon District Council of the Philippines Assemblies of God, the largest Protestant denomination in the country. He received a good theological education, which is a growing trend among Asian Pentecostals, through Asia Pacific Theological Seminary, a premier Pentecostal school in Asia. He has finished the Master of Divinity and Master of Theology degrees and is presently studying toward the Doctor of Ministry degree from the same school.

They have two Sunday morning worship services at 9:00 a.m. and 10:30 a.m. More people (around 150) attend the first service than the second one (around 120). I normally participate in the second worship service, partly because this one has less time constraints (especially when I preach). By the time the first gathering is about to end, early comers for the second one experience the highlights of the first service.

Their Sunday morning service began with what is called 'worship', that is singing with a call to worship as we experienced on our visitation day (June 4, 2006). After a short prayer inviting God's presence among them, a group of musicians and singers lead more than a half-an-hour segment. One can hardly see any clergy as being a part of this section. The songs are highly 'contemporary', such as the music by Hill Song of Australia. The atmosphere is lively and the music is loud with electric guitars, a keyboard and a drum set. Incidentally, all the music team members are either in their teens or twenties, with one leader perhaps in his early thirties. There is no traditional church music instrument such as a piano and organ; and several young girls dance with cymbals in their hands. There is no hymn book, and songs are projected through an overhead projector. Most of this time, the congregation not only stands, but also clap and raise their hands, and some even dance. Between songs, often a spontaneous prayer and praise burst forth and the whole congregation freely joins in with their own prayers in a loud voice, and the leader seems to guide the congregation through this process. During the singing session, the auditorium becomes filled with young and old members and visitors. After many fast and lively songs, toward the end, a little slower song is introduced to calm the heightened atmosphere, evidently to prepare the audience for reflection and

---

[3] National Statistics Office, 'Summary of Projected Population by Region, by Single-Year Interval, Philippines: 1995-2005' (http://www.census.gov.ph/data/sectordata/ poproj09. txt), accessed: June 23, 2006.

listening to the Word of God. This celebrative session comes to an end with a loud round of applause and shouts of 'Amen'.

The second portion of the service began with the pastor giving a welcome remark and a report on the recent missionary trip to Malaysia and Cambodia. His report is met by an excited response from the audience; he also makes several announcements. And, just before he proceeds to his preaching, he acknowledges the presence of new members.

However, this portion of the service is dedicated to sharing the word of God. And typically, although not on this particular day perhaps due to time constraints, this portion is further divided into two periods: testimonies by several members of the congregation, normally not prearranged, and the proclamation of the word by the preacher. Pastor Conrado Lumahan reads almost the entire chapter of Acts 2. Noting that it is Pentecost Sunday, his message traces the appearance of God in the Old Testament through 'fire', and then the presence of the 'tongues of fire' on the day of Pentecost. Frequently repeated are words such as 'fire', and 'empowerment', and placing emphasis on the 'empowering aspect' of the Holy Spirit in the lives of believers. The preaching was quite long, almost an hour. And yet, the response of the congregation was active with an occasional 'Amen', as well as various expressions, such as the nodding of their heads in agreement and clapping their hands. In fact, toward the end of the sermon, the audience enthusiastically responded in unison with 'Amen'. The sermon is concluded with the entire congregation standing and joining in the pastor's prayer for the baptism in the Holy Spirit with the sign of speaking in tongues. The prayer eventually turns into a communal prayer as the audience is divided by threes and fours and prays for one another, particularly for the baptism in the Holy Spirit.

At other times, the church has a long 'altar service', when people are invited to come forward for prayer, often to respond to the message just preached. In addition, people come forward for prayer for healing, baptism in the Spirit, and for various other needs. The ministers lay their hands on the heads and offer special prayer, and this is often accompanied with expressed responses from the people, including sobbing, raising of hands, crying, or even 'slaying in the Spirit'. This is the time when various spiritual gifts are best exercised, such as a word of knowledge, speaking in tongues, interpretation, prophecy, healing, casting out of demons, etc. The entire congregation spends a good twenty to thirty minutes for this characteristically Pentecostal part of worship.

The next segment of the service may be termed a 'koinonia' time. First, is the recognition of birthday celebrants; on this Sunday, about six or seven come to the front. After the congregation sings 'Happy Birthday to You' (not necessarily a Christian song!), the pastor prays for God's blessings upon them. I recognized that this is not necessarily a 'Pentecostal' feature as many Pentecostal churches do not have this part in their service.

Then, after the collection of offerings and tithes, the pastor pronounced a benediction through an elaborate prayer of God's blessings, along with a commitment to reach out to our own neighbours. What is also noted is his prayer for his members to speak in tongues in order to live a powerful Christian life. The facial expressions of the people indicate their enthusiastic reception of the prayer of blessing. The entire worship ends with a burst of applause and another time of joyous singing. The service lasts close to two hours.

Characteristics and Theological Reflection

In a number of ways, this worship service represents a typical Pentecostal worship. It contains all the three major 'foundational clusters or rites: the worship and praise rite...the sermon or biblical-pastoral message rite, and the later response rite'.[4] Also in agreement is all the 'values, expressions, and sensibilities', some of which we will discuss. Several characteristics noted in the worship of All Gospel Church, as well as in many other Asian Pentecostal churches, will be enumerated, particularly in comparison with traditional or evangelical churches in Asia. I will try to bundle them under several headings. For each, I will attempt to offer its theological rationale, as commonly held by Pentecostals, although seldom explicated.

Intensity and Liveliness

Perhaps the most striking element in Pentecostal worship is its intensity and liveliness, often represented by verbal expressions and body movements. In the worship we just observed, such characteristics are abundant in every segment of it. The 'worship and praise' is characteristically intense and lively with plenty of body motions, lively music, dances, lifted hands, clapping of hands, and even jumping by some members. The message part is again lively, not only by the preacher's enthusiastic communication with constant motions and body movements (including walking across the pulpit), but also by the response of the congregation. The last part is much like a celebration which prompts more expressive response from the congregation.

When I first attended a small Pentecostal church in a Korean city, after having spent my early teen years in a small town, but in a large Presbyterian church, my first impression was of its 'noisiness'. They enthusiastically prayed loud, sang loud, and clapped their hands (which people in my previous church never did). For example, we were expected to be reverently silent during the preaching in the previous church; but, in the Pentecostal church, we were now expected to respond to particular segments of the message with a loud 'Amen', 'Hallelujah' or even with exuberant hand clapping.[5]

This intensity and liveliness may have come from at least two theological orientations. In Pentecostal worship, there is a high expectancy of experiencing God. Both 'expectancy' and 'experience' can immediately prompt enthusiastic

---

[4] Albrecht, 'An Anatomy of Worship', 78.

[5] Albrecht, 'An Anatomy of Worship', 78 calls this and similar oral or verbal expressions 'sacred expletives'.

responses. God is never abstract, but concrete; He is never static, but dynamic. And particularly to Asians, a deity is always acting, either bringing curses or blessings, thus constantly interacting with humans, deeply involved in human affairs. Many Asians coming from other religious backgrounds, although quite different in the case of the Philippines, may have gone though the process of functional substitution in their Christian development. Their new God is to interact with his worshipers, listening to their prayers, responding to their worship and providing for their needs, which is quite different from the version of Christianity which western missionaries once propagated, except for Pentecostalism.

Another theological reasoning for this liveliness may have come from the restorationalist nature of Pentecostalism. With the Pentecostal's high regard for the scriptures and their literalistic interpretation, there is a sense that they are reaching all the way back to apostolic times, characterized by heroic faith and daily experience of God's miraculous power. This notion, like early Reformers, has made Pentecostals 'odd' or 'anti-cultural' to many contemporaries including Christians, and yet they remain consciously satisfied with their understanding of their unique locus in God's economy. One example may be found among Chinese Christians of some house church networks.[6] They are literally surrounded by forces of persecution, but their Christian outlook is amazingly positive, due to their self-understanding of being true people of God, and the understanding of God's unique calling, for example, as expressed in the highly publicized 'Back-to-Jerusalem' missionary movement.

This feature has its own weaknesses which are already apparent. There is a simplistic popular notion that 'louder worship' is a better one. In many rural Pentecostal churches, I have seen that, at the top of their shopping list is a powerful audio system, electric guitars and a drum set, even if the church does not have enough copies of their hymn book. A potential danger is that the loudness may become an empty shell, if hearts are not committed to meaningful worship. However, a more serious danger is that Pentecostals, already well used to loudness, may have lost their ability for meditation and reflective spiritual discipline. If this is true, then Pentecostalism, in spite of its lively forms, may indeed represent a religion of shallow spirituality. Also often mentioned are the possible emotional excesses of Pentecostal worship. While being given credit that the movement has rediscovered the importance of the affective dimension of

---

[6] Whether they are 'Pentecostal' is highly debated. For recent studies on the topic, see Luke Wesley, *The Church in China: Persecuted, Pentecostal and Powerful* (Baguio, Philippines: AJPS Books, 2004). There are three useful chapters in Allan Anderson and Edmond Tang (eds.), *Asian and Pentecostal: The Charismatic Face of Christianity in Asia* (Oxford: Regnum; Baguio: APTS Press, 2005): see Gotthard Oblau, 'Pentecostals by Default? Contemporary Christianity in China' (411-38); Zhaoming Deng, 'Indigenous Chinese Pentecostal Denominations' (439-68); and Edmond Tang, "Yellers' and Healers: Pentecostalism and the Study of Grassroots Christianity in China' (469-88).

human religiosity, emotions can become uncontrollable during a time of religious excitement. Also to be guarded against is the 'feeling-oriented expectation' of worshipers. Such an attitude can turn worship into a sort of religious entertainment, thus creating a theological environment where worshipers develop an expectation of 'receiving' through the worship experience or simply an unengaged spectator attitude and forgetting that we are to offer ourselves as a living sacrifice.

Participatory Worship

The full participation of many (often lay) members of the church in various segments of their worship is quite noticeable. In fact, the psychological distance between the pulpit area and the pews is very narrow. This is an obvious contrast with the notion I had during my Presbyterian years, in that the pulpit was unapproachable for the 'rest of us'. This 'open stage' nature of Pentecostal worship is evident in all the three major 'rites'. The worship and praise is marked not only by the group of musicians (most of them are on the stage) and singers primarily coming from the laity, but also the full and enthusiastic participation of the congregation blurs the demarcation between the leaders and the led. In the message 'rite', the most significant democratized feature of ministry is the testimony time. As I elaborated elsewhere,[7] this session brings anticipation to the church, but also anxiety to the worship leadership. Although some members regularly testify about their experiences with or of God in their daily lives, there could be a visitor who comes forward to share his or her experiences. Often hosted by a lay leader, this time becomes an 'open pulpit', and the 'prophethood of all believers' is at its best in a corporate worship setting. As discussed below, this has an enormous implication to the theologizing process of Pentecostal beliefs in a local church context. Ministry for the altar service is not restricted to clergy. Lay leaders, friends, family members, or church members of those who have come to the altar area for a special prayer can come and join them. Often by laying their hands on the shoulders or even the head of their friends, they freely minister to them. The fellowship time is obviously celebrative and everyone joins in expressing their welcome to visitors and fellow members.

One significant theological foundation for such democratized ministry is the Pentecostal emphasis on the Holy Spirit's empowering role. Based on their cardinal scripture, Acts 1:8, Pentecostals believe that the primary role of the Holy Spirit in the believer's life is to empower them for service.[8] This is a considerable departure from Pauline pneumatology which stresses the Spirit's role in regeneration. As Peter rightly quotes Joel 2:28-29 to explain the advent of the Holy Spirit on the Day of Pentecost (Acts 2:17-21), the strong emphasis was

---

[7] Wonsuk Ma, 'Doing Theology in the Philippines: A Case of Pentecostal Christianity', *AJPS* 8:2 (2005), 220-21.

[8] The most articulate theological treaty is by Roger Stronstad, *Charismatic Theology of St. Luke* (Peabody, MA: Hendrickson, 1984).

on the 'democratization' of the Spirit's endowment without regard to age, gender and social status. The modern Pentecostal movement has seen the same egalitarian nature of the Spirit's experience. With a strong link between the baptism in the Spirit and empowerment for witness, Pentecostal believers are literally 'liberated' to serve the Lord and his church. This theological understanding widely opens ministry opportunities to people, clergy as well as laity, and that is what happens in Pentecostal worship.

Already strongly alluded to is the democratization of ministry. Against the ministerial scene where clergy monopolized in the established churches, the Azusa Street Mission, for instance, saw the ministry now fully open to the whole church. The Mission further overcame the strong social hurdle of racial division. The Azusa leader, William Seymour's leadership included not only male and female, but also white and African-Americans. In the Asian context, where social hierarchy is still recognized, be it by age, economic status, educational attainment, or social positions, clergy-laity has been clearly demarked. In some countries, such as Japan and Korea, even among Pentecostal churches, the clergy-laity demarcation is more evident than in the Philippines, for instance, primarily due to their own cultural contexts. Nonetheless, an increased involvement of laity in Christian ministry is quite obvious among Pentecostals. One example, in spite of the cultural surroundings, is David Yonggi Cho's revolutionary involvement of lay women leaders for his renowned cell group system. This liberation of ministry from the hands of a few elite (that is, clergy) to the mass of the church is a significant theological impact of Pentecostalism.

Also implicit is a general belief that the presence of the Holy Spirit is not necessarily assumed, or at least the presence is in varying degrees. One of the most common terms used by Pentecostals associated with worship is 'anointing'. Arguably based on the Old Testament usage,[9] but appropriated by Pentecostals, this term is used in how the preacher, song leader, musicians, singers, or the whole ambiance of worship 'touches' individuals or if the Lord has 'spoken' to worshipers. Normally liveliness and spontaneity are two ingredients of 'anointed' worship. For this, worshipers are urged to 'submit' themselves to the move of the Holy Spirit, so that he will have full 'freedom' to minister to his people. Inherent in this is also the conditionality of the presence and work of the Holy Spirit in a worship setting.

These theological contributions can also produce negative consequences if not properly guided. Prevalent among Pentecostal-charismatic churches, particularly among independent ones, is the casual attitude toward ministry.

---

[9] The closest is Isa. 61:1.

Spontaneity

Spontaneity is another strong characteristic of Pentecostal worship.[10] In the worship of All Gospel Church, this 'improvisation' occurs frequently in all the three 'rites' of the service. During the 'worship and praise', although songs were pre-selected and the music team rehearsed previously, the leaders are prepared to be 'led by the Spirit', a common expression among Pentecostals to refer to an unexpected urge to do something not planned at all. This sensitivity to the move of the Spirit is crucial in Pentecostal worship, and as a result, a singing segment can turn into a season of congregational prayer or corporate worship, often with individuals voicing their praises and thanksgiving to the Lord, or 'singing in the Spirit'. In the message segment, Pentecostal spontaneity is best seen in the testimonials. Anyone among the congregation may rise and share his or her experience with the rest of the church; this part is seldom prearranged. Even the preaching by the minister contains sufficient room for spontaneity. Most Pentecostal preachers preach from a set of outlines, seldom from a full text.[11] The altar service again is full of spontaneity, as this is not structured at all. It is often the case among Pentecostal churches that participants are dismissed as they wish, while others remain in prayer around the altar area. The fellowship time, which often extends even beyond the benediction, is another less organized part of worship. Humanly speaking, the pastor should be open to the changing scenes of human responses and be able to lead the congregation into a suitable mode of worship.

A couple of theological themes may have contributed to this distinct characteristic of Pentecostal worship. The first is the fundamental understanding of worship and the role of the Holy Spirit. As Albrecht rightly asserts, 'For Pentecostals, worship is not strictly a human activity…. Believers expect God to come and meet with them. Pentecostals believe that God alone inaugurates such a meeting by God's gracious acts and presence'.[12] This experience with the presence of God is made possible through the work of the Holy Spirit, according to common Pentecostal notion. And this is where the creativity of the Holy Spirit is manifested and Pentecostals are to leave 'enough room' for his activity. Often a prayer is said to the Holy Spirit 'to take full charge over the worship'. Also the worshipers are prepared to be surprised by the Holy Spirit, as 'God 'comes' to meet with God's people, that God listens and responds to worshipers'[13] and this takes place through the Holy Spirit. As people sense the move (or often said as 'prompting') of the Holy Spirit, the whole congregation is to follow the move,

---

[10] This is also a 'value' of Pentecostal worship that Albrecht, 'An Anatomy of Worship', 76, includes.

[11] Vincent Leoh, 'Pentecostal Preaching: A Century Past, a Century Forward' (a paper presented at the 8th annual meeting of Asian Pentecostal Society, Kuala Lumpur, Malaysia, September 2006), 3, calls this 'sanctified illiteracy'.

[12] Albrecht, 'An Anatomy of Worship', 72.

[13] Albrecht, 'An Anatomy of Worship', 74.

and this requires sensitivity and spontaneity. The surprise role of the Holy Spirit in Pentecostal worship can best be epitomized by utterances, either in tongues (preferably followed by an interpretation) or as prophecies. Although absent in the worship we visited, this 'interception' by the Spirit in worship is a distinct feature of Pentecostal worship. In common minds, any tightly prescribed order of worship which fails to leave room for such work of the Spirit is viewed as 'grieving the Spirit', by not allowing him to minister to his people.

Closely related to the preceding discussion is the expectation of an encounter with God's presence throughout worship. In fact, 'the personal encounter with the Holy remains at the centre of Pentecostal spirituality and worship'.[14] This expectancy naturally heightens the sensitivity of worshipers to what God speaks to individuals and to the collective gathering. Impressions in the heart, audible voice, dreams, visions, any scriptural passage or words of a song 'that stand out' are all perceived as means of God speaking to his people. This dynamic view of God's word is in stark contrast with the static view of God's revelation, that is, the 'closed' view of the word of God. However, this is not necessarily God's words 'outside of the scriptures', as Pentecostals diligently measure any 'revelation' by the written scripture. The high regard Pentecostals have toward the scripture has been a critical safeguard toward 'private' interpretation of God's revelation. This 'open' view of God's revelation is particularly relevant to Asian believers. Asian traditional religious traditions have oriented most Asians to the communication between humans and the divine. Although it takes different ritual procedures, almost every religion has a common belief in such experiences, and this prepares Asian Pentecostals to be more attentive to the revealing of the Lord.

What is observed in a Pentecostal worship service is the absence of written liturgy. Although Korean Pentecostal churches have adopted more liturgical elements, such as the Apostle's Creed or a responsive reading of the scripture as part of their Sunday worship, most Pentecostal churches have not incorporated any prescribed liturgy. As Hollenweger argues, Pentecostals do have rich liturgical components in their worship, but they are primarily non-verbal and unprescribed. For instance, spontaneous congregational response to certain points of a sermon by saying an 'Amen' is a good case of Pentecostal liturgical practice. Body gestures, such as the raising of hands during the praise time, are also liturgical expressions. [15]

---

[14] Albrecht, 'An Anatomy of Worship', 74.

[15] This oral tradition is part of what is called the 'Black Root' of Pentecostalism. See the elaborate discussion of W.J. Hollenweger, *Pentecostalism*, 17-131, particularly illuminating is his discussion on Black Pentecostalism in the United States and African Pentecostalism.

Experience of the Transcendental

The experiential aspect of Pentecostal spirituality has often been cited as one of the most distinct Pentecostal values.[16] At the Azusa Street Mission, for example, experience of God's presence and his working was their hallmark. It is true that every Christian tradition has an experiential aspect included in their religious life. What stands out in the Pentecostal tradition is more than cognitive awareness of God's being. It is rather a tangible encounter with the great God, and such an experience affects the whole human being including one's feelings and will power. This unique feature makes Pentecostalism a 'religion with flesh and bones',[17] that is, a religion that brings an encounter with God to the daily living of believers, and this experience is marked by its tangibility. In the worship of the All Gospel Church, the impact of the divine encounter was expressed in various ways by the worshippers, and some parts of the worship in fact highlighted these tangible experiences, such as healing, repentance, and baptism in the Holy Spirit with an emphasis on speaking in tongues as a sign. Prayers are often offered for the healing of family members who are not present in the worship service, family problems (such as financial matters), relationship issues, and even for tuition payments for their children. We notice that the nature of God's work can be 'natural' as well as 'supernatural'. God is believed to be not only good, but also capable, indeed answering their prayers in the 'here and now'.

Even communion, which Pentecostal churches celebrate every month, typifies this tendency. Pentecostals typically take a 'low' theological view of the Lord's presence in communion, that is, the elements are received to symbolize or to 'remember' the Lord's body and blood. However, it is often expected that through this experience physical healing takes place. Passages such as 'By his wounds, you have been healed' (Isa. 53:5; 1 Pet. 2:24, NIV) is often recited by the minister to remind the congregation that communion is a special occasion with its powerful ritual elements when healing indeed takes place.

A few roots of such expectation can be cited. The first is the 'primal' nature of Pentecostal religious values. This expression, coined by Harvey Cox,[18] may also indicate the Pentecostal ethos to bring back to the modern Christian life the spirituality and patterns of worship of the early church as recorded in the book of Acts. This restorative impetus is further enhanced by general Asian religious worldview which makes little distinction between the natural and supernatural. For example, Julie Ma convincingly demonstrates how such tangible

---

[16] For example, see R.P. Spittler, 'Spirituality, Pentecostal and Charismatic', *DPCM*, 804-805.

[17] Wonsuk & Julie C. Ma, 'Jesus Christ in Asia: Our Journey with Him as Pentecostal Believers', *IRM* 94 (Oct 2005), 498.

[18] Harvey Cox, *Fire from Heaven: The Rise of Pentecostal Spirituality and the Reshaping of Religion in the Twenty-First Century* (Reading, MA: Addison-Wesley, 1995), 82-83, 88-89.

demonstration of God's power, often in miraculous ways, has impacted many tribal groups in the northern Philippines, resulting in mass conversions. She partly contributes this movement to the similarities in the Pentecostal worldview and that of the tribes.[19] Thus, Pentecostalism has become a corrective of traditional Christianity which was characterized by its worldview with an 'excluded middle'.[20] As I argued elsewhere, Christianity in a non-western (or majority-world) setting may be inherently charismatic in type, if left without any theological interference from outside, especially from a western church.[21] The very fact that many 'indigenous' forms of Christianity is of Pentecostal-charismatic varieties may attest to this, be it in Africa (such as African Initiate Church) or in Asia (Chinese house church networks, for example). This recovery of 'primitive' elements of Christianity by Pentecostalism has also 'renewed' the existing churches in the West as seen in the Charismatic movement during the 1960s.

The other contributing factors may also be found in the social context of Asia. In many Asian societies, suffering is the most urgent social context in which Pentecostal believers find themselves. Today, some political systems often oriented to a certain religious system pose a formidable challenge to Christians. Pentecostals, as the more vibrant form of Christianity, tend to attract hostile treatments from political, religious environments. Wiyono, an Indonesian Pentecostal, informs us that the most number of churches which militant Muslims burned, vandalized, or destroyed were Pentecostal-Charismatic ones.[22] Believers in house church networks in China or Pentecostal believers in some Middle Eastern countries may fall in the same category. Or, some political systems simply do not allow room for religious activities, and this applies to some churches in Vietnam, Laos, Bhutan, North Korea and others. However, the most serious daily challenge comes from suffering out of poverty. The Asian Development Bank has a quick summary of the current state: 'Asia and the Pacific are still home to 900 million poor people—nearly one third of the region's population. South Asia alone has more than 500 million poverty-stricken people, twice as many as in the whole of Africa. Two-thirds of

---

[19] J. Ma, *When the Spirit Meets the Spirits*, esp. 167-232. Recently a similar study was published by Lalsangkima Pachuau, 'Mizo '*sakhua*' in transition: Change and Continuity from Primal Religion to Christianity', *Missiology* 34:1 (Jan. 2006), 41-57, particularly 51-53 for the incorporation of their worldviews into Christianity.

[20] Paul G. Hiebert, Daniel R. Shaw, and Tite Tiénou, *Understanding Folk Religion: A Christian Response to Popular Beliefs and Practices* (Grand Rapids: Baker, 1999), 89.

[21] Ma and Ma, 'Jesus Christ in Asia', 503.

[22] Gani Wiyono, 'Pentecostals in Indonesia', in *Asian and Pentecostal*, 319-320. For a more comprehensive study of the subject, see Harold D. Hunter and Cecil M. Robeck, Jr., eds., *The Suffering Body: Ecumenical and International Perspectives on the Persecution of Christians* (Waynesboro, GA: Paternoster, 2006).

Asia's poor are women'.[23] Such daily struggle has made people turn to religions which promise divine answers, and Pentecostal-Charismatic Christianity has presented the most attractive message. The nine-million strong El Shaddai Catholic Charismatic group in the Philippines exemplifies the flight of poverty-stricken masses to the miracle-performing God.[24] And David Yonggi Cho's message of God's blessing is another instance of such an approach.[25] The fundamental difference between the controversial prosperity gospel and what is preached in Asia may not necessarily be found in their messages, but in their motivations. The West preaches it for what people 'want', while the majority world offers the prosperity message for what people 'need'. Such struggle of suffering brings people to God out of desperation and their resultant expectation for God's help in their daily sustenance. Considering that Pentecostalism is basically a religion of the 'poor',[26] their worship reflects this felt need.

There could be a few other features of Pentecostal worship that have theological implications. For example, the emphasis on and operation of spiritual gifts, and emphasis on evangelism and mission could be included in the list.

Concluding, Theologically...

Now, how Pentecostal worship in Asia interacts with their theological orientation is an interesting inquiry. There are several aspects of this discussion.

Worship as Theological Expression

What is the relationship between worship and theology? It is obvious that they are closely linked. First of all, theology informs how one worships, and Asian Pentecostals are not an exception. As I suggested, several theological underpinnings for each feature of Pentecostal worship in Asia, their theological orientation, although often implicit in articulation, contributes greatly to how Asian Pentecostals worship. Practically, what they believe makes who they are. In addition to the 'received' theology from western Pentecostal hands, each socio-cultural context plays an important role in the process of theologization.

---

[23] Asian Development Bank, 'Fighting Poverty in Asia and the Pacific' (http://www.adb.org/Documents/Brochures/Fighting_Poverty/default.asp?p=poverty, 2006), accessed: June 26, 2006.

[24] For a recent study on miracles claimed by the El Shaddai group, see Katharine L. Wiegele, *Investing in Miracles: El Shaddai and the Transformation of Popular Catholicism in the Philippines* (Honolulu: University of Hawaii Press, 2005).

[25] For theological reflections on Cho's message, see Wonsuk Ma, William W. Menzies, and Hyeon-sung Bae (eds.), *David Yonggi Cho: A Close Look at His Theology and Ministry* (Baguio, Philippines: APTS Press, 2004).

[26] See the characterization of Pentecostals as the poor in Wonsuk Ma, '"When the Poor Are Fired Up": The Role of Pneumatology in Pentecostal-charismatic Mission', *Transformation* 24:1 (2007), 28-34.

Secondly, the re-enactment through various expressions of worship affirms, reinforces, and strengthens its theology. Worship is the formal and corporative platform where such process takes place. Due to the high relevancy to the worshipper's daily experiences, their theology is lived out as it is tangibly expressed and experienced in the worship context.

Thirdly, worship is also a place where theological revision, reinterpretation and even alteration take place. This can take place in various ways: 1) inclusion or choice (of certain songs, sermon topics, etc.), 2) emphases, 3) reinterpretation (particularly in a changing social context), and more seriously, 4) by omission. The decreasing message of the Lord's return, for example, is a case of the latter.[27]

Worship as Theological Formation

The 'democratic' nature of Pentecostal worship promises a good possibility for the formation of 'people's theology'. How the worship leader selects songs for a given worship service and how the emcee for the testimony time offers 'interpretation' for presented testimonies are all part of the corporate theologizational process. However, the most significant element of corporate theologization is the testimonial tradition. Here is my own assessment of the role of testimonies in the theologization process:

> Even in tribal churches in the Cordillera mountain region of the Philippines, old and young members stand or come forward to the pulpit to share their experiences with God. Sometimes this lasts more than an hour.... This tradition provides a place not only for participation in theology-making, but also a space for the rest of the congregation to reflect, evaluate, and commonly share, once accepted as genuine and valid, the theological experiences of one member as a community possession. This has made Pentecostal theology inevitably a 'people's theology'. The uniqueness of this feature should be understood in the context where theologizing has been left exclusively in the hands of theological and ecclesial elites in most Christian traditions. [28]

However, it is unfortunate that this unique Pentecostal tradition has not been practiced in some countries like Korea, perhaps due to cultural reasons such as those in Korea. Also true is that in large Pentecostal churches, for obvious practical reasons, this practice is slowly disappearing. As a result, the theologization process is steadily shifting to the clergy's hands.

Who is Behind the Wheel?

In spite of the revolutionary feature of the democratization of theologization, the most critical role is played by pastors. They are practically behind the wheel as

---

[27] See Wonsuk Ma, 'Pentecostal Eschatology: What Happened When the Wave Hit the West End of the Ocean', in Harold Hunter and Cecil M. Robeck, Jr. (eds.), *The Azusa Street Revival and Its Legacy* (Cleveland, TN: Pathway), 227-42.

[28] W. Ma, 'Doing Theology in the Philippines', 220-21.

worship takes place under their leadership, and also the message is proclaimed by them. They have a weekly opportunity to shape the theological orientation of their parishioners. Also, due to frequent contact with members, either through formal worship, house visitation, daily dawn prayer meetings (as in Korea) or house meetings (such as in China), the pastor has the best possibility for theological formation of his or her church.

The influence of the pastor for theological formation does not stop there. Often future Pentecostal and Charismatic pastors and Christian workers are raised up and trained in a local church setting. Obviously the pastor functions as the mentor for the future pastors and workers.

It is estimated that about 80% of pastors in the Philippines have never received any formal theological and ministerial training. It is plausible that the Pentecostal and Charismatic counterparts may be even less formally trained, at least for two reasons: 1) considering its general anti-intellectual tendency, and 2) some well known and successful pastors with little or no ministerial training themselves have served as powerful role models for many who are turning to a ministerial vocation. Also challenging is the pressure which a Pentecostal preacher would feel to address life's issues in his or her preaching and teaching. In spite of its advantage of relevancy, this approach may promote a consumerist tendency in the process of theological formation.

Now the challenge for the pastor is surmountable. One possible answer to this dilemma is a close partnership between the ever-increasing Pentecostal ministers and emerging theological minds in the Asian Pentecostal circle. Asia has already seen more than a dozen Pentecostal graduate schools, many national Pentecostal societies, academic journals and publications; and this is the time that scholars can begin to produce materials that are pastor-friendly in language and subject matter. By 'translating' their existing scholar work into popular versions, pastors, lay leaders and Bible school students will greatly benefit from such contributions. Such partnership will bring churches and theological schools closer to the healthy future of Asian Pentecostalism.

Chapter 16

Korean Pentecostal Spirituality: A Case Study of Jashil Choi

Introduction

The majority of sincere Korean believers are carrying on a constant prayer life. Some of them leave their daily routines, find a secluded place and have a period of prayer and fasting, for particular occasions or for the solution of serious problems. And, the spirituality of Korean Pentecostals will never be complete, if the spiritual traditions of prayer and fasting are removed, as they are two of several key components needed to build one's spirituality and successful church work. Prayer is a direct communication to and with a Divine Being, through which one can keep one's spiritual life intact and obtain spiritual power to do God's work. Prayer, coupled with fasting, intensifies one's spiritual life and in turn, the spirituality of individuals, especially church leaders, which directly affects community ministry.

Jashil Choi epitomizes such spirituality among Korean Pentecostals. I met her in 1983, during the third year of our missionary lives in the Philippines, when Yonggi Cho held a mass public crusade in Manila, and many Korean residents, students and missionaries enthusiastically participated in the event.

On the second day, Jashil Choi, the mother-in-law of Cho, invited several Korean ministers to her hotel room. I had not met her before then, but she warmly welcomed us, and she also asked us to lay hands on her twisted ankle for a complete healing. At some point during this time, she held my hand and comforted me as if she had known me for many years. She even handed me a substantial offering for my struggling missionary family. This fond memory swelled immediately in my heart while I was reading her autobiography.

This book thoroughly delineates the spirituality reflected in her life of prayer and fasting and its effect on her ministry, particularly through the Yoido Full Gospel Church (YFGC) and the Choi Jashil International Fasting and Prayer Mountain (CJIFPM). While reading the book, I was often awestruck by the extraordinary accounts of her life. Choi's life literally consisted of fasting and prayer, often through the night, and each challenging moment in her life and ministry was overcome by her fervent prayer. And, having experienced the power of prayer, she was determined to establish a prayer mountain, with distinct emphasis on fasting, in spite of strong opposition from some church leaders. Her determination was so strong that even Cho himself could not stand in her way, though seemingly every circumstance was not favourable towards it.

The evidence of her spirituality was felt strongly even from the pioneering year of the YFGC, originally called Full Gospel Central Church, to its growth today as the world's largest church. Undoubtedly, Yonggi Cho's spiritual leadership has single-handedly influenced the development of the church; but he has frequently acknowledged the powerful spiritual and ministerial role of Choi's sacrificial prayer, with fasting, in the growth and development of his ministry. 'Pastor Choi, my mother-in-law, is the person whom I would never forget in my life. If she was not my pastoral companion I would not be a pastor in the world's largest church'.[1]

This study is designed to investigate various elements of Choi's spirituality as a representative of Korean Pentecostalism. Her spirituality not only shows her deep spiritual commitment to the Lord, but it is also a case of creative contextualization of Pentecostal faith.

What Is Spirituality?

There are many ways to define spirituality. It can be broad or narrow depending on how one comprehends its content. Perhaps a traditional approach to spirituality focuses on seeking the presence of God in prayer, meditation, contemplation and fasting to learn God's heart, desires and to adopt his character. This spiritual life is necessary to carry on a solid pattern of Christian living. It is furthermore encouraged in order to generate and to put into practice the fruit of the Spirit: love, joy, peace, patience, kindness…' (Galatians 5:22-23). It takes a period of time to bear fruit in one's Christian life, just as a tree never bears a single fruit immediately. This implies that spiritual formation does not take place in a split-second, but perhaps requires a life-long process. Spirituality makes life worth living and produces a valuable life through reflecting its maturity.

C.S. Lewis, a great Christian thinker, sought to form his spiritual life through self-giving, that is, the giving of one's whole self to Christ, including all personal wishes and precautions. Instead of being self-centred and focusing on worldly pleasure or ambition, one has to be honest and humble to be in conformity with good; in other words, giving-up self desire. Lewis contemplates seriously on how one can keep such a valuable life. He states that, 'a thistle cannot produce figs. If I am a field that contains nothing but grass-seed, I cannot produce wheat. Cutting the grass may keep it short, but I shall still produce grass and no wheat. If I want to produce wheat, the change must go deeper than the surface. I must be

---

[1] Yonggi Cho expressed it in the Preface of Jashil Choi, *I Was a Hallelujah Woman* (in Korean; Seoul: Seoul Books, 1978). The book will be referred to as Choi, *Hallelujah Woman*.

ploughed up and re-sown'.[2] Lewis is obviously aware of the value of being good, and this shows his degree of spiritual maturity.

St. Augustine, who was born in North Africa in 354 and lived in a monastic community for thirty-four years, confessed his own struggle to nurture spirituality. He has been considered as one of the most significant thinkers in the history of the Christian church. Augustine's spirituality focuses on an on-going debate to surrender to the will of Christ, through which he believed he could get into deep faith. He desired to live according to the will of God, but he could not fully conform to it; thus he agonized under such a growing process. He explained the process of spiritual growth with this analogy:

> The mind gives an order to the body and is at once obeyed, but when it gives an order to itself, it is resisted. What causes it? The mind commands the hand to move and is so readily obeyed that the order can scarcely be distinguished from its execution. Yet the mind is mind and the hand is part of the body. But when the mind commands the mind to make an act of will, these two are one and the same and yet the order is not obeyed. Why does this happen? The mind orders itself to make an act of will, and it would not give this order unless it willed to do so; yet it does not carry out its own command. But it does not fully will to do this thing and therefore its orders are not fully given. It gives the order only insofar as it wills, and insofar as it does not will, the order is not carried out.[3]

As Paul cried out against the struggle of the law of Spirit and body (Rom. 7:14-25), Augustine likewise experienced the same degree of dilemma. His sole desire was to be fully conformed to the will of God and live according to Christ's will for him. Here, 'the will' most likely contains all biblical teachings and follows the promises of Christ, thus living a true spiritual life.

How do Pentecostals understand spirituality? Russell Spittler, who is noted for his interest in the subject, agrees that spirituality consists of behaviours and contemplations that are learned by the beliefs and values that identify a particular religious fellowship.[4] Russell presents five specific values ruling Pentecostal spirituality.[5]

First, he refers to personal experience in accomplishing religious contentment. The personal experience, especially for Pentecostals, is truly guided by the presence of the Holy Spirit. Their desire is to know more of God through a spiritual journey.

---

[2] C.S. Lewis, 'Excerpts from Mere Christianity', in Richard J. Foster and James B. Smith (eds.), *Devotional Classics* (San Francisco: Harper San Francisco, 1993), 7-9.
[3] St. Augustine in Foster and Smith (eds.), *Excerpts from Confessions*, 52-53.
[4] Russell Spittler, 'Spirituality, Pentecostal and Charismatic', *DPCM*, 804.
[5] Spittler, 'Spirituality', 804-805.

Secondly, orality[6] is one of the important ways to express what the Divine Being has accomplished in their lives through his love, goodness, faithfulness and mercy, and such affective dimension, which is eminently developed, will be demonstrated orally. Thus, Pentecostals value orality as high as the written record in terms of sharing their empirical experience with Jesus Christ.

Thirdly, spontaneity is counted as Pentecostal devoutness. Spirituality is being exercised in intensity during worship time, and this is because the Holy Spirit comes upon those worshippers who wait on and welcome the Spirit to lead. Thus, Pentecostals cannot keep themselves in silence.

Fourthly, the notion of otherworldliness is strongly imbedded in their spiritual life. The true world is not the visible world, but the invisible and eternal world. Such perception prevails, perhaps more among the grass-root level, than the upper-middle class. I have noticed that tribal people in Northern Luzon[7] are fond of songs containing ideas of 'hope' and 'heaven', or songs of the Second Coming of Christ. Their dire living conditions cause them to draw closer to the Saviour and to increase their hope in the eternal world.

Lastly, making allegiance to biblical authority is one of the Pentecostals' spiritual characteristics. Their high consideration for biblical authority, and diligent leaning to take the message of the scriptures at face value, are common among Pentecostals.[8] Balancing both beliefs and practices is a significant value that Pentecostals highly regard. Thus, Pentecostal spirituality is not transcendental or philosophical, but practical and tangible and such spirituality facilitates an encounter with God in a unique way.

Biblical Perspectives on Prayer and Fasting

The Scriptures often emphasize the importance of prayer in the believer's life. The Book of Psalms contains a variety of prayers and supplications offered by the psalmist. The people of God cry out in times of trouble, moments of grief, and on many other occasions.

In Psalm 50:15, God urges his people 'Call upon me in the day of trouble; I will deliver you, and you will honour me'. Also Psalm 38:15 notes, 'I wait for you, O Lord; you will answer, O Lord my God'. Mark 14:32-36 describes how, with a troubled heart, Jesus spent time in prayer. Verse 34 reads, 'My soul is overwhelmed with sorrow to the point of death'. He asks the Father, if it is possible, to take the 'cup' from him. In Chapters 3 and 4, the Book of Esther

---

[6] Also W.J. Hollenweger, 'Pentecostal Research: Problems and Promises', in Charles E. Jones (ed.), *A Guide to the Study of the Pentecostal Movement* (Metuchen, NJ: Scarecrow, 1983), vii-ix.

[7] Pentecostal churches among the grass-root animistic tribal groups were established through intensive power manifestations around 1947-1955. For more detail, see J. Ma, *When the Spirit Meets the Spirits*.

[8] Spittler, 'Spirituality', 805.

details the difficulties Esther faced as a result of the evil plot by her enemy, Haman. Esther 4:16 reveals how determined Esther was to rescue her people, as it records Esther's words to Mordecai: 'Go, gather together all the Jews who are in Susa, and fast for me. Do not eat or drink for three days, night or day. I and my maids will fast as you do'. These texts all highlight the significant role which prayer plays in the spiritual life of God's people.

More specifically in Esther, fasting is presented as an integral part of prayer, especially in times of extreme need. The Psalmist also fasts, possibly to get rid of shame. II Kings 18:5-8 speaks of Hezekiah's spiritual life before God; he not only places full trust in God, but also fasts and prays. He obeys the commands the Lord gave Moses. God blesses all aspects of Hezekiah's activities and makes him a successful king (v. 7). Deuteronomy 13:4 also highlights the importance of fasting for maintaining an upright heart and keeping the commands of the Lord. The text declares: 'It is the Lord your God you must follow, and him you must revere'.

The above Scriptures all clearly demonstrate the importance of prayer and fasting. Prayer and fasting are presented as significant in solving personal problems, establishing peace in the family, healing the sick, dealing with grief, and sharing the gospel.

Choi's Personal Background

Choi was born in 1915 in Haeju City in Hwang-hae Province of North Korea during the Japanese occupation. While she was still young, her father died and she had to take up the heavy responsibility of assisting her mother, who made a tiny income from her sewing job. At the age of twelve, she and her mother had a chance to attend a tent revival meeting led by Sung-Bong Lee, a well-known Holiness preacher in early Korean Christian history. During this meeting they accepted Christ as their personal Savior. Their great desire was to be able to overcome poverty and become rich. To achieve this goal, Choi entered a nursing school to become a nurse and to work as a midwife as well. During those days nurses earned good money, while enjoying a decent life and respect. Choi's diligence and hard work led her closer to her goal, and she later married an affluent and educated man.

After moving to Seoul, South Korea from the North, she opened a new business and it became successful. However, the more money she made the more empty her heart became. And yet, she refused to go to church. Then a tragedy befell her: her mother and the oldest daughter died, within about a ten-day interval of each other. That incident shook Choi so badly that she developed complex illnesses. She interpreted this as a penalization from God for her ambition and worldly desires and for her life away from him. Coincidentally, her business failed miserably. In 1956, she attempted to kill herself as she was losing all hope to live.

During this desperate period, she turned to the Lord. She headed to a prayer mountain, where the famous revival speaker Sung-Bong Lee was conducting a revival meeting, and there she came back to the Lord. Lee's message strongly ministered to her heart and helped her open up to the Holy Spirit. During the prayer time, she experienced fire running throughout her body from above, and her tongue became twisted and she spoke in a strange language, as the Holy Spirit baptized her. She had a true encounter with the Lord and made a full commitment to him. She entered the Full Gospel Bible College to prepare for her future ministry.[9]

Prayer and Fasting in Choi's Life

The spirituality of Choi's life can be attributed to two key components: prayer and fasting. This spiritual practice has long been recognized as vital in a Christian's life. According to Roberta C. Bondi, prayer is the fundamental reality of a Christian life. Prayer actualizes believers as they discover their focus in God.[10] Prayer leads God's people into growth knowledge of, and deepening love for, God. E. M. Bounds notes that prayer has to be the basis of Christian character, one's life and living. This is Christ's law of prayer, forming it into the very being of the Christian. It should be the primary step and breath.[11] 'Prayer is the Christian's vital breath, The Christian's native air; His watchword at the gates of death; He enters heaven with prayer'.[12]

Choi, in her book, *Way of Receiving Answer*,[13] illustrates the power of prayer as found in Exodus 17:8-16. Israel's war against the invading Amalekites at Rephidm was entirely dependent on Moses' praying hands. If he continually held up his hands, victory was on the Israelites; but when his hands came down, the enemy won. To win the battle, Moses had to sit on a rock while his assistants held up his hands. Choi emphasizes the importance of unceasing prayer, particularly in the midst of life's difficulties.

Choi's prayer life was shaped during her Bible school years. In a sense, her life of being a student in her older age could have been exciting, but it was not. She had many responsibilities, including the burden of leaving her children to someone else's care, and supporting them. Such difficult situations drew her closer to God and her spirituality in prayer was developed. Choi not only prayed at designated hours she set up, but she also prayed constantly. Her spirituality was not confined just to her private life, but was often demonstrated in her life of ministry, and such display of concern for others was part of her spiritual exercise.

[9] Choi, *Hallelujah Woman*, 1-125.
[10] Roberta C. Bondi, *To Pray and to Love* (Minneapolis: Fortress Press, 1991), 12.
[11] E.M. Bounds, *The Complete Works of E.M. Bounds on Prayer* (Grand Rapids, MI: Baker, 1995), 247.
[12] Bondi, *To Pray and to Love*, 247.
[13] Jashil Choi, *How to Pray for Answer* (in Korean; Seoul: Seoul Books, 1997), 11.

She recalled the time during Bible school days, when Yonggi Cho was terribly ill with tuberculosis. While no one else paid any attention to him, or cared for him, she showed her affection towards him with intense prayer for his healing.[14] Perhaps this incident encouraged them to cultivate a close relationship with each other.

Choi fasted as often as her spirit was led. She firmly believed that fasting could draw one closer to the Divine presence and enable more powerful prayer. As a result, she found that problems were solved rather quickly through intense prayer and fasting.

Arthur Wallis believes that spirituality is exercised in a form of fasting for enduement of power, for spiritual gifts and for physical healing, and specific answers to prayer.[15] Choi also argued similarly on the prominence of fasting. This discovery was made through her long and deep spiritual journey. Her desire for a sound spiritual life, led her to the establishment of a prayer mountain dedicated to fasting. Long and intensive prayer with frequent fasting naturally characterized this process. The more time she spent in prayer and fasting, the stronger her faith became for the very first prayer mountain, with distinct emphasis on fasting.

In the meantime, she began to search for a good location for the prayer facility. While she was praying and fasting, one night she clearly heard the voice of God directing her to a parcel of land for the prayer mountain. The place had been a cemetery for many years and she may have felt a strong reluctance about using it. However, when she made an immediate visit to the place called Osan-ni Village, she knelt down on her knees on the barren ground, surrounded by graves, and prayed.

After her daily ministry in the fast growing church pastored by Yonggi Cho, she would go alone to the cemetery and spent hours in prayer every night.[16] A woman with no company, praying in the desolate field, must have been a strange sight; but it demonstrated her unreserved trust in God's promise and her strong commitment to him. These short accounts of her early life and ministry suffice to illustrate her unique spiritual life.

The Influence of Choi's Spirituality on Her Ministry

Personal Evangelism

Choi had a marvellous heart for serving lost souls. She always made herself available to be used for the work of God's kingdom. During her training in the Bible school, she took every opportunity to bring the unsaved to Christ.

---

[14] Choi, *Hallelujah Woman*, 147-52.

[15] Arthur Wallis, *God's Chosen Fast* (Fort Washington, PA: Christian Literature Crusade, 1968), 55-59.

[16] Choi, *Hallelujah Woman*, 429-33.

Donald Whitney points out that evangelism is an intrinsic overflow of the Christian life. It is also the call of a *disciple,* that all Christians should follow the Lord, not only in obedience, but also in evangelism. Each Christian, therefore, has to be active in witnessing, rather than waiting for a moment to come.[17] Matthew 5:16 well fits this context: 'Let your light shine before men, that they may see your good deeds and praise your Father in heaven'. Whitney correctly interprets that, to 'let' the light shine before others means more than 'don't do anything to keep your light from shining'. The closest rendering is: 'Let there be the light of good works shining in your life, let there be the evidence of God-honouring change radiating from you. Let it begin! Make room for it!'[18]

Choi's unique evangelism strategy was to approach children, as Choi had a natural ability to draw children to her. Even in evangelism, prayer was the bedrock of her ministry. She in fact spent more time in prayer and fasting than in actual evangelism.

In 1957 Choi graduated from the Bible school, but was not certain about her future ministry. In order to discover God's direction for her, she fervently prayed and fasted for many days. At one point, Choi seriously considered operating an orphanage since she had a heart for children, but soon learned that was not God's best intention for her. Nonetheless, Choi continually exerted herself in children's evangelism. Her autobiography includes many incidents that illustrate her love for the souls of children. Every night her intense prayer always included children.[19]

She gradually expanded her evangelistic activities to include adults. Each Sunday, Choi had about 70 attendees in fellowship, plus a good number of children. As there was no suitable meeting place, their gathering often took place under a pine tree. Thus, rainy days posed extreme challenges. Once, during her regular prayer time in a quiet place, she heard the voice of God instructing her to start a tent church. 'Hearing God's voice' was a regular part of her prayer life.

The Bible provides a good number of cases where people spent time to listen to God. I Kings 19:11-13 notes Elijah's effort to hear the gentle voice of God in a segregated Mount Horeb. Habakkuk (2:1) also stood on the guard post and kept attention to see or hear what God would speak to him. The depth of Choi's faith and trust is certainly comparable with Bible characters, particularly in her desire and endurance to hear the Divine voice.

With God's assurance, and joy bubbling in her heart, Choi began to proceed immediately with the purchase of a tent. In those days, a tent was expensive and not of good quality, but eventually a tent was pitched on the outskirts of Seoul, surrounded by makeshift houses and graves. Her zeal for soul winning increased, and many were added to the Kingdom.

---

[17] Donald Whitney, *Spiritual Disciples for the Christian Life* (Colorado Springs, CO: NavPress, 1993), 100.

[18] Whitney, *Spiritual Disciples*, 100.

[19] Choi, *Hallelujah Woman*, 213.

Bounds contends that in prayer, trust in faith becomes absolute, validated, accomplished. Trust is solid belief and faith is 'full flower'. It is an alert act, a fact to which believers are sensitive. According to the biblical notion, it is the eye of the infant soul and the ear of the regenerated soul. Such belief brings no wakefulness of their presence, no 'joy unspeakable and full of glory' results from their exertion.[20]

Christ showed that trust is the basic foundation of prayer. The central issue of Christ's ministry and work was his unreserved trust in his Father. When trust is complete, prayer is simply an outstretched hand ready to receive.[21] Trust always operates in the present tense, not in the past.

Sensitivity to Felt Needs

Choi found herself frequently caring for the needy and sick. Residents around the church were extremely poor, many were physically ill, and some were demon-possessed. One day a poor family invited her to visit the mother, who had been greatly suffering for seven years with a severe case as a paralytic. To make her situation worse, the mother had given birth recently and was not able to afford nutritious food needed for recuperation. As a result, she was very sick. When Choi entered the room, a strong odor caused nausea and she almost threw up. She immediately prayed to get over the difficult smell and embraced the family with love. The Lord spoke into her heart: 'Do not just ask for love, get water and wash her body'.[22] Upon hearing the voice of God, Choi washed the malodorous body of the woman and even her children. Bondi characterizes God's love, not as the love of a disinterested and unjust king for his aloof subjects. It is close, tender and defenseless, as a mother's is for her child.[23]

Choi's deep spirituality is a tangible embodiment of what Abba Poemen stated:

> There is nothing greater in love than that a (person) lay down (that person's) life for his (or her) neighbour. When a (person) hears a complaining word and struggles against himself (or herself) and does not...begin to complain; when a (person) bears an injury with patience, and does not look for revenge; that is when a (person) lays down his (or her) life for his (or her) neighbours.[24]

Choi's action revealed the genuine love of God toward her neighbour in an extreme need and she often cried with pain in her heart for this family; and with compassion, she constantly visited them and offered deep prayers for their healing, as well as their conversion. The family's situation was worsened by the heavy drinking of the husband day and night, who never paid any attention to the

[20] Bounds, *The Complete Works*, 24.
[21] Bounds, *The Complete Works*, 26.
[22] Choi, *Hallelujah Woman*, 227.
[23] Bondi, *To Pray and to Love*, 29.
[24] Bondi, *To Pray and to Love*, 112.

family. Choi, even in her own financial difficulty, brought bread and rice for the family.[25] She understood how God treats the poor: 'Has not God chosen those who are poor in the eyes of the world to be rich in faith and to inherit the kingdom...' (James 2:5). Verse 6 continues, 'But you have insulted the poor'. Matthew records the attitude of the Lord: 'If you want to be perfect, go, sell your possessions and give to the poor, and you will have treasure in heaven...' (Matthew 9:21).

In a similar way, George Soares Prabhu argues that, to be a follower of Christ means experiencing God the way that Jesus had experienced God. One essential element for Christian self-definition is the experience of God's love, which encourages us to love in effectual compassion to those in want.[26] The poor are indeed the object of God's concern and care. To appropriate God's compassion toward the needy is an important element of Christian spirituality.

Choi's spirituality is a good example. It was expressed in cleaning smelly rooms and bathing children regularly. In addition, she once fasted for three days for the mother's healing and the salvation of the entire family. She constantly read the Bible and prayed to encourage her faith. Through her persevering prayer, the paralytic woman began to rise and take fragile steps. Awesome Divine power was manifested, and fifteen days later, the woman was able to work for the family. Such events caused others to open their eyes and come to the Lord.

Choi was assured of the power of fasting in supplication for healing. She expounded the prominence of fasting in prayer in her book,[27] *How to Pray for Answer*, drawing examples from the scriptures. Hezekiah was her outstanding example. He was a spiritual man who put total trust in the Lord for the peace of a nation (2 Kings 18:6). When he was fatally ill and about to die, he wept bitterly before God for healing. His supplication resulted in Divine grace and his life was expanded by fifteen more years.

Spiritual Warfare

Throughout her ministry, Choi encountered many demon-possessed cases. After a Sunday worship service, a member from a neighbouring church rushed to Choi, asking her to visit her friend, who was tormented by a terrible sickness. The sick woman was not a Christian, and she was always referred to shamans for healing and advice. One day the shaman gave a striking revelation: 'If she fails to become a shaman through a special ritual, she will die soon'. Upon hearing such a dreadful verdict, her family fiercely opposed the idea and out of great anxiety,

---

[25] Choi, *Hallelujah Woman*, 232-33.

[26] George Soares Prabhu, 'The Jesus of Faith: A Christological Contribution to an Ecumenical Third World Spirituality', in K.C. Abraham and Bernadette Mbuy-Beya (eds.), *Spirituality of the Third World* (Maryknoll, New York: Orbis, 1994), 153.

[27] Choi, *How to Pray for Answer*, 105-106.

shared her problem with her Christian friend.[28] This proves that Choi was quite well known in the area as a woman filled with the Spirit and that she had an earnest desire to minister to people who were going through difficulties.

Bounds notes that religion has to do with everything but our hearts. It requires our hands and feet to give full devotion. It takes hold of our voices to praise. It lays its hands on our material concern. But it does not take hold of personal affections, desires and enthusiasm.[29] One may add that our sincere heart is not only for worship and praise, but also to serve with our hands and feet with it, laying down human selfishness and fervour.

Choi, and her ministry partner Yonggi Cho, were brought to the house of the sick woman. When they entered the room, she suddenly sat down and stared at them like an angry rooster. Choi and the accompanying members quietly sat on the floor and began to sing hymns. Choi instantaneously knew that Satan would attempt to attack.[30]

Ephesians 6:10-20 well states such a spiritual struggle. Believers are caught in the idea of eschatological tension that is 'already, but not yet'. The Apostle Paul was well aware of two different realms of power: God and the devil. It is also obvious that in the world, the dominion of darkness is on one side, while Christ, Christians with the power and authority of God, are on the other.[31]

With this understanding, Choi and her group sang continually and rebuked the evil spirit in the woman with the authority of Christ. In the middle of singing and prayer, the woman abruptly uttered in Japanese, 'Let's go. Let's go to Japan'. (Choi spoke Japanese like many Koreans who endured Japanese occupation.) Then, she seemed to be back to normal. The Japanese language was not spoken by the woman, but by Satan. According to the woman, she had gone to Japan for study when she was a young girl and had stayed there for several years. During this period she became a member of a religious group, and then she later returned to Korea and married. While she was pregnant with her first child, she was terribly ill and the sickness continued until Choi's ministry to her. Through the power of God displayed in prayer, the woman was delivered from her bondage. Such manifestation of God's power led her entire family and relatives to the Lord.

Power encounter is a regular part of Christian spiritual life, especially among Pentecostals. Thus, the concept has been used among Asian Christians without question. But some believers feel reluctant to use such a term because of its military connotation. This term was first used by Alan Tippett to refer to a

---

[28] Choi, *Hallelujah Woman*, 315-16.
[29] Bounds, *The Complete Works*, 92.
[30] Choi, *Hallelujah Woman*, 317.
[31] Clinton E. Arnold, *Ephesians: Power and Magic* (Grand Rapids, MI: Baker, 1992), 156-57.

conflict between the kingdom of God and the kingdom of Satan.[32] It frequently takes place, especially among tribal groups who believe in the spiritual world and the involvement of spirits in their life.

During the ministry of Jesus, he drove out many demons from people. This demonstration of God's power was also frequent in the Old Testament. One of the outstanding instances is the story of Elijah, confronting the four hundred and fifty prophets of Baal on Mount Carmel (I Kings 18:16-45). Oscar Cullmann notes that Satan still has great power, power that can destroy any human being and his or her plan if they remained without encumbrance.[33] Thus, Divine power and authority is essential for effective work in God's kingdom. John Wimber argues that unity also facilitates believers to experience God's power.[34] In the Book of Acts, when believers came together in one accord, the power of God was manifested.

The Establishment of Prayer Mountain

The church Choi had pioneered with Yonggi Cho in the outskirts of Seoul moved to town to accommodate the growing members. After the move, the membership soon grew to 18,000, and the growth continued during the next seven years. During these exceptional years of church growth, Cho was perfectly complemented by Choi's spiritual insights and gifts. The church became particularly known for its healing ministry. When the church held a tent revival meeting, together with missionary Sam Todd, about 200 people received healing.[35]

As the church constantly grew in number, Cho and the church began to search for another location for a new church building. When Yoido Island was suggested, odds were against Cho. First, Yoido was too far from the city centre, and the future of the deserted military airfield was uncertain. This challenge took Choi frequently to a prayer mountain near Seoul. While she was asking God about the future of the church, suddenly the idea of starting a prayer mountain for her own church entered her mind. She immediately noticed that it was not merely a human thought, but it was from God. With this assurance, Choi prayed every day for God's direction. In addition to the huge financial needs, the timing seemed to be wrong: the church was preparing for a new and huge facility. However, Choi did not abandon the vision. In fact, the vision grew stronger through her prayers. Every night she went to the cemetery in Osan-ri and spent

---

[32] Alan R. Tippet, *People Movements in Southern Polynesia* (Chicago: Moody Press, 1971), 81.

[33] Oscar Cullmann, *Christ and Time* (Philadelphia: Westminster, 1964), 64.

[34] John Wimber and Kevin Springer, *Power Evangelism* (New York: Harper Collins, 1984), 58.

[35] Choi, *Hallelujah Woman*, 355-56.

her time in prayer. Through the ministry of the prayer mountain, she wanted to bring the people of God to a prayer life.[36]

More than once Yonggi Cho has underscored the importance of prayer: 'We Koreans have made prayer our first priority. From prayer has come communion and fellowship with the Holy Spirit. Today the Holy Spirit guides us in our daily lives, and we have power with God through prayer'.[37] Bondi had a holistic view of prayer: the possibilities of prayer influence all things. Whatever deals with people's highest well-being, and whatever has to do with God's scheme and will concerning human beings on earth, is a subject for prayer. Prayer opens doors for the access of the gospel.[38]

In addition to the financial challenge, some leaders of the church questioned the choice of the location. First of all, it was located in the northern part that was too close to the border with North Korea. In case of a North Korean invasion, the area would be devastated instantly. Secondly, there was no running water or trees, but only graves. Such negative feedback caused Choi to feel that the prayer mountain no longer seemed a possibility, and she was indeed despondent. Once, she spent the whole night with some church members in prayer. During her prayer, God gave her scriptures that uplifted her enormously: John 14:1, 'Do not let your hearts be troubled. Trust in God; trust also in me'. Also Philippians 2:13, 14 was another passage: 'For it is God who works in you to will and to act according to his good purpose. Do everything without complaining or arguing…'. From these verses Choi was assured that God would accomplish this vision through her.[39]

It is rather common among Pentecostals to expect the 'leading of the Spirit', as Pentecostals have a sense of hearing what the Spirit is speaking to them, not only through the word of God, but also through a personal encounter with God.

The Lord then showed a clear sign of his will: People from different places flocked into Osan-ri, even though it was not yet purchased and was still barren. Those people who came prayed with fasting, and this became a rule of this prayer mountain. Soon the place began to attract people from Japan and other parts of the world and they too discovered a new spiritual dimension through prayer with fasting. The Osan-ri Prayer Mountain became the first international facility for prayer and fasting. An increasing number of sick came to experience divine healing. Soon many experienced healing from incurable sicknesses through intensive and fervent prayer accompanied with fasting. Such news soon spread throughout the nation and more people who were in a desperate situation came to pray.

---

[36] Choi, *Hallelujah Woman*, 415-32.

[37] Yonggi Cho, 'Prayer Can Change the Course of Your Life', *Pentecostal Evangel*, Oct. 18, 1998, 11.

[38] Bondi, *To Pray and to Love*, 163.

[39] Choi, *Hallelujah Woman*, 432-33.

An emphasis on the power of prayer and fasting became the hallmark of Choi's spirituality. Joel 2:12 notes the significance of fasting: 'Yet even now', says the Lord, 'return to me with all your heart, with fasting...'. First Kings 21:27-29 also illustrates a similar point. After the murder of Naboth and Ahab's obligatory obtainment of his vineyard, God sent Elijah to declare Divine judgment upon him. 'When Ahab heard those words, he rent his clothes, and put sackcloth upon his flesh, and fasted'. God then declared, 'Because he has humbled himself before me, I will not bring evil in his days; but in his son's days' (1 Kings 21:27-29). Judgment was postponed because even such an evil person as Ahab humbled himself by fasting. God's mercy is never limited to only righteous people, but is extended to anyone who seeks God's mercy.

Fasting displays how earnest the people of God are, especially in time of need. Arthur Wallis notes that 'fasting makes prayer ascend up as on eagle's wings. It is meant to usher the supplicant into the spectators' room of the Lord and to extend to him the golden scenery. It may be anticipated to drive back the oppressing powers of darkness and loosen their grip on the prayer objective. It is counted to give a brim to a man's intercessions and power to his petitions. The Lord is eager to listen when someone prays with fasting'.[40]

Undoubtedly, fasting is an important aspect of the Christian life, and is often the ultimate form of earnest and extended supplication. Fasting is indeed a spiritual wrestling between the supplicant and the Divine Being, and Andrew Murray affirms that 'fasting helps to express, to deepen, and to confirm the resolution that we are ready to sacrifice anything, to sacrifice ourselves, to attain what we seek for the kingdom of God'.[41]

In the CJIFPM, originally called the Osan-ri Prayer Mountain, some fasted for forty days. Such testimonies and the increasing number of visitors to Osan-ri, even though it was located in a desolate place, moved the hearts of church leaders to establish the prayer mountain. Ultimately, however, it was the Holy Spirit who accomplished the vision, as during the early period of the prayer mountain, Choi fasted as frequently as three days a week. Her exemplary prayer life has encouraged many to follow her example and they have been drawn into deep spiritual experiences.

Choi's International Ministry

Choi's spiritual ministry soon crossed national boundaries and expanded to other countries. God opened a door for her to reach the Japanese, as church leaders repeatedly invited her to come. Prior to her preaching, Choi would customarily spend the whole night in prayer for the next day's service. The effects of her prayers were so evident, that many people in the service were filled with the Holy Spirit. Also, a variety of manifestations of the Spirit regularly took place. Choi's anointed message, accompanied by the work of the Spirit, impacted many

---

[40] Wallis, *God's Chosen Fast*, 50.
[41] Wallis, *God's Chosen Fast*, 50.

Japanese churches. Common themes of her messages were repentance, prayer and the Spirit-led life.

When she visited a place, Choi eagerly ministered in as many churches as she could and offered a marvellous ministry. Her autobiography illustrates her eagerness as well. The Spirit was at work particularly in healing and often unprecedented miracles took place. Soon, many people in Japan with sicknesses began to visit the prayer mountain in Osan-ri and spent days in prayer and fasting, during which time a variety of spiritual gifts were manifested, including speaking in tongues and interpretation.

Many in the United States were called into the ministry through her influence. Her ministry in Thailand, Hong Kong, Germany and other places produced similar results. Choi's international ministry was also her commitment to the missionary call found in Acts 1:8, 'But you will receive power when the Holy Spirit comes on you; and you will be my witnesses in Jerusalem, and in all Judea and Samaria, and to the ends of the earth'.[42]

Prior to such trips, Choi spent two or three weeks in prayer and fasting. She was not only preparing for a forthcoming ministry, but was also making herself a living message of God's power through prayer and fasting'.

Assessment of Choi's Spirituality

Her Influence on Korean Christianity

As discussed above, Choi's distinctive spirituality had strong implications on her ministry: it was founded on prayer and fasting. Perhaps it is fair to say that such spirituality had been a part of the spiritual traditions in various religions, and particularly in Korean Christianity.

In the early revival in Pyungyang (1939) for instance, the entire 3,000 members in Suemoon Church fasted, while praying the whole night. The preacher was Jun, Jasun, one of the great evangelists. Such incident caused the members to encounter the power of the Holy Spirit, repentance and a spiritual renewal.[43]

During the post-exilic period in the Old Testament, Jews commonly fasted as a form of prayer, and fasting became a part of their spirituality. Even in New Testament times Jews frequently fasted (Matthew 6:16-18). Thus, fasting is a long Jewish tradition.

However, Choi's practice of prayer and fasting may not be strictly identified with the Jewish practice. As everyone would agree, prayer is an essential part of Christian spiritual life; but, fasting requires additional commitment and effort. Perhaps an experience or two of fasting, especially in a desperate circumstance,

---

[42] Choi, *Hallelujah Woman*, 437-60.

[43] International Theological Institutes, *A History of the Korean Assemblies of God* (in Korean; Seoul: Seoul Books, 1998), 183-84.

could be possible without much serious discipline. However, fasting regularly as part of one's spiritual life was probably a new concept, at least in Korean Christianity.

From the beginning of her Christian life, Choi considered fasting very important for cultivating her spiritual growth and development of an intimate relationship with the Lord. This also led her to wider and deeper spiritual experiences; for instance, before engaging in cases of demon possession, she fasted with fervent prayer. She frequently experienced God's power to drive out the demon. Thus, one can acknowledge the importance of fasting in spiritual warfare.

Fasting also enhanced many Christian works such as evangelism, preaching, missions, church growth, healing and solving diverse problems. As discussed above, Choi's ministry was characterized by prayer and fasting. In fact, her spiritual leadership and contribution through her intense prayer and fasting was an integral part of the unprecedented growth of the YFGC. Yonggi Cho acknowledges it openly, '…if she was not my co-worker, I am not able to accomplish such a successful pastoral ministry now'.[44]

Challenges of Choi's Spirituality

Fasting and prayer have been the main features of Choi's spirituality. Her deep communion with God through prayer and fasting greatly heightened her sensitivity in the Spirit. Choi's unique spirituality, especially through her prayer mountain ministry, set forth a new paradigm for Christian spirituality, and this became identified as Korean Pentecostal spirituality.

Choi's teaching on prayer and fasting spread quickly to the entire Korean Christianity and beyond, not only through the prayer mountain, but also through her popular conferences which she conducted in various countries. One such conference was held in Jerusalem in October, 1980, when around 500 people came from different countries and had a four-day prayer rally with fasting. Thirty-four ministers from South Africa attended this conference and experienced a deep working of the Spirit. The participants learned how to pray with fasting and this became a significant part of their spiritual life, as well as that of their churches. Consequently, fasting has become a common and even important spiritual religious tradition across many countries. For example, I have seen an American fast for one day, before he delivered a special lecture.

Choi's life-long devotion to, and campaign for, prayer and fasting changed the spiritual paradigm of the Korean church forever. Her life and ministry demonstrated that prayer is not just part of the Christian life, but prayer *is* the Christian life. When prayer is accompanied by fasting, the intensity of prayer is significantly enhanced. This is because fasting signifies a total surrender to God and a serious commitment to prayer itself. The example of Jesus shows this clearly in the Gospels. In the desert, he prepared himself in prayer, with forty-day

---

[44] Foreword to Choi, *Hallelujah Woman*.

fasting for the Messianic mission. After a long period of prayer he returned to Galilee in the power of the Spirit and was ready to launch his earthly mission (Luke 4:14).

The unique spirituality of Choi is something that the people of God must adapt and apply to their spiritual life. Such a spiritual exercise is perhaps more required in our increasingly secularized modern societies, so that the church can be the true light in a darkened post-modern era.

Summary

Choi's distinctive spirituality has been investigated and, as we have seen, everywhere she went, her prayer life with fasting impacted practically millions of believers through her pastoral and international ministries. Subsequently, several more prayer mountains with special emphasis on fasting were established, sometimes by her; but many others were established by people who had been impacted by her ministry. Until her death, prayer and fasting were the hallmark of her life and ministry. I was personally amazed by her solid spiritual devotion to prayer with fasting, and how deeply it was embedded in her life.

I personally received a paramount challenge from her life of prayer and fasting, as fasting is particularly difficult for me. I have done it on a few occasions; but, as the years went by, that laborious exercise slowly disappeared from my spiritual life. However, as I studied Choi's spirituality, I came to realize the significance of fasting. As a consequence, prayer and fasting have again slowly become a part of my spiritual journey.

Many believers, who were influenced by Choi, were boldly involved in extensive fasting. Particularly, members of the YFGC have been well taught. Cell group heads and church leaders are taken to the CJIFPM during the very first days of a new year to pray and fast. In fact, regular bus trips leave the church many times a day to go to the prayer mountain. I witnessed many people riding a bus to spend at least a night for prayer, right after the church service.

Spirituality is the human response to God, prompted by theology's intersection with a believers' real life.[45] Choi's life and ministry was shaped through an intense and continuous interaction with God. Surely prayer is one of the most meaningful ways to experience the presence of God.

Choi has taught us how to have a more successful and deeper experience with God, through prayer with fasting. My prayer is that Choi's rich spiritual legacy and heritage will continue to encourage and challenge many believers to

---

[45] Leslie C. Allen, 'Spirituality of the Psalms' (William Menzies Annual Lectureship, Asia Pacific Theological Seminary, Baguio, Philippines, January 2001), 3.

cultivate their spirituality through prayer and fasting. There is nothing more important in the Christian life than experiencing God himself on a regular basis.

Chapter 17

Spirit, Mission, and Unity: A Personal Journal

Introduction

If we were to reflect on our journey as individuals and as people corporately, it would reveal how the human race has made amazing progress in every aspect of human life, particularly in the past one hundred years or so. From a distinctly Christian perspective, God has also revealed His own plan for His creation as well as His will to fulfill this plan. In this divine economy, the people of God, called collectively the church, has been graciously invited by God to join God's own journey of restoring His creation.[1]

My own reflection will look back at the last one hundred years and highlight what God has been doing with his people as his 'mission partners'. Therefore, the two major themes of our gathering are understood in plain language: mission is what we are called for in relation to the world and God's creation, and 'churches together' in unity is how we relate to each other as God's missionary people.

I will begin with myself and then extend to others, and I will also begin with the past and move to the present. I do this as a second generation Christian, having grown up in a family where Christianity was always viewed as 'weird' and abnormal. This was also a common experience for many of my friends from the non-western world. At the end of each section, I will add comments that I have learned about what God has been doing with his people. I will discuss my own stories in this reflection, my own cultural and ethnic orientation as a Korean, and my own Christian experience as a Pentecostal. Hence, the presentation is oral in style.

What Have We Learned?

What have we observed in God's work with His people in the last one hundred years? What have we learned from this observation about His intention and our response?

---

[1] My statement of 'Mission as the Restoration of God's Creation' is found in ch. 2.

Christ: The Best Thing That Can Happen in Life

My first encounter with Christian truth was extremely personal and real. I had been a 'good' Sunday school boy, and church events were all part of my 'fun' life, as I hardly remember what the Korean War was like, not to mention the harsh Japanese colonial rule which predated the war. When I was a teenager, one day my mother decided to take my younger sister, who had suffered from polio, to a healing crusade in a nearby town. Mom asked me to get up early in the morning (5 a.m.!) and join the dawn prayer meeting at the church. My first reaction was, 'She can't be serious, that God could heal my sister, who had been given up by my own uncle, who was a surgeon!' Then, I realized that all the things I had learned from the Sunday school class may not be 'just old stories' at all; they may be real, if Mom is taking my sister to the same God. I had never before heard of a God who can, and will, do such a thing, and much more than that, or who as Christ in fact died in my place. Although my sister did not experience a radical healing as expected, my conversion process was well under way. Christ's coming into my life had become the crucial experience for the rest of my life.

Christian mission begins with this conviction of the uniqueness of Christ and His offer of salvation. That explains why my Mom was so zealous in bringing the people around us to the church. Even though she struggled as a new member of the church, and as the only Christian in a practically non-religious family by marrying my Dad, she thought all along that she was the only person in the family with 'real life'. The first fruit of her missionary engagement was all five of us, and then my cousins, later my Dad and my Grandma, both of whom used to be the fiercest critics of her faith. For her and us, this was a sure proof that this God was the very best and we were among the lucky few in this Buddhist country. We had eternal life and we were children of God! This God continued to prove His love and mercy as my Mom regularly resorted to Him when everything else failed.

It was one of the critical moments of my life, when I gave up my hope to go to university, and temporarily stopped my high school studies to help my younger siblings to continue their studies, when both parents were gravely ill. The only 'lifeline' my Mom had was a small Pentecostal church which was known for 'weeping in prayer'. Desperate (and dedicated, I supposed), these people braved the cold winter and a dark path to 'hang on' to the only hope for their daily survival. After the dawn prayer meeting, my Mom would tread the still dark path back home, worrying about what to cook for her five children. She recalled, having started the fire 'by faith' with water in the pot, she heard something drop outside the door. She ran out to the doorstep and saw a sack of rice. Two shadows hurriedly disappeared under the cover of darkness. For her, they were, and are, the angels, and God had miraculously provided for her needs. Such stories as this were repeated throughout her life.

The reality of the Christian message as Christ's good news to the poor (Luke 4:18-19) is particularly felt among the marginalized. The humble and yet desperate desire of my parents for their children was for them to receive an education much higher than elementary education, which they could only attain under Japanese colonial rule. There are millions of the 'poor' in the world to whom Christ's good news has been offered. Some of them are the millions of Indian Dalit parents, who struggle so that their children will be able to break the chain of oppression and poverty; also the ever-increasing refugees in various parts of the world, dislocated from their homes by force; hundreds of thousands of children, who are enslaved in city brothels and industries, forfeited of their basic rights to be children under care and protection; and millions of people under oppressive rulers, who fight for their freedom, as seen recently in Myanmar. This list goes on endlessly.

The steady and exponential growth of churches in the Global South (or 'Southern Church') has been in part attributed to the 'poor' hearts finding the unique 'good news' offered by Christianity. There is no doubt that such growth, for example in Korea, owes much to the missionary efforts of the western church (that is from Europe and North America, as well as Oceania), in spite of some criticisms, particularly as Christianity often came as part of a colonial enterprise. Moreover, as experienced by the Pentecostal movement in the twentieth century, the 'poor' are the most eager recipients of the gospel.

Mission: So Natural for God's People

Someone has brilliantly defined evangelism as 'a beggar telling another beggar where to get bread'. Then it is not difficult to follow my Mom's reasoning, that sharing any good news with those who are in need is natural, whether at 'home' or 'out there'. She was a genuine 'Great Commission' Christian, although she never spoke about the Great Commission. According to her, sometimes people simply do not know what they so desperately need. This simplistic and deep conviction has made many first-generation Christians extremely zealous in their faith, be they Korean, Chinese, Brazilian or Nigerian. Often their speeches are neither politically correct nor religiously tolerant, nor is their behaviour culturally refined or properly informed. In fact, they may appear religiously imperialistic and culturally ignorant, with their unswerving dedication and overflowing energy. The recent hostage incident involving the Korean short-term mission group in Afghanistan is a case in point. However, I became one of them: a Korean missionary to the Philippines.

Church history is a history of missionary work, be it good or bad. The missionary instinct of Christianity has been recently confirmed by the 'Back to Jerusalem' missionary movement of the Chinese house church movement.[2] This modern laboratory case of Christianity went through an entire generation, with

---

[2] David Aikman, *Jesus in Beijing: How Christianity Is Transforming China and Changing the Global Balance of Power* (Washington, DC: Regnery, 2003), 193-205; Paul Hattaway, *Back to Jerusalem: Three Chinese House Church Leaders Share their Vision to Complete the Great Commission* (Waynesboro, GA: Authentic Media, 2003).

almost no outside interference, under the extreme persecution of a brutal totalitarian political system. When the world finally had a chance to glance at the Chinese church, the big surprise was that the church had not only survived, but that it had also grown. An even bigger surprise has been its resolute commitment to 'reach back to Jerusalem', while still struggling to survive in the midst of persecution. The understanding of the nature of the church ('ecclesiology') cannot be complete without this outward mission to the world.

The Edinburgh Missionary Conference of 1910 was a co-ordinated effort among Protestant churches to bring this intuitive mission into a carefully crafted plan to evangelize the world in their own generation. As more than 80% of the world was under the political control of the western 'Christian' nations, there was optimism to finally complete the great commission. Plans and resources were at their disposal and they earnestly believed that they could 'finish the job'.[3] But instead, in this generation, two of the greatest world wars humans have ever known were fought among 'Christian' nations. The second half of the century witnessed the weakening of the western churches, while new churches emerged in the non-western world. Accordingly, the missionary mobilization was initially from the north and west to the east and the south. However, the last quarter of the twentieth century witnessed an increasing missionary movement from the south to the south (such as Brazilian missionaries to Malta). This does not in any way undermine the dedicated missionary service of so many from the western church, who willingly gave their lives to share the very 'good news' of Christ.[4]

What have we learned from this? The missionary call of the church begins with the uniqueness of Christ, and only those who affirm Him as the way of life can obey Christ's invitation to join in God's ultimate goal of restoration. Although viewed as problematic in the religiously pluralistic world, this mission is carried out by those who believe and experience that Christ is the best thing that happens in life. Often God raises His people from the margins, be it in the church world (ecclesiastically) or in the socio-economic context (socially). In fact, it is the 'beggar' who values the piece of 'bread' he receives and is then willing to share this good news with other 'beggars'. The second half of the last century demonstrated incredibly diverse missionary dynamics: laity as well as clergy; evangelism as well as social engagement; western as well as non-western; preachers as well as professionals. The Pentecostal movement has

---

[3] The conference theme, 'The Evangelization of the World in This Generation', was indeed the watchword of the missionary community in the western world.
[4] I have personally been impacted by a young, single, woman missionary, Ruby Rachel Kendrick (1883-1908), who died in Korea within a short time after her arrival. Her tombstone reads, 'If I had a thousand lives to give, Korea should have them all'. Taek-bu Jun, *Yanghwa-jin Missionary Biographies* [in Korean], rev. ed. (Seoul: Hongsung, 2005) includes many of such records of early missionaries in Korea.

forcefully presented what is called the 'prophethood of all believers', arguing that every believer has a missionary call.

Divided Body in the Name of Mission I: Which Life?

A 'Korean missionary' was as strange a concept to me as to my hosts. Until then, at least according to the common perception, 'missionaries' were white and lived in a large compound away from people in the country, eating food they brought from home. A missionary who needed to learn to speak English did not fall into the existing stereotype. However, this was not the first time that my unique value was not recognized: I saw it happen to my Mom long ago.

However, I quickly learned that 'not all mission is created equal', and not everyone means the same thing when they talk of mission. The biggest divide I soon encountered was the emphasis on human life in reference to death: one group has a mission to preach 'life after death', while the other has a mission to work for 'life before death'. This divide was particularly evident among the normal (or western) missionaries, and soon I also realized that 'mainline' churches are distinguished from 'evangelical' ones by their mission emphases.

These groups started together in the Edinburgh Missionary Conference in 1910 when carefully crafted theological agendas were presented for Christian (at least Protestant in this case) mission. Championing the marginalized and oppressed masses in society, particularly in the developing world, the 'life before death' camp purported to prepare God's people and its church to play an important role to create a just society. The move from Edinburgh to the formation of the World Council of Churches (WCC) caused the 'life after death' group to gradually drop out. To mainstream missiology, issues that hinder the creation of a just society are all mission topics: oppressive political systems, unjust socio-cultural structures, wide-spread poverty, the HIV-AIDS pandemic, ethnic genocide, human trafficking, among many others. The famous liberation theology from Latin America with its variations is but one example of the mission engagement of this group.

My early missionary life in the newly adopted country of the Philippines was during the time of the Marcos dictatorship. Home-grown (mostly Catholic) liberation theologians often led the armed resistance movement called the New People's Army. Many political 'enemies' of the Marcos regime found this movement to be the only 'home' for their social and political life. Such an approach often requires its missionaries not only to be in sympathy with the victims, but also to be involved in the struggle with them. Such solidarity with suffering fellow humans is indeed a noble cause, although sometimes the absence of 'Christian-ness' is criticized.

The other 'life after death' camp, to which I considered myself to belong, is extremely committed to the 'soul saving' business. Having correctly diagnosed that human problems have their roots in sin and the spiritual severance from the Lord of all lives, Christ the saviour is the answer to all human needs. Over the decades, this camp has strengthened its commitment to evangelism and church planting, just as the 'before' camp has concentrated its efforts on issues in 'this life'. This evangelical mission was further reinforced by the surge of Pentecostal-Charismatic Christianity, resulting in the rapid growth of evangelical Christianity, particularly in 'southern' countries. Theologically some topics on the 'liberal' agenda, such as church unity, inter-religious dialogue, and social engagement, were left to the other camp. The Lausanne Congress on World Evangelization (1974) commonly viewed as the best expression of an organized evangelical mission, was a watershed event in that it positively embraced social service as an integral part of Christian mission.[5]

What is logically apparent (without even mentioning the Biblical teaching) is that these two approaches are complementary to each other, as we need to live our life both before and after death. My eager church planting among mountain tribal groups quickly taught me that the presentation of the Christian 'good news' meant very little when many children were losing their lives because there was no medical facility available. The 'good news' has to include this earthly aspect as well as the heavenly one. At the same time, generous humanitarian aid without the presentation of Christ cannot be called Christian mission. Several years into this missionary journey, my wife and I came to conclude that each 'life' camp has part of the whole truth. This does not make their claim only a half truth. It is part of the full truth. However, each does not represent the full truth. Both are equally credible works of God's mission, but each is never complete without the other.

Divided Body in the Name of Mission II: Which Church?

Our family's move from a small town to a nearby city was also a move from a one-church community to a many-church setting. In the new city, by my Mom's choice, we all moved to a small Pentecostal church under a woman pastor. In Korean society this is by no means a respected congregation even among fellow Christians. This 'weeping church' so aptly described, because of various emotional expressions freely displayed, was where desperate youths, mothers and families came to weep and find hope for life. Even my Christian uncles (on my mother's side) urged us to get out of this 'cultish and indecent' church, where nonsensical claims of healing and miracles were regularly made, not to mention the controversial 'speaking in tongues'. But my mother weathered the years of hardship, and this time criticisms from fellow Christians were added to the struggles with non-believing in-laws and other family members. I used to think that we needed to overcome the 'world', but this time I also found out that we needed to overcome our fellow believers! With hindsight, I can see that there were doctrinal issues that divided the church. But I have also experienced enough cases to realize that small differences (often relational) or utterly

---

[5] Lausanne Committee for World Evangelization, 'The Lausanne Covenant' (July 1974) found, among others, at http://www.lausanne.org/lausanne-1974/lausanne-covenant. html, accessed on Sept. 11, 2007.

'worldly' cravings for power and control have divided local congregations. From one Presbyterian church (in fact, only one 'Korean Church' as early Presbyterian and Methodists decided) in Korea about 120 years ago, there are now more than 100 Presbyterian denominations, some due to 'imports', but most are due to domestic divisions. Each group's claim for authenticity and truth, at the cost of others, is blatantly un-Christian.

My Pentecostal 'table' was turned around as the Pentecostal movement spread its wings globally. By the time my wife and I were deeply involved in tribal areas in the northern Philippines, my Pentecostal denomination was the biggest and strongest, and still is the fastest growing. When we opened a church in a deep mountain village some years ago, one existing 'liberal' church simply died, and we 'praised' the Lord for his wonderful work. We thought that Christ's 'full gospel' had finally arrived in this place. However, I quickly realized that there were hundreds of small villages in the mountains without a single Christian family, let alone a church. As most zealous missionaries from 'new' (or 'Southern') churches would do, we were busy trying to evangelize everyone, including other Christians. In fact, we seem to have spent more energy in 'converting' other Christians into our form of Christianity than we did non-believers. (Local) church growth was equated with the Kingdom growth, even if sheep-stealing is part of the strategy. The extremely individualistic nature of 'evangelical' Christianity has spent much time and energy trying to figure out who is in and who is out. Anyone who is out should be 'evangelized', be they Catholic or otherwise.

It was only when I began to meet with brothers and sisters from other Christian churches did it become apparent that I was not only ignorant, but also arrogant. In fact, when I saw a good post-Pentecostal scholar enjoying his cigar, my confusion was at its height: how can the mouth which smokes speak 'heavenly language' (or tongues)? I was genuinely worried about the Holy Spirit who might have to look for fresh air. My understanding of church (ecclesiology), the Holy Spirit (pneumatology) and mission was hopelessly shallow and narrow. Later did I also realize that the gift of the Holy Spirit in the twentieth century was intended for the whole church. Only a few courageous Pentecostals like David du Plessis understood the mind of the Holy Spirit and took this very good news to other Christian churches, while they received severe criticism from their own churches.[6]

It is also noticeable that the ecumenical movement which has worked to bring various Christian churches together has created, ironically, an environment for some churches to find it simply impossible to approach the network. It has inadvertently formed a 'game plan' to know which belong to the 'in church' and which are 'outside' of the circle. How the Catholic Church has defined a genuine church and a second class church is a similar practice.

---

[6] David J. Du Plessis, and Bob Slosser, *A Man Called Mr. Pentecost* (Plainfield, JL: Logos, 1977).

My 'evangelize-everyone' attitude began to change when I started meeting wonderful new friends who dress and worship differently than I do. After all, I found out that I must look quite strange to them as well. This 'church unity by fellowship' (*koinonia*) has been something I have observed from my youth: average Christians care very little about denominations. I also noted that from diverse orientations, common experiences of the Holy Spirit bring together God's people for celebration. This 'spontaneous ecumenism'[7] was noted from the Azusa Street Mission, the very birthplace of the modern Pentecostal movement. My own experience of working with various church traditions in mission settings suggests that common commitment to mission is another platform where church unity can be experienced. This still leaves a legitimate place for a structural effort to create church unity.

A Tale of Two Siblings

My first exposure to the Edinburgh Missionary Conference (1910) was almost by accident. I was a mission practitioner whose academic training was in Biblical study. Even the second Lausanne Congress on World Evangelism in Manila (1989) was not of interest to me, even if it did take place in the same county where I was working. Only when I was invited to participate in the preparatory conference for the Edinburgh centenary (2005), did I become aware of this historic event and its enduring effect since then. As a Pentecostal, this was a new discovery. The following is a story of the two global missionary movements of the twentieth century, the Edinburgh Conference and the Pentecostal movement, born in the same decade (1900s) but with very little contact with each other. Yet both have exerted an enormous influence on Christianity today, like a tale of two siblings who never met each other.

The Edinburgh gathering in 1910, the first concerted effort to bring Christian mission agencies and churches together, resolved and devised plans to finish the job in 'this [their] generation'. This primarily western 'mainline' Christian gathering was filled with optimism that this was at last achievable, not only because of the corporate efforts, but also through the progress of western civilization and colonial powers which controlled most of the 'heathen' world. The conference adopted well-prepared documents to guide Christians to complete the Great Commission soon. As it explored critical mission themes over the first half of the last century, the two world wars shattered the optimism that prevailed at the conference. Soon after the second war ended, many 'heathen' nations gained their independence, and the tradition crystallized into an ecumenical movement so giving birth to the WCC, although a mission commission, the heir of the Edinburgh Conference, joined the body a few years

---

[7] This term was used in describing an unexpected ecumenical phenomenon among Pentecostals and Catholic Charismatics by Koichi Kitano, 'Spontaneous Ecumenicity Between Catholics and Protestants in the Charismatic Movement' (PhD dissertation, Centre Escolar University, Manila, Philippines, 1981).

later. The second half of the century was a story of ecumenism but by the end of the first fifty years of its existence serious issues had surfaced.

The WCC was born out of a missionary movement, which recognized that church unity is an integral part of, or prerequisite for, mission. To an outsider, it is an unfortunate development that the WCC should have been a mission body with the ecumenical unit under its wing. To be truthful to the original idea, church unity should have been explored always in the context of mission, but in reality, mission has been truncated into the discussion of church unity. Some believe that this is one reason why the traditional 'mainline churches' (particularly in the West) have steadily lost their influence, membership and resources.

By contrast, the Pentecostal movement began as a marginalized fringe Christian phenomenon in the downtown of Los Angeles. Although mockery from the society was harsh, the most unbearable attacks were lodged by fellow Christians.[8] In every aspect, they were the powerless, as the Azusa Street Mission was headed by an African-American preacher William J. Seymour.[9] The marginalized and 'poor' were attracted to the message of God's immanent presence by manifestations such as healing, miracles, and religious ecstatic experience (or 'baptism in the Holy Spirit'). With its missionary fervour instantly recognizable,[10] the Pentecostal movement was predominantly a revival phenomenon. This 'religion of the poor' survived through its endless divisions and doctrinal controversies and also never-ending external marginalization and criticisms. Thus, for the first half century of its existence it remained as a fringe movement.

However, its adherents hold a strong conviction that the 'best thing' (Christ) in their life was even bettered by the empowerment of the Holy Spirit, and they were extremely eager to spread the good news to the fellow 'poor'. This 'fired-up poor' brought the movement during the second half of the last century into a global expansion in various shapes and forms. This movement of 'primal spirituality' has had a particular appeal to those who are 'poor' in many ways (economically, socially, politically etc.), and who live in the developing countries. Many 'indigenous' types of Christianity, closely resembling the Pentecostal spirituality, but without any historic tie to the North American 'springhead', have been 'discovered'. This spiritual and renewal movement,

---

[8] Cecil M. Robeck, Jr., *The Azusa Street Mission and Revival: The Birth of the Global Pentecostal Movement* (Nashville, TN: Thomas Nelson, 2006), 134, reprints such a cartoon ridiculing the Pentecostal movement.

[9] Robeck, *The Azusa Street Mission and Revival*, esp. 87-128, describes the pivotal role of Seymour in the Mission.

[10] For example, Allan Anderson, *Spreading Fires: The Missionary Nature of Early Pentecostalism* (Maryknoll, NY: Orbis, 2007), 149-190 notes that as early as 1906 (the same year when the Azusa Street Mission began), a Pentecostal missionary was present in the 'Bible Lands' (152-53).

without any global structure or umbrella organisation, has become a powerful missionary movement, evident in its exponential growth.[11] In its zeal for mission, however, church unity was completely ignored, even though the Azusa Street Mission demonstrated the powerful potential of the Spirit for church unity.[12]

These two most powerful mission movements of the twentieth century have contrasting birth stories. What is equally noticeable is their ethos of mission: the ecumenical initiative is a 'gathering into' movement (centripetal), while the Pentecostal-charismatic movement is a 'spreading out' movement (centrifugal). Now with a century of experience behind them, each one has begun to reflect on itself: recognizing its own strength and achievements as well as being self-critical about its weaknesses and mistakes. Understandably the WCC views one in a more organized way, while the other one in a 'spontaneous' way. The recent general assemblies of the WCC highlighted the person and work of the Holy Spirit,[13] and took steps to intentionally include some Pentecostal delegates. Its latest Conference on World Mission and Evangelism in Athens (2005) is another case in point: its theme was 'Come Holy Spirit, and Heal and Reconcile'.[14] The presence of Pentecostal Christianity in the gathering was evident, not only in the plenary speeches, but also in the workshops and worship programmes. The creation of a more neutral and new space such as the Global Christian Forum is an indication of this growing awareness.

From the Pentecostal perspective, some churches, particularly from the 'southern' continents, have slowly joined various gatherings of the WCC or its national councils. Often this move comes with much criticism from their fellow Pentecostal churches, sister organisations and their own constituencies. Ecumenical dialogues are in progress with the Roman Catholic Church,[15] the

---

[11] Patrick Johnston and Jason Mandryk, *Operation World*, 21st century edition (Cumbria, UK: Paternoster, 2001), 3, predicts close to one billion Pentecostal-Charismatic believers by 2010.

[12] The inter-racial and ecumenical nature of the Azusa Street Mission has been well documented. For the recovery of this tradition, specifically for Asian Pentecostals, see Robeck, Cecil M., Jr. 'Pentecostal Ecumenism: An Introductory Essay for Asian Pentecostals'. *AJPS* 2:1 (1999), 87-103.

[13] The most obvious is the theme of the seventh general assembly in Canberra, Australia (1991): 'Come Holy Spirit, Renew Thy Whole Creation'. The theme of the latest ninth general assembly still maintains the emphasis, although less explicit: 'God, in Your Grace, Transform the World'.

[14] 'Conference on World Mission and Evangelism' (http://www.mission2005.org/, May 19, 2005), accessed: Oct 25, 2007.

[15] For example, 'Evangelism, Proselytism and Common Witness: The Report from the Fourth Phase of the International Dialogue 1990-1997 Between the Roman Catholic Church and Some Classical Pentecostal Churches and Leaders', *AJPS* 2:1 (1999), 105-151.

Reformed Churches,[16] Lutherans as well as the WCC at the global level, while growing national or local dialogues take place. Unlike their dialogue partners, Pentecostal delegates are all individuals without any representing authority from their Pentecostal churches.

This self-critical reflection and growing awareness of each other through various (sometimes courageous) contacts has led the two siblings much closer to each other than was possible decades ago. As the Edinburgh centenary celebration is being planned, this may be a historic opportunity to bring the divided church together for its mission. Even the 2010 Edinburgh conference is correcting its mistakes by becoming as inclusive as possible, ecclesiastically (as now Catholics, evangelicals and Pentecostals are included) and geographically (with an intentional effort to reflect the current global Christian status with the 'southern' majority).[17] We have to confess that this divided history was not the Lord's intent, but human short-sightedness and a failure to recognize the divine intent. In spite of human failure, the Spirit with creativity and grace brought forward God's mission and now brings His church together for the same mission.

Massive Fringe: 'Southern' Christianity

Earlier we discovered that one division among the churches was between the 'mainline' and evangelical churches. The former was generally regarded as 'liberal' in their attitude toward the scriptures, mission and the world (including other religions), while the latter was 'conservative' in the same areas. The former is generally found in the fold of the WCC, while the latter 'outside' of it. Regardless of their theological stance, however, in earlier days the western churches were the missionary-sending entities (benefactors, thus 'Christian' as they were 'missioning'), while the nations and states of the Global South were considered the mission field (beneficiaries, 'heathens', thus, 'missioned'). This global divide was the setting one hundred years ago (e.g. in the time of the Edinburgh Conference).

Now the rule of dividing the Christian world has changed drastically. The southward move of the centre of the global Christian gravity means there are far more (about four times more) Christians in the Global South than in the north (or 'west'). The rapid increase of 'southern' missionaries is also a natural consequence, already outnumbering their traditional western counterparts. For example, Korea is the second largest missionary-sending nation after the United States, while the highest missionary-sending country per capita is surprisingly

---

[16] For example, 'Word and Spirit, Church and World: The Final Report of the International Dialogue Between Representatives of the World Alliance of Reformed Churches and Some Classical Pentecostal Churches and Leaders 1996-2000', *AJPS* 4:1 (2001), 41-72.

[17] Towards 2010, 'Edinburgh 2010 – Mission in Humility and Hope' (http://www.towards 2010.org.uk/int_June_2005_doc.htm): accessed: Oct 25, 2007.

Mongolia.[18] The ambitious plan (but not at all surprising considering the huge Christian population that is still growing) of the Chinese house church networks to raise 200,000 missionaries in the near future to reach 'Back to Jerusalem' can be a reality. These are just numbers. However, equally significant is what is 'under the hood'.

Southern Christianity has exhibited several important characteristics. The first is its holistic understanding of the Christian faith. It is not only the spiritual aspect of salvation that is important, but also the material and physical aspects as well. In a way 'life before death' and 'life after death' come together to form a complete spectrum of human life. In fact, a supreme God who cannot bring physical healing today, while promising an eternal life after one dies, is not convincing at all to people, who regularly expect their ancestor spirits to bring healing and good fortune. Equally holistic is the understanding of the natural and supernatural world. In the religious worldview where spirits, gods and demons are perceived to be extremely active in human affairs, it is no wonder that Southern Christianity includes spiritual beings in religious life, and phenomena such as miracles and exorcism. Socially speaking, becoming Christian often comes with a high cost in many parts of the southern world, where Christianity is a minority 'foreign' religion.[19] Only with the strong conviction that the best thing in life is Christ can Christians persevere in this hostile environment. Furthermore, generally speaking, these Southern Christians take the scripture at its face value,[20] unlike western sophisticated methods of Biblical interpretation with their high degree of scepticism and suspicion. Unquestionable acceptance of religious teaching is part of their culture. This explains why the same church (e.g. Anglican) demonstrates a remarkable difference between the West and the South (e.g. Uganda) over issues like human sexuality. Now the clearest divide in global Christianity is between the North and the South. This too-good-to-be-true picture is not without problems. There is a great danger for Christianity to be reduced to old religion where deities are 'used' for human consumption. Nonetheless, Southern Christianity has shown great potential to renew global Christianity, while deeply engaging in a completely non- or even anti-Christian society. This makes today's Christian mission extremely viable and effective.

Conclusion

The last one hundred years have shown us the remarkable work of God, as global Christianity has gone through unprecedented world crises and yet faced

---

[18] It could be India for the total number, which includes many cross-cultural missionaries within the country. Johnston and Mandryk, *Operation World*, 6.

[19] A personal account of this sort is found in Wonsuk Ma and Julie C. Ma, 'Jesus Christ in Asia: Our Journey with Him as Pentecostal Believers', *IRM* 94 (2005), 493-94.

[20] Philip Jenkins, *The New Faces of Christianity: Believing the Bible in the Global South* (Oxford: Oxford University Press, 2006).

incredible opportunities. Christian unity will continue to remain a major challenge for Christian communities. There will be more reasons why divisions will further intensify, on the one hand, and a more urgent and predominant reason why the church should work together, on the other hand. The mission of God is to bring complete restoration to His creation through the life-giving power of the Holy Spirit. If mission has divided the church, it is entirely due to human faults. In fact, mission is to bring the church together.

Thus, our journey as fellow Christians has taught us that church unity is like riding a bicycle. We will fall unless we go forward. Church unity was rightly perceived within the context of mission, and this should continue. Called by one God, redeemed through the one Lord, and empowered through the presence of the one Spirit, church-together is not only a dream but also a possibility. There is a potential for spontaneous ecumenism through loving fellowship and Spirit-led worship. Working together for the cause of God's kingdom is another viable arena for church-together. We have sufficient experience to further this aim.

Then how can organic or spontaneous ecumenism be structurally regulated so as to perpetuate it? This represents a serious challenge as the history of ecumenism in the last half a century exemplifies. For this reason, we should not overlook the role of learning and reflection: the earnest desire to learn from the scripture and from fellow Christians should lead us to develop a desire to be one. Occasions like this have the potential to foster such authentic ecumenism by combining open *koinonia*, Spirit-filled worship, and diligent learning to discern what the Lord is doing in different Christian communions. It is all for God's mission's sake that we are called together to be in one body so that the world may know that we are the people of God (John 17:21, 23). An African saying may encourage us: 'If you want to go fast, go alone. If you want to go far, go together'.

PART THREE

Looking Ahead

Chapter 18

Reflective Mission Practice:
Suggested Areas for Pentecostal Mission Research

The global Pentecostal community celebrated its centennial not long ago, and it has since been in the mode of reflection on the past, and agenda-setting for the future. Considering the rapid and sustained growth of the movement, to become the second largest global Christian block in its first hundred years of existence, its contribution to evangelism and mission is unquestionable. For this reason, we are seeing a growing number of studies on the subject, and this study is part of the large thrust of reflection and agenda-setting.[1]

I am not a trained missiologist but a biblical scholar who has been serving as a field missionary. I also represent a 'Southern' church, which once received, and is now sending missionaries. The perspective of this reflection is global. The topics are divided into two large categories: issues around Pentecostal mission theories and Pentecostal mission practices. It is hard to treat theories and practices separately, but for the former, I would include basic issues of missiology, theological and historical aspects, while the latter has to be a selection of practical topics.

Considering its highly pragmatic approach, Pentecostals have been more 'mission doers' than mission reflectors. And mission reflection, however scant it may be, has been more born out of missionary experiences rather than deep and serious literary research. One good example is Melvin Hodges, the most celebrated Pentecostal missiologist.[2] More substantial works, since then, have appeared through younger reflective practitioner-theologians, while an increasing number of doctoral researchers provide for the promising future.[3] To date, however, the reality is that Pentecostal colleges and seminaries throughout the world must find a Pentecostal mission textbook for classroom use, most likely from the list of evangelical publications. Even to undergird the global

---

[1] One such study is the 45:1 (Jan. 2007) issue of *Missiology: An International Review* under the theme of 'Mission and Pentecost'.

[2] His books include Melvin L. Hodges, *The Indigenous Church: A Complete Handbook on How to Grow Young Churches* (Springfield, MO: Gospel Publishing House, 1976).

[3] Significant are Murray W. Dempster, Byron D. Klaus, Douglas Petersen, eds., *Called and Empowered: Global Mission in Pentecostal Perspective* (Peabody, MA: Hendrickson, 1991); Paul A. Pomerville, *The Third Force in Missions: A Pentecostal Contribution to Contemporary Mission Theology* (Peabody, MA: Hendrickson, 1985).

growth of the movement, reflective work on Pentecostal mission is an urgent task. Here are some critical issues which require immediate attention.

Basics of Mission

There are several key foundational questions of mission that Pentecostals are required to explore, along with the larger Christian community.

What is Mission?

This foundational question is an unsettled issue among church groups and mission organisations. A careful examination of Pentecostal mission practice reveals that Pentecostals have been extremely concentrated on the 'how tos' of mission rather than foundational issues such as the definition of mission. What has always been assumed among Pentecostal mission leaders and practitioners is the narrowly defined evangelical understanding of mission: to establish viable local churches through evangelism. The most celebrated Pentecostal missiology, *The Indigenous Church* by Melvin Hodges, may epitomize this wide-spread understanding. To Pentecostals, Christian mission is every activity which is undertaken in order to achieve the ultimate goal, be it training, caring ministry or other.

The Lausanne Covenant defines the mission of God as 'the extension of his kingdom, the building up of Christ's body, and the glory of his name', and its concluding statement suggests that evangelism is the means to achieve this goal.[4] C. Wright identifies mission as 'our committed participation as God's people...in God's own mission...for the redemption of God's creation'.[5] Concepts such as *Missio Dei*, mission as transformation, holistic mission, and recently, integral mission, are some expressions of the serious struggle to define Christian mission. It is an opportune time for the Pentecostal mission community to join this important discussion through various platforms, be it the Lausanne movement, Edinburgh centenary, or the Commission on World Mission and Evangelism (of the World Council of Churches). This may be a continuing process rather than one definitive task. As the global mission community dialogues with one another and reflects on the scripture, context and history, Pentecostal mission thinkers will need to work together in this process. This will challenge pragmatic Pentecostal missiology to be more comprehensive and reflective.

---

[4] Lausanne Committee for World Evangelization, 'The Lausanne Covenant' (July 1974) found, among others, at http://www.lausanne.org/lausanne-1974/lausanne-covenant.html, accessed on Sept. 11, 2007.

[5] Christopher J. H. Wright, *The Mission of God: Unlocking the Bible's Grand Narrative* (Nottingham: Inter-Varsity Press, 2006), 23.

What is Pentecostal Mission?

The definition of 'Pentecostal mission' is a challenging task, primarily because the precise meanings of both terms are hotly debated. Having briefly discussed the second word, how do we understand the first one, 'Pentecostal'? For the present discussion, the issue is not primarily about the meaning of it, but rather the scope of it. That is, whether a 'Pentecostal mission' discussion should be restricted to classical Pentecostals or also includes the charismatic movement and the wide-range of indigenous Pentecostals, as well as the Third Wave. For the Charismatic communities, they tend to add the Spirit element to their 'mother' church's theological and missiological position, while neo-charismatic or indigenous Pentecostals have become a catch-all category, and its diversity makes it just impossible to construct any coherent missiology. To make the present exercise workable and meaningful, I am restricting my discussion on classical Pentecostals. This group maintains the hallmark missionary thrust of the early Pentecostal believers.

Then for our inquiry, the logical step toward the definition of Pentecostal mission is to analyze classical Pentecostal mission practices and their missiological characteristics and assumptions. Obviously, not everything that Pentecostals are doing in mission is Pentecostal mission. At the same time, things that are done by non-Pentecostals could bear some characteristics of Pentecostal mission. Several useful studies are available on the characteristics of Pentecostal mission.[6] And such analysis should continue not only to add more characteristics to the existing list, but more importantly, to trace their theological roots.

Considering the diversity we now see even in the classical Pentecostal churches throughout the world, the process of identifying Pentecostal mission practices and theology should be an international endeavour. The traditional Pentecostal missionaries from North America and Europe introduced their mission practices and underlying theological assumptions. In the mission 'field', different expressions of Pentecostal mission may have surfaced over the years, as they have become new missionary-sending churches. For example, how Korean Pentecostal missiologists perceive Pentecostal mission may be different from how their colleagues from North America, India or Nigeria think and practice. The meaningful participation and contribution of the Pentecostal mission communities from the Global South is critical to the construction of a comprehensive picture of global Pentecostal mission.

Even within the smallest segment of global Pentecostal church families, however, it is important to carefully 'recover' creative Pentecostal mission practices outside of, but often born out of, classical Pentecostal churches. The most important among them would be Youth With A Mission (YWAM). As an independent mission group, it is understandable that they do not necessarily

---

[6] For example, Allan Anderson, 'Towards a Pentecostal Missiology for the Majority World', *AJPS* 8:1 (Jan 2005), 29-47.

adopt one particularly doctrinal tradition. However, their mission practices evidently demonstrate many characteristics of Pentecostal mission, and such groups should be carefully included in Pentecostal mission studies.

Biblical Basis of Pentecostal Mission

Biblical foundation for Pentecostal mission is commonly found in Acts 1:8. One can quickly realize, however, that this has to do with the 'enhancing' of the missionary process. Thus, this Pentecostal contribution assumes the general Evangelical mission understanding based on the Great Commission found in Matthew 28:18-20. Even Evangelical mission thinking, however, has diligently searched the root of Christian mission and this is well evidenced in the Lausanne Covenant and the Manila Manifesto. They rightly suspect that the basis of God's mission is found from the very beginning of human history: creation.

One natural theme which Pentecostals can fruitfully explore is the role of the Spirit of God in creation as God's life-giving force, its empowering role among selected leaders and prophets, and its eschatological role in God's plan of restoration.[7] Another useful biblical framework is the kingdom motif, which shares evangelical mission theology. The good news of Christ is the coming of God's kingdom breaking into human life. This theological framework certainly provides convincing basis for Christian mission. Pentecostals then need to explore this theme from a distinctly Pentecostal perspective.[8] Another possibility may be 'mission as restoration:' the full restoration of creation intent, if Genesis is taken as the beginning of God's mission. With Pentecostalism's instinct on the restoration motif, this may be a possibility.[9] It is encouraging that there is growing interest in exploring the biblical bases of Pentecostal mission.[10] With this positive trend, it is also expected to see increasing efforts to articulate distinctively Pentecostal mission thinking and its biblical basis.

The Scope of Mission

The foregoing discussion definitely affects the scope of Pentecostal mission. Pentecostal missionaries have concentrated on evangelism and church planting supported through the training of workers. Intuitively, however, their missionary

---

[7] For a Charismatic mission reflection, see Andrew Lord, *Spirit-Shaped Mission: A Holistic Charismatic Missiology* (Bletchley, UK: Paternoster, 2005). For the Third Wave, C. Peter Wagner's idea of spiritual warfare may epitomize the group's mission thinking, although its conceptual consensus is far from being realized.

[8] For example, Gordon D. Fee, 'The Kingdom of God and the Church's Global Mission', in *Called and Empowered*, pp. 7-21; Murray Dempster, 'A Theology of the Kingdom: A Pentecostal Contribution', in Vinay Samuel and Chris Sugden (eds.), *Mission as Transformation* (Oxford: Regnum, 1999), 45-75.

[9] For more discussion, see ch. 2.

[10] John V. York, *Missions in the Age of the Spirit* (Springfield, MO: Logion, 2000); Julie C. Ma, *Mission Possible: Biblical Strategy for Reaching the Lost* (Oxford: Regnum, 2005).

practice includes social aspects such as education, care of children, ministry to drug addicts, etc. They do this for practical reasons in order to meet some dire needs of life. Theoretically, such 'social' activities are understood to be a preliminary for evangelism. At least, like their evangelical cousins, Pentecostals have developed some significant mission programs to 'care for victims' of social injustice. Vaguely, such missionary activity is linked to the Messianic mission proclaimed in Luke 4:18-19.

Overall, however, Pentecostals have been 'other-worldly' and their missionary focus has been on 'soul saving'. With strong inclination toward the pre-millennial dispensationalistic eschatology, life in this world is viewed as incidental as compared with life in heaven. However, the century-old deposit of experience and reflection has led and has helped Pentecostals to recognize that God's mission should be holistic, as some parts of Pentecostal theology informs. New frontiers of Pentecostal mission reflection include the care for the marginalized through education, meeting poverty needs, HIV-AIDS, children at risk, women's issues and disaster relief, and Pentecostals' distinct contribution, not only to mission practices, but also mission reflection in this area, is encouraging.[11]

Considering another further step towards frontier mission discussion will take a long time and further debate, and the discussion will inevitably focus on the limit and scope of Christian (and here Pentecostal) mission. This is more than a choice of mission operation, but often is determined by one's understanding of sin and redemption. For example, mission scope of the World Council of Churches (WCC) has been based on its affirmation: 'The evangelistic witness will also speak to the structures of this world; its economic, political and social institutions'.[12] Its 'evangelistic witness' is defined as 'the call to conversion, as a call to repentance and obedience', thus, the 'structures of this world' are viewed as the object of evangelism and conversion [13]. Therefore, Pentecostal response to human sexuality, social injustice, unjust political systems, structural oppression, environmental issues, ecumenism, and inter-religious issues will require far more than an administrative decision. Admittedly such engagement is possible without subscribing to the WCC-like statement; Pentecostals need to make sure that their involvement in such life issues is conscious and based on an alternative scriptural and theological basis. Unlike the previous mode of operation, reflection after action, Pentecostal missiologists and theologians need to proactively provide serious and conscious theological groundwork and

---

[11] For a recent example of a sociological look at a Pentecostal response to urban social problems in the United States using the Dream Centre of Los Angeles, see Michael Wilkinson, 'Faith-Based Social Services: Some Observations for Assessing Pentecostal Social Action', *Transformation* 24:2 (April 2007), 71-79.

[12] CWME, *The WCC Mission and Evangelism: An Ecumenical Affirmation* (Geneva: WCC, 1982), section 15.

[13] CWME, *Mission and Evangelism*, section 12.

framework for mission practices. On the one hand, Pentecostals are not called to join every popular missionary bandwagon. Conscious choices are to be made with the help of reflective minds for each challenging mission topic. At the same time, Pentecostals are to bring their own distinct contribution to mission thinking and practice, and this requires them to be active and reflective.

Theology of Pentecostal Mission

Mission practice is deeply rooted in one's theological belief. Although Pentecostal theology often lacks articulation, building a sound Pentecostal missiology will require careful investigation of several areas of Pentecostal theology. Only selected topics are discussed here, and for each topic, a serious biblical foundation should be established.

Eschatology

Early popular literature urged Pentecostal believers to engage in mission, partly because of their urgent expectation of the Lord's return. Evidence points to the fact that many early Pentecostal missionaries, as well as sending Pentecostal congregations, were mostly motivated by this eschatological urgency. These missionaries with 'one-way tickets' served with zeal and commitment, again fueled by the same urgency, although some did not stay long in the field as often disease took their lives. However, Pentecostal mission continued with the same amazing zeal and commitment even into the second and third generations. Today, however, among Pentecostal mission circles, very little evidence is found to prove that eschatological urgency is even preached in Pentecostal congregations, mission agencies or by missionaries. This leaves us with several important questions: 'What then was the motivating force of early Pentecostal mission, if eschatological was not the main one?'; 'Exactly what role did Pentecostal understanding of eschatological urgency play in its missionary movement?'; 'What changes did Pentecostals and their mission communities go though in their eschatological understanding?'; 'What effect did the change bring to mission thinking and practices?'; and, 'Was there any conscious attempt to revise their eschatology?'

Another important area of the eschatological study may be undertaken from the recipient's perspective in the missionary equation. A very general study was recently done to examine how the evolution (by default) of Pentecostal eschatology has affected the development of Asian Pentecostalism.[14] In this study, the author argues that the waning other-worldly orientation quickly gave way to a this-worldly invasion, and two of its expressions in Asia are church renewal or growth instead of cross-cultural mission, and the prosperity gospel instead of empowerment for mission. Pentecostals' theological abandonment of eschatology is critically worrying. The theological and missionary communities

---

[14] W. Ma, 'Pentecostal Eschatology', 227-42.

of Pentecostal circles need to undertake a serious reflection on its default theological 'development' and recover a balanced Pentecostal eschatology with a critical reflection and conscientious investigation. In a way, the decrease of an eschatological emphasis is widespread in modern Christianity and this should motivate Pentecostals to work closely with other Christian thinkers and mission communities for this theological process.

Pneumatology

Mission pneumatology in the Pentecostal circles centres around two topics, empowerment and supernatural work. Both are distinctly Pentecostal, and these topics should be reflected on and explored. First of all, the empowerment emphasis of the Spirit's work may have provided a significant impetus to some characteristics of, and continuing motivation to, Pentecostal mission. Often the Pentecostal notion of empowerment is linked to supernatural power based on Acts 1:8. The contribution of this theological foundation deserves more than a quick consideration of the supernatural equipment for mission. First of all, the biblical notion of the Spirit's empowerment needs to be broadly explored, beyond the Lukan literature. Empowerment is not always linked to triumphal victory. The case of Jesus' empowered life demonstrates that empowerment includes the staying power needed in harsh circumstances to fulfill a God-given task (e.g., Luke 4:1). It is the Spirit's empowerment that enabled Jesus to bear the cross (Hebrews 9:14). The book of Acts itself displays that the 'empowered' ministries of Paul, Peter and Stephen, for example, were not always prosperous cases in human expectation. This seriously challenges Pentecostals to expand their understanding and scope of Christian mission. Another important area of this reflection will be the application of the beliefs to Pentecostal mission practices. Here Hodge's indigenous church principle can be reviewed from an intentionally Pentecostal perspective. To begin with, the indigenous church principle was around long before Hodge's time. Then what makes his presentation distinctly Pentecostal? One possibility is to place his indigenous argument within the framework of empowerment theology. For example, developing local leadership as early as possible can be explained through the empowerment motivation, and so can all other 'self' principles. Another obvious example may be the YWAM theology of mobilization of youth for mission. This can only be explained as a logical application of this cardinal Pentecostal mission principle. How the vision of its founder Loren Cunningham was rejected by his Pentecostal mission leadership is another powerful example of the lack of proper understanding. A third example may be David Yonggi Cho's renowned cell group system. The mobilization of laity, and particularly women in what is a male dominant culture, can find powerful theological support, and this will add a significant Pentecostal contribution to this program.

The supernatural manifestation of the work of the Holy Spirit is an important part of Pentecostal mission, be it healing, exorcism, miracles, prophecy, word of wisdom, etc.[15] This also includes God's sovereign provision for missionaries. For example, healing has played an important role in evangelism and mission, as, almost always, popular Pentecostal evangelistic crusades feature divine healing. In animistic settings, healing is in fact an integral part of the religious experience and this may partly explain the growth of Pentecostalism in the missionary setting. When analyzed carefully, however, healing is not necessarily a distinctly Pentecostal agenda, as the expectation is based either on the atonement of Christ (for which Isa. 53 is often quoted), the gift of healing, or simply as God's gracious response to an earnest petition. The most Pentecostal part of it may be the 'power of the Holy Spirit' as often pronounced in prayer or declaration. What has been seriously overlooked is the creation role of the Holy Spirit, and also in restoration, be it material, physical, relational, communal, ethical or spiritual (e.g., Isa. 32:15ff.). This not only appropriates healing to the Pentecostal framework of theology, it opens vast territory for the Spirit's creative and restorative potential, and this will definitely enlarge the potential of Pentecostal mission thinking and practice. Equally crucial is the issue of non-healing or suffering. Many helpful studies are available, and yet popular minds perceive healing and suffering as being caused by various elements: due to the presence or absence of faith, sin, spiritual power, inter-generational curse, or a host of other things. This requires Pentecostals to be more than triumphalistic or proud as if the secret code of evangelism has been broken.

In the area of pneumatology, at least two areas await Pentecostal reflection. The first is the works of the Holy Spirit, outside of empowerment and supernatural manifestation. As mentioned briefly, the Spirit's work in creation and re-creation needs to be appropriated into Pentecostal pneumatology and its missional application. Also often missing in Pentecostal discussion is the abiding presence of the Spirit as presented by the Johannine literature, as well as, in a less serious degree, the Pauline notion of the Spirit's work in regeneration, and their missionary implications. The second area is what is called the 'new agenda', which has been brought forward by the Third Wave writers. This includes concepts such as power encounter, territorial spirits, inner healing, deep healing, inter-generational curses, the demonization of believers, and others.[16] Each one of them has a significant mission implication, thus requiring not only a close biblical and theological examination, but also a dialogue for mutual understanding and benefit. Equally fruitful will be the participation of non-western Pentecostal thinkers and practitioners as some of the topics seem to have a significant implication to animistic minds.

---

[15] For a helpful study, see Gary B. McGee, 'The Radical Strategy in Modern Mission: The Linkage of Paranormal Phenomena with Evangelism', in C. Douglas McConnell (ed.), *The Holy Spirit and Mission Dynamics*, Evangelical Missiological Society Series 5 (Pasadena, William Carey Library, 1997), 69-95.

[16] See ch. 12.

Theology of the World

How an individual understands the world, influences his or her mission thinking and practice in a significant way. There is evidence that the early Pentecostals, primarily due to their eschatological urgency, viewed the world as the object of God's immanent judgment. Mission was therefore perceived as a rescue operation to save condemned lives from destruction. The negative notion of the world was also influenced by the holiness dichotomy between sacred and secular. The emergence of some exclusive Christian communities may be an expression of this dualistic notion. Such an extreme attitude toward the world and present life may have produced an extreme zeal and commitment for mission. Now after three generations of development, there seems to be a gradual shift in values, and even a movement toward the other extreme. Coinciding with the waning eschatological expectation, the material provisions of God began to receive more stress in the Pentecostal pulpit. A fruitful area of study can be found by following the trajectory of this change, which is by no means uniform in church groups and geographical areas.

Practical challenges have arisen, however, in the mission setting, where socio-cultural contexts demand that missionary work is more than just a rescue operation of 'perishing souls'. For example, Indonesian Pentecostals need to be oriented to live within their Muslim social and religious context. This will require a serious re-examination of the theology of the world with accompanying questions. And this value shift should come not just from missionary convenience but through a serious study of the scriptures. In fact, ecumenical circles have raised a challenging question: Is the Spirit present outside of the church? Based on the theology of creation, it is not difficult to respond positively. However, the question will inevitably lead to a more challenging one: would the Spirit work in cultures and in other religions? Pentecostals are no longer in a comfortable position of free choice, but are now forced to engage in serious reflection. For this reason, some recent studies have opened new discussions on the Pentecostal theology of religions.[17] This re-visitation of the theology of the world will open new territories for research. Some of these research areas could be the role of cultures, stewardship of creation (including natural disasters), inter-religious issues (such as religious conflicts and terrorism), racial issues, and others. These are in addition to the issue of social and political engagement as part of mission.

On a very different front, many mission contexts view the material world as part of a holistic reality, animated by a host of spirits and gods. This worldview will clash with the Christian worldview as soon as the gospel is communicated. As one can expect, this is where a critical success point is found in Pentecostal

---

[17] For example, Amos Yong, *Beyond the Impasse: Toward a Pneumatological Theology of Religion* (Grand Rapids: Baker, 2003).

mission.[18] But my point here is how Pentecostal missionaries can present a healthy view of the world, drawn from the scriptures. There is much work to be done.

Historical Study

Historical studies can provide a valuable contribution to the formulation of Pentecostal missiology. For example, the century of Pentecostal mission will reveal how theological mission assumptions have been expressed in changing social context and diverse mission settings.

In the Context of the Modern Missionary Movement

This is a uniquely opportune time to study the locus of Pentecostal mission in the history of modern Christian mission. The last hundred years were not only the century of Pentecostalism, but also that of organized Protestant missionary movements. The latter was signaled by the Edinburgh Missionary Conference in 1910, while the former was signaled by the Azusa Street Mission (1906-09). The two powerful missionary movements of the twentieth century, however, have seldom intersected with each other, thus, they have benefited little from each other's strengths. The Lausanne movement from 1974 was not much different from the Edinburgh-WCC tradition with regards to the Pentecostals. Only in its second Congress in Manila (1989) did Pentecostal leaders participate in the programs, but not without controversy, and some delegates expressed their discontent at the Pentecostal's presence in the conference.

In the meantime, the mission world has recognized the unique contribution of the Pentecostal churches in mission. The explosive growth of Pentecostal-charismatic churches worldwide is the surest proof of it. Academic mission journals have published an increasing number of studies on Pentecostal mission. This should be perceived by Pentecostals, however, not only as a sign of growing recognition and acceptance, but also as a challenge to meaningfully join the wider global mission discussion by contributing their thoughts on self-examination and reflection in mission practices and their perceived assumptions. For example, a comparative story of the birth of the Azusa Street Mission and the Edinburgh Missionary Conference may partly explain why these two mission movements have had a radically different and yet parallel mission history. The subsequent developments of both movements will be a useful study. For the Edinburgh-WCC tradition, studies abound following its thirteen conferences and their theological agenda. For the Pentecostal side, much work is left to be done. Major western Pentecostal denominations may have their studies on mission development, but an overarching study on Pentecostal mission is yet to be written. A similar study on Pentecostal mission in relation to the Lausanne

---

[18] For example, for a worldview comparison between Pentecostal and tribal groups, see J. Ma, 'A Comparison of Two Worldviews', 265-90.

tradition would be fruitful. Such studies will pave the way for Pentecostal mission communities to participate in the global mission movements with their unique historical, theological and practical contributions.

Historical Development of Pentecostal Mission

As alluded to above, two levels of mission history are essential: micro and macro. For each Pentecostal denomination or group, an increasing number of mission history books are now available.[19] As long as they are self-critical and honest, each study will be useful. Such researches should not only trace the historical development of one organisation's mission work, but also probe how the organisation and doctrinal development has affected their mission work. For similar inquiries, in-depth historical studies will be useful on other 'Pentecostal' mission groups such as YWAM, Full Gospel Business Men's Fellowship, Teen Challenge, as well as large and influential Pentecostal congregations. Even regional mission programs should be diligently studied before the pioneers, and their memories, are lost. Such would include Latin American Childcare, Calcutta Mercy Ministries, and a host of others.[20] Equally fruitful will be the biographies of Pentecostal missionaries which would not only keep the memories in posterity, but more importantly demonstrate unique missionary approaches that are genuinely Pentecostal. From my own region, I would like to see biographies of Louis Richard, who influenced David Yonggi Cho in a significant way, Cho himself, Mammie Williams, who impacted the Muslim-powerful Mindanao Islands of the Philippines, and many more. As Allan Anderson passionately urges, the contribution of national and local Pentecostal leaders needs urgent attention as often they are simply buried under missionary stories and eventually lost with memories.[21]

The macro level will take much cooperation and intentional efforts to be fruitful. At a national level, various Pentecostal denominations, including their expatriate missionaries as well as national leaders, need to come together to shape the development of the national Pentecostal movement. Expatriate missionaries can play an important part in this process, as they can provide valuable financial and research resources, whilst enabling the national counterpart to build a workable structure. Then this has to move to the regional level until a global picture of Pentecostal history can surface. Such cooperative work can take place through interdenominational working bodies such as seminaries, research centres, academic societies and theological associations.

---

[19] For example, for the Assemblies of God, U.S.A., McGee, *This Gospel Shall Be Preached*, 2 vols.; for the Church of God, Cleveland, TN, see Charles W. Conn, *Where the Saints Have Trod* (Cleveland, TN: Pathway Press, 1959).

[20] A good study is available by Douglas Petersen, *Not by Might, Nor by Power: A Pentecostal Theology of Social Concern in Latin America* (Oxford: Regnum, 1996).

[21] Anderson, *Spreading Fires*, 5-9.

Some Areas of Practice

It is simply impossible to discuss a long list of important topics that arise from the actual missionary setting, so only selected topics are chosen here.

Pentecostal Missionaries

It will be revealing to trace the process of the making of a Pentecostal missionary, both in the West and in the Global South. First is the calling. Many testimonies indicate that Pentecostal missionaries go through a unique vocational calling, and this needs to be carefully studied. At this stage one may already be able to find a clue to the unique missionary ethos of Pentecostal mission. With the swelling number of non-western Pentecostal missionaries now in the field (e.g., Indian, Brazilian, Korean, Nigerian, etc.), this can be proven to be a fruitful area of study. The next will be processing. The call experience can take place early in one's life and how the subsequent events and developments are viewed providentially as God's leading will be a useful exploration. The role of the baptism in the Holy Spirit should receive special attention as it relates to the call and its nurturing. Then would come the actual preparation stage including a vocational appointment, be it formal or informal. Deployment will reveal the Pentecostal organisational ethos in undertaking mission. However, a more important consideration would be the missionary's attitude toward the missionary vocation and toward the new socio-cultural environment. Having received varying degrees of pre-field training, the balance between the expectation of the divine involvement and human planning may differ from other evangelical missionaries. The inquiry can continue in the actual ministry attitude, the analysis of newsletters and reports, the goal of their missionary work, and the like.

Such studies will have the potential to make a contribution in several areas. Considering the diversity of Pentecostal missionaries, now that Asians, Latin Americans and Africans are fast outnumbering the traditional western contingent, the process is going to be increasingly diverse, and this will reveal the changing demography of Pentecostal missionaries. Also revealed will be the typical as well as the new creative expressions of Pentecostal mission beliefs.

Revival and Social Change

Even 'progressive Pentecostals' would not resort to the kind of social engagement that the WCC has advocated.[22] Its spiritually centred holism will view a list of changes beginning with the spiritual conversion. Therefore, if Pentecostals are going to engage in social issues, it will inevitably begin with a personal and spiritual change, that will soon have a ripple effect on family life, work habits, and the individual's role in society. The effect is soon expanded to

---

[22] For this term, see Donald E. Miller, 'Pentecostalism and Social Transformation', in Harold D. Hunter and Cecil M. Robeck, Jr. (eds.), *The Azusa Street Revival and Its Legacy* (Cleveland, TN: Pathway Press, 2006), 335-48.

the family, community and the society. This is the Pentecostal plan for social transformation. Teen Challenge provides a good model. However, criticism has often been heard that this bottom up approach lacks any programmatic intentionality, and everything is left to each individual. This may partly explain why Latin American Pentecostals, for example, have achieved social upward mobility, while they constantly face a challenge of expanding among the masses and advancing their conditions, presumably by no longer 'remaining of the masses'.[23]

One case to explore, as a response to such criticism, may be revival movements, as old as the Ezra's reform and as recent as the Pensacola Revival, and everything in between. Revivals in the non-western world should not be ignored either.[24] The historical study of a revival movement will quickly reveal that it can have a powerful social impact, as was noted during the Wesley revival. The impact is often measurable, as official reports are available that show a decline in crime rates, alcohol consumption, prostitution industry, and the like, while recording an increase in volunteerism, philanthropic activities, work productivity, and most likely active evangelism. A big question to be asked is: 'Did the stakeholders of the revival movement understand its impact and intentionally plan to increase its effect and prolong the life of revival?' Often a revival runs its own life course, sometimes not without spiritual controversy or personal issues, and it is inevitable to expect the end of the revival. However, its social impact can be nurtured, promoted, and supported with adequate programs and structures. Such a study will be valuable so that the next revival can be maintained longer, and its impact, be it spiritual or social, be preserved for a long time, even after the closure of the revival itself. The historical study may also be able to recover various revival attempts and present several workable models to increase their effect and life. An international conference on this theme may be a useful platform to recover many revival stories, especially 'hidden' ones, and their effects.

Contextualization

An increasing number of studies have proven that the genius of Pentecostal mission is its adaptability to a given socio-cultural context. Often empirical studies unlock the success secrets of Pentecostal mission, particularly in animistic tribal settings. Suggested conclusions range from similar worldviews to Pentecostal responses to their felt needs, including the physical and the spiritual, often through power encounters. These 'successes' are particularly significant when compared with similar efforts of other Christian groups. The case of a successful contextualization, however, is questionable, if it refers to the

---

[23] David Martin, *Tongues of Fire: The Explosion of Protestantism in Latin America* (Oxford: Blackwell, 1990), 232.

[24] For example, Gani Wiyono, 'Timo Revival: A Historical Study of the Great Twentieth-century Revival in Indonesia', *AJPS* 4:2 (2001), 269-93.

process where a native symbol is properly redefined with a new Christian meaning. Often the Pentecostal interaction with a local context appears to be more a case of the overwhelming imposition of Pentecostal worldview rather than a careful negotiation which gives due respect to the local culture. This 'upper hand' phenomenon is possible through the demonstration of an unquestionably superior spiritual power. At least, this, in part, provides an explanation of the exponential growth of the movement in non-western settings. Exactly what is happening as Pentecostal Christianity is introduced or demonstrated in an animistic setting requires a closer look at the process from anthropological, social, and religious points of view.

Equally successful has been Pentecostal mission among the urban poor. The study by Cox, for example, suggests clues to success in their unique social circumstances: dislocation and marginality.[25] However, it is likely that the majority of the urban poor are urban immigrants from rural areas, often for economic reasons. This situation creates a social setting where varying dynamics play important roles: animistic orientation now seriously challenged by modern civilization of urban centres, stability brought by the drastic change in life, and the sheer challenge to survive in a hostile environment. The encounter between Pentecostal spirituality and the deprived socially 'disinherited' results in the explosive growth of Pentecostal churches in urban centres. This phenomenon deserves careful study from theological, sociological and anthropological perspectives.

The contextual adaptability of Pentecostalism is also increasingly evident among the established class of society. There is a growing trend that Pentecostal churches now attract professionals who are socially and economically established and better educated. This may also have to do with the general improvement of Pentecostal believers' social standards over the years. This upward social mobility and the addition of socially established members have fast changed the demography of some Pentecostal churches. In the West, this trend is now an accepted norm rather than an exception. In places like China, more intellectuals, such as university professors and journalists, are attracted to Pentecostal-type house churches.[26] This evolution also requires careful study. This phenomenon has already suggested a notion that Pentecostalism is not just for the poor. The acceptance of Pentecostal spirituality by the middle class mainline churches during the emergence of the Charismatic movement provides

---

[25] Cox, *Fire from Heaven*, 120, discusses Pentecostal's ability to provide 'despondent people with an alternative metaphor, a life vision at variance from the image of the 'good life''. This 'deprivation theology', however, has been contested not as the principle explanation of Pentecostal's growth. Miller & Yamamori, *Global Pentecostalism*, 162-77, engages with Max Weber's argument of Protestant ethics and its applicability to Pentecostalism.

[26] David Aikman, *Jesus in Beijing: How Christianity Is Transforming China and Changing the Global Balance of Power* (Washington, DC: Regnery, 2003).

a useful example. And yet, social and economic stability poses a formidable challenge to Pentecostal Christianity, as it usually flourish in a crisis setting. Therefore, studies exploring a correlation between socio-economic change and spiritual dynamics will be quite useful. Pentecostal churches in Korea, for example, are grappling with this challenge: the more affluent one becomes, the less spiritual one tends to be. For the future health of the movement, studies on this issue will prove to be useful.

Proselytism and Ecumenism

In almost all the ecumenical dialogues that Pentecostals have engaged, the Pentecostal practice of evangelism is often viewed as sheep-stealing or proselytism.[27] The phenomenon is more complex than it appears, as Pentecostals would certainly have something to say about their own experience of losing their sheep to other churches. However, everyone agrees that there is an overwhelming migration pattern towards Pentecostal churches, and such a movement has posed a serious threat to church unity and cooperation. For this reason, it is plausible that Pentecostals should legitimately be blamed for working against church unity.

There are two issues that Pentecostals need to be re-oriented in, in order to be a meaningful partner in the global mission of the church. The first is the understanding of the church (ecclesiology) and the diverse work of the Holy Spirit in different church traditions. Often in reading the book of Acts, the Pentecostal claim of apostolicity tends to ignore the two thousand year gap between the early church and the present. Although Pentecostals have rightly recovered 'primal' spirituality, this does not deny the continuing work of the Spirit through the history of the church. Pentecostals would easily agree that the sporadic revivals throughout church history are definitely the work of the Spirit. This understanding can easily be expanded to apply to the rise of various church traditions often with a renewal impetus, such as the Reformation and Methodism. Then it is not too difficult to accept that the Spirit called them with a clear missional purpose to rise as a member of his universal church. Unique spirituality, the mode of public worship and the church governance and structure of each church tradition should be understood within this larger historical context. This would help Pentecostals to appreciate the diversity found in the church on one hand, and also to avoid 'evangelizing other Christians' into the Pentecostal-type of Christianity, on the other. Such mutual understanding and appreciation is critical in the non-western settings, where often Christianity struggles under the pressure of other religions and socio-cultural structures. Good research is available on the continuity of charismatic manifestations

---

[27] For example, 'Evangelization, Proselytism and Common Witness: The Report from the Fourth Phase of the International Dialogue 1990-1997 Between the Roman Catholic Church and Some Classical Pentecostal Churches and Leaders', *AJPS* 2:1 (1999), 105-151.

throughout church history and comparative studies between Pentecostalism and other church traditions are also useful.[28]

The second issue is the development of the unique contribution of Pentecostals toward church cooperation. Considering the Pentecostal ethos of practicality and mission-orientation, an active participation in selected global missionary movements would be an easy step forward. Since, from the second congress, Pentecostals have played an increasingly important role in the Lausanne process. As it moves toward its third congress in 2010, it is critical that an intentional effort is made by various Pentecostal mission bodies. If the 2006 biannual leadership conference is any indication of a Pentecostal role, judging from the list of participants and the discussion topics, Pentecostals have not demonstrated that they are ready to make a significant contribution to this evangelical mission movement. Another important event is the centenary of the Edinburgh missionary conference in 2010. The organizer is keenly aware of the surprise move of the Holy Spirit in the last one hundred years, squarely against the optimism of the western church to evangelize the whole world 'in our generation'.[29] History tells us of two important facts: 1) The Holy Spirit, the main mover of God's mission, has his own way of doing mission, and 2) the modern Pentecostal movement never entered in the discussion of the original conference, nor its subsequent missionary conferences. Like its 1910 conference, the centenary will leave another legacy by producing mission documents to assist Christian mission in the coming decades. Pentecostals are urged to actively participate in the nine study themes and processes. Related to the Edinburgh event is the mission wing of the World Council of Churches. The latest conference of the Commission on World Mission and Evangelism in Athens (2005) adopted 'Healing' as its theme, a typical Pentecostal issue, and included Pentecostal speakers.[30] There are sufficient indications that, partly from the shrinking size of their member churches, this world mission body is open to dialogue with Pentecostals for future mission work. A careful study can help the Pentecostal mission leaders to compare each one's mission theology and their

---

[28] For example, with Orthodox faith, see Edmund J. Rybarczyk, *Beyond Salvation: Eastern Orthodoxy and Classical Pentecostalism on Becoming Like Christ* (Milton Keynes, UK: Paternoster, 2004).

[29] For example, a number of articles published by Kenneth R. Ross in *IBMR*, e.g., 'The Centenary of Edinburgh 1910: Its Possibilities', 30:4 (Oct. 2006), 177-79, and *Edinburgh 2010: Springboard for Mission* (Pasadena, CA: William Carey International University Press, 2009). Also David Kerr and Kenneth R. Ross (eds.), *Edinburgh 2010: Mission Then and Now* (Oxford: Regnum Books, 2009).

[30] Jacques Matthey (ed.), *Come Holy Spirit, Heal and Reconcile: Report of the WCC Conference on World Mission and Evangelism, Athens, Greece, May 2005* (Geneva: WCC Publications, 2008).

mode of missionary engagement. As one study reveals, mission is one area where church cooperation can take place with relative ease.[31]

Ecumenism should be part of mission thinking, as Christians working together bring credibility to their witness. For this reason, Pentecostal 'divisiveness' should come under self-scrutiny. Highly individualistic and entrepreneurial modes of operation among western Pentecostal missionaries have not helped mission churches. The fact that the same church in different (western) countries established separate national bodies and training programs, remains as a painful reminder of this destructive trait of Pentecostal divisiveness. It is the national church that struggles often in a hostile environment, and church unity becomes an urgent necessity for the very survival of the church in such a setting. As historical studies reveal, there is a powerful potential for believers from all church traditions to unite and celebrate the presence of the Holy Spirit as one body.[32] As several ecumenical dialogues are on-going with Pentecostals, it is unfortunate that Pentecostal delegates do not often represent their churches, while their partners, be they Catholic, Reformed or Lutheran, are duly empowered to represent their churches. The learned community has been exploring this uneasy territory, and its fruit is already seen in the attitude of some churches toward Pentecostal-charismatic Christianity. Furthermore, with its robust growth, Pentecostal churches are now expected to play a key role in bringing Christ's church together in mission and unity. This is another promising area of further exploration.

A Word on Methodology

For many topics, particularly in theoretical (e.g. theological) areas, traditional research methodologies can be employed. Shaping theoretical foundations, be it biblical, theological or simply conceptual, will require epistemological approaches, while interpreting phenomena that are uniquely Pentecostal from various contexts will require interpretive or hermeneutical methodologies. However, in Pentecostal mission research the role of mission practice remains critical, and this will require another set of research methodologies.[33]

---

[31] Cecil M. Robeck, Jr. 'The Assemblies of God and Ecumenical Cooperation', in *Pentecostalism in Context*, 107-150.

[32] For example, Peter Hocken, *The Challenges of the Pentecostal, Charismatic and Messianic Jewish Movements: The Tensions of the Spirit* (Surrey, UK: Ashgate, 2009), 1, views all the three movements as an expression of ecumenism.

[33] The seriousness of methodology was seen in a criticism against Wagner's attempts to use anecdotic (or narrative) data to turn it into a more general from of knowledge: A. Scott Moreau, 'Broadening the Issues: Historiography, Advocacy, and Hermeneutics: Response to C. Peter Wagner', in Douglas McConnell (ed.), *The Holy Spirit and Mission Dynamics*, EMSS 5 (Pasadena, CA: William Carey Library, 1997), 123-35.

There are two modes of practice-based research.[34] The first is one that has been around for some time in Christian circles. By using the researcher's professional experience, the study not only includes an analysis of the practice itself, but also its epistemological foundations, with the goal of creating general or universal knowledge in the field. For example, one can take up the cell group system of Yoido Full Gospel Church, Seoul, Korea, study its history and practices by applying analytical and evaluative tools. Through this process, this particular case within its unique social, church and personal context is turned into a set of generally and universally applicable knowledge. At the same time, the practice can also be grounded in a theoretical foundation. For example, the Pentecostal epistemology of the 'prophethood of all believers', perhaps never intended by the initiator, can be successfully introduced as a valid theoretical foundation, thus appropriating this successful ministerial practice as a *bona fide* Pentecostal practice. Because of its goal to create general knowledge, the particulars of the practice are valuable in the process but no longer serve a primary purpose after the creation of knowledge. It is like a set of scaffolding for the construction of a building. Perhaps pioneered by other disciplines such as business studies, this form of practice-based study has been adopted in Christian higher education through professional doctorates such as Doctor of Ministry or Doctor of Missiology programs. There is no doubt that this mode of study will continue to serve Pentecostal mission researches.

Pentecostal mission will have little meaning if sophisticated theories are fully developed but its actual practice is no longer in operation. For this reason, a reflective process to continue to enhance its practice and the creation of universal knowledge is essential. The second pattern of research is known by various names including action research. For such research to achieve the best possible results, a long-term process is necessary and the researcher should remain in the mission setting. Most likely a cycle of a period of mission practice and a limited time of reflective research should be repeated several times. Each smaller research segment often involves the analysis and evaluation of a practice in a given time frame and context, and is used to inform the next stage of the practice. In the process, the story of mission practice is an important element of reflection. The smaller research studies and their subsequent applications in practice would constitute the trajectory of the research journey. Social science has already tried various models of practice-based and practice-oriented researches, and

---

[34] The professional post-graduate programmes that Oxford Centre for Mission Studies developed represented a commitment to such methodological explorations, although the proposed programmes were short-lived due to reasons external to the school. See for example, David Adams, 'Putting Heart and Soul into Research: An Inquiry into Becoming 'Scholar-Practitioner-Saint'', *Transformation* 25:2-3 (April/July, 2008), 144-57, for a plea for mission practitioners to become reflective practitioners as well as practitioner-reflectors. For a methodological discussion, see David Adams and Bernard Farr, 'Researching Christian Action', *Transformation* 25:2-3 (April/July, 2008), 158-64.

Pentecostals can learn much from them. In truth, both action/practice and narratives are characteristically Pentecostal, thus, Pentecostal mission practitioners may be able to contribute significantly to the development of new research tools.

Conclusion

The list in the study could go on, but space limits this luxury. If I may suggest, however, the following topics deserve close examination by Pentecostal mission thinkers.

Various families of global Pentecostal-Charismatic Christianity share some important commonalities whilst also having their own unique emphases: an interaction between such Pentecostal 'waves' will help each family to unearth their missional gift in their theology and spirituality. It is particularly true with controversial new issues such as identificational repentance, spiritual technology, strategic level power encounter, modern apostles and prophets, inter-generational curses, inner healing, and others. Serious attempts to learn from and assist one another are critical.

Church Growth and Church Revitalization is another topic, as Pentecostal churches have led this movement, although theorists are mostly non-Pentecostals. The sudden 'abandonment' of this movement by some of its own advocates has left the Christian world in bewildering confusion. There is a good possibility that this can be developed in the missionary context and prove a good impetus to many growing Pentecostal-charismatic churches. Also relevant is church revitalization, as once large Pentecostal churches may face the challenge of decline. What will be useful is the correlation between church growth and missionary motivation, as some western Pentecostal churches begin to lose membership and the question of how we can sustain the missionary movement will be a grave challenge.

Leadership will be an important area for further reflection. Particularly bewildering is the grave moral failures of some Spirit-gifted church leaders. With the global spread of the movement, there is no guarantee that the unfortunate failures in the West can be improved elsewhere. Various dynamics that lead one to moral failure in the midst of seemingly Spirit-empowered ministry need serious attention.

To conclude this reflection, I wish to make several practical suggestions to the Pentecostal mission communities and their learned minds. The first is networking. When international mission communities wish to invite international Pentecostal representatives to join them in dialogue or conference, there is simply no counterpart where they can make such a request. There is no international fellowship of Pentecostal missiology or Pentecostal mission organisations. A similar lack of networking is also found at the regional and national levels, although some denominational gatherings are noted in some areas. Without a networking structure in place, it is impossible to undertake any meaningful joint projects to represent the whole Pentecostal scope. It is encouraging to note an increasing number of Pentecostal academic societies at the regional level. International mission movements, such as the Lausanne process toward the Lausanne III congress in 2010 and the Edinburgh Centenary in the same year, can be an important opportunity for networking the global Pentecostal mission minds to provide a valuable contribution towards them.

Another practical proposal is a Pentecostal version of the mission perspectives book. It was more than a quarter of a century ago that a group of Pentecostal missiologists brought forth an extremely useful book, *Called and Empowered: Global Mission in Pentecostal Perspective.*[35] Now it is high time for global Pentecostal mission minds to form a small editorial body to carefully plan such a book, which can be handily used throughout Pentecostal Bible schools and missionary training programs, as well as the growing contingent of international Pentecostal missionaries. It will likely need to take similar major divisions: biblical-theological, historical and practical perspectives. Already there is a good pool of published studies to be considered, while it will also be likely that some topics need to be commissioned from various authors. For such a publication, it will be critically important that global, particularly the non-western, Pentecostal contributions are carefully sought after, in order that any one denomination will not exert an undue influence.

There are two sectors from which global mission communities have been eagerly anticipating contributions toward future Christian mission: Pentecostal and the non-western churches. For this reason, the international Pentecostal mission thinkers must take full advantage of this openness and intentionally plan to network and produce reflections. The twenty-first century may be truly a century of Pentecostal Christianity, particularly in the area of mission.

---

[35] Dempster, Klaus, & Petersen (eds.), *Called and Empowered.*

Selected Bibliography

Abeysekera, Fred. *The History of the Assemblies of God of Singapore* (Singapore: Abundant Press, 1992).

Adams, David. 'Putting Heart and Soul into Research: An Inquiry into Becoming "Scholar-Practitioner-Saint"', *Transformation* 25:2-3 (April/July 2008), 144-57.

_____, and Bernard Farr, 'Researching Christian Action', *Transformation* 25:2-3 (April/July, 2008), 158-64.

Ahmad, Aminah. *Women in Malaysia* (Manila: ADB, 1998).

_____. *Women in the People's Republic of China* (Manila: ADB, 1998).

Aigbe, Sunday. 'Pentecostal Mission and Tribal People Groups', in Murray A. Dempster, Byron D. Klaus, and Douglas Petersen (eds.), *Called and Empowered: Global Mission in Pentecostal Perspective* (Peabody, MA: Hendrickson, 1991), 172-75.

Aikman, David. *Jesus in Beijing: How Christianity Is Transforming China and Changing the Global Balance of Power* (Washington, DC: Regnery, 2003).

Albrecht, Daniel E. 'An Anatomy of Worship: A Pentecostal Analysis', in Wonsuk Ma and Robert P. Menzies (eds.), *The Spirit and Spirituality: Essays in Honor of Russell P. Spittler* (London: T. & T. Clark, 2004), 70-82.

Anderson, Allan. *Spreading Fires: The Missionary Nature of Early Pentecostalism* (London: SCM Press, 2007).

_____. 'Towards a Pentecostal Missiology for the Majority World', *AJPS* 8:1 (January 2005), 29-47.

Anderson, Gordon L. 'Pentecostals Believe in More Than Tongues', in *Pentecostals from the Inside Out* (Wheaton: Victor, 1990), 53-64.

Asian Conference of Third World Theologians, 'Asia's Struggle for Full Humanity: Toward a Relevant Theology', in Douglas J. Elwood (ed.), *Asian Christian Theology* (Philadelphia: Westminster, 1980).

Asian Development Bank. *Poverty in Viet Nam* (Manila, Philippines: ADB, 1995).

Bagamasped, A. and Z. Hamada-Pawid, *A People's History of Benguet* (Baguio, Philippines: Baguio Printing, 1985).

Baker, Carolyn Denise and Frank D. Macchia, 'Created Spirit Beings', in Stanley M. Horton (ed.), *Systematic Theology: A Pentecostal Perspective* (Springfield, MO: Logion Press, 1994), 179-213.

Baldemor, Oscar C. 'The Spread of Fire: A Study of Ten Growing Churches in Metro-Manila' (Th. M. thesis, Fuller Theological Seminary, 1990).

Barret, David B., George T. Kurian, and Todd M. Johnson (eds.), *World Christian Encyclopedia A Comparative Survey of Churches and Religions in the Modern World* (2nd ed., 2 vols.; Oxford: Oxford University Press, 2001).

Bartleman, Frank. *Azusa Street* (Plainfield, NJ: Logos International, 1980).

Bautista, Lorenzo C. 'The Church in the Philippines', in Saphir Athyal (ed.), *Church in Asia Today: Challenges and Opportunities* (Singapore: Asia Lausanne Committee for World Evangelization, 1996), 175-202.

Berthrong, John. 'Sages and Immortals: Chinese Religions', in Pat Alexander, et al. (eds.), *Eerdman's Handbook to the World's Religions* (Grand Rapids, MI: Eerdmans, 1994), 245-54.

Bondi, Roerta C. *To Pray and to Love* (Minneapolis: Fortress Press, 1991).

Bounds, E.. *The Complete Works of E.M. Bounds on Prayer* (Grand Rapids, MI: Baker, 1995).

Bridges, John Cheryl. *Pentecostal Formation: A Pedagogy among the Oppressed* (JPTSS 2; Sheffield: Sheffield Academic Press, 1993).

_____. 'Pentecostals and the Praxis of Liberation: A Proposal for Subversive Theological Education'. *Transformation* 11:1 (January/March, 1994), 34-46.

Brother Yun with Paul Hattaway. *The Heavenly Man: The Remarkable True Story of Chinese Christian Brother Yun* (London: Monarch Books, 2002).

Cavaness, Barbara. 'God Calling: Women in Assemblies of God Mission', *Pneuma: The Journal of the Society for Pentecostal Studies* 16:1 (1994), 49-62.

Chan, Simon. *Spiritual Theology: A Systematic Study of Christian Life* (Downers Grove, IL: InterVarsity Press, 1998).

Cho, David [Paul] Yonggi. 'City Taking in Korea', in Peter Wagner (ed.), *Engaging the Enemy: How to Fight and Defeat Territorial Spirits* (Ventura: Regal Books, 1991), 117-20.

_____. 'Prayer Can Change the Course of Your Life', *Pentecostal Evangel*, Oct. 18, 1998, 11.

_____. 'The Secret Behind the World's Biggest Church', in L. Grant McClung (ed.), *Azusa Street and Beyond: Pentecostal Missions and Church Growth in the Twentieth Century* (South Plainfield, NJ: Bridge Publishing, 1986), 99-104.

Choi, Jashil, *How to Pray for Answer* (in Korean; Seoul: Seoul Books, 1997).

_____. *I Was a Hallelujah Woman* (in Korean; Seoul: Seoul Books, 1978).

Chua, Wee Hian. 'The Worship of Ancestors', in Pat Alexander, et al. (eds.), *Eerdman's Handbook of World Religions* (Grand Rapids, MI: Eerdmans, 1994), 248-50.

Clark, Mathew. 'The Challenges of Contextualization and Syncretism to Pentecostal Theology and Missions in Africa', *JAM* 3:1 (2001), 79-99.

Coker, Dan. 'New Mission Opportunities in Communist Countries-Latin America' (Lectures delivered at Abilene Christian University Lectureship, Feb. 20, 2002, Abilene, TX).

Cole, Harold R. 'A Model of Contextualized Deliverance Ministry: A Case Study: The Cordillera Rehabilitation Centre', *JAM* 5:2 (2003), 259-273.

Conn, Charles W. *Where the Saints Have Trod* (Cleveland, TN: Pathway Press, 1959).

Covell, Ralph R. *Confucius, the Buddha, and Christ: A History of the Gospel in Chinese* (Maryknoll, NY: Orbis, 1986).

Cox, Harvey. *Fire from Heaven: The Rise of Pentecostal Spirituality and the Reshaping of Religion in the Twenty-First Century* (Reading, MA: Addison-Wesley, 1995).

David, Rina and Penny Azarcon de la Cruz, 'Towards Our Own Image: An Alternative Philippines Report on Women and Media' (Pamphlet Series No. 1, Philippines Women's Research Collective, Quezon City, 1985).

Dempster, Murray A.H. 'A Theology of the Kingdom: A Pentecostal Contribution', in Vinay Samuel and Chris Sugden (eds.), *Mission as Transformation* (Oxford: Regnum, 1999), 45-75.

_____, Byron D. Klaus, and Douglas Petersen (eds.), *Called and Empowered: Global Mission in Pentecostal Perspective* (Peabody, MA: Hendrickson, 1991).

Deng, Zhaoming, 'Indigenous Chinese Pentecostal Denominations', in Allan Anderson and Edmond Tang (eds.), *Asian and Pentecostal: The Charismatic Face of Christianity in Asia* (Oxford: Regnum, 2005), 439-68.

Douglas, Elwood, and Magdamo Patricia. *In Christ in Philippine Context* (Quezon City, Philippines: New Day Publishers, 1971).

Du Plessis, David J. *The Spirit Bade Me Go* (Plainfield, NJ: Logos, 1970).

_____, and Bob Slosser. *A Man Called Mr. Pentecost* (Plainfield, NJ: Logos, 1977).

Duffield, Guy P. *Pentecostal Preaching: The L.I.F.E. Bible College Alumni Association Lectureship on Preaching for 1956* (New York: Vantage, 1957).

Dyrness, William. *Learning About Theology From the Third World* (Grand Rapids: Zondervan, 1990).

Eim, Yeol-soo. 'Pentecostalism and Public School: The Case Study of Rev. Dr. Seen-ok Ahn' (A Paper presented in the first Asian Pentecostal Society at Four Square Seminary, Daejon, Korea, May 21, 1999).

Elliston, Edgar J. 'Response to 'Power Evangelism in Pioneer Mission Strategy'', in C. Peter Wagner and F. Douglas Pennoyer (eds.), *Wrestling with Dark Angeles: Toward a Deeper Understanding of the Supernatural Forces in Spiritual Warfare* (Ventura, CA: Regal Books, 1990), 297.

Elwood, Douglas and Patricia Magdamo, *In Christ in Philippine Context* (Quezon City, Philippines: New Day, 1971).

Esperanza, T.C. 'The Assemblies of God in the Philippines' (M.R.E. thesis, Fuller Theological Seminary, 1965).

'Evangelism, Proselytism and Common Witness: The Report from the Fourth Phase of the International Dialogue 1990-1997 Between the Roman Catholic Church and some Classical Pentecostal Churches and Leaders', *AJPS* 2:1 (1999), 105-151.

Fee, Gordon D. 'The Kingdom of God and the Church's Global Mission', in Murray A. Dempster, Byron D. Klaus, and Douglas Petersen (eds.), *Called and Empowered*, (Peabody, MA: Hendrickson, 1991), 7-21.

_____. 'Toward a Pauline Theology of Glossolalia', in Wonsuk Ma and Robert P. Menzies (eds.), *Pentecostalism in Context: Essays in Honor of William W. Menzies* (JPTSS 11; Sheffield: Sheffield Academic, 1997), 24-37.

Flora, Tabora. 'Some Folk Beliefs and Practices among the Mountain People of Northern Luzon', *SLU Research Journal* 9:3-4 (1978), 59-72.

Gammage, Albert W. Jr., *How To Plant a Church* (Makati, Philippines: Church Strengthening Ministry, 1995).

Glasser, Arthur and Donald McGavran. *Contemporary Theories of Mission* (Grand Rapids: Baker, 1983).

Goff, James R. Jr., 'Initial Tongues in the Theology of Charles Fox Parham', in Gary B. McGee (ed.), *Initial Evidence: Historical and Biblical Perspectives on the Pentecostal Doctrine of Spirit Baptism* (Peabody, MA: Hendrickson, 1991), 57-71.

Guidelines of the Catholic Charismatic Renewal Movement in the Archdioceses of Manila (Manila: Archdiocesan Office for Research and Development, 1983).

Hammer, Raymond. 'Approaches to Truth: The Great Interpreters', in Pat Alexander, et al. (eds.), *Eerdman's Handbook to the World's Religions* (Grand Rapids, MI: Eerdmans, 1994), 183.

_____. 'Concepts of Hinduism', in Pat Alexander, et al. (eds.), *Eerdman's Handbook to the World's Religions* (Grand Rapids, MI: Eerdmans, 1994), 185-92.

_____. 'Karma and Dharma: Hindu Ethics', in Pat Alexander, et al. (eds.), *Eerdman's Handbook to the World's Religions* (Grand Rapids, MI: Eerdmans, 1994), 190.

Harper, George W. 'Philippine Tongues of Fire? Latin American Pentecostalism and the Future of Filipino Christianity', *JAM* 2:2 (2000), 225-59.

Harvey, Cox. *Fire from Heaven: The Rise of Pentecostal Spirituality and the Reshaping of Religion in the Twenty-First Century* (Reading, MA: Addison-Wesley, 1995).

Hattaway, Paul. *Back to Jerusalem: Three Chinese House Church Leaders Share their Vision to Complete the Great Commission* (Waynesboro, GA: Authentic Media, 2003).

Hayes, Jeanne. *Sowing the Grains of Peace: A Resource Handbook for Building Peace* (Okinawa, Japan: Northeast Asia Subregional Women's Consultation Gionowan Seminar, June 1992).

Henry, Rodney L. *Filipino Spirit World: A Challenge to the Church* (Manila: OMF Lit., 1986).

Hesselgrave, David J. and Edward Rommen. *Contextualization: Meanings, Methods, and Models* (Grand Rapids: Baker, 1989).

Hiebert, Paul G. *Anthropological Insights for Missionaries* (Grand Rapids: Baker, 1991).

_____. *Anthropological Reflections on Missiological Issues* (Grand Rapids: Baker, 1994).

_____. *Konduru* (Minneapolis: University of Minnesota Press, 1974).

_____, R. Daniel Shaw, and Tite Tiénou, *Understanding Folk Religion: A Christian Response to Popular Beliefs and Practices* (Grand Rapids: Baker, 1999).

Hocken, Peter. *The Challenges of the Pentecostal, Charismatic and Messianic Jewish Movements: The Tensions of the Spirit* (Surrey, UK: Ashgate, 2009).

Hodges, Melvin. *A Guide to Church Planting* (Chicago, Moody Press, 1973).

_____. *The Indigenous Church: A Complete Handbook on How to Grow Young Churches* (Springfield, MO: Gospel Publishing House, 1976).

Hollenweger, Walter J. 'Pentecostal Research: Problems and Promises', in Charles E. Jones (ed.), *A Guide to the Study of the Pentecostal Movement* (Metuchen, NJ: Scarecrow, 1983), vii-ix.

_____. *Pentecostalism: Origin and Developments Worldwide* (Peabody, MA: Hendrickson, 1997).

_____. 'Syncretism and Capitalism', *AJPS* 2:1 (1999), 47-61.

Hong, Young-gi. 'Revisiting Church Growth in Korean Pentecostalism: A Theological Reflection', *International Review of Mission* 89/353 (2000), 190-202.

Horton, Stanley. *Reflections of an Early American Pentecostal* (Baguio, Philippines. APTS Press, 2001).

Howard, Rick. 'David du Plessis: Pentecost's "Ambassador-at-Large"', in Wonsuk Ma and Robert P. Menzies (eds.), *The Spirit and Spirituality: Essays in Honor of Russell P. Spittler* (London: T. & T. Clark, 2004), 271-97.

Hughes, Ray H. 'The Uniqueness of Pentecostal Preaching', in L. Grant McClung, Jr. (ed.), *Azusa Street and Beyond: Pentecostal Missions and Church Growth in the Twentieth Century* (South Plainfield, NJ: Bridge, 1986).

Hunter, Harold D. and Cecil M. Robeck, Jr. (eds.), *The Suffering Body: Ecumenical and International Perspectives on the Persecution of Christians* (Waynesboro, GA: Paternoster, 2006).

Hwa Yung, 'A Systematic Theology that Recognises the Demonic', in A. Scott Moreau, et. al. (eds.), *Deliver Us from Evil: An Uneasy Frontier in Christian Mission* (Monrovia, CA: MARC, 2002), 3-27.

_____. 'Endued with Power: The Pentecostal-Charismatic Renewal and the Asian Church in the Twenty-first Century', *AJPS* 6:1 (2003), 63-82.

Igualdo, Lolito. 'The Social World of the Kankana-eys' (Ed.D. dissertation, Baguio Central University, 1988).

Illo, Frances Jeanne I. *Women in the Philippines* (Manila: ADB, 1997).

Inez, Sturgeon. *Give Me This Mountain* (Oakland, CA: Hunter Advertising, 1960).

International Theological Institutes, *A History of the Korean Assemblies of God* (in Korean; Seoul: Seoul Books, 1998).

Jenkins, Philip. *The New Faces of Christianity: Believing the Bible in the Global South* (Oxford: Oxford University Press, 2006).

_____. 'Next Christianity', *The Atlantic Monthly*, Oct 2002 (http://www.theatlantic.com/past/docs/issues/ 2002/10/jenkins.htm).

Jenks, Albert E. *The Bontoc-Igorot* (Manila, Philippines: Bureau of Printing, 1905).

Johns, Cheryl Bridges. *Pentecostal Formation: A Pedagogy Among the Oppressed* (JPTSS 2; Sheffield: Sheffield Academic Press, 1993).

_____. 'Pentecostals and the Praxis of Liberation: A Proposal for Subversive Theological Education', *Transformation* 11:1 (1994), 8-20.

Johnson, Todd M., and Sun Young Chung, 'Christianity's Centre of Gravity, AD 33-2100', in Todd M. Johnson and Kenneth R. Ross (eds.), *Atlas of Global Christianity* (Edinburgh: Edinburgh University Press, 2009), 50-53.

Johnston, Patrick, and Jason Mandryk, *Operation World*, 21st century edition (Cumbria, UK: Paternoster, 2001).

Jun, Taek-bu. *Yanghwa-jin Missionary Biographies* [in Korean], rev. ed. (Seoul: Hongsung, 2005).

Kamps, Timothy J. 'The Biblical Forms and Elements of Power Encounter' (M.A. thesis, Columbia Graduate School of Bible and Missions, Columbia, SC, 1986).

Karkkainen, Veli-Matti. 'Theology of the Cross: A Stumbling Block to Pentecostal/Charismatic Spirituality?', in Wonsuk Ma and Robert P. Menzies (eds.), *The Spirit and Spirituality: Essays in Honour of Russell P. Spittler* (London: T & T Clark, 2004), 150-63.

_____. '"What in the World Is the Spirit Doing?": A Pentecostal-Charismatic Inquiry into the Theology of Religions' (A paper presented at the International Symposium on Pentecostal Mission, Baguio, Philippines, February 2003).

Kearney, Michael. *World View* (Novato, CA: Chandler & Sharp, 1984).

Keith, Minus. 'Missions and Indigenisation in World Missions', in Met Castillo (ed.), *The Asian Challenge: A Compendium of the Asia Missions Congress '90*, (n.p.: Asian Missions Congress, 1991).

Kerr, David, and Kenneth R. Ross (eds.), *Edinburgh 2010: Mission Then and Now* (Oxford: Regnum Books, 2009).

Kim, Dongsoo. 'The Healing of *Han* in Korean Pentecostalism', *JPT* 15 (1999), 123-39.

Kim, Soon Young. 'Enough Shame for a Woman: The Story of Jungshindai', in John C. England and Alan J. Torrance (eds.), *Doing Theology with the Spirit's Movement in Asia* (ATESEA Occasional Papers 11; Singapore: ATESEA, 1991), 184-93.

Kim, Yong Bock. 'Doing Theology in Asia Today: A Korean Perspective', in Douglas J. Elwood (ed.), *Asian Christian Theology* (Philadelphia: Westminster, 1980).

Kirk, Andrew J. *What Is Mission?: Theological Explorations* (Minneapolis, MN: Fortress, 2000).

Kitano, Koichi. 'Socio-Religious Distance Between Charismatics and Other Religious Group Members: A Case Study of the Philippines in the 1980s', *JAM* 5:2 (2003), 231-42.

_____. 'Spontaneous Ecumenicity Between Catholics and Protestants in the Charismatic Movement' (Ph.D. dissertation, Centro Escolar University, Manila, Philippines 1981).

Kraft, Charles H. *Anthropology for Christian Witness* (Maryknoll, NY: Orbis, 1996).

_____. '"Christian Animism" or God-Given Authority?', in Robert J. Priest, Thomas Campbell, and Bradford A. Mullen (eds.), *Spiritual Power and Missions: Raising the Issues* (EMSS 3; Pasadena, CA: William Carey Library, 1995), 88-136.

_____. *Christianity With Power: Your Worldview and Your Experience of the Supernatural* (Ann Arbor, MI: Servant, 1988; reprint by Manila, Philippines: OMF Literature, 1990).

_____. 'Contemporary Trends in the Treatment of Spiritual Conflict', in A. Scott Moreau, et al. (eds.), *Deliver Us from Evil: An Uneasy Frontier in Christian Mission* (Monrovia: MARC, 2002), 177-202.

_____. 'Dealing with Demonization', in Charles H. Kraft, Tom White, Ed Murphy, et al. (eds.), *Behind the Enemy Lines: An Advanced Guide to Spiritual Warfare* (Ann Arbor, MI: Vine, 1994), 79-120.

_____. *Defeating Dark Angeles: Breaking Demonic Oppression in the Believer's Life* (Ann Arbor, MI: Servant, 1992).

_____, Tom White, Ed Murphy, et al. (eds.), *Behind the Enemy Lines: An Advanced Guide to Spiritual Warfare* (Ann Arbor, MI: Vine, 1994).

Layda, William V. 'Mobilizing the Church for Missions', in Met Castillo and Katie Sisco (eds.), *Into the 21st Century Asian Churches in Mission: A Compendium of the Asia Missions Congress II* (n. p.: Evangelical Fellowship of Asia, n.p.d.), 115-117.

Lee, Diana S. and Kendall Laurel. *An Initiation of Kut for a Korean Shaman* (videotape; Honolulu: University of Hawaii Press, 1991).

Lee, Jae-bum. 'Pentecostal Type Distinctives and Korean Protestant Church Growth' (Ph.D. dissertation, Fuller Theological Seminary, 1986).

Leoh, Vincent. 'Pentecostal Preaching: A Century Past, a Century Forward' (A paper presented at the 8th annual meeting of Asian Pentecostal Society, Kuala Lumpur, Malaysia, September 2006).

Lewis. Jonathan, *World Mission: An Analysis of the World Christian Movement, Part 2: Strategic Dimension* (Pasadena, CA: William Carey, 1987).

Loito, Igualdo. 'The Social World of the Kankana-eys' (Ed.D. dissertation, Baguio Central University, 1988).

Lord, Andrew. *Spirit-Shaped Mission: A Holistic Charismatic Missiology* (Bletchley, UK: Paternoster, 2005).

Lua, Norma. *Fiction in the Traditional Kankanay Society* (Baguio, Philippines: Cordillera Studies Centre, 1984).

Ma, Julie C. 'Animism and Pentecostalism', in Stanley M. Burgess (ed.), *The Encyclopedia of Pentecostal and Charismatic Christianity* (New York: Routledge, 2006), 26-27.

_____. 'Animism and Pentecostalism: A Case Study', in Stanley M. Burgess and Eduard M. van der Maas (eds.), *NIDPCM* (Grand Rapids, MI: Zondervan, 2002), 315-18.

_____. 'A Comparison of Two Worldviews: Kankana-ey and Pentecostal', in Wonsuk Ma and Robert Menzies (eds.), *Pentecostalism in Context: Essays in Honor of William W. Menzies* (Sheffield: Sheffield Academic Press, 1997), 265-90.

_____. 'Elva Vanderbout: A Woman Pioneer of Pentecostal Mission Among Igorots', *JAM* 3:1 (2001), 121-40.

_____. 'Korean Pentecostal Spirituality: A Case Study of Jashil Choi', in Wonsuk Ma & Robert P. Menzies (eds.), *Spirit and Spirituality: Essays in Honor of Russell P. Spittler* (London: T & T Clark, 2004), 298-313.

_____. *Mission Possible: Biblical Strategy for Reaching the Lost* (Oxford: Regnum Books, 2005).

_____. 'A Missionary Challenge to Asian Pentecostals: Power Mission and Its Effect' (A Paper Presented at Asian Pentecostal Society Annual Meeting, Manila, Philippines, 2000).

_____. *When the Spirit Meets the Spirits: Pentecostal Ministry Among the Kankana-ey Tribe in the Philippines* (Frankfurt am Main: Peter Lang, 2000).

Ma, Wonsuk. 'Asian Pentecostalism: A Religion Whose Only Limit Is the Sky', *Journal of Beliefs and Values* 25:2 (Aug 2004), 191-204.

_____. 'Doing Theology in the Philippines: A Case of Pentecostal Christianity', *AJPS* 8:2 (2005), 215-33.

_____. 'The Effect of Rev. Cho's Sermon Style for Church Growth on the Development of Theology', in Sung-hoon Myung and Young-gi Hong (eds.), *Charis and Charisma: David Yonggi Cho and the Growth of Yoido Full Gospel Church* (Oxford: Regnum Books, 2003), 159-71.

_____. 'The Empowerment of the Spirit of God in Luke-Acts: An Old Testament Perspective', in Wonsuk Ma and Robert P. Menzies (eds.), *The Spirit and Spirituality: Essays in Honor of Russell P. Spittler* (London: T. & T. Clark, 2004), 28-40.

_____. 'A "First Waver" Looks at the "Third Wave": A Pentecostal Reflection on Charles Kraft's Power Encounter Terminology', *Pneuma* 19:2 (1997), 189-206.

_____. 'Full Cycle Mission: A Possibility of Pentecostal Missiology', *AJPS* 8:1 (2005), 5-27.

_____. '"If It Is a Sign": An Old Testament Reflection on the Initial Evidence Discussion', *AJPS* 2:2 (1999).

_____. 'The Spirit of God in Creation: Lessons for Christian Mission', *Transformation* 24:3 & 4 (2007), 222-30.

_____. 'The Spirit of God upon Leaders of the Ancient Israelite Society and Igorot Tribal Churches', in Wonsuk Ma and Robert P. Menzies (eds.), *Pentecostalism in Context: Essays in Honor of William W. Menzies* (JPTSS 11; Sheffield: Sheffield Academic Press, 1997), 291-316.

_____. '"When the Poor Are Fired Up": The Role of Pneumatology in Pentecostal-charismatic Mission', *Transformation* 24:1 (2007), 28-34.

_____, and Julie C. Ma, 'Jesus Christ in Asia: Our Journey with Him as Pentecostal Believers', *IRM* 94 (Oct 2005), 493-506.

_____, William W. Menzies, and Hyeon-sung Bae (eds.), *David Yonggi Cho: A Close Look at His Theology and Ministry* (Baguio, Philippines: APTS Press, 2004).

Martin, David. *Tongues of Fire: The Explosion of Protestantism in Latin America* (Oxford: Blackwell, 1990).

Martin, Larry. *The Life and Ministry of William J. Seymour* (Joplin, MO: Christian Life Books, 1999).

Matthey, Jacques (ed.), *Come Holy Spirit, Heal and Reconcile: Report of the WCC Conference on World Mission and Evangelism, Athens, Greece, May 2005* (Geneva: WCC Publications, 2008).

McClung, L. Grant, Jr. 'Introduction: Truth on fire: Pentecostals and an Urgent Missiology', in L. Grant McClung, Jr. (ed.), *Azusa Street and Beyond: Pentecostal Missions and Church Growth in the Twentieth Century* (South Plainfield, NJ: Bridge Publishing, 1986), 47-54.

_____. '"Try to Get People Saved": Revisiting the Paradigm of an Urgent Pentecostal Missiology', in Murry W. Dempster, Douglas P. Petersen, and Byron D. Klaus (eds.), *The Globalization of Pentecostalism: A Religion Made to Travel* (Oxford: Regnum Books, 1999), 30-51.

McDonald, Margaret. *Women in Development: Viet Nam* (Manila: ADB, 1995).

McGavran, Donald A. 'What Makes Pentecostal Churches Grow?' in L. Grant McClung (ed.), *Azusa Street and Beyond: Pentecostal Missions and Church Growth in the Twentieth Century* (South Plainfield, NJ: Bridge Publishing, 1986), 120-23.

McGee, Gary B. 'Mission, Overseas (North American)', Stanley M. Burgess, Gary B. McGee, and Patrick H. Alexander (eds.), *DPCM* (Grand Rapids: Zondervan, 1988), 610-25.

_____. 'The Radical Strategy in Modern Mission: The Linkage of Paranormal Phenomena with Evangelism', in C. Douglas McConnell (ed.), *The Holy Spirit and Mission Dynamics* (EMSS 5; Pasadena, William Carey Library, 1997), 69-95.

_____. *This Gospel Shall Be Preached: A History and Theology of Assemblies of God Foreign Missions*, 2 vols. (Springfield, MO: Gospel Publishing House, 1986-89).

Menzies, Robert P. *Empowered for Witness: The Spirit in Luke-Acts* (Sheffield: Sheffield Academic Press, 1994).

_____. 'Spirit-baptism and Spiritual Gifts', in Wonsuk Ma and Robert P. Menzies (eds.), *Pentecostalism in Context: Essays in Honor of William W. Menzies* (JPTSS 11; Sheffield: Sheffield Academic Press, 1997), 48-59.

Menzies, William W. 'Non-Wesleyan Origins of Pentecostal Movement', in Vinson Synan (ed.), *Aspects of Pentecostal-Charismatic Origins* (Plainfield, NJ: Logos, 1975).

_____. 'Reflection on Suffering: A Pentecostal Perspective', in Wonsuk Ma and Robert P. Menzies (eds.), *The Spirit and Spirituality: Essays in Honour of Russell P. Spittler* (London: T & T Clark, 2004), 141-49.

Mercado, Leonardo N. *Elements of Filipino Theology* (Tacloban City, Philippines: Divine Word University, 1975).

Metz, Wulf. 'The Enlightened One: Buddhism', in Pat Alexander, et al. (eds.), *Eerdman's Handbook to the World's Religions* (Grand Rapids, MI: Eerdmans, 1994), 222-32.

Miller, Donald E. 'Pentecostalism and Social Transformation', in Harold D. Hunter and Cecil M. Robeck, Jr. (eds.), *The Azusa Street Revival and Its Legacy* (Cleveland, TN: Pathway Press, 2006), 335-48.

_____, and Tetsunao Yamamori, *Global Pentecostalism: The New Face of Christian Social Engagement* (Berkley: University of California Press, 2007).

Montague, George T. *The Holy Spirit: Growth of a Biblical Tradition* (New York: Paulist, 1976).

Moreau, A. Scott. 'Broadening the Issues: Historiography, Advocacy, and Hermeneutics: Response to C. Peter Wagner', in Douglas McConnell (ed.), *The Holy Spirit and Mission Dynamics* (EMSS 5; Pasadena, CA: William Carey Library, 1997), 123-35.

_____, et. al. (eds.), *Deliver Us from Evil: An Uneasy Frontier in Christian Mission* (Monrovia, CA: MARC, 2002).

Myung, Sung-Hoon. 'Spiritual Dimensions of Church Growth as Applied in the Yoido Full Gospel Church' (Ph.D. dissertation, Fuller Theological Seminary, 1990).

Nagasawa, Makito. 'Makuya Pentecostalism: A Survey', *AJPS* 3:2 (2000), 203-218.

Neil, Stephen C. *Christian Faith and Other Faiths* (New York: Oxford, 1970).

Neill, Stephen. *Creative Tension* (London: Edinburgh House, 1959).

Nicholls, Bruce J. 'Theological Education and Evangelization', in J.D. Douglas (ed.), *Let the Earth Hear His Voice* (Minneapolis: World Wide, 1975), 647.

Nida, Eugene. *Customs and Cultures: Anthropology for Christian Mission* (Pasadena, CA: William Carey, 1954).

Oblau, Gotthard. 'Pentecostals by Default? Contemporary Christianity in China', in Allan Anderson and Edmond Tang (eds.), *Asian and Pentecostal: The Charismatic Face of Christianity in Asia* (Oxford: Regnum Books, 2005), 411-38.

Oscar, Baldemor C. 'The Spread of Fire: A Study of Ten Growing Churches in Metro-Manila' (Th. M. Thesis, Fuller Theological Seminary, 1990).

Pachua, Lalsangkima. 'Mizo "*sakhua*" in Transition: Change and Continuity from Primal Religion to Christianity', *Missiology* 34:1 (Jan. 2006), 41-57.

Parham, Charles F. *The Sermons of Charles F. Parham* (New York/London: Garland, 1985).

Park, Myung Soo. 'Korean Pentecostal Spirituality as Manifested in the Testimonies of Believers of the Yoido Full Gospel Church', *AJPS* 7:1 (2004), 35-56.

Parshall, Phil. *Bridges to Islam* (Grand Rapids: Baker, 1983).

Petersen, Douglas. *Not by Might, Nor by Power: A Pentecostal Theology of Social Concern in Latin America* (Oxford: Regnum Books, 1996).

Piker, Steven. 'Buddhism and Modernization in Contemporary Thailand', *Contributions to Asian Studies* IV (1973).

Poloma, Margaret. *The Assemblies of God at the Crossroads* (Knoxville: University of Tennessee Press, 1989).

Pomerville, Paul A. *The Third Force in Missions: A Pentecostal Contribution to Contemporary Mission Theology* (Peabody, MA: Hendrickson, 1985).

Prabhu, George Soares. 'The Jesus of Faith: A Christological Contribution to an Ecumenical Third World Spirituality', in K.C. Abraham and Bernadette Mbuy-Beya (eds.), *Spirituality of the Third World* (Maryknoll, NY: Orbis, 1994).

Priest, Robert J., Thomas Campbell, and Bradford A. Mullen, 'Missiological Syncretism: The New Animistic Paradigm', in *Spiritual Power and Missions: Raising the Issues* (EMSS 3; Pasadena, CA: William Carey Library, 1995), 9-87.

Raymond, Hammer. 'Approaches to Truth: The Great Interpreters', in Pat Alexander, et al. (eds.), *Eerdman's Handbook to the World's Religions* (Grand Rapids, MI: Eerdmans, 1994), 183.

_____. 'Concepts of Hinduism', in Pat Alexander, et al. (eds.), *Eerdman's Handbook to the World's Religions* (Grand Rapids, MI: Eerdmans, 1994), 185.

_____. 'Karma and Dharma: Hindu Ethics'. in Pat Alexander, et al. (eds.), *Eerdman's Handbook to the World's Religions* (Grand Rapids, MI: Eerdmans, 1994), 190.

Reyes, Erlinda. 'A Theological Framework for Non-healing in the Pentecostal Perspective' (ThM thesis, Asia Pacific Theological Seminary, 2007).

Richard, H. L. 'Evangelical Approaches to Hindus', *Missiology: An International Review* 29 (July 2001), 307-16.

Rina, David and Azarcon-de la Cruz Penny. 'Towards Our Own Image: An Alternative Philippines Report on Women and Media' (Pamphlet Series No. 1, Philippines Women's Research Collective, Quezon City, 1985).

Ringgren, Helmer. *The Messiah in the Old Testament* (David E. Green, trans.; Philadelphia: Fortress, 1966).

Ro, Bong Rin. 'The Korean Church: Growing or Declining?', *Evangelical Review of Theology* 19 (1995), 344-45.

Robeck, Cecil M., Jr. 'The Assemblies of God and Ecumenical Cooperation', in Wonsuk Ma and Robert P. Menzies (eds.), *Pentecostalism in Context: Essays in Honor of William W. Menzies (JPTSS* 11; Sheffield: Sheffield Academic Press, 1997), 107-150.

_____. *The Azusa Street Mission and Revival: The Birth of the Global Pentecostal Movement* (Nashville, TN: Thomas Nelson, 2006).

_____. 'Pentecostal Ecumenism: An Introductory Essay for Asian Pentecostals'. *AJPS* 2:1 (1999), 87-103.

Roebuck, David G. 'Go and Tell My Brother?: The Waning of Women's Voices in American Pentecostalism' (A paper presented at the Twentieth Annual Meeting of the Society for Pentecostal Studies, Dallas, TX, Nov. 8-10, 1990).

Rommen, Edward (ed.), *Spiritual Power and Missions: Raising the Issues* (EMSS 3; Pasadena, CA: William Carey Library, 1995).

Ross, Kenneth R. 'The Centenary of Edinburgh 1910: Its Possibilities', *International Bulletin of Missionary Research* 30:4 (Oct. 2006), 177-79.

_____. *Edinburgh 2010: Springboard for Mission* (Pasadena, CA: William Carey International University Press, 2009).

Rybarczyk, Edmund J. *Beyond Salvation: Eastern Orthodoxy and Classical Pentecostalism on Becoming Like Christ* (Milton Keynes, UK: Paternoster, 2004).

Sacla, D. Wasing. *Treasury of Beliefs and Home Rituals of Benguet* (Baguio, Philippines: BCF Printing, 1987).

Schumitsch, Charlotte. 'Missionettes in the Philippines', *Pentecostal Evangel*, March 25, 1962, 1.

Scott, William H. 'Cultural Changes Among Igorots in Mining Companies', *Church and Community*, Jan.-Feb., 1967, 27-30.

_____. *On the Cordillera: A Look at the Peoples and Cultures of the Mountain Province* (Manila: MSC Enterprises, Inc., 1969).

Seccombe, D.P. 'Luke and Isaiah', *New Testament Studies* 27 (1981), 258-59.

Shaull, Richard and Waldo Cesar. *Pentecostalism and the Future of the Christian Churches: Promises, Limitations, Challenges* (Grand Rapids: Eerdmans, 2000).

Shaw, Daniel R. *Kandila* (Ann Arbor, MI: University of Michigan Press, 1990).

Shemeth, S. 'Trasher, Lillian Hunt', *IDPCM*, 1153.

Sklba, Richard J. ''Until the Spirit from on High Is Poured out on Us' (Isa 32:15): Reflections on the Role of the Spirit in the Exile', *Catholic Biblical Quarterly* 46 (1984), 1-17.

Soriano, Juan B. 'Pentecost in the Philippines', *Pentecostal Evangel* (7 August 1948), 2-4.

Sowing the Grains of Peace: A Resource Handbook for Building Peace (Okinawa, Japan: Northeast Asia Subregional Women's Consultation Ginowan Seminar, June 1992).

Spittler, Russell P. 'Glossolalia', in Stanley M. Burgess and Eduard M. van der Maas (eds.), *NIDPCM* (Grand Rapids, MI: Zondervan, 2002), 338-39.

_____. 'Spirituality, Pentecostal and Charismatic', in Stanley M. Burgess, et al. (eds.), *DPCM* (Grand Rapids: Zondervan, 1988), 804-809.

Spradley, James. 'Worldview and Values' (A reader used in Worldview and Worldview Change class, School of World Mission, Fuller Theological Seminary, 1994).

Stephens, Sunil H. 'Doing Theology in a Hindu Context', *JAM* 1:2 (Jan 1999), 181-203.

Steyne, M. *Gods of Power* (Houston, TX: Touch, 1992).

Stronstad, Roger. *Charismatic Theology of St. Luke* (Peabody, MA: Hendrickson, 1984).

Sturgeon, Inez. *Give Me This Mountain* (Oakland, CA: Hunter Advertising, 1960).

Synan, H. Vinson. 'Preaching, A Pentecostal Perspective', in Stanley M. Burgess and Gary B. McGee (eds.), *DPCM* (Grand Rapids, MI: Zondervan, 1988), 722.

_____. *The Spirit Said 'Grow': The Astounding Worldwide Expansion of Pentecostal and Charismatic Churches* (Monrovia, CA: MARC, 1992).

Tabora, Flora. 'Some Folk Beliefs and Practices Among the Mountain People of Northern Luzon', *SLU Research Journal* 9:3-4 (1978), 494-515.

Tang, Edmond. '"Yellers" and Healers: Pentecostalism and the Study of Grassroots Christianity in China', in Allan Anderson and Edmond Tang (eds.), *Asian and Pentecostal: The Charismatic Face of Christianity in Asia* (Oxford: Regnum Books, 2005), 469-88.

Tano, Rodrigo D. 'Theological Issues in the Philippine Context', *Evangelical Review of Theology* 19 (1995).

Tarr, Del. 'Preaching the Word in the Power of the Spirit: A Cross-cultural Analysis', in Byron D. Klaus and Douglas Petersen, eds., *Called and Empowered: Global Mission in Pentecostal Perspective* (Peabody, MA: Hendrickson, 1991), 127.

Tippet, Alan R. *People Movement in Southern Polynesia* (Chicago: Moody Press, 1971).

Van Rheenen, Gailyn. *Communicating Christ in Animistic Contexts* (Grand Rapids: Baker, 1991).

Vanderbout, Elva. 'Here and There', *Midland Courier*, Jan. 26, 1958, 3.

_____. 'Salvation-Healing Meetings in Mountain Province', *Missionary Challenge*, Feb. 1958, 2-3.

_____. 'Salvation-Healing Revival in Baguio City, Philippines', *Pentecostal Evangel*, June 1955, 2-4.

_____. 'A Westward Move', *Our Missionary*, Aug. 1962, 1-3.

_____. 'A Work of Mercy in the Philippines', *Foreign Field Report*, July 1954.

Wacker, Grant. 'Wild Theories and Mad Excitement', in Harold B. Smith (ed.), *Pentecostals from the Inside Out* (Wheaton: Victor, 1990).

Wagner, C. Peter. 'Characteristics of Pentecostal Church Growth', in L. Grant McClung (ed.), *Azusa Street and Beyond: Pentecostal Missions and Church Growth in the Twentieth Century* (South Plainfield, NJ: Bridge Publishing, 1986), 124-32.

_____. *On the Crest of the Wave: Becoming a World Christian* (Ventura, CA: Regal Books, 1983).

Wallis, Arthur. *God's Chosen Fast* (Fort Washington, PA: Christian Literature Crusade, 1968).

Walls, Andrew F. *The Missionary Movement in Christian History: Studies in the Transmission of Faith* (Maryknoll, NY: Orbis, 1996).

Wesley, Luke. *The Church in China: Persecuted, Pentecostal and Powerful* (Baguio, Philippines: AJPS Books, 2004).

Whitney, Donald. *Spiritual Disciples for the Christian Life* (Colorado Springs, CO: NavPress, 1993).

Wiber, Melanie. 'The Canayao Imperative: Changes in Resource Control, Stratification and the Economy of Ritual Among the Ibaloi of Northern Luzon', in Susan Russell and E.C. Clark (eds.), *Changing Lives Changing Rites: Ritual and Social Dynamics in Philippines and Indonesian Up-lands* (Ann Arbor, MI: University of Michigan, 1988), 45-62.

Wiegele, Katharine L. *Investing in Miracles: El Shaddai and the Transformation of Popular Catholicism in the Philippines* (Honolulu: University of Hawaii Press, 2005).

Wilkinson, Michael. 'Faith-Based Social Services: Some Observations for Assessing Pentecostal Social Action', *Transformation* 24:2 (April 2007), 71-79.

Wimber, John. 'Power Evangelism: Definitions and Directions', in C. Peter Wagner and F. Douglas Pennoyer (eds.), *Wrestling With Dark Angeles: Toward a Deeper Understanding of the Supernatural Forces in Spiritual Warfare* (Ventura: Regal Books, 1990), 13-14.

_____, and Kevin Springer, *Power Evangelism* (New York: Harper Collins, 1984).

Winter, Ralph. *Crucial Dimensions in World Evangelism* (Pasadena, CA: William Carey Library, 1976).

Wiyono, Gani. 'Pentecostals in Indonesia', in Allan Anderson and Edmond Tang (eds.), *Asian and Pentecostal: The Charismatic Face of Christianity in Asia* (Oxford: Regnum Books, 2005), 307-328.

_____. 'Timo Revival: A Historical Study of the Great Twentieth-century Revival in Indonesia', *AJPS* 4:2 (2001), 269-93.

'Word and Spirit, Church and World: The Final Report of the International Dialogue Between Representatives of the World Alliance of Reformed Churches and Some Classical Pentecostal Churches and Leaders 1996-2000', *AJPS* 4:1 (2001), 41-72.

Wright, Christopher J.H. *The Mission of God: Unlocking the Bible's Grand Narrative* (Nottingham: Inter-Varsity Press, 2006).

Yang, C.K. *Religion in Chinese Society* (Berkley: University of California Press, 1967).

Yong, Amos. *Beyond the Impasse: Toward a Pneumatological Theology of Religion* (Grand Rapids: Baker Book, 2003).

Yoo, Boo-Woong. *Korean Pentecostalism: Its History and Theology* (Frankfurt am Main: Peter Lang, 1988).

York, John V. *Missions in the Age of the Spirit* (Springfield, MO: Logion, 2000).

Young, John D. *East-West Synthesis: Matteo Ricci and Confucianism* (Hong Kong: Hong Kong Centre of Asian Studies, University of Hong Kong, 1980).

Zurcher, E. *The Buddhist Conquest of China: The Spread and Adaptation of Buddhism in Early Medieval China* (Leiden: Brill, 1972).

Index of Names